Vol. 1

By Aya Kanno

HAMBURG // LONDON // LOS ANGELES // TOKYO

Soul Rescue Volume 1
Created by Aya Kanno

Translation - Christine Schilling
English Adapation - Meadow Jones
Retouch and Lettering - Corey Whitfield
Graphic Designer - John Lo

Editor - Katherine Schilling
Digital Imaging Manager - Chris Buford
Pre-Production Supervisor - Erika Terriquez
Art Director - Anne Marie Horne
Production Manager - Elisabeth Brizzi
VP of Production - Ron Klamert
Editor-in-Chief - Rob Tokar
Publisher - Mike Kiley
President and C.O.O. - John Parker
C.E.O. and Chief Creative Officer - Stuart Levy

A  Manga

TOKYOPOP Inc.
5900 Wilshire Blvd. Suite 2000
Los Angeles, CA 90036

E-mail: info@TOKYOPOP.com
Come visit us online at www.TOKYOPOP.com

ISBN: 1-59816-672-7

First TOKYOPOP printing: December 2006
10 9 8 7 6 5 4 3 2 1
Printed in the USA

Soul Rescue

Aya Kanno

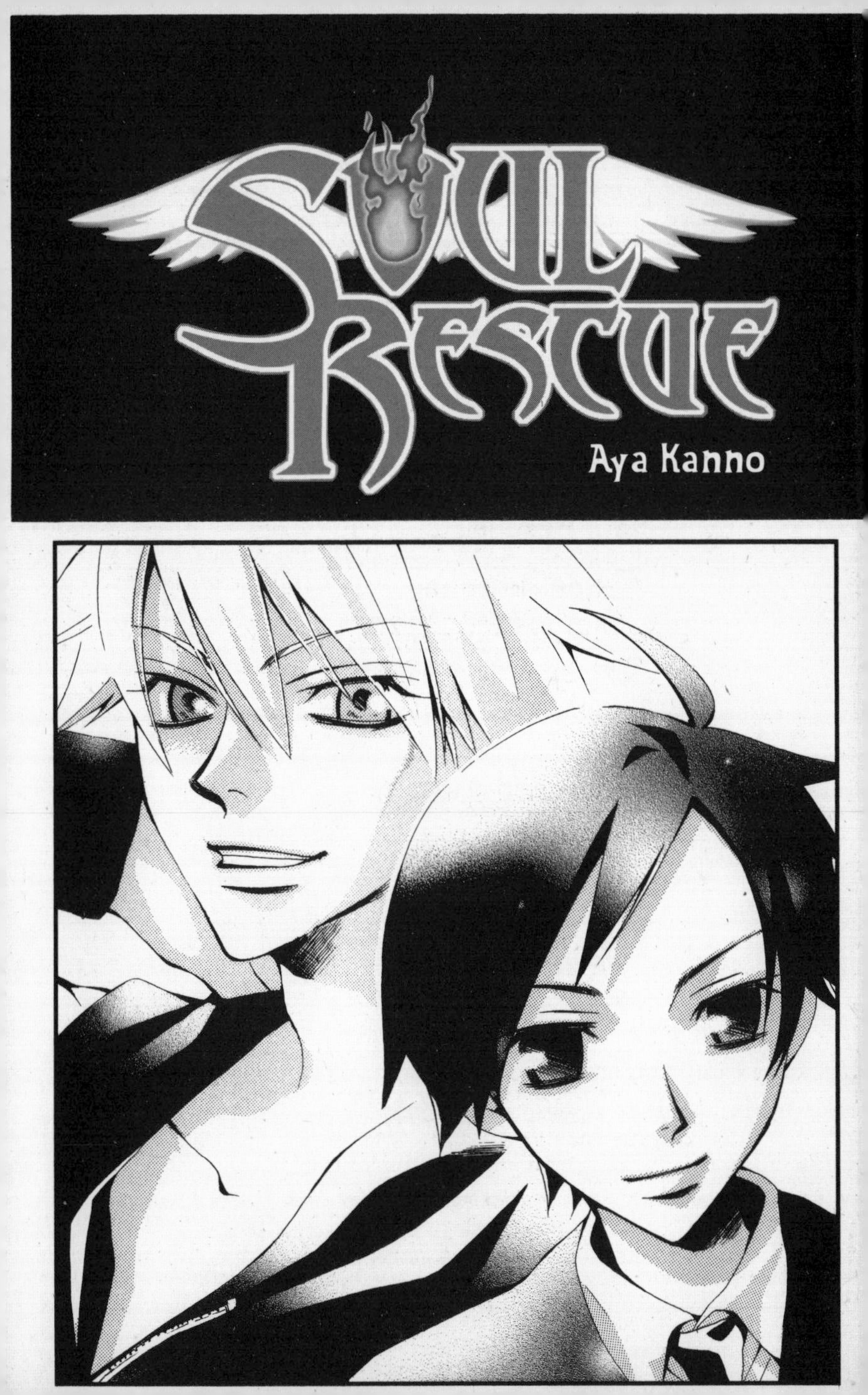

Table of Contents

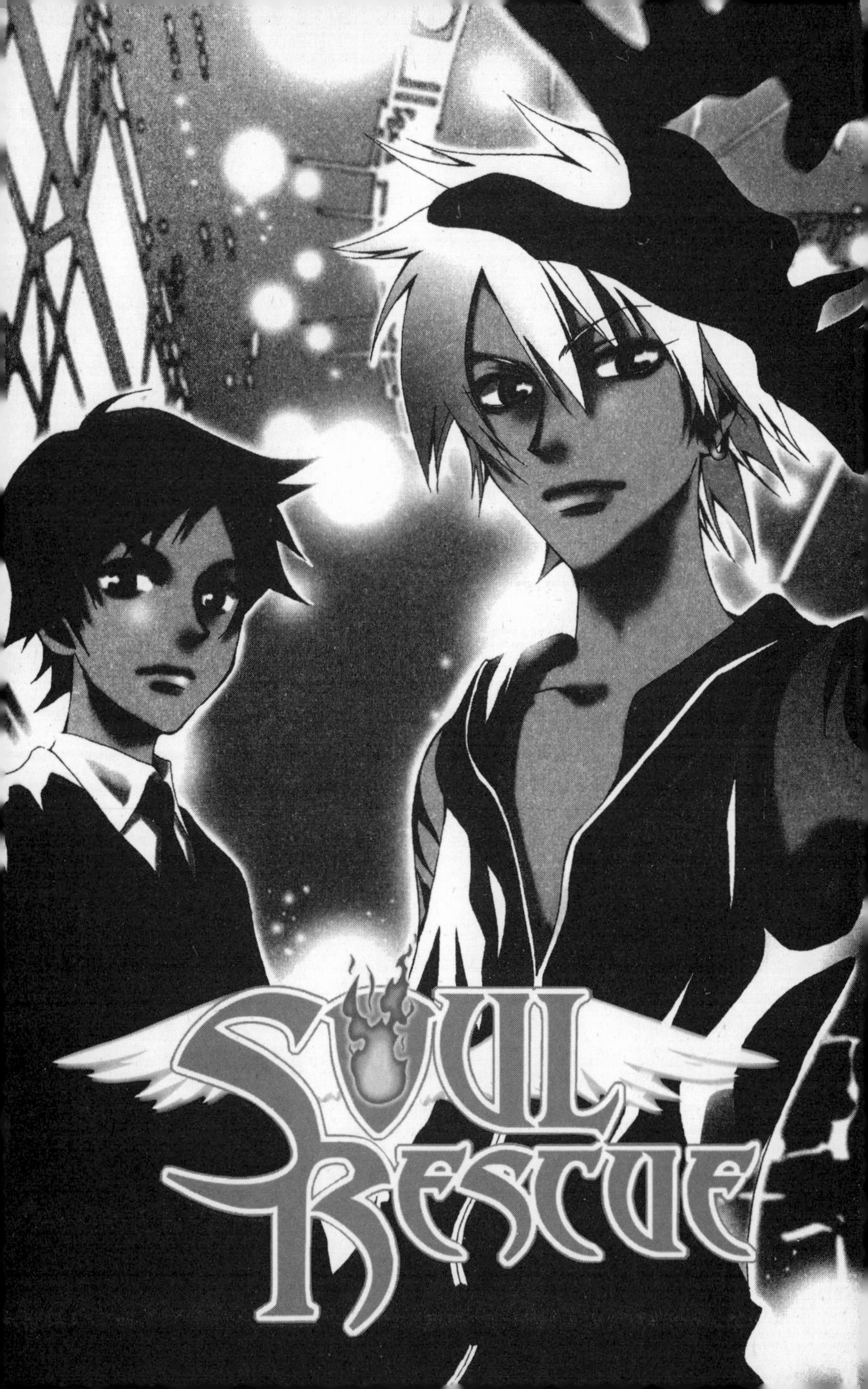
SOUL RESCUE

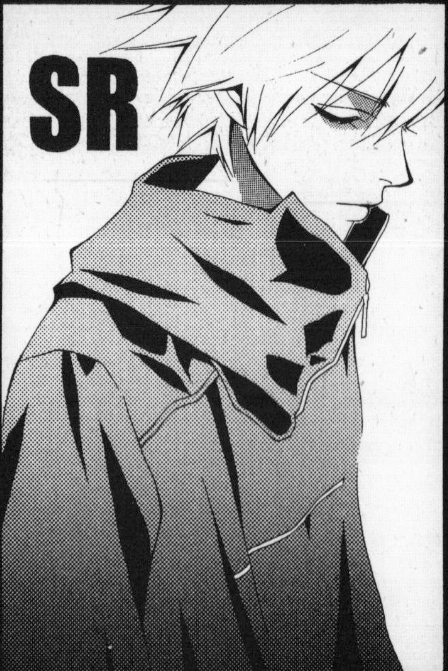
SR

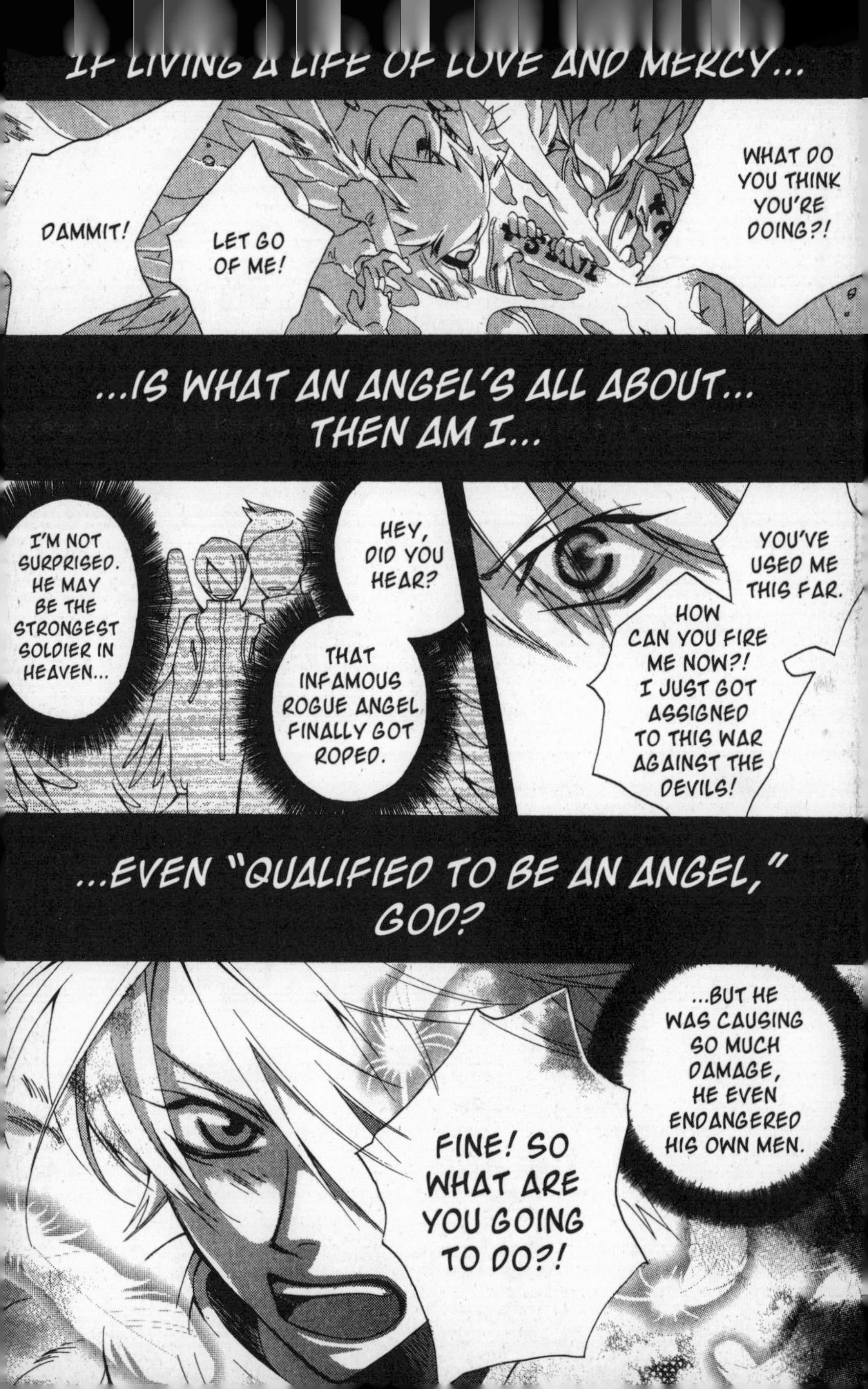
IF LIVING A LIFE OF LOVE AND MERCY...
WHAT DO YOU THINK YOU'RE DOING?!
LET GO OF ME!
DAMMIT!
...IS WHAT AN ANGEL'S ALL ABOUT... THEN AM I...
YOU'VE USED ME THIS FAR.
HOW CAN YOU FIRE ME NOW?! I JUST GOT ASSIGNED TO THIS WAR AGAINST THE DEVILS!
HEY, DID YOU HEAR?
THAT INFAMOUS ROGUE ANGEL FINALLY GOT ROPED.
I'M NOT SURPRISED. HE MAY BE THE STRONGEST SOLDIER IN HEAVEN...
...EVEN "QUALIFIED TO BE AN ANGEL," GOD?
...BUT HE WAS CAUSING SO MUCH DAMAGE, HE EVEN ENDANGERED HIS OWN MEN.
FINE! SO WHAT ARE YOU GOING TO DO?!

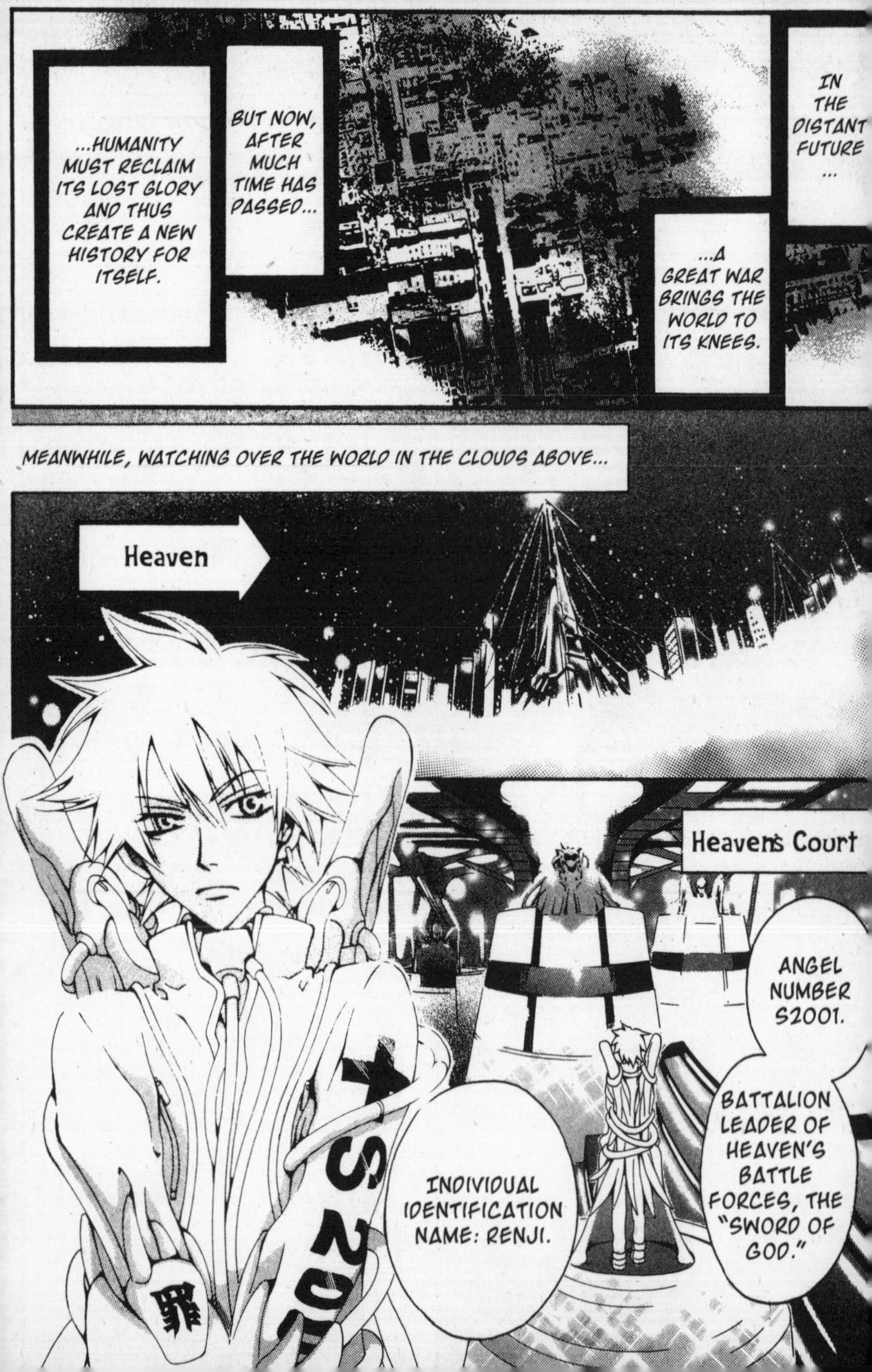
IN THE DISTANT FUTURE...
...A GREAT WAR BRINGS THE WORLD TO ITS KNEES.
BUT NOW, AFTER MUCH TIME HAS PASSED...
...HUMANITY MUST RECLAIM ITS LOST GLORY AND THUS CREATE A NEW HISTORY FOR ITSELF.
MEANWHILE, WATCHING OVER THE WORLD IN THE CLOUDS ABOVE...
Heaven
Heaven's Court
ANGEL NUMBER S2001.
BATTALION LEADER OF HEAVEN'S BATTLE FORCES, THE "SWORD OF GOD."
INDIVIDUAL IDENTIFICATION NAME: RENJI.

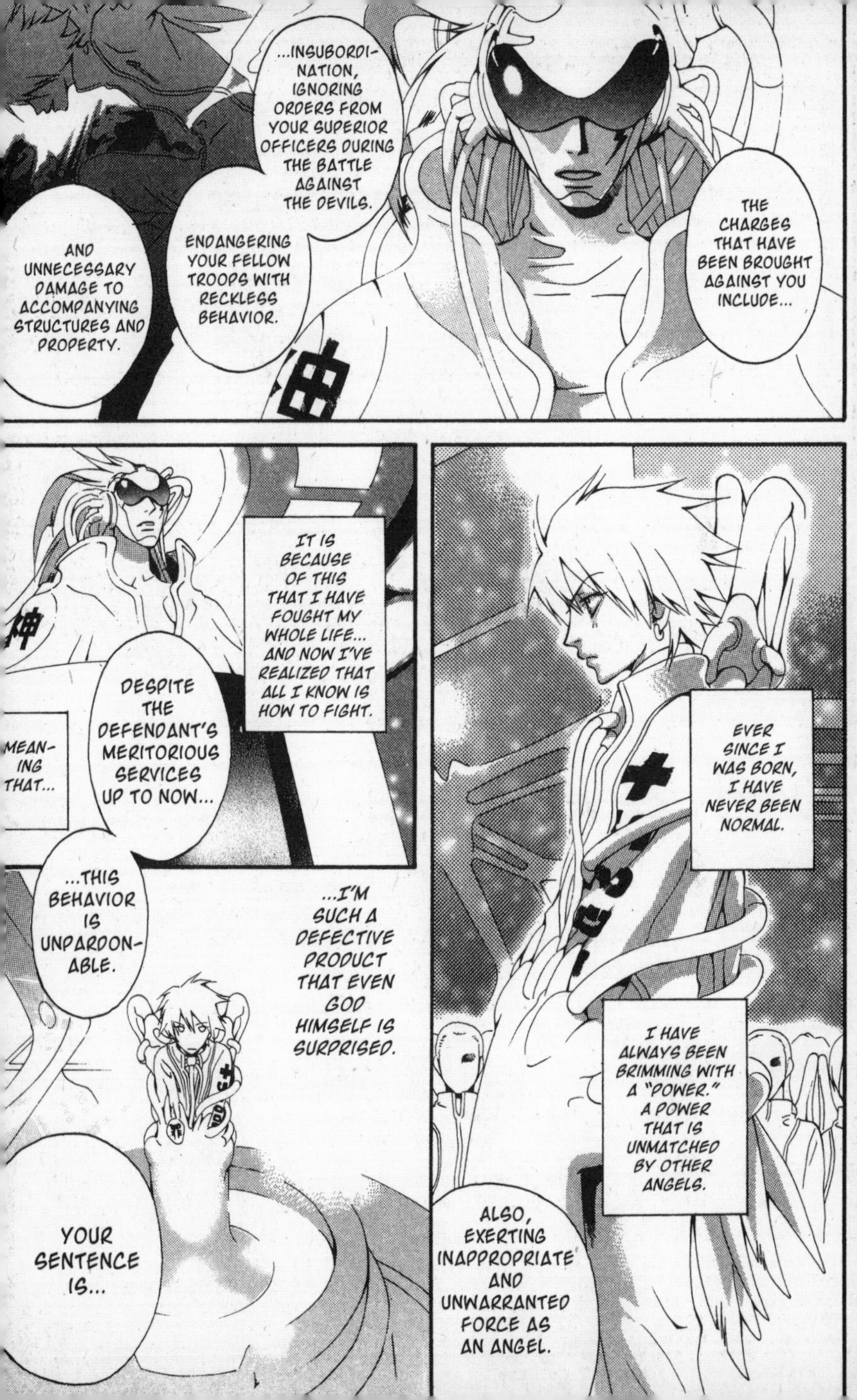
THE CHARGES THAT HAVE BEEN BROUGHT AGAINST YOU INCLUDE...
...INSUBORDINATION, IGNORING ORDERS FROM YOUR SUPERIOR OFFICERS DURING THE BATTLE AGAINST THE DEVILS.
ENDANGERING YOUR FELLOW TROOPS WITH RECKLESS BEHAVIOR.
AND UNNECESSARY DAMAGE TO ACCOMPANYING STRUCTURES AND PROPERTY.
EVER SINCE I WAS BORN, I HAVE NEVER BEEN NORMAL.
I HAVE ALWAYS BEEN BRIMMING WITH A "POWER." A POWER THAT IS UNMATCHED BY OTHER ANGELS.
ALSO, EXERTING INAPPROPRIATE AND UNWARRANTED FORCE AS AN ANGEL.
IT IS BECAUSE OF THIS THAT I HAVE FOUGHT MY WHOLE LIFE... AND NOW I'VE REALIZED THAT ALL I KNOW IS HOW TO FIGHT.
DESPITE THE DEFENDANT'S MERITORIOUS SERVICES UP TO NOW...
MEANING THAT...
...I'M SUCH A DEFECTIVE PRODUCT THAT EVEN GOD HIMSELF IS SURPRISED.
...THIS BEHAVIOR IS UNPARDONABLE.
YOUR SENTENCE IS...

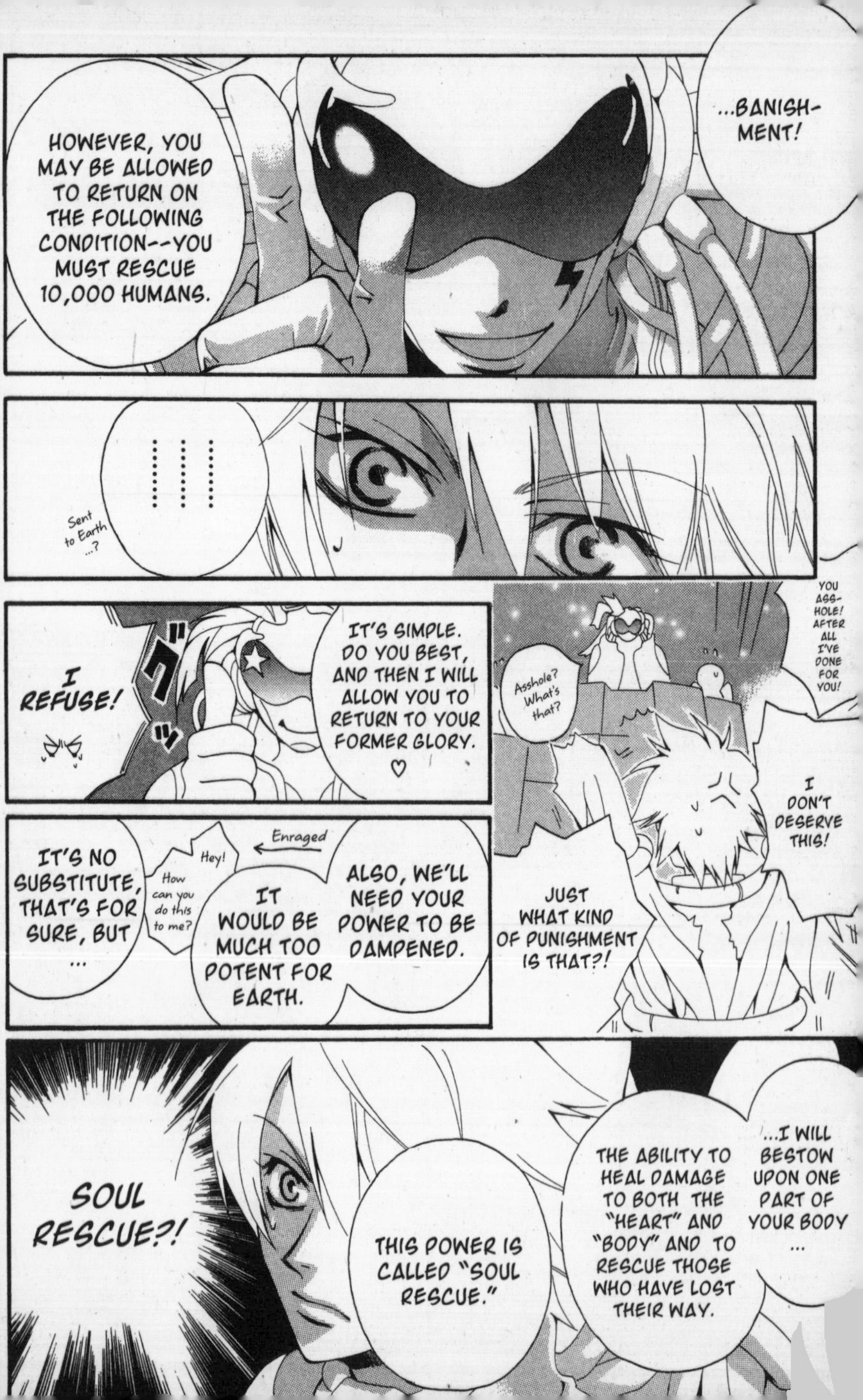
...BANISHMENT!
HOWEVER, YOU MAY BE ALLOWED TO RETURN ON THE FOLLOWING CONDITION--YOU MUST RESCUE 10,000 HUMANS.
......
Sent to Earth ...?
YOU ASSHOLE! AFTER ALL I'VE DONE FOR YOU!
Asshole? What's that?
I DON'T DESERVE THIS!
JUST WHAT KIND OF PUNISHMENT IS THAT?!
IT'S SIMPLE. DO YOU BEST, AND THEN I WILL ALLOW YOU TO RETURN TO YOUR FORMER GLORY. ♡
I REFUSE!
ALSO, WE'LL NEED YOUR POWER TO BE DAMPENED.
Enraged
IT WOULD BE MUCH TOO POTENT FOR EARTH.
Hey!
How can you do this to me?
IT'S NO SUBSTITUTE, THAT'S FOR SURE, BUT ...
...I WILL BESTOW UPON ONE PART OF YOUR BODY ...
THE ABILITY TO HEAL DAMAGE TO BOTH THE "HEART" AND "BODY" AND TO RESCUE THOSE WHO HAVE LOST THEIR WAY.
THIS POWER IS CALLED "SOUL RESCUE."
SOUL RESCUE?!

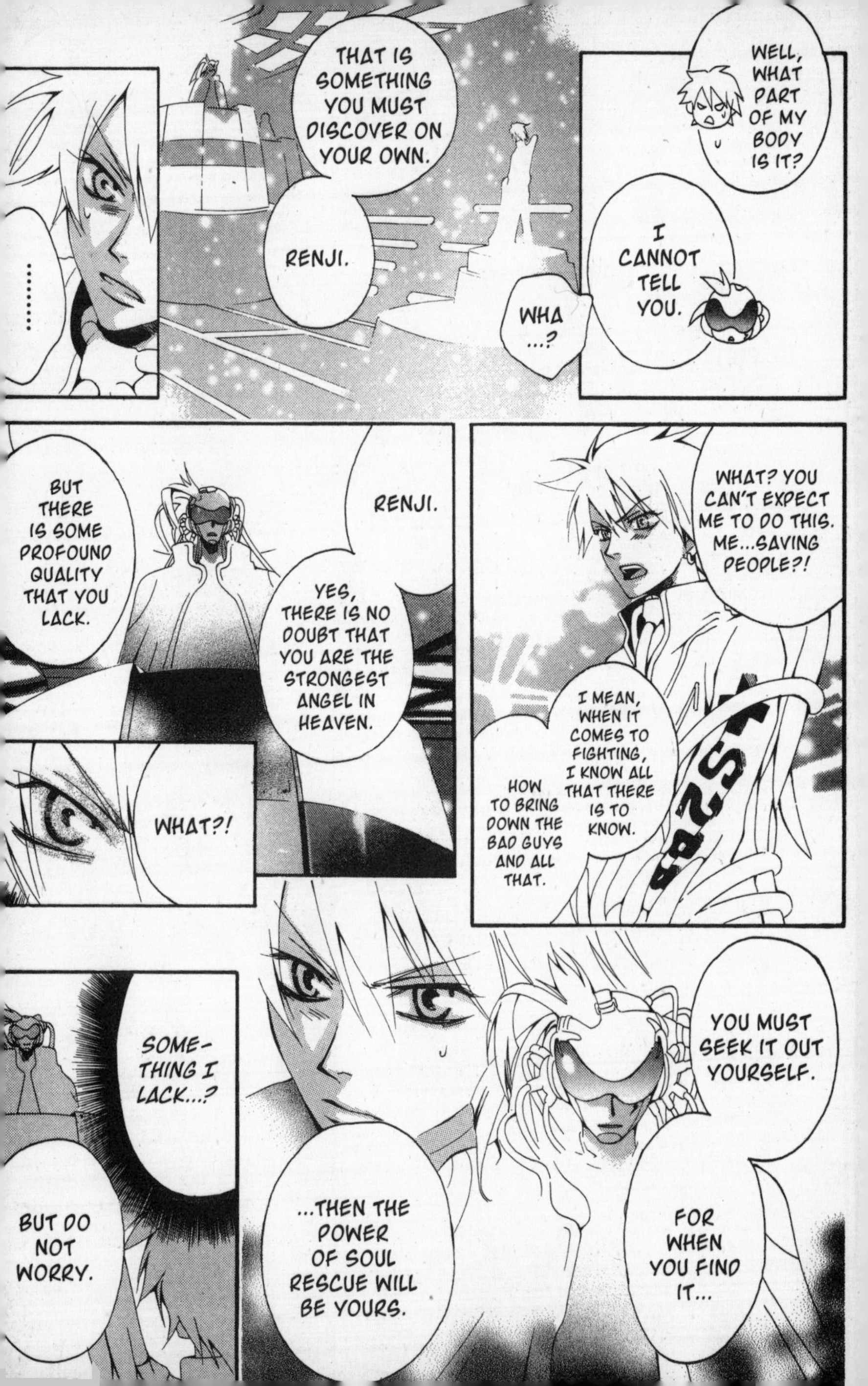
WELL, WHAT PART OF MY BODY IS IT?
I CANNOT TELL YOU.
WHA ...?
THAT IS SOMETHING YOU MUST DISCOVER ON YOUR OWN.
RENJI.
......
WHAT? YOU CAN'T EXPECT ME TO DO THIS. ME...SAVING PEOPLE?!
I MEAN, WHEN IT COMES TO FIGHTING, I KNOW ALL THAT THERE IS TO KNOW.
HOW TO BRING DOWN THE BAD GUYS AND ALL THAT.
RENJI.
YES, THERE IS NO DOUBT THAT YOU ARE THE STRONGEST ANGEL IN HEAVEN.
BUT THERE IS SOME PROFOUND QUALITY THAT YOU LACK.
WHAT?!
SOME-THING I LACK...?
BUT DO NOT WORRY.
YOU MUST SEEK IT OUT YOURSELF.
FOR WHEN YOU FIND IT...
...THEN THE POWER OF SOUL RESCUE WILL BE YOURS.

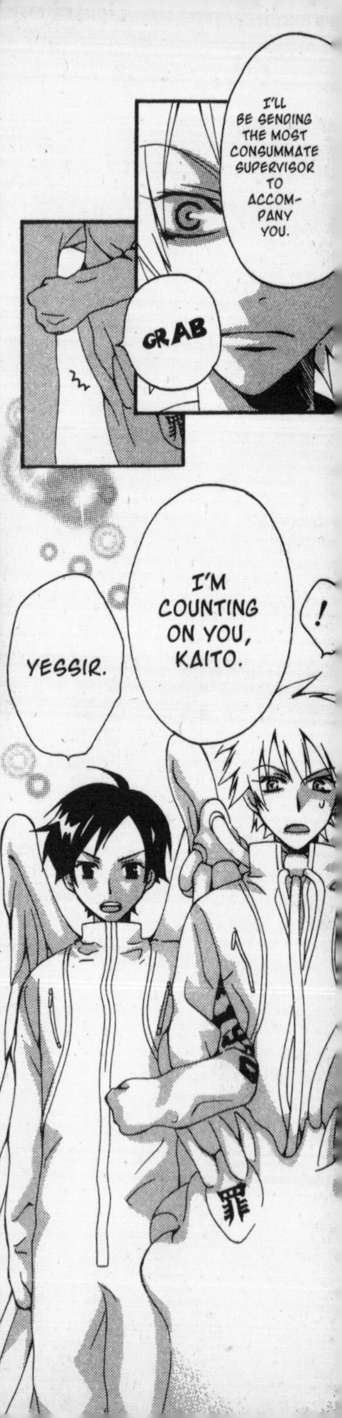
I'LL BE SENDING THE MOST CONSUMMATE SUPERVISOR TO ACCOMPANY YOU.
GRAB
I'M COUNTING ON YOU, KAITO.
!
YESSIR.

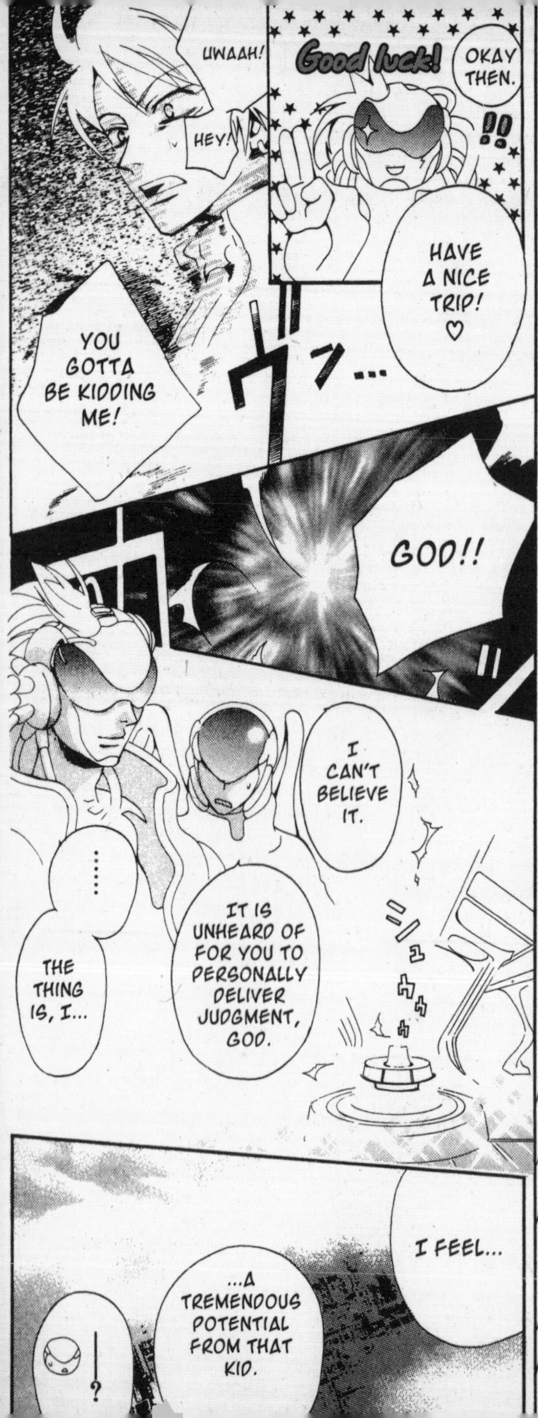
OKAY THEN.
Good luck!
!!
HAVE A NICE TRIP! ♡
UWAAH!
HEY!
YOU GOTTA BE KIDDING ME!
GOD!!
I CAN'T BELIEVE IT.
IT IS UNHEARD OF FOR YOU TO PERSONALLY DELIVER JUDGMENT, GOD.
......
THE THING IS, I...
I FEEL...
...A TREMENDOUS POTENTIAL FROM THAT KID.
—?

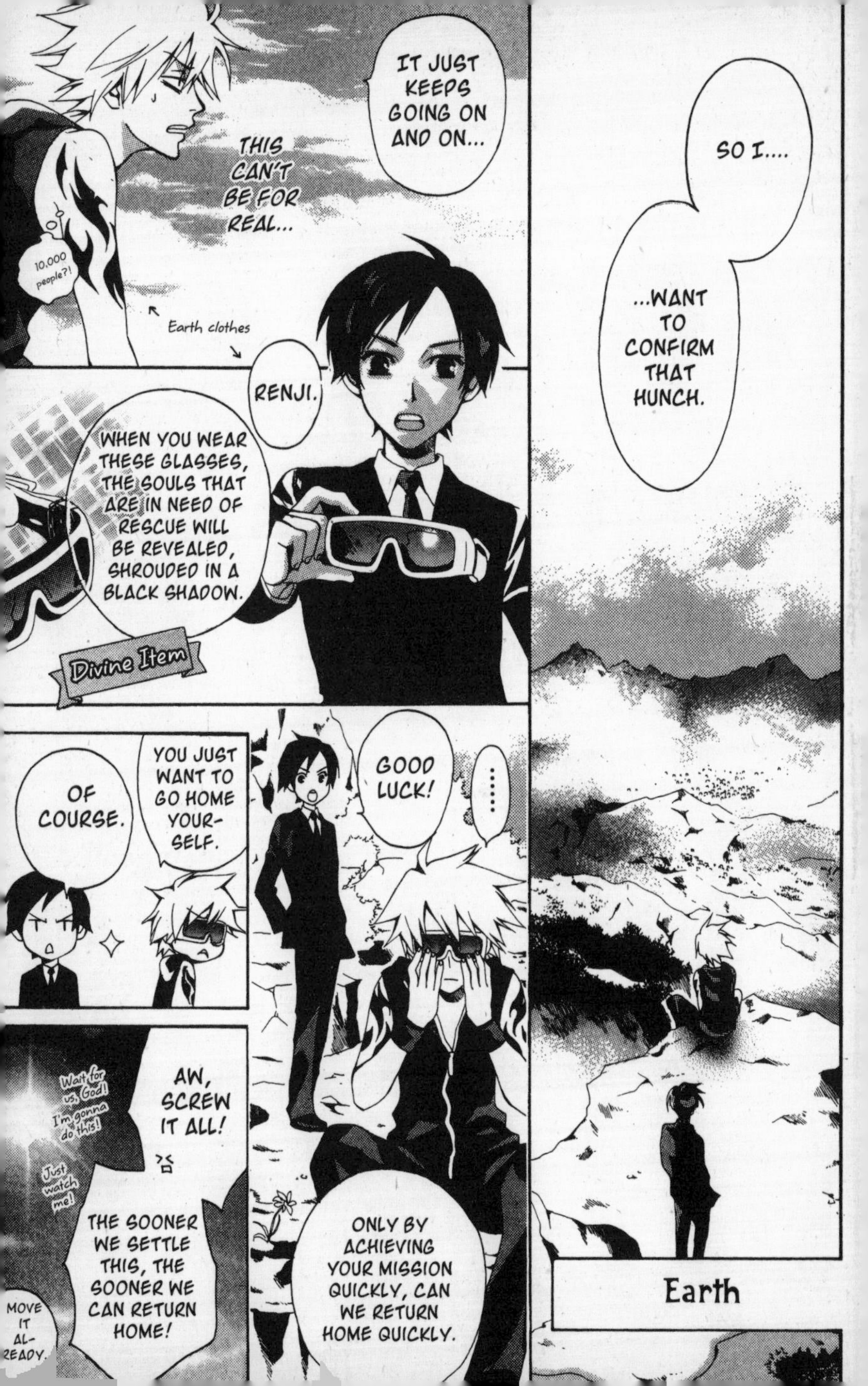
SO I....
...WANT TO CONFIRM THAT HUNCH.
Earth
IT JUST KEEPS GOING ON AND ON...
THIS CAN'T BE FOR REAL...
10,000 people?!
Earth clothes
RENJI.
WHEN YOU WEAR THESE GLASSES, THE SOULS THAT ARE IN NEED OF RESCUE WILL BE REVEALED, SHROUDED IN A BLACK SHADOW.
Divine Item
GOOD LUCK!
......
ONLY BY ACHIEVING YOUR MISSION QUICKLY, CAN WE RETURN HOME QUICKLY.
YOU JUST WANT TO GO HOME YOUR-SELF.
OF COURSE.
AW, SCREW IT ALL!
Wait for us, God! I'm gonna do this!
Just watch me!
THE SOONER WE SETTLE THIS, THE SOONER WE CAN RETURN HOME!
MOVE IT AL-READY.

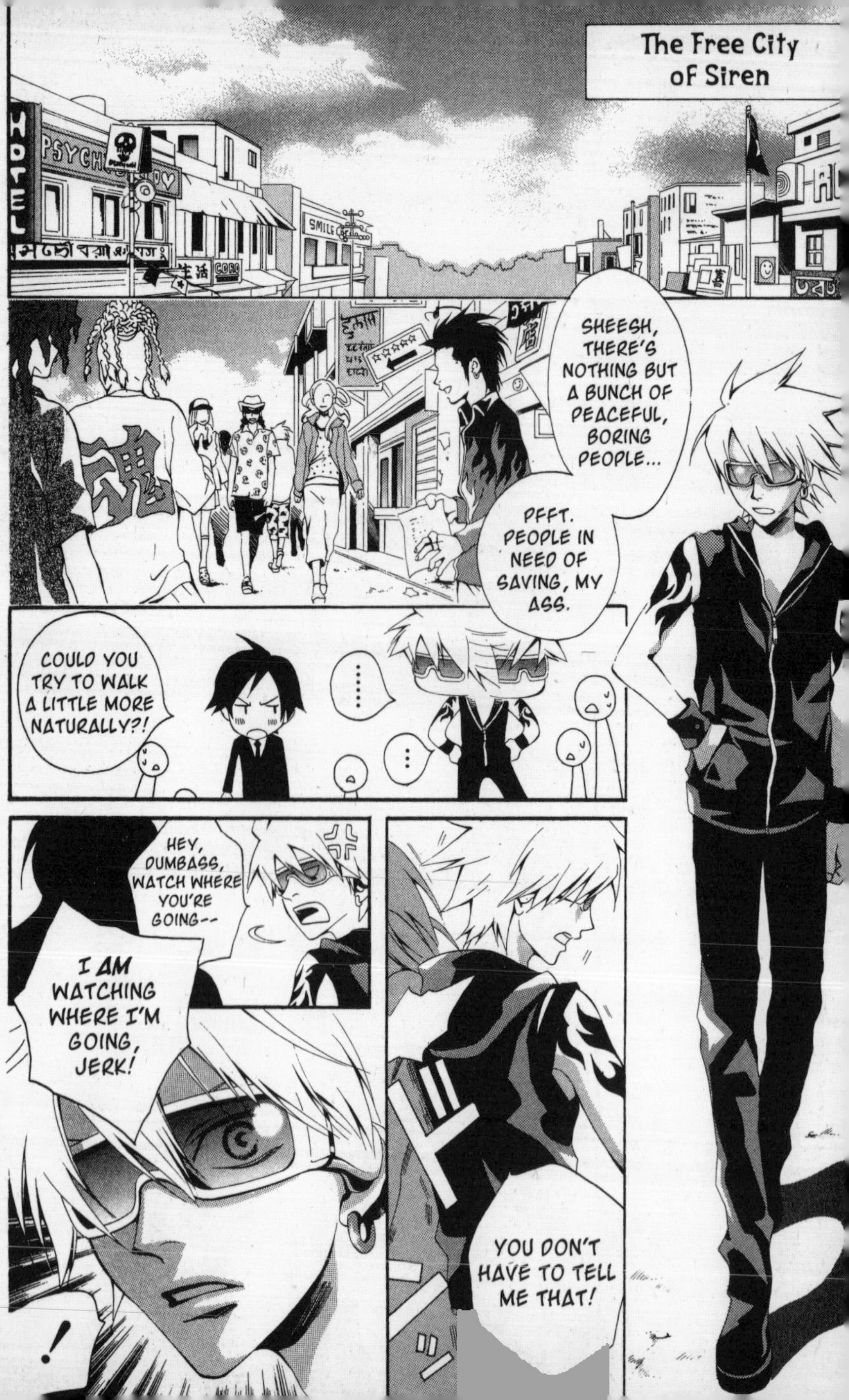

The Free City of Siren
SHEESH, THERE'S NOTHING BUT A BUNCH OF PEACEFUL, BORING PEOPLE...
PFFT. PEOPLE IN NEED OF SAVING, MY ASS.
......
COULD YOU TRY TO WALK A LITTLE MORE NATURALLY?!
...
YOU DON'T HAVE TO TELL ME THAT!
HEY, DUMBASS, WATCH WHERE YOU'RE GOING--
I AM WATCHING WHERE I'M GOING, JERK!
!

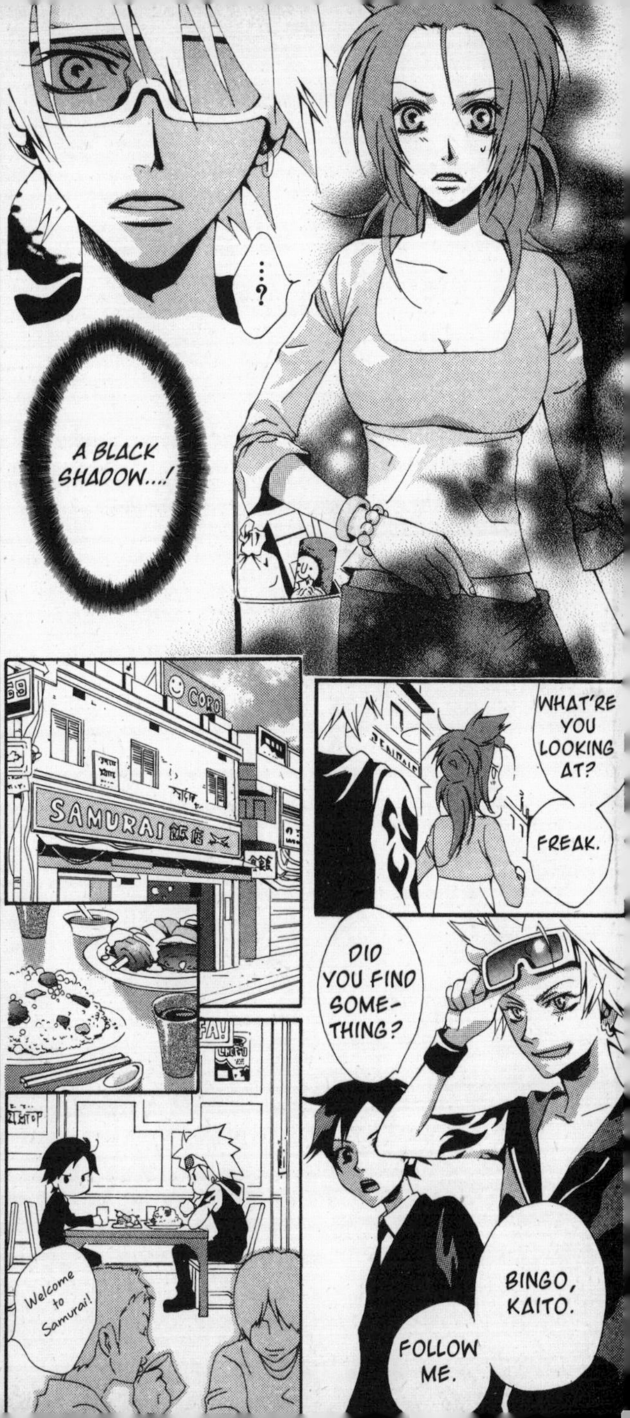
...?
A BLACK SHADOW...!
WHAT'RE YOU LOOKING AT?
FREAK.
SAMURAI 飯店
DID YOU FIND SOME-THING?
BINGO, KAITO.
FOLLOW ME.
Welcome to Samurai!

SR

Hello and nice to meet you. This is Aya Kanno, And this is my tankobon! Uwaaah... Well, this is nice... I mean, I'm ecstatic over this! And it's all thanks to you! That's right, you reading this right now! Have I done well not to betray all your expectations? I do hope you enjoy this even a little bit. And that's the truth. ☺

At any rate, I'm feeling the sharp sting of my inadequacy as I write. Sure I've got the story down, but the illustrations! They are too crappy... I'm working on it, though...

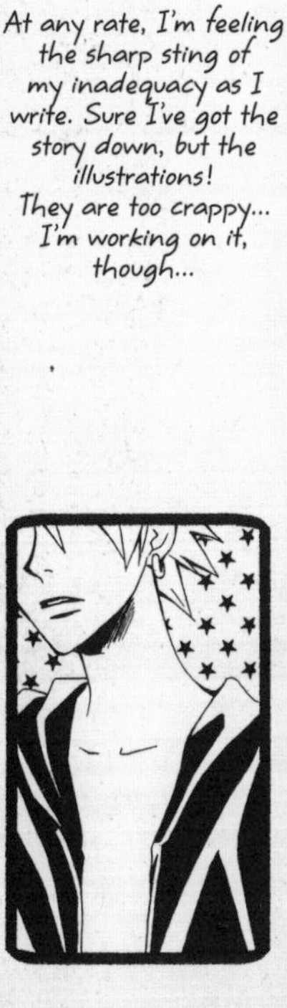

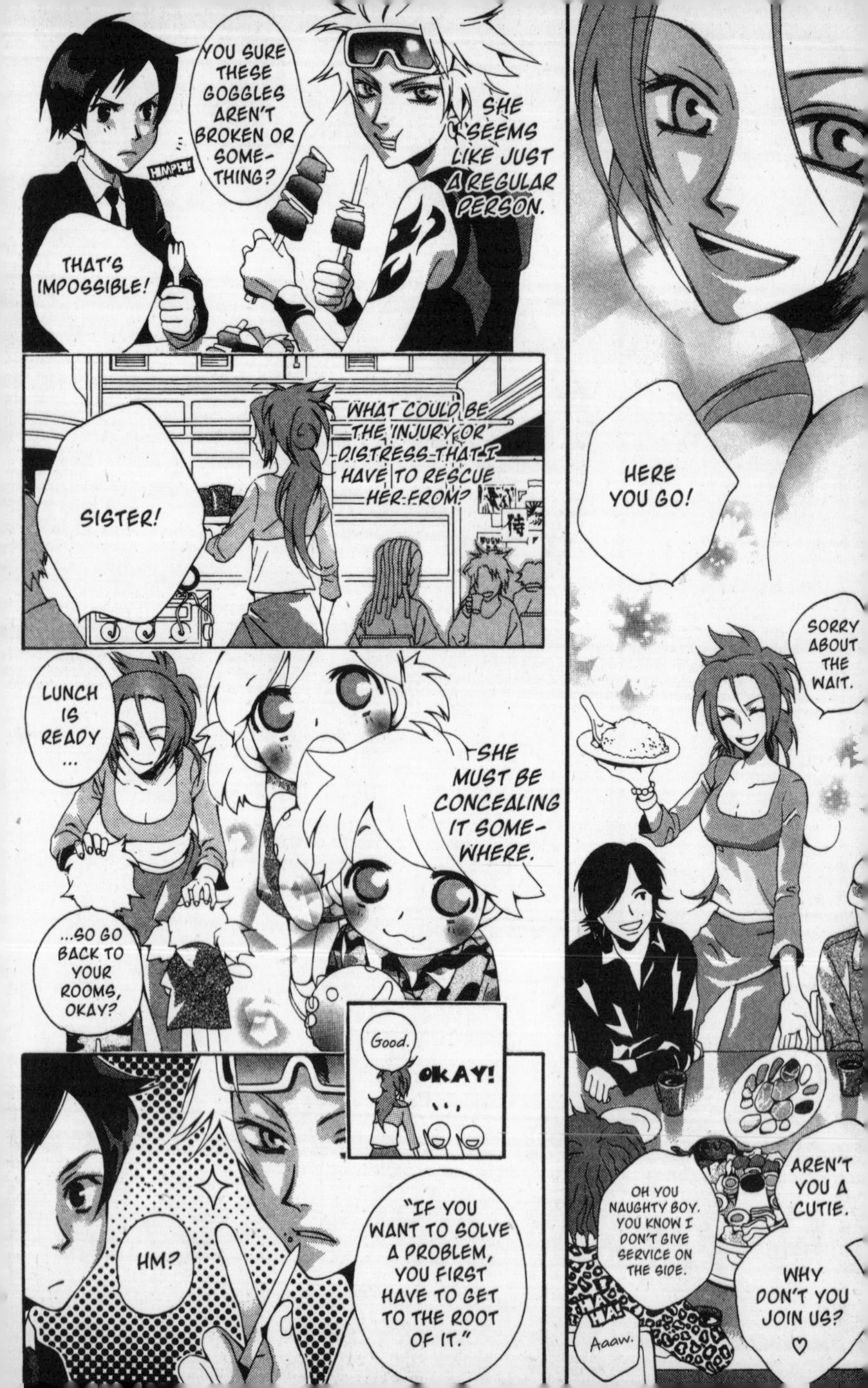
HERE YOU GO!
SORRY ABOUT THE WAIT.
AREN'T YOU A CUTIE.
WHY DON'T YOU JOIN US? ♥
OH YOU NAUGHTY BOY. YOU KNOW I DON'T GIVE SERVICE ON THE SIDE.
HA HA!
Aaaw.
SHE SEEMS LIKE JUST A REGULAR PERSON.
YOU SURE THESE GOGGLES AREN'T BROKEN OR SOMETHING?
HMPH!
THAT'S IMPOSSIBLE!
WHAT COULD BE THE INJURY OR DISTRESS THAT I HAVE TO RESCUE HER FROM?
SISTER!
SHE MUST BE CONCEALING IT SOMEWHERE.
LUNCH IS READY...
...SO GO BACK TO YOUR ROOMS, OKAY?
Good.
OKAY!
"IF YOU WANT TO SOLVE A PROBLEM, YOU FIRST HAVE TO GET TO THE ROOT OF IT."
HM?

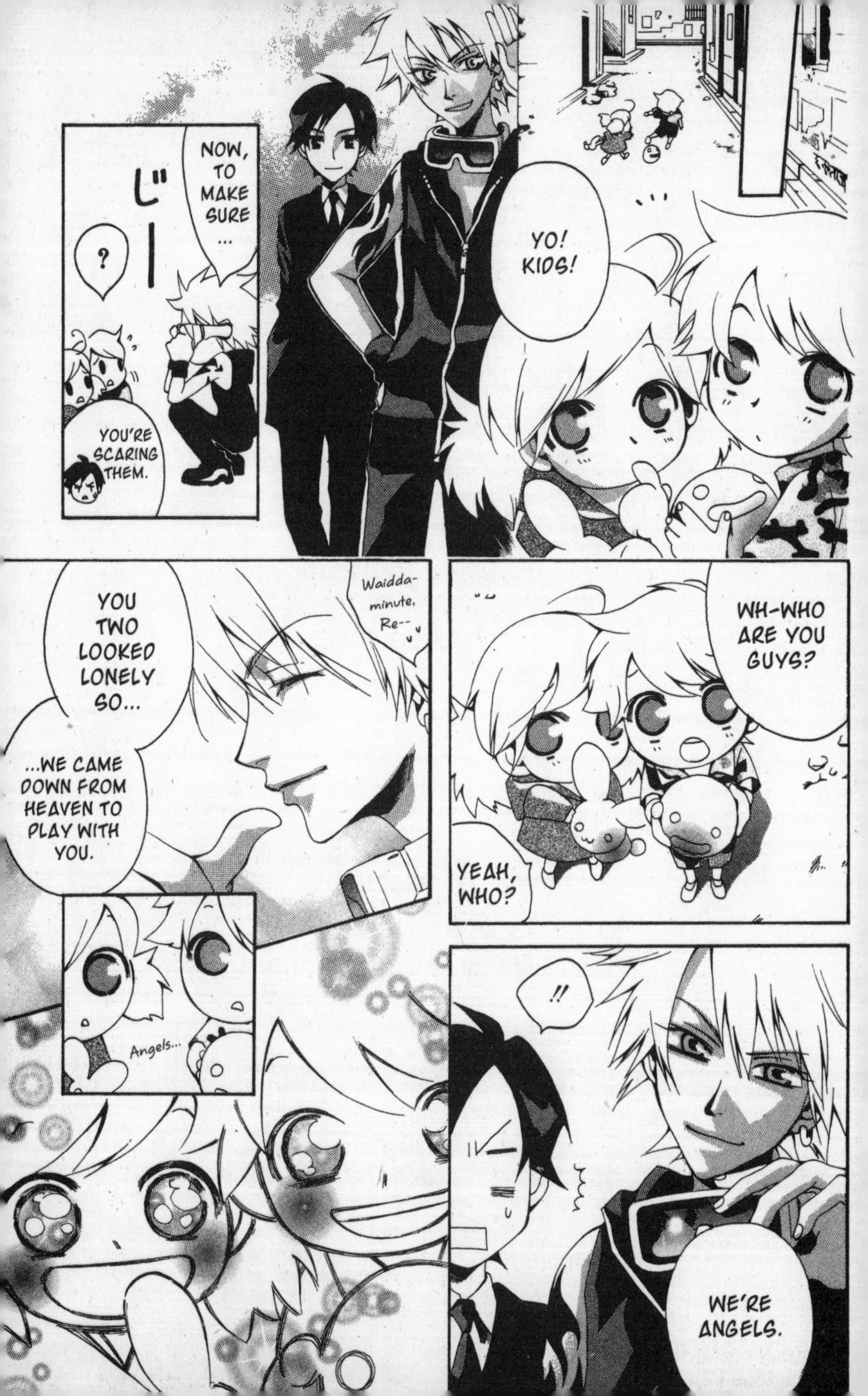
...
YO! KIDS!
NOW, TO MAKE SURE...
じー
?
YOU'RE SCARING THEM.
WH-WHO ARE YOU GUYS?
YEAH, WHO?
Waidda-minute, Re--
YOU TWO LOOKED LONELY SO...
...WE CAME DOWN FROM HEAVEN TO PLAY WITH YOU.
!!
WE'RE ANGELS.
Angels...

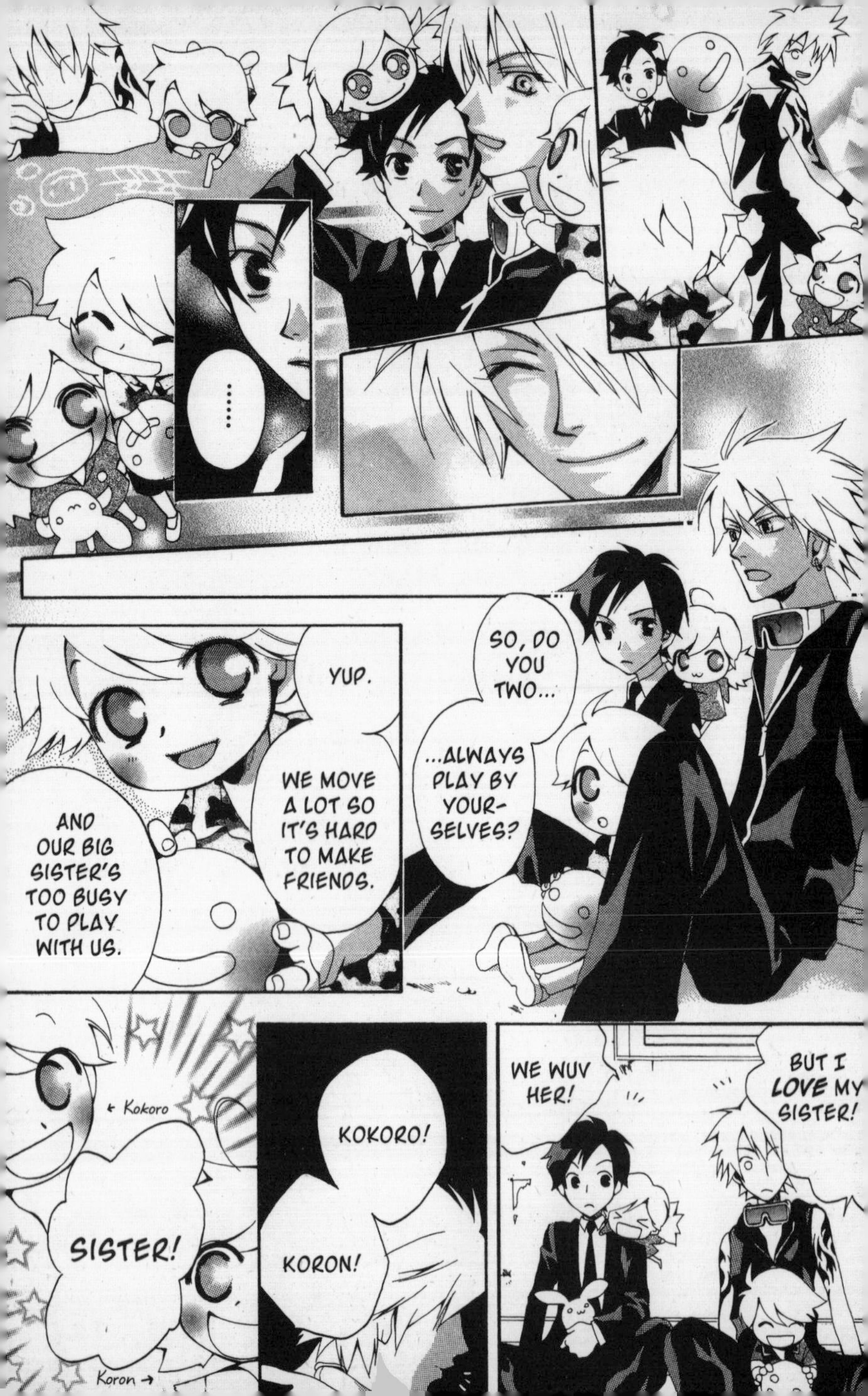
......
SO, DO YOU TWO...
...ALWAYS PLAY BY YOUR-SELVES?
YUP.
WE MOVE A LOT SO IT'S HARD TO MAKE FRIENDS.
AND OUR BIG SISTER'S TOO BUSY TO PLAY WITH US.
BUT I *LOVE* MY SISTER!
WE WUV HER!
KOKORO!
KORON!
← Kokoro
SISTER!
Koron →

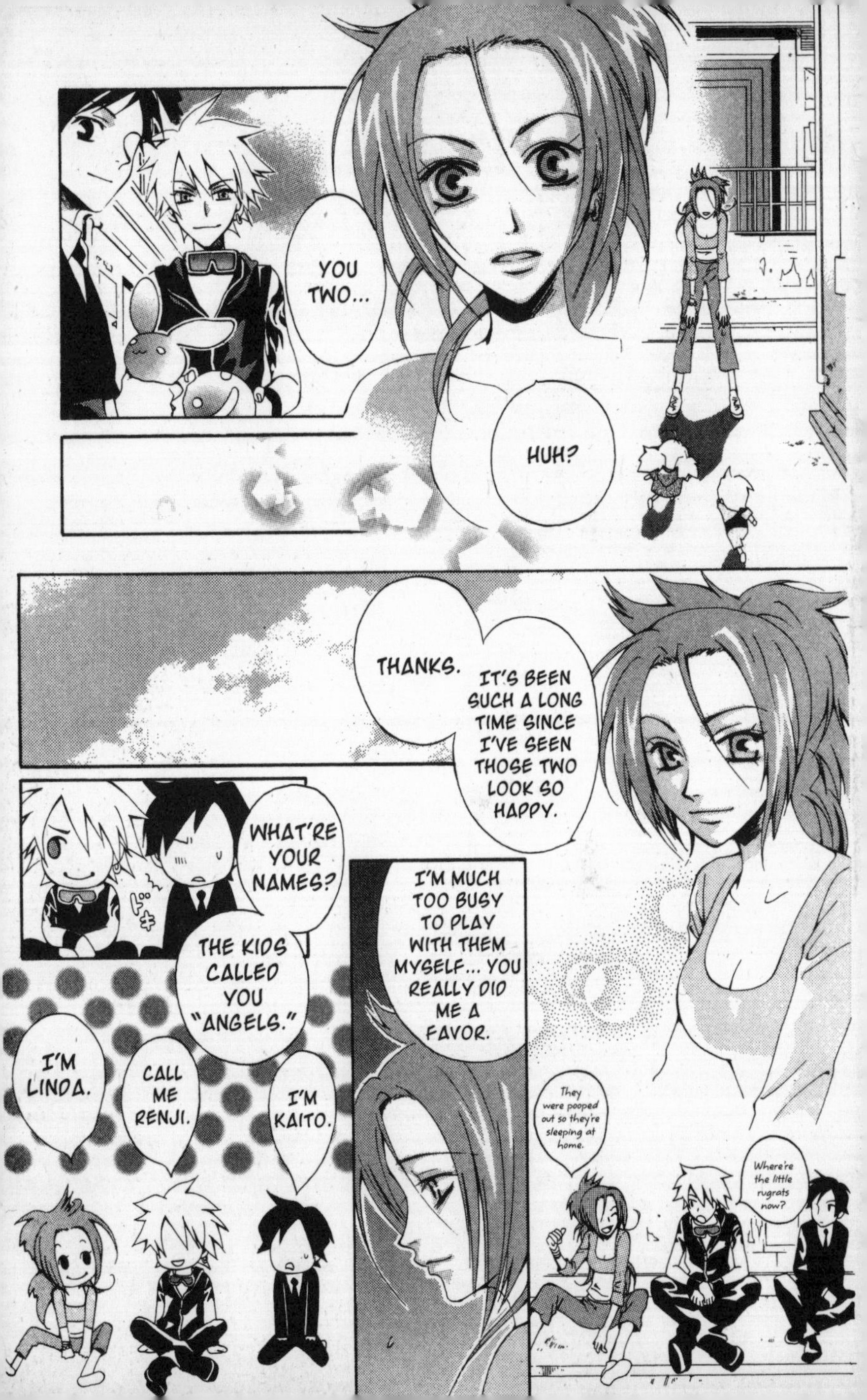
YOU TWO...
HUH?
THANKS.
IT'S BEEN SUCH A LONG TIME SINCE I'VE SEEN THOSE TWO LOOK SO HAPPY.
I'M MUCH TOO BUSY TO PLAY WITH THEM MYSELF... YOU REALLY DID ME A FAVOR.
WHAT'RE YOUR NAMES?
THE KIDS CALLED YOU "ANGELS."
Where're the little rugrats now?
They were pooped out so they're sleeping at home.
I'M KAITO.
CALL ME RENJI.
I'M LINDA.

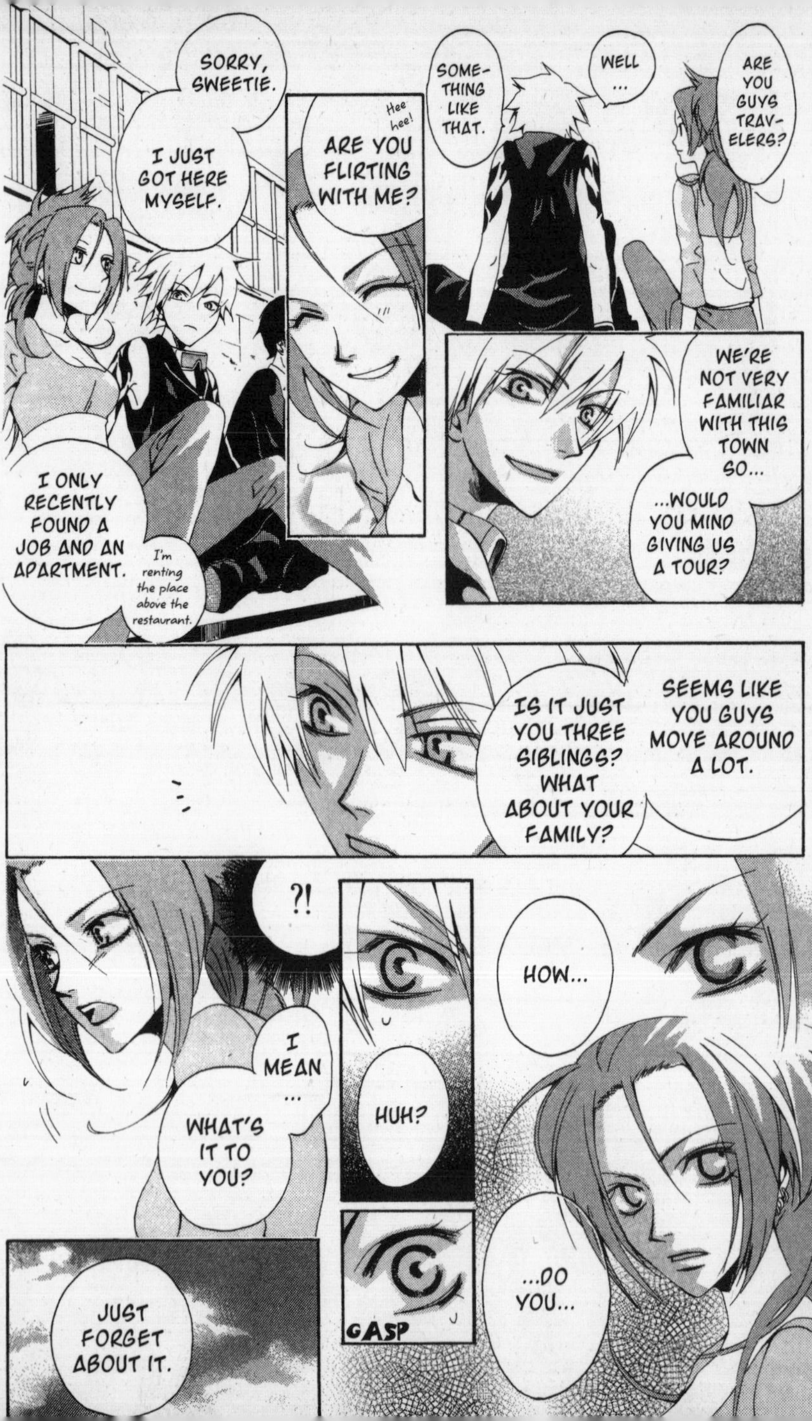
ARE YOU GUYS TRAV-ELERS?
WELL ...
SOME-THING LIKE THAT.
WE'RE NOT VERY FAMILIAR WITH THIS TOWN SO...
...WOULD YOU MIND GIVING US A TOUR?
Hee hee!
ARE YOU FLIRTING WITH ME?
SORRY, SWEETIE.
I JUST GOT HERE MYSELF.
I ONLY RECENTLY FOUND A JOB AND AN APARTMENT.
I'm renting the place above the restaurant.
SEEMS LIKE YOU GUYS MOVE AROUND A LOT.
IS IT JUST YOU THREE SIBLINGS? WHAT ABOUT YOUR FAMILY?
HOW...
...DO YOU...
?!
HUH?
GASP
I MEAN ...
WHAT'S IT TO YOU?
JUST FORGET ABOUT IT.

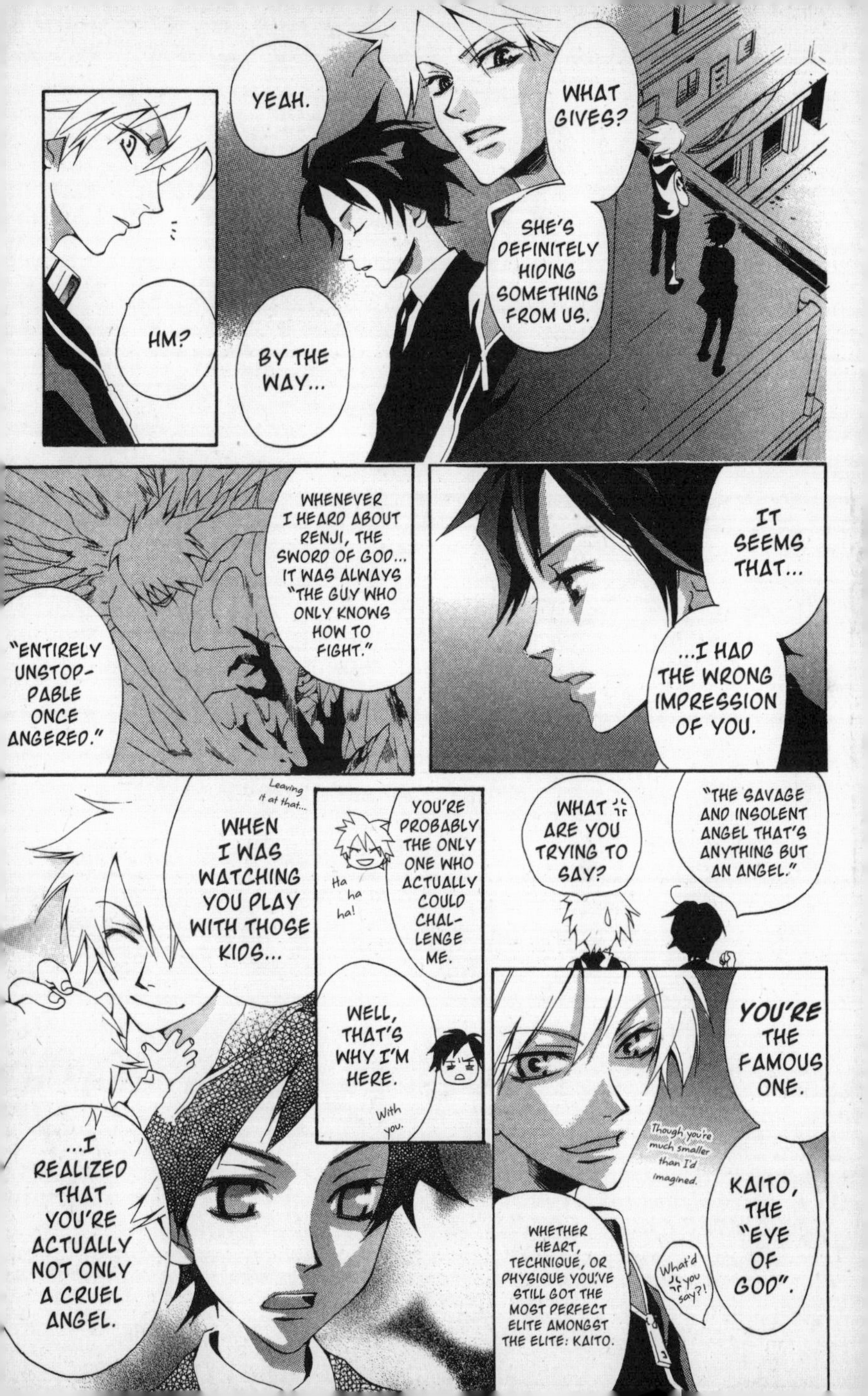
WHAT GIVES?
YEAH.
SHE'S DEFINITELY HIDING SOMETHING FROM US.
BY THE WAY...
HM?
IT SEEMS THAT...
...I HAD THE WRONG IMPRESSION OF YOU.
WHENEVER I HEARD ABOUT RENJI, THE SWORD OF GOD... IT WAS ALWAYS "THE GUY WHO ONLY KNOWS HOW TO FIGHT."
"ENTIRELY UNSTOP-PABLE ONCE ANGERED."
"THE SAVAGE AND INSOLENT ANGEL THAT'S ANYTHING BUT AN ANGEL."
WHAT ARE YOU TRYING TO SAY?
YOU'RE THE FAMOUS ONE.
KAITO, THE "EYE OF GOD".
Though you're much smaller than I'd imagined.
WHETHER HEART, TECHNIQUE, OR PHYSIQUE YOU'VE STILL GOT THE MOST PERFECT ELITE AMONGST THE ELITE: KAITO.
What'd you say?!
YOU'RE PROBABLY THE ONLY ONE WHO ACTUALLY COULD CHAL-LENGE ME.
Ha ha ha!
Leaving it at that...
WELL, THAT'S WHY I'M HERE.
With you.
WHEN I WAS WATCHING YOU PLAY WITH THOSE KIDS...
...I REALIZED THAT YOU'RE ACTUALLY NOT ONLY A CRUEL ANGEL.

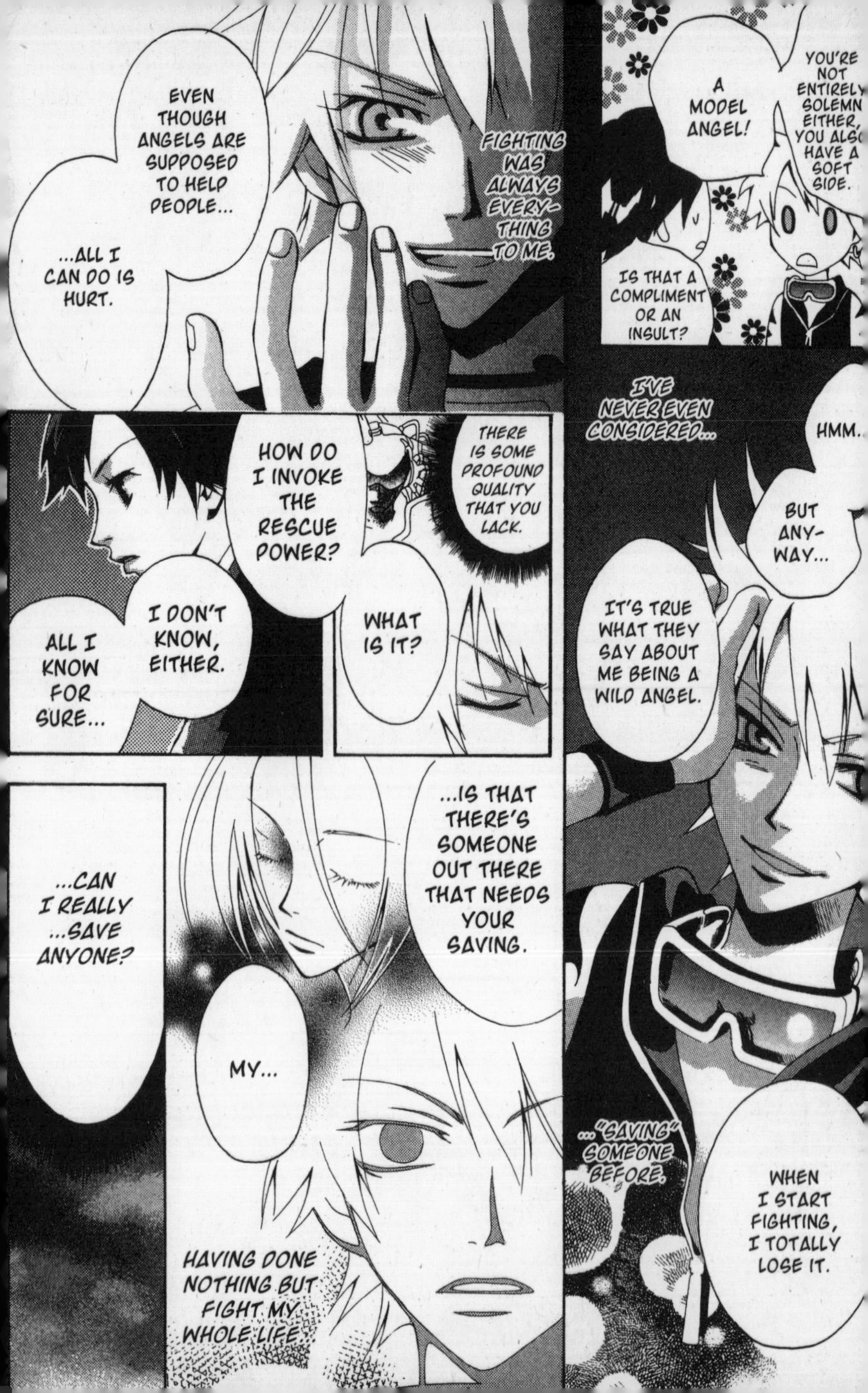
YOU'RE NOT ENTIRELY SOLEMN EITHER, YOU ALSO HAVE A SOFT SIDE.
A MODEL ANGEL!
IS THAT A COMPLIMENT OR AN INSULT?
FIGHTING WAS ALWAYS EVERYTHING TO ME.
EVEN THOUGH ANGELS ARE SUPPOSED TO HELP PEOPLE...
...ALL I CAN DO IS HURT.
HMM..
BUT ANYWAY...
I'VE NEVER EVEN CONSIDERED...
IT'S TRUE WHAT THEY SAY ABOUT ME BEING A WILD ANGEL.
WHEN I START FIGHTING, I TOTALLY LOSE IT.
..."SAVING" SOMEONE BEFORE.
THERE IS SOME PROFOUND QUALITY THAT YOU LACK.
WHAT IS IT?
HOW DO I INVOKE THE RESCUE POWER?
I DON'T KNOW, EITHER.
ALL I KNOW FOR SURE...
...IS THAT THERE'S SOMEONE OUT THERE THAT NEEDS YOUR SAVING.
MY...
HAVING DONE NOTHING BUT FIGHT MY WHOLE LIFE...
...CAN I REALLY ...SAVE ANYONE?

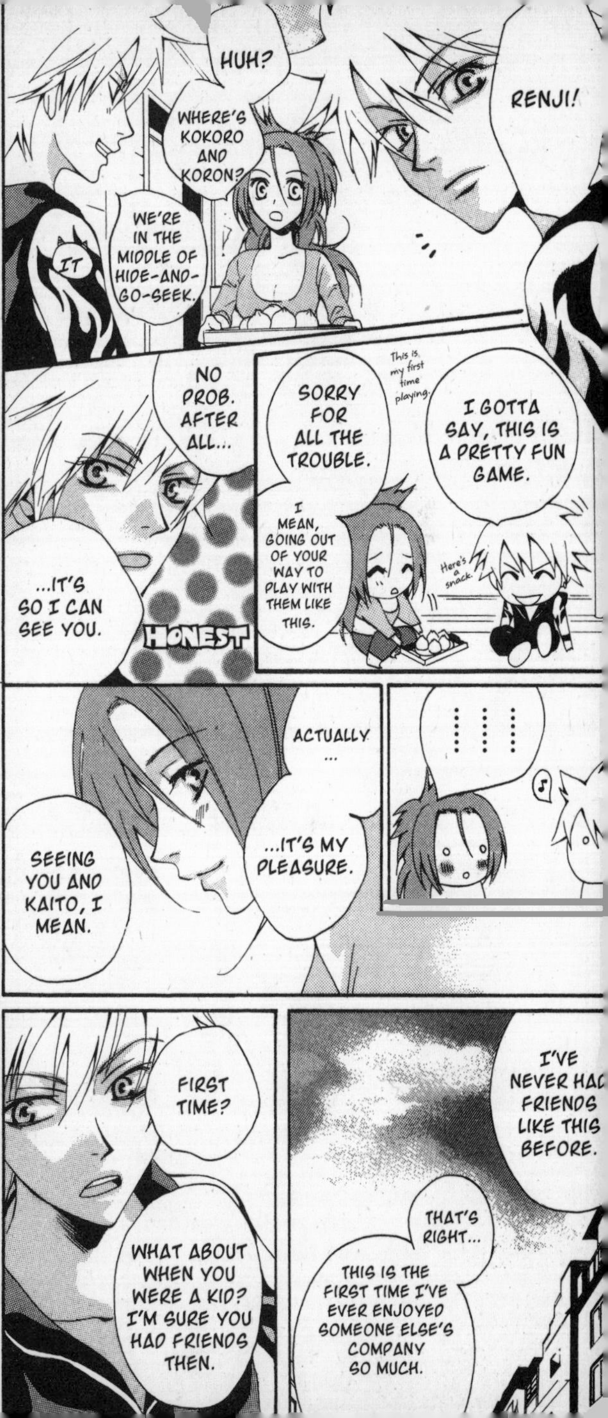
RENJI!
HUH?
...
WHERE'S KOKORO AND KORON?
WE'RE IN THE MIDDLE OF HIDE-AND-GO-SEEK.
IT
I GOTTA SAY, THIS IS A PRETTY FUN GAME.
This is my first time playing.
SORRY FOR ALL THE TROUBLE.
Here's a snack.
I MEAN, GOING OUT OF YOUR WAY TO PLAY WITH THEM LIKE THIS.
NO PROB. AFTER ALL...
...IT'S SO I CAN SEE YOU.
HONEST
......
♪
ACTUALLY...
...IT'S MY PLEASURE.
SEEING YOU AND KAITO, I MEAN.
I'VE NEVER HAD FRIENDS LIKE THIS BEFORE.
THAT'S RIGHT...
THIS IS THE FIRST TIME I'VE EVER ENJOYED SOMEONE ELSE'S COMPANY SO MUCH.
FIRST TIME?
WHAT ABOUT WHEN YOU WERE A KID? I'M SURE YOU HAD FRIENDS THEN.

SR

People sometimes ask this in their letters to me, so here's the answer: I first started drawing manga when I was in third grade. I think it was about that time, yes. I've always loved drawing. I think it was in sixth grade that I actually started penning my drawings in properly. I would basically serialize (...) my stories on notebook paper and written in pencil, and show them to my friends. God, I was so dumb! Uuh...now I'm going to borrow this little space to give a message to my friends from back then: Please return those manga notebooks I gave you! I'm serious! They serve as the greatest embarrassment of my life! (sniffle)

★★★★★★★★

About Chapter 1.
I'm actually very bad at drawing women and children... Even so, my readers were quite taken by the three characters below so I'm very pleased by that. ☺

Take care!

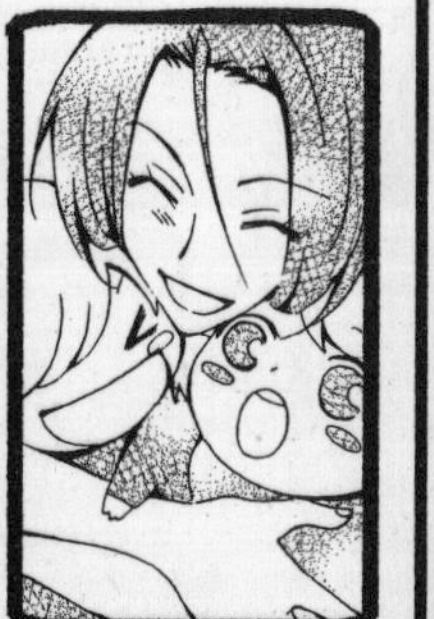

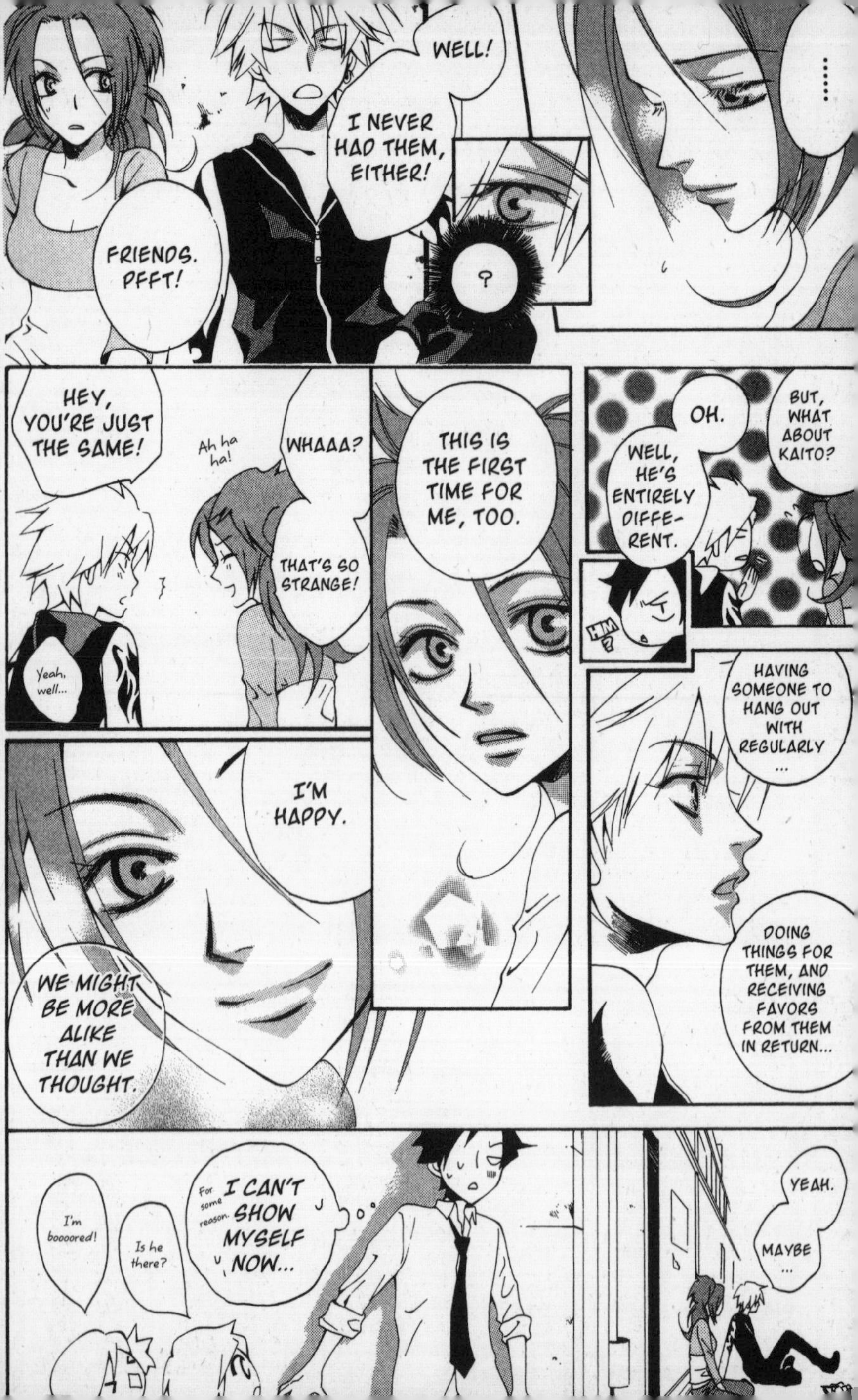
......
?
WELL!
I NEVER HAD THEM, EITHER!
FRIENDS. PFFT!
BUT, WHAT ABOUT KAITO?
OH.
WELL, HE'S ENTIRELY DIFFE-RENT.
HM?
HAVING SOMEONE TO HANG OUT WITH REGULARLY ...
DOING THINGS FOR THEM, AND RECEIVING FAVORS FROM THEM IN RETURN...
THIS IS THE FIRST TIME FOR ME, TOO.
WHAAA?
THAT'S SO STRANGE!
Ah ha ha!
HEY, YOU'RE JUST THE SAME!
Yeah, well...
I'M HAPPY.
WE MIGHT BE MORE ALIKE THAN WE THOUGHT.
YEAH.
MAYBE ...
I CAN'T SHOW MYSELF NOW...
For some reason.
Is he there?
I'm booored!

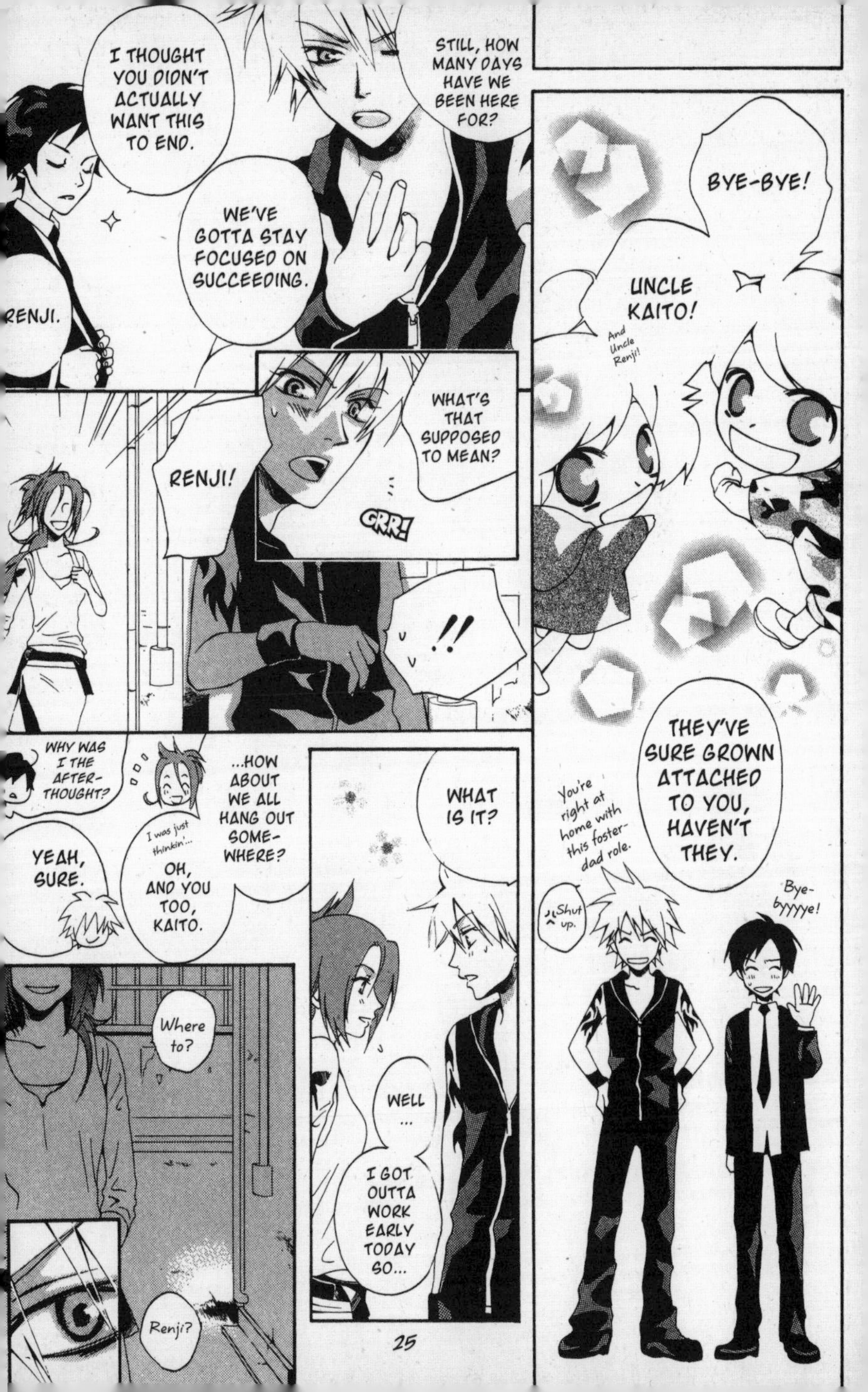
BYE-BYE!
UNCLE KAITO!
And Uncle Renji!
THEY'VE SURE GROWN ATTACHED TO YOU, HAVEN'T THEY.
You're right at home with this foster-dad role.
Shut up.
Bye-byyyye!
STILL, HOW MANY DAYS HAVE WE BEEN HERE FOR?
I THOUGHT YOU DIDN'T ACTUALLY WANT THIS TO END.
WE'VE GOTTA STAY FOCUSED ON SUCCEEDING.
RENJI.
WHAT'S THAT SUPPOSED TO MEAN?
GRR!
RENJI!
!!
WHAT IS IT?
WELL...
I GOT OUTTA WORK EARLY TODAY SO...
...HOW ABOUT WE ALL HANG OUT SOMEWHERE?
WHY WAS I THE AFTER-THOUGHT?
I was just thinkin'...
OH, AND YOU TOO, KAITO.
YEAH, SURE.
Where to?
Renji?

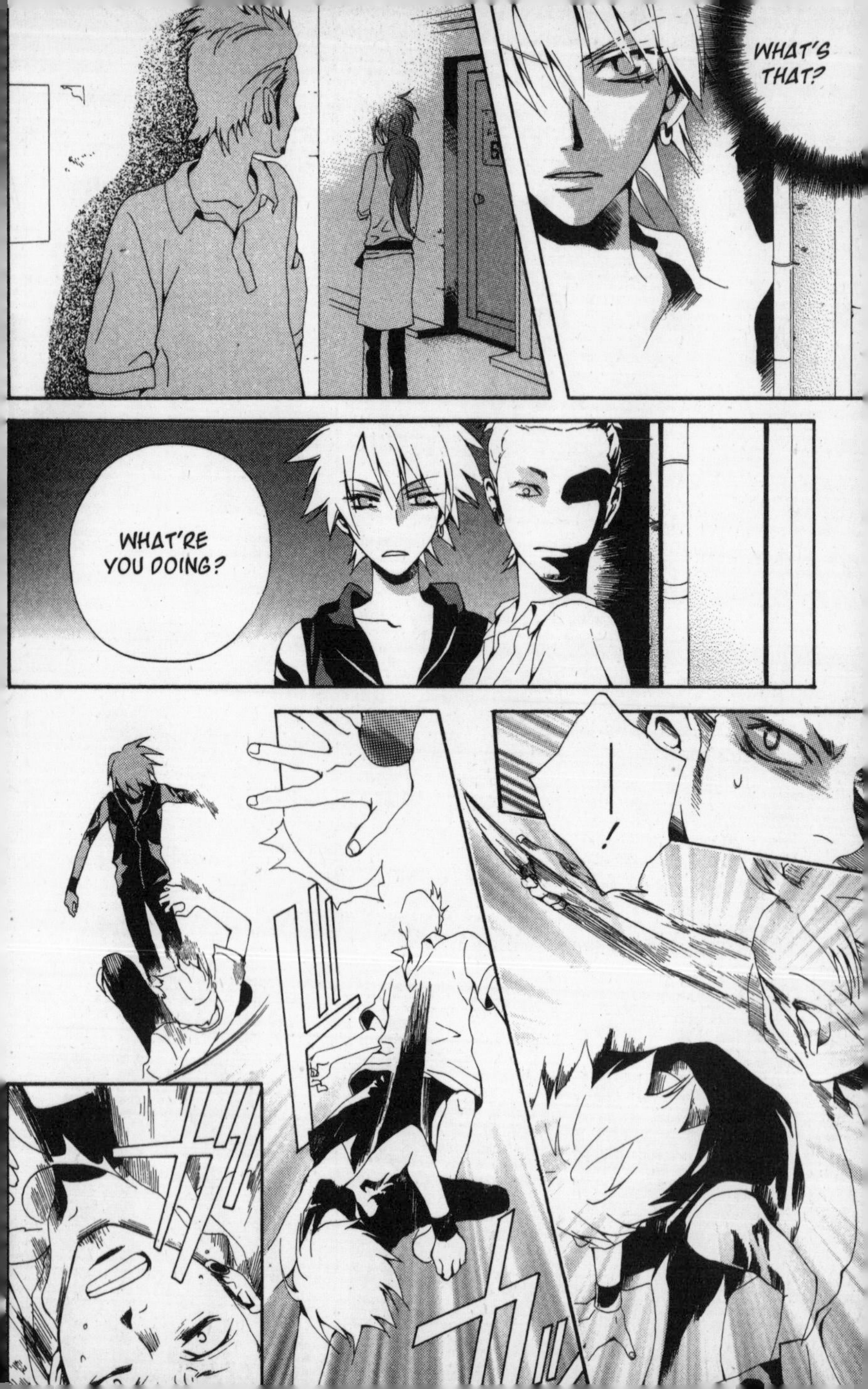
WHAT'S THAT?
WHAT'RE YOU DOING?
!

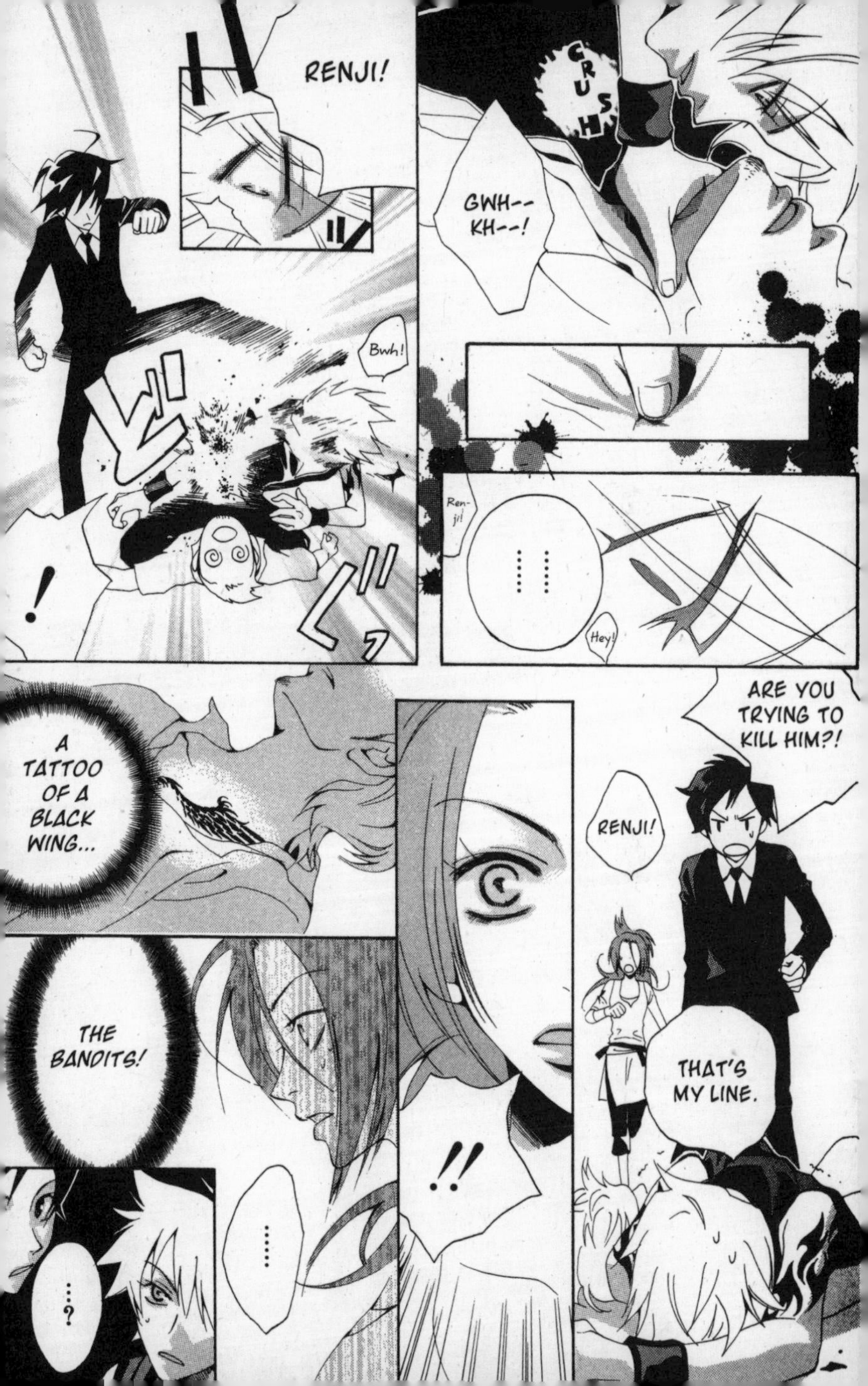
CRUSH
GWH-- KH--!
Ren-ji!
......
Hey!
RENJI!
Bwh!
!
ARE YOU TRYING TO KILL HIM?!
RENJI!
THAT'S MY LINE.
!!
A TATTOO OF A BLACK WING...
THE BANDITS!
......
...?

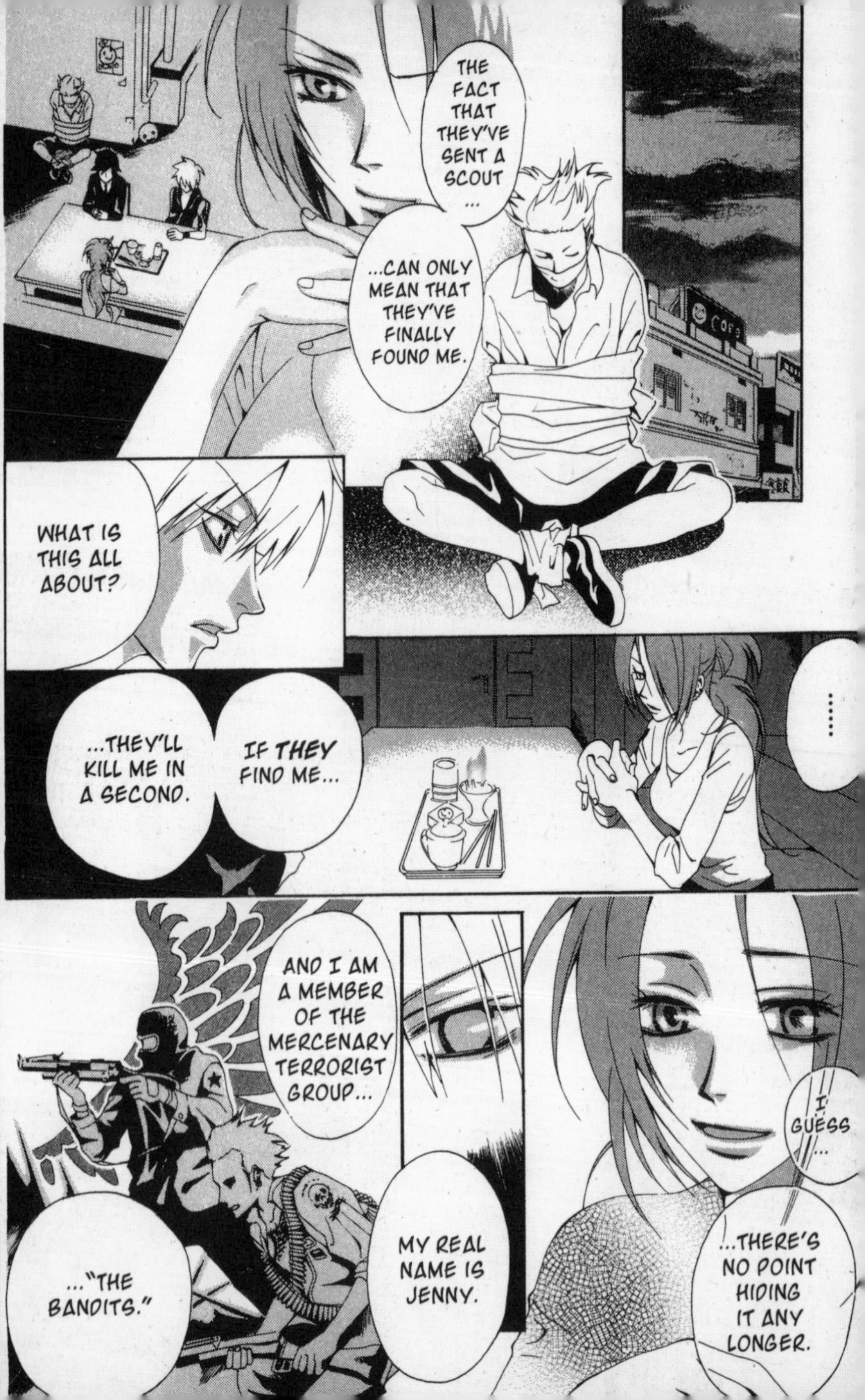
THE FACT THAT THEY'VE SENT A SCOUT...
...CAN ONLY MEAN THAT THEY'VE FINALLY FOUND ME.
WHAT IS THIS ALL ABOUT?
......
IF *THEY* FIND ME...
...THEY'LL KILL ME IN A SECOND.
I GUESS...
...THERE'S NO POINT HIDING IT ANY LONGER.
MY REAL NAME IS JENNY.
AND I AM A MEMBER OF THE MERCENARY TERRORIST GROUP...
..."THE BANDITS."

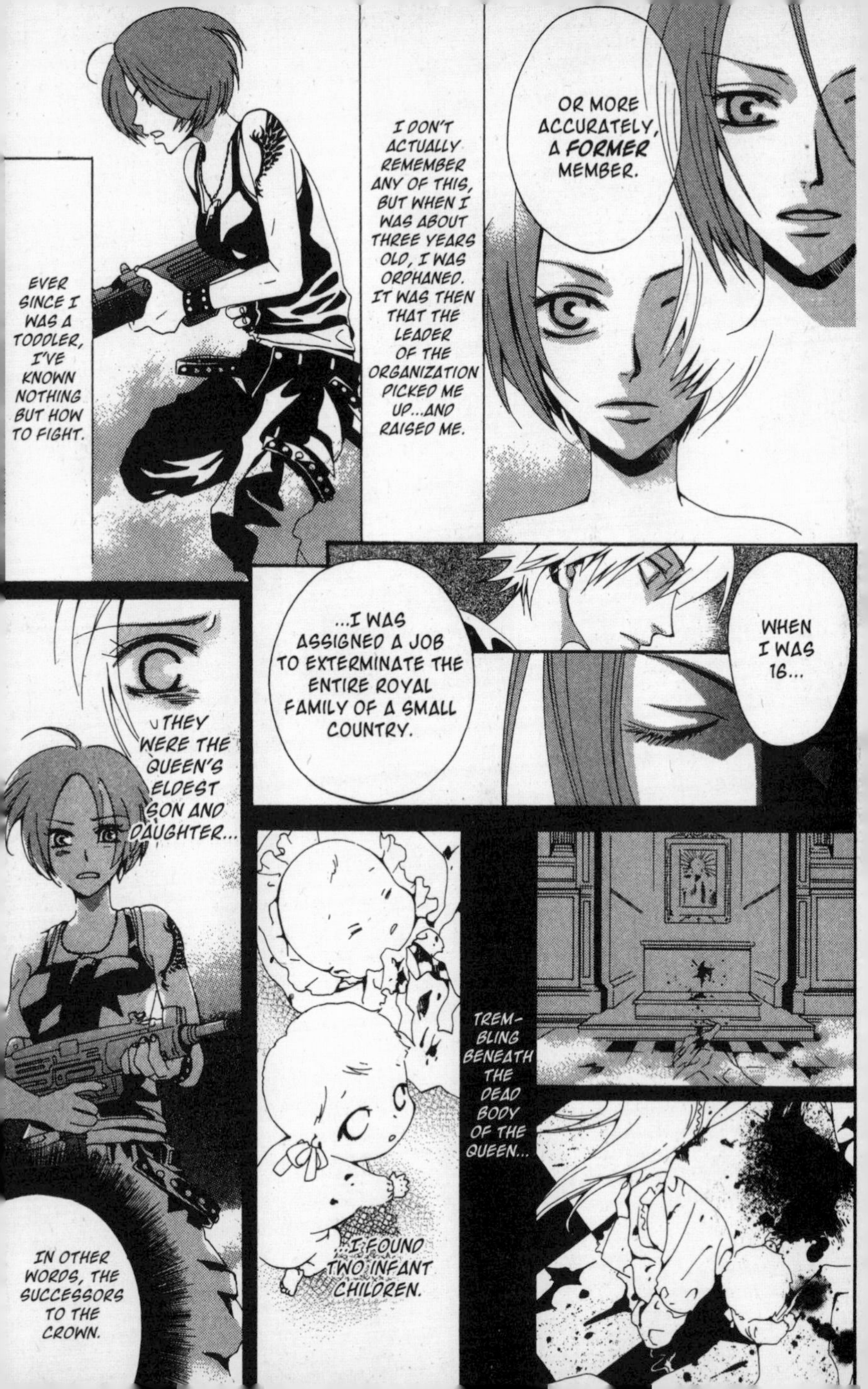
OR MORE ACCURATELY, A **FORMER** MEMBER.
I DON'T ACTUALLY REMEMBER ANY OF THIS, BUT WHEN I WAS ABOUT THREE YEARS OLD, I WAS ORPHANED. IT WAS THEN THAT THE LEADER OF THE ORGANIZATION PICKED ME UP...AND RAISED ME.
EVER SINCE I WAS A TODDLER, I'VE KNOWN NOTHING BUT HOW TO FIGHT.
WHEN I WAS 16...
...I WAS ASSIGNED A JOB TO EXTERMINATE THE ENTIRE ROYAL FAMILY OF A SMALL COUNTRY.
TREMBLING BENEATH THE DEAD BODY OF THE QUEEN...
...I FOUND TWO INFANT CHILDREN.
THEY WERE THE QUEEN'S ELDEST SON AND DAUGHTER...
IN OTHER WORDS, THE SUCCESSORS TO THE CROWN.

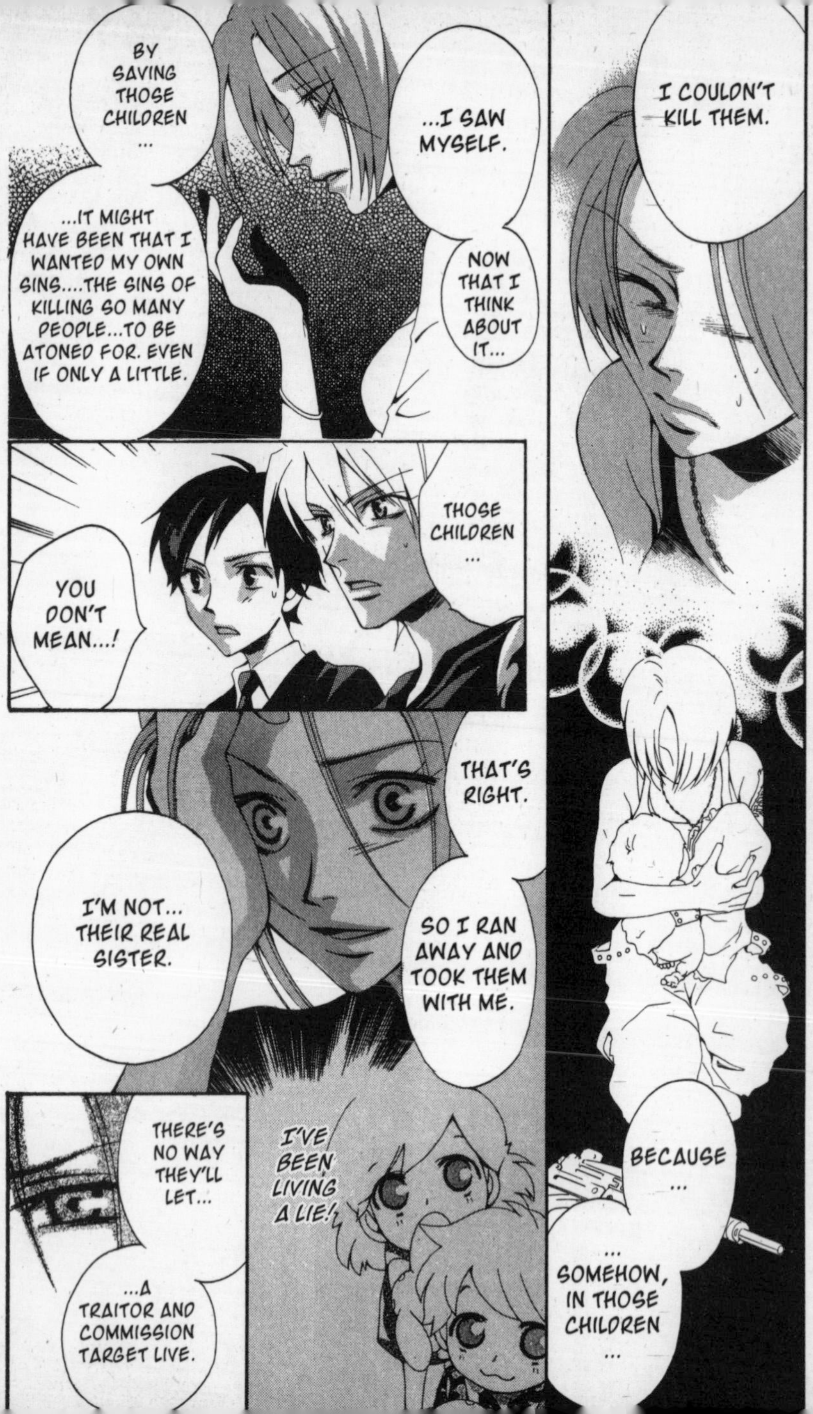
I COULDN'T KILL THEM.
BECAUSE...
...SOMEHOW, IN THOSE CHILDREN...
...I SAW MYSELF.
BY SAVING THOSE CHILDREN...
NOW THAT I THINK ABOUT IT...
...IT MIGHT HAVE BEEN THAT I WANTED MY OWN SINS....THE SINS OF KILLING SO MANY PEOPLE...TO BE ATONED FOR. EVEN IF ONLY A LITTLE.
THOSE CHILDREN...
YOU DON'T MEAN...!
THAT'S RIGHT.
I'M NOT... THEIR REAL SISTER.
SO I RAN AWAY AND TOOK THEM WITH ME.
I'VE BEEN LIVING A LIE!
THERE'S NO WAY THEY'LL LET...
...A TRAITOR AND COMMISSION TARGET LIVE.

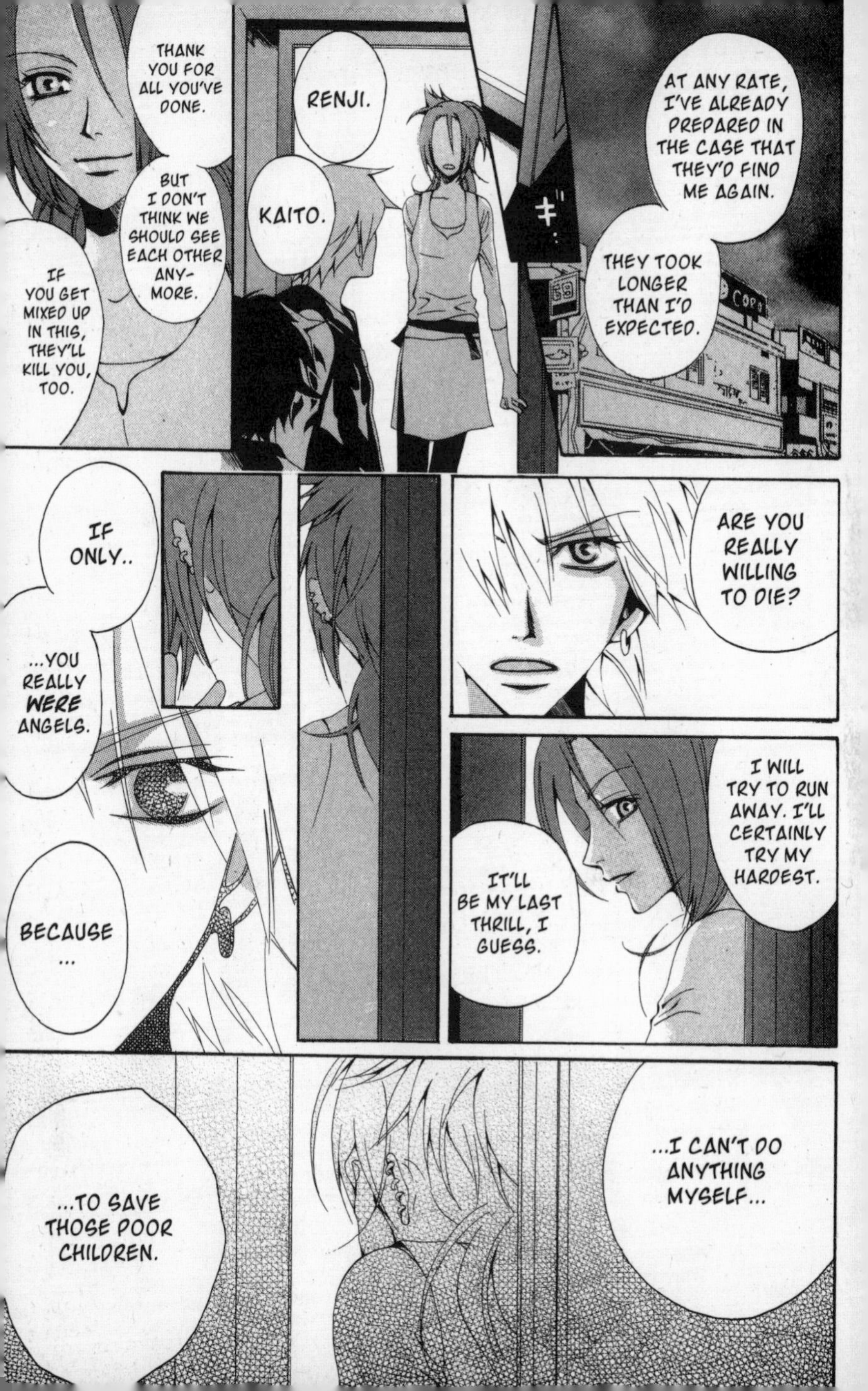
AT ANY RATE, I'VE ALREADY PREPARED IN THE CASE THAT THEY'D FIND ME AGAIN.
THEY TOOK LONGER THAN I'D EXPECTED.
RENJI.
KAITO.
THANK YOU FOR ALL YOU'VE DONE.
BUT I DON'T THINK WE SHOULD SEE EACH OTHER ANYMORE.
IF YOU GET MIXED UP IN THIS, THEY'LL KILL YOU, TOO.
ARE YOU REALLY WILLING TO DIE?
I WILL TRY TO RUN AWAY. I'LL CERTAINLY TRY MY HARDEST.
IT'LL BE MY LAST THRILL, I GUESS.
IF ONLY..
...YOU REALLY *WERE* ANGELS.
BECAUSE ...
...I CAN'T DO ANYTHING MYSELF...
...TO SAVE THOSE POOR CHILDREN.

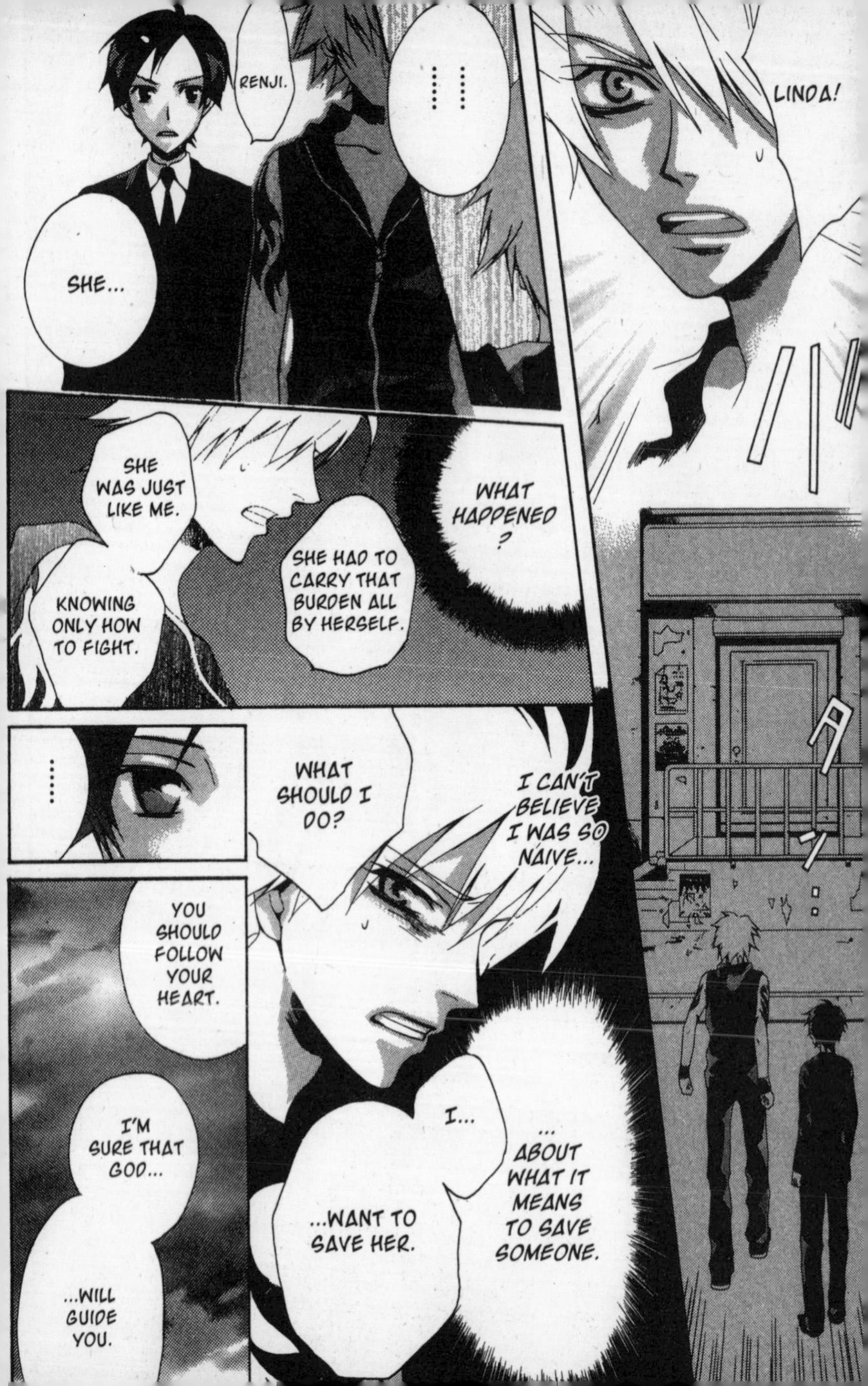
LINDA!
......
RENJI.
SHE...
WHAT HAPPENED?
SHE WAS JUST LIKE ME.
SHE HAD TO CARRY THAT BURDEN ALL BY HERSELF.
KNOWING ONLY HOW TO FIGHT.
WHAT SHOULD I DO?
......
I CAN'T BELIEVE I WAS SO NAIVE...
...ABOUT WHAT IT MEANS TO SAVE SOMEONE.
I...
...WANT TO SAVE HER.
YOU SHOULD FOLLOW YOUR HEART.
I'M SURE THAT GOD...
...WILL GUIDE YOU.

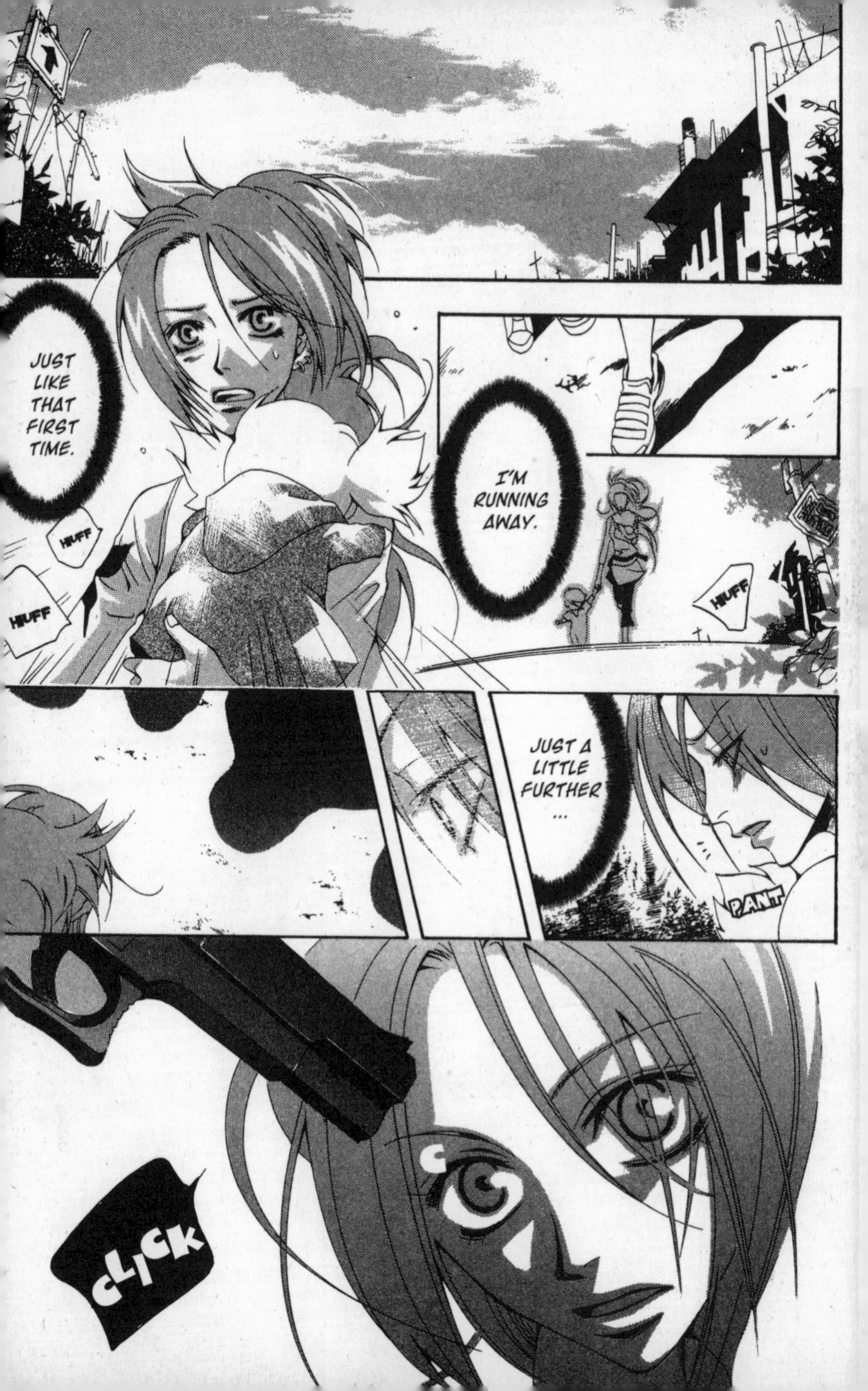
I'M RUNNING AWAY.
HUFF
JUST LIKE THAT FIRST TIME.
HUFF
HUFF
JUST A LITTLE FURTHER ...
PANT
CLICK

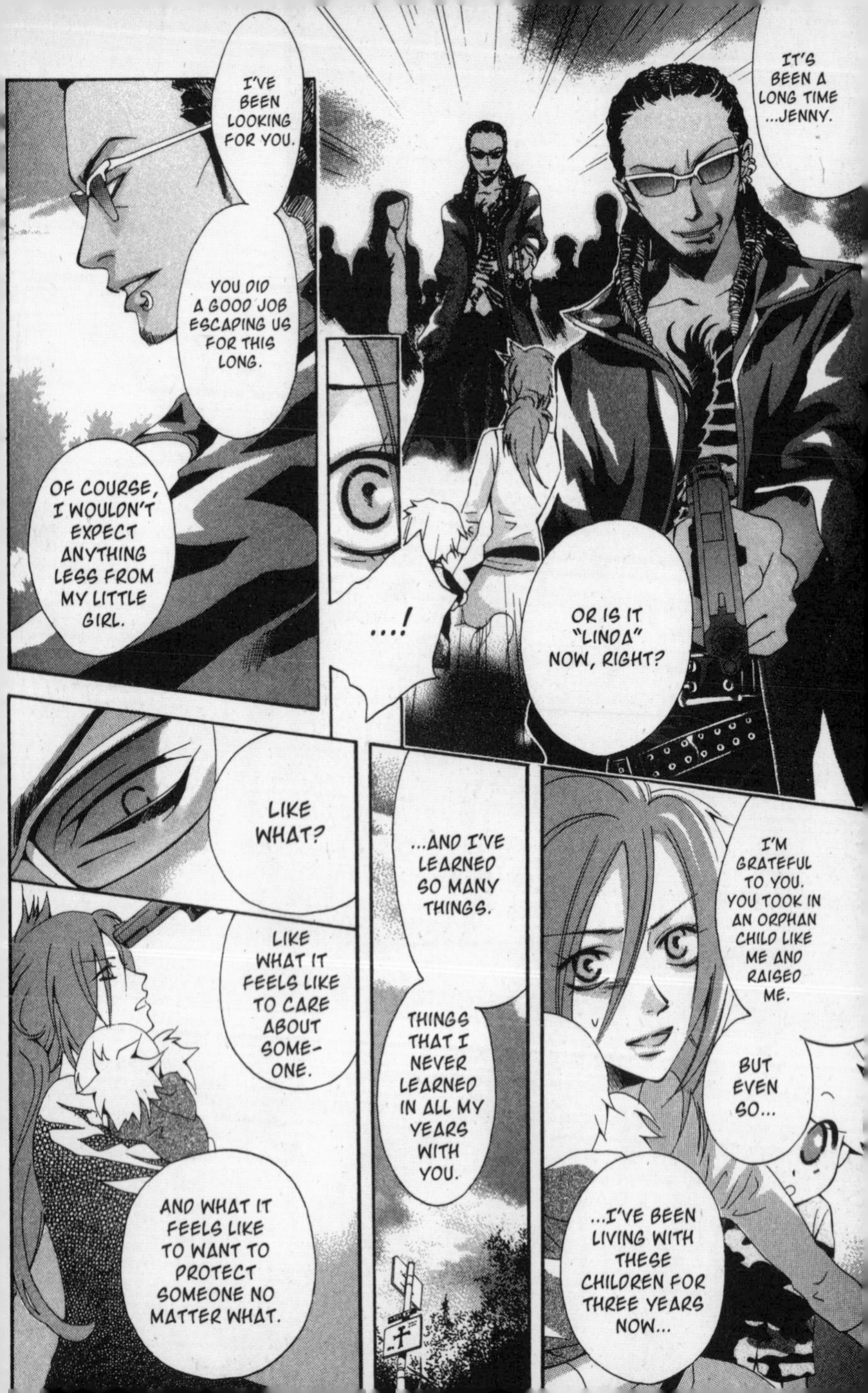
IT'S BEEN A LONG TIME ...JENNY.
OR IS IT "LINDA" NOW, RIGHT?
...!
I'VE BEEN LOOKING FOR YOU.
YOU DID A GOOD JOB ESCAPING US FOR THIS LONG.
OF COURSE, I WOULDN'T EXPECT ANYTHING LESS FROM MY LITTLE GIRL.
I'M GRATEFUL TO YOU. YOU TOOK IN AN ORPHAN CHILD LIKE ME AND RAISED ME.
BUT EVEN SO...
...I'VE BEEN LIVING WITH THESE CHILDREN FOR THREE YEARS NOW...
...AND I'VE LEARNED SO MANY THINGS.
THINGS THAT I NEVER LEARNED IN ALL MY YEARS WITH YOU.
LIKE WHAT?
LIKE WHAT IT FEELS LIKE TO CARE ABOUT SOME-ONE.
AND WHAT IT FEELS LIKE TO WANT TO PROTECT SOMEONE NO MATTER WHAT.

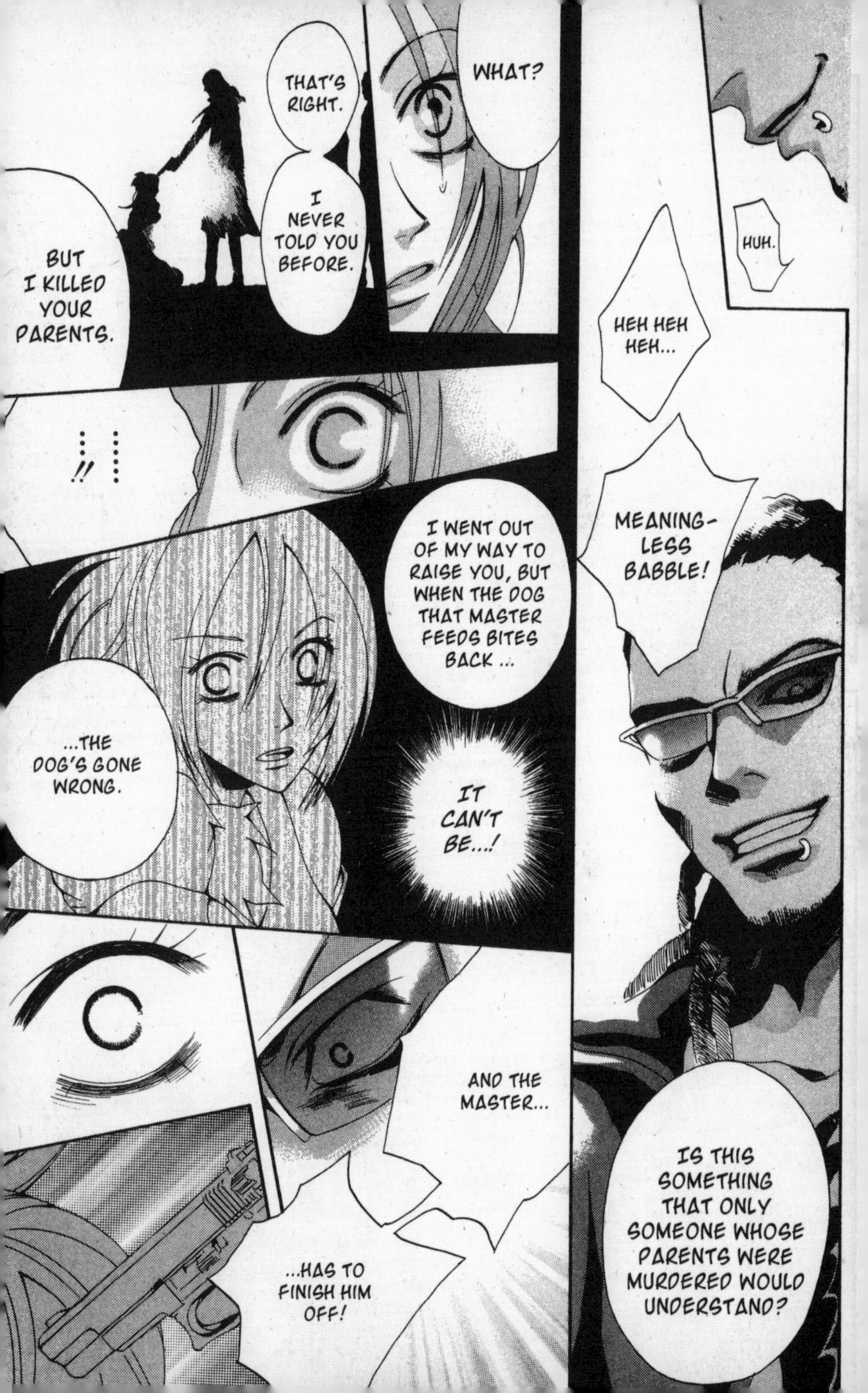
HUH.
HEH HEH HEH...
MEANING-LESS BABBLE!
IS THIS SOMETHING THAT ONLY SOMEONE WHOSE PARENTS WERE MURDERED WOULD UNDERSTAND?
WHAT?
THAT'S RIGHT.
I NEVER TOLD YOU BEFORE.
BUT I KILLED YOUR PARENTS.
......!!
I WENT OUT OF MY WAY TO RAISE YOU, BUT WHEN THE DOG THAT MASTER FEEDS BITES BACK ...
IT CAN'T BE...!
...THE DOG'S GONE WRONG.
AND THE MASTER...
...HAS TO FINISH HIM OFF!

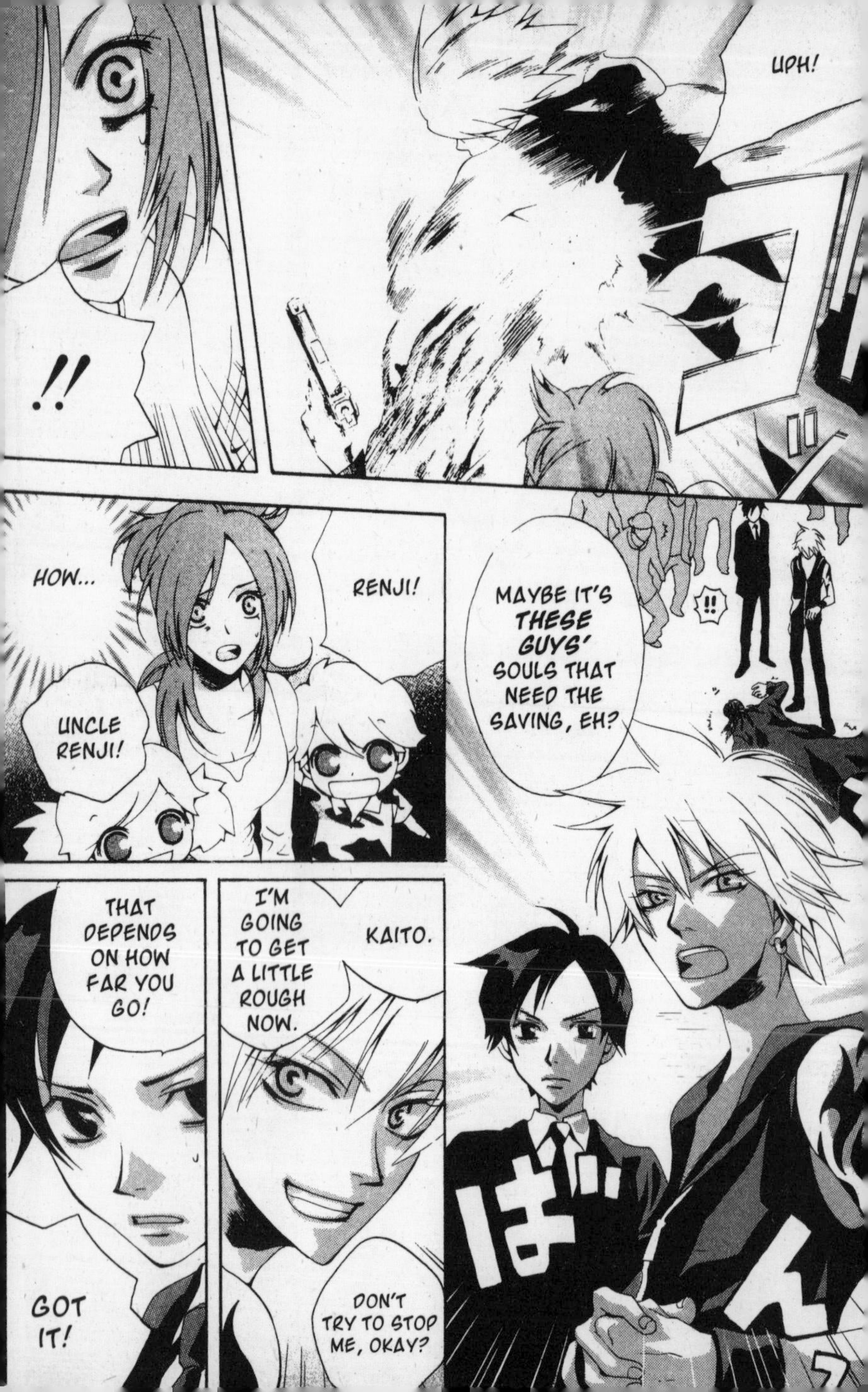
UPH!
!!
MAYBE IT'S THESE GUYS' SOULS THAT NEED THE SAVING, EH?
!!
RENJI!
HOW...
UNCLE RENJI!
KAITO.
I'M GOING TO GET A LITTLE ROUGH NOW.
DON'T TRY TO STOP ME, OKAY?
THAT DEPENDS ON HOW FAR YOU GO!
GOT IT!

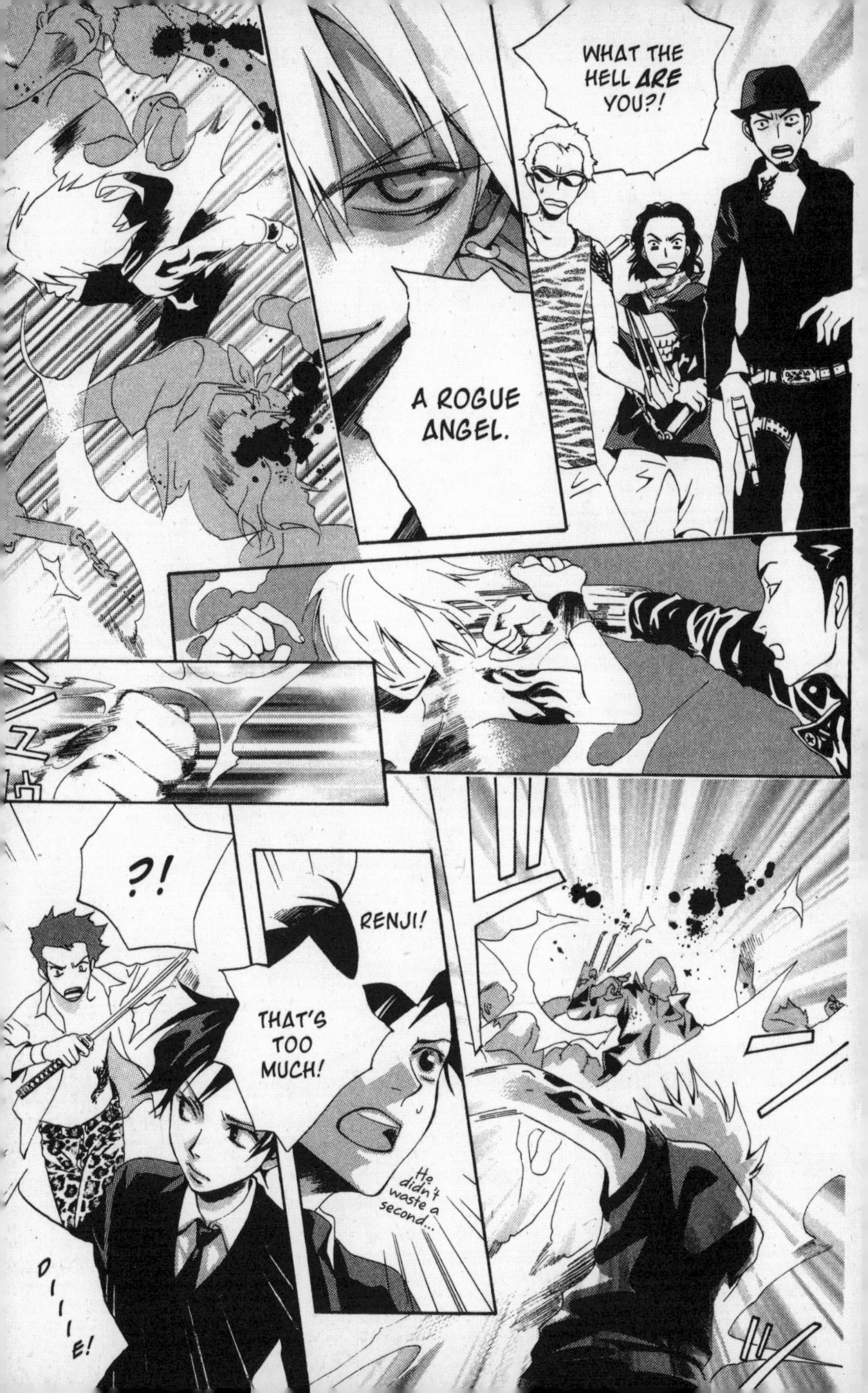
WHAT THE HELL ARE YOU?!
A ROGUE ANGEL.
RENJI!
THAT'S TOO MUCH!
He didn't waste a second...
?!
DIIIIE!

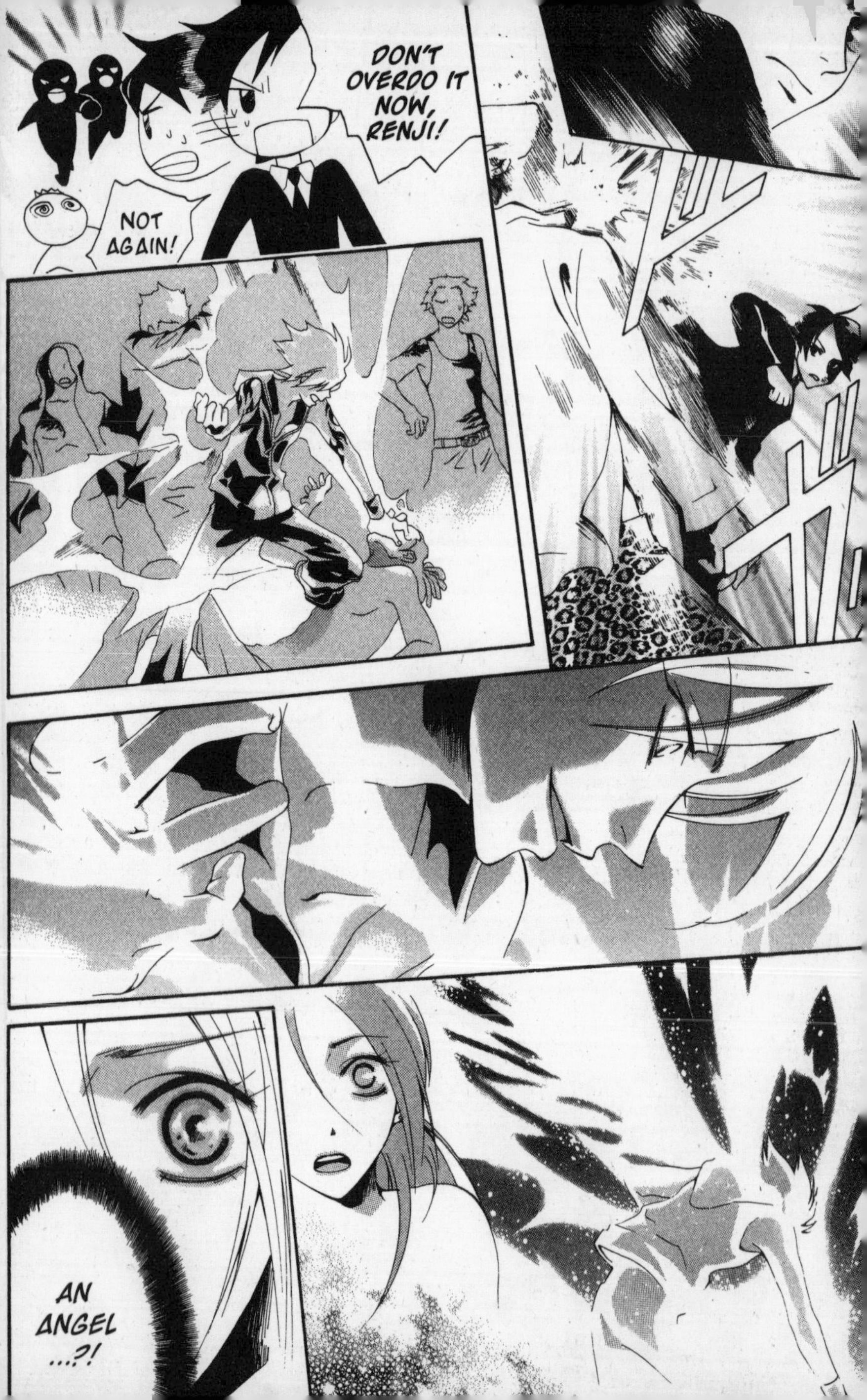
DON'T OVERDO IT NOW, RENJI!
NOT AGAIN!
AN ANGEL ...?!

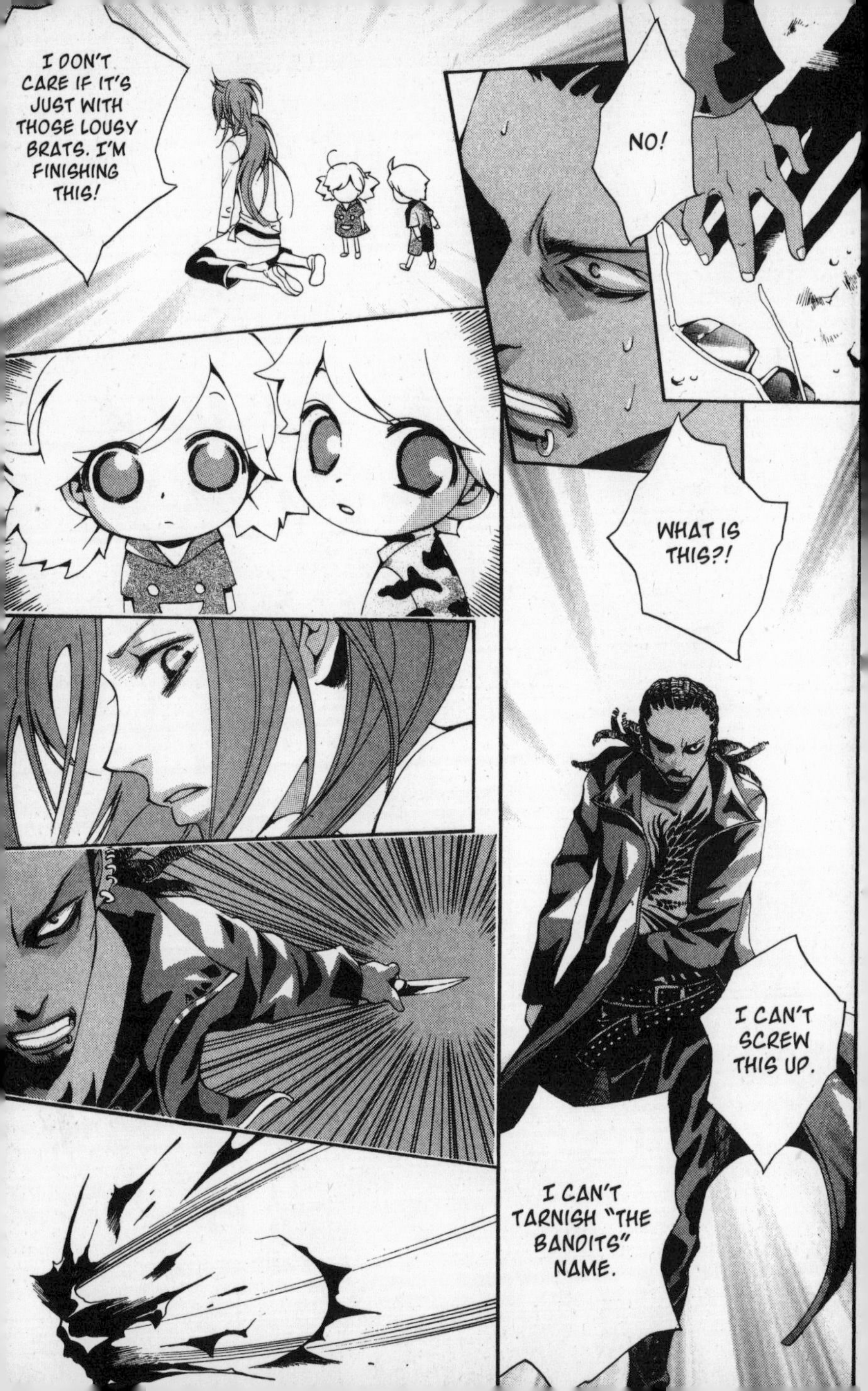
NO!
WHAT IS THIS?!
I CAN'T SCREW THIS UP.
I CAN'T TARNISH "THE BANDITS" NAME.
I DON'T CARE IF IT'S JUST WITH THOSE LOUSY BRATS. I'M FINISHING THIS!

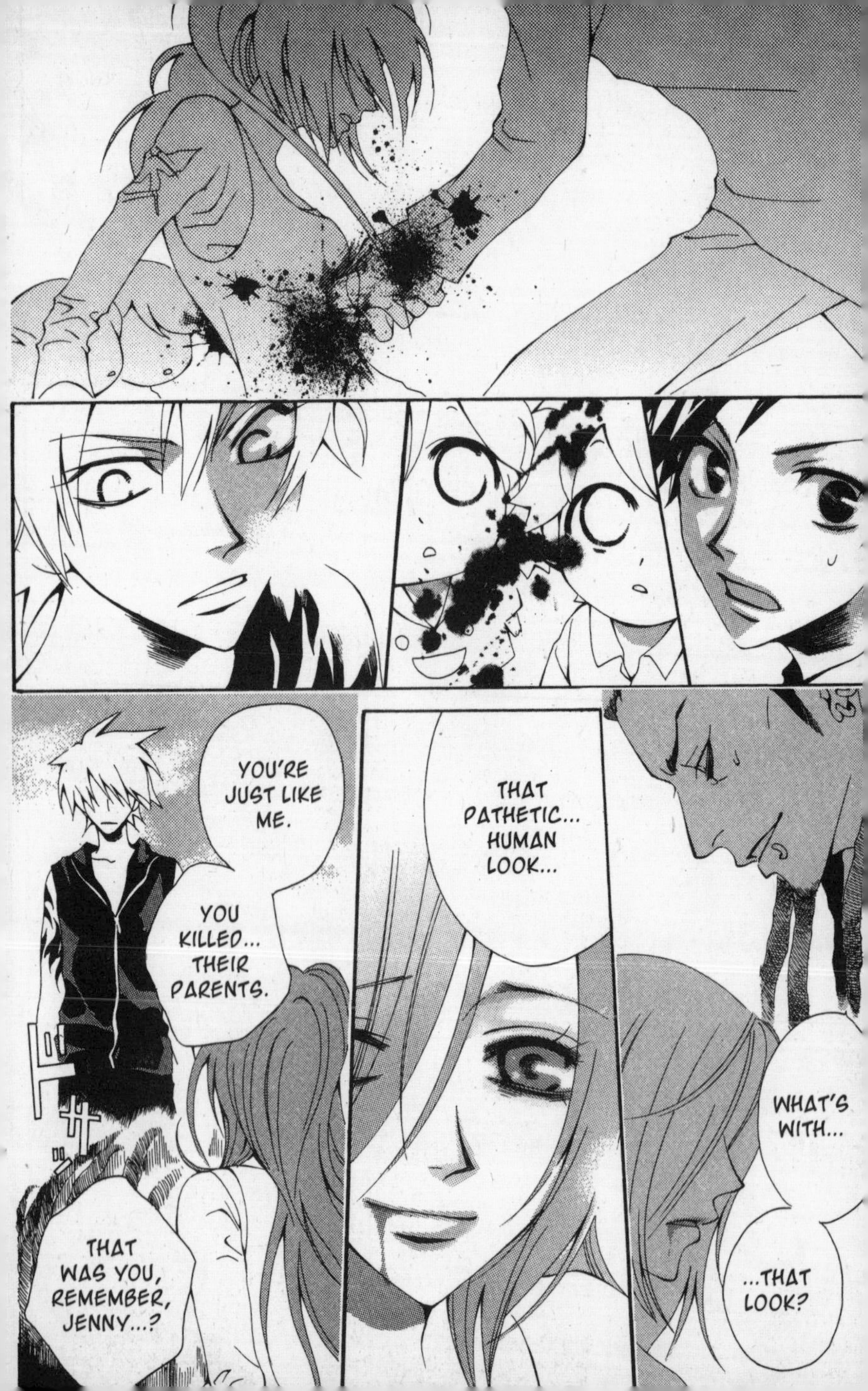
WHAT'S WITH...
...THAT LOOK?
THAT PATHETIC... HUMAN LOOK...
YOU'RE JUST LIKE ME.
YOU KILLED... THEIR PARENTS.
THAT WAS YOU, REMEMBER, JENNY...?

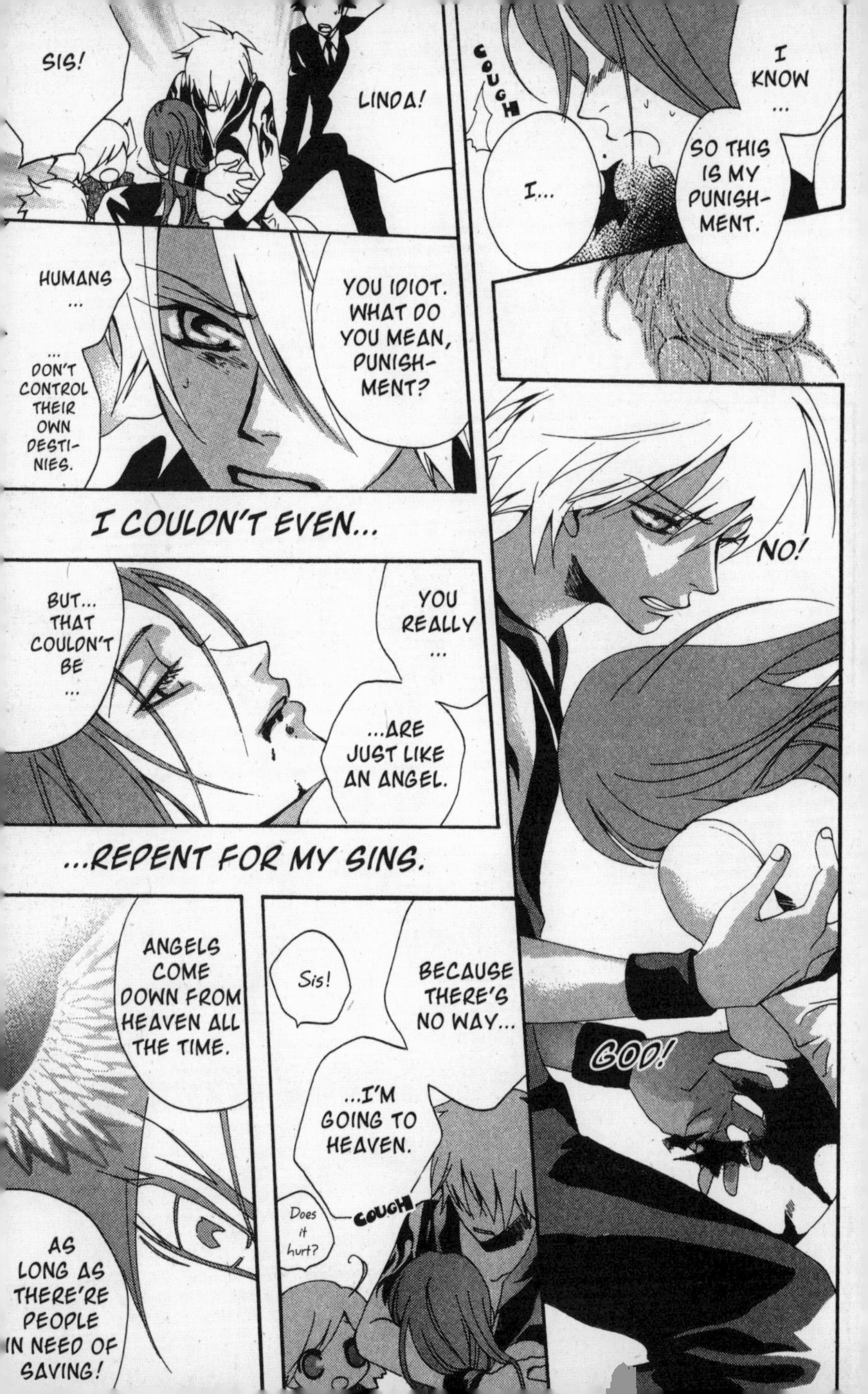
COUGH
I KNOW ...
SO THIS IS MY PUNISH-MENT.
I...
SIS!
LINDA!
YOU IDIOT. WHAT DO YOU MEAN, PUNISH-MENT?
HUMANS ...
... DON'T CONTROL THEIR OWN DESTI-NIES.
I COULDN'T EVEN...
YOU REALLY ...
...ARE JUST LIKE AN ANGEL.
BUT... THAT COULDN'T BE ...
...REPENT FOR MY SINS.
Sis!
BECAUSE THERE'S NO WAY...
...I'M GOING TO HEAVEN.
Does it hurt?
COUGH
ANGELS COME DOWN FROM HEAVEN ALL THE TIME.
AS LONG AS THERE'RE PEOPLE IN NEED OF SAVING!
NO!
GOD!

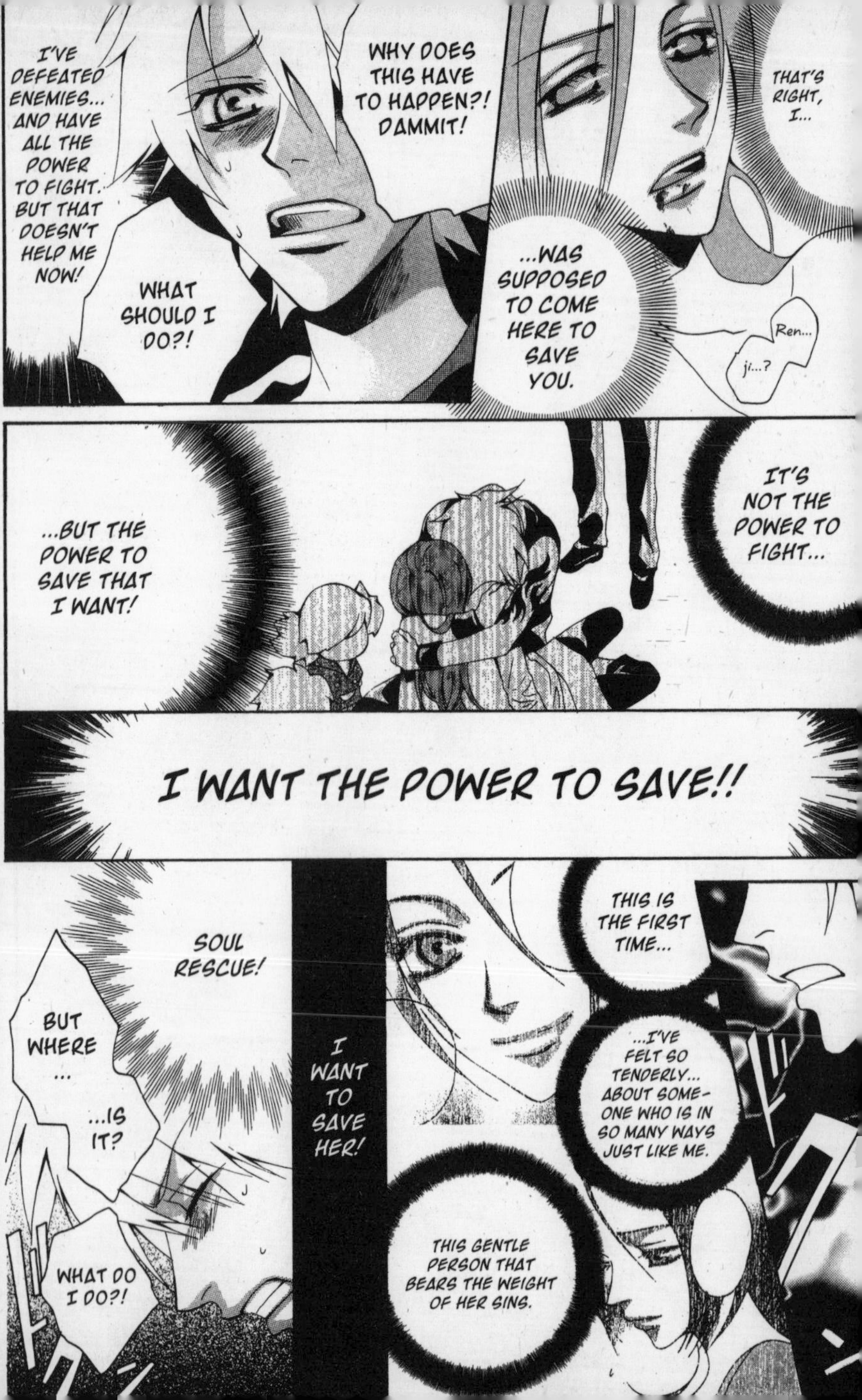
THAT'S RIGHT, I...
...WAS SUPPOSED TO COME HERE TO SAVE YOU.
Ren...
ji...?
WHY DOES THIS HAVE TO HAPPEN?! DAMMIT!
I'VE DEFEATED ENEMIES... AND HAVE ALL THE POWER TO FIGHT. BUT THAT DOESN'T HELP ME NOW!
WHAT SHOULD I DO?!
IT'S NOT THE POWER TO FIGHT...
...BUT THE POWER TO SAVE THAT I WANT!
I WANT THE POWER TO SAVE!!
THIS IS THE FIRST TIME...
...I'VE FELT SO TENDERLY... ABOUT SOME-ONE WHO IS IN SO MANY WAYS JUST LIKE ME.
THIS GENTLE PERSON THAT BEARS THE WEIGHT OF HER SINS.
I WANT TO SAVE HER!
SOUL RESCUE!
BUT WHERE ...
...IS IT?
WHAT DO I DO?!

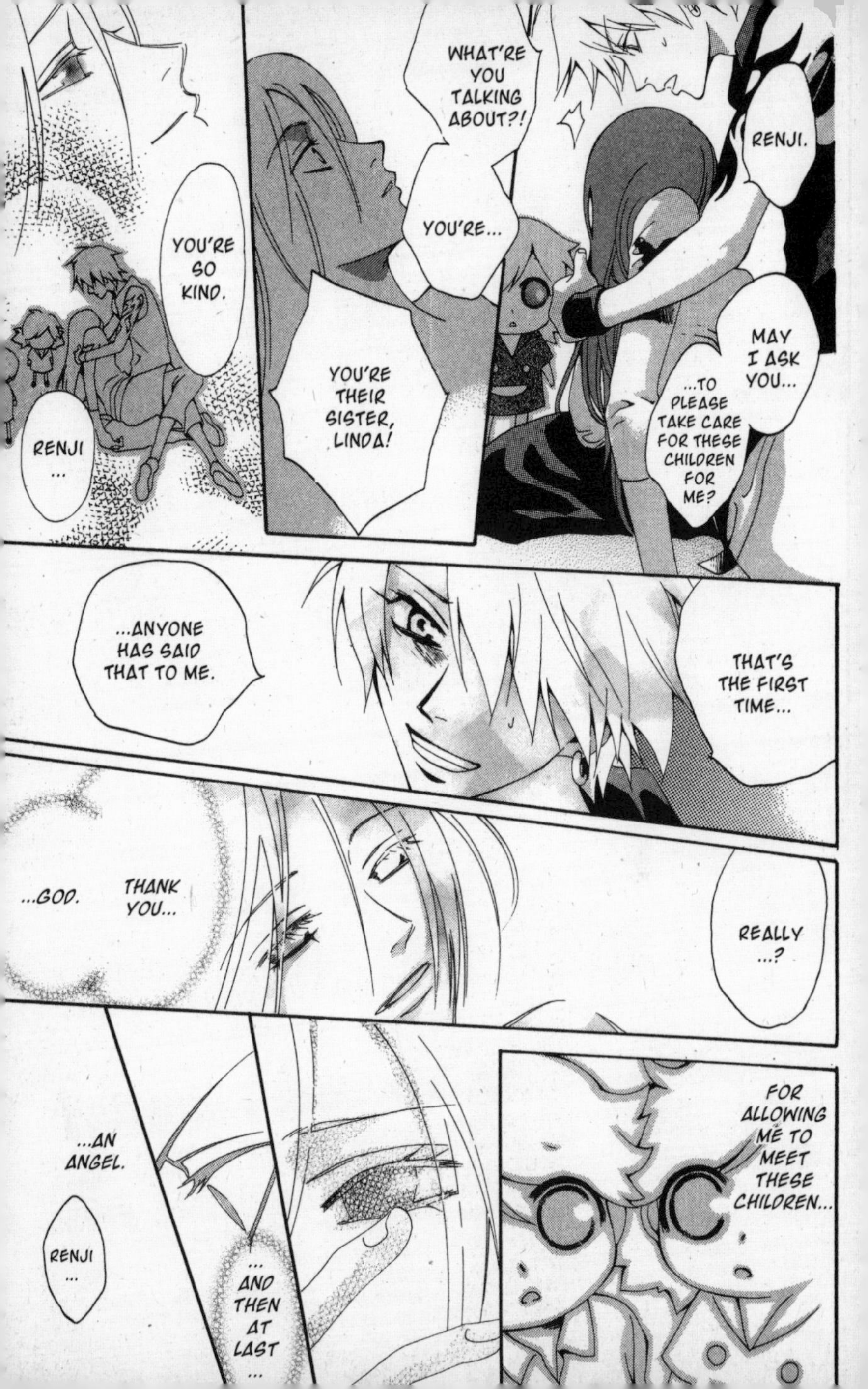
RENJI.
MAY I ASK YOU...
...TO PLEASE TAKE CARE FOR THESE CHILDREN FOR ME?
WHAT'RE YOU TALKING ABOUT?!
YOU'RE...
YOU'RE THEIR SISTER, LINDA!
YOU'RE SO KIND.
RENJI ...
THAT'S THE FIRST TIME...
...ANYONE HAS SAID THAT TO ME.
REALLY ...?
THANK YOU...
...GOD.
FOR ALLOWING ME TO MEET THESE CHILDREN...
... AND THEN AT LAST ...
...AN ANGEL.
RENJI ...

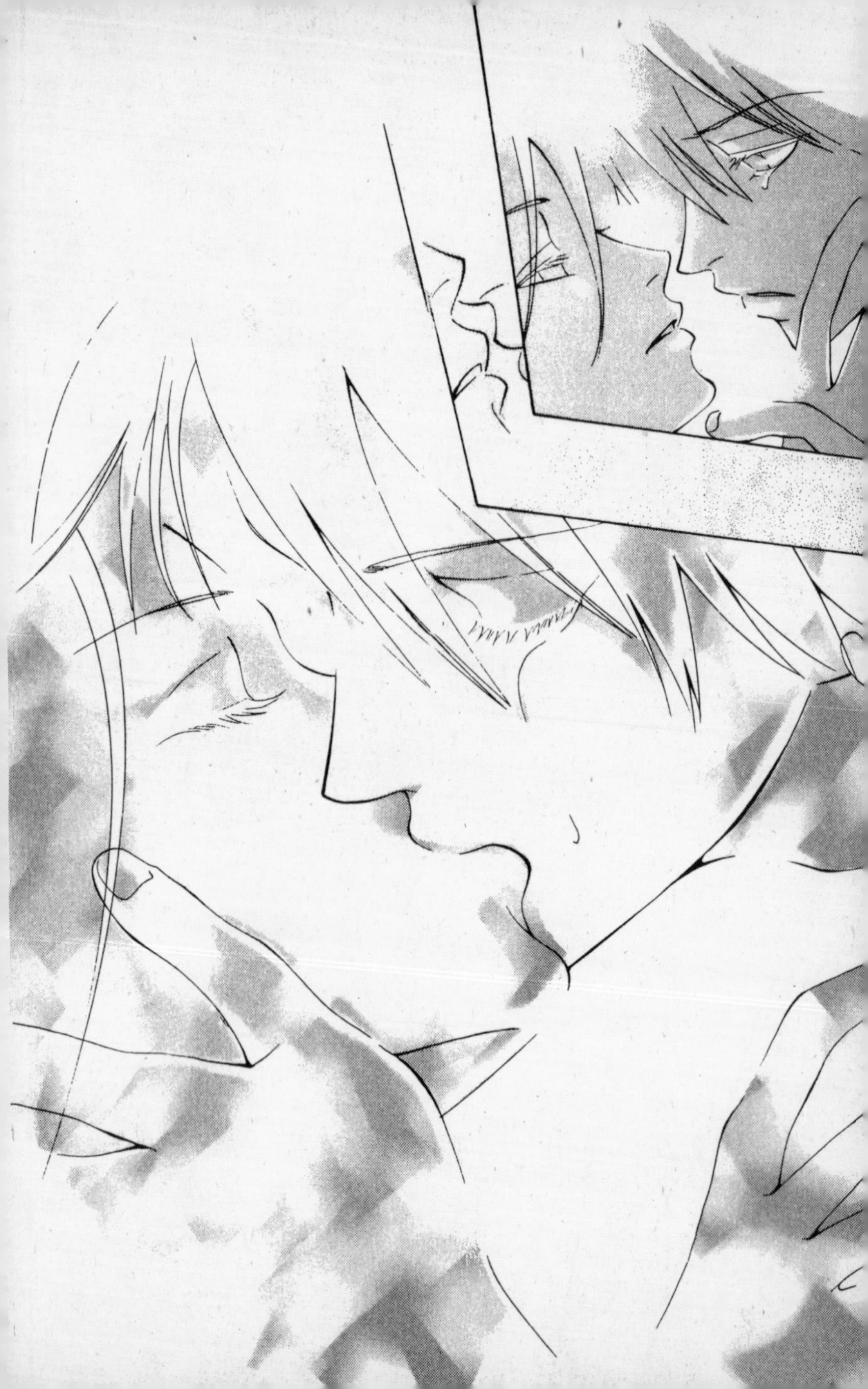

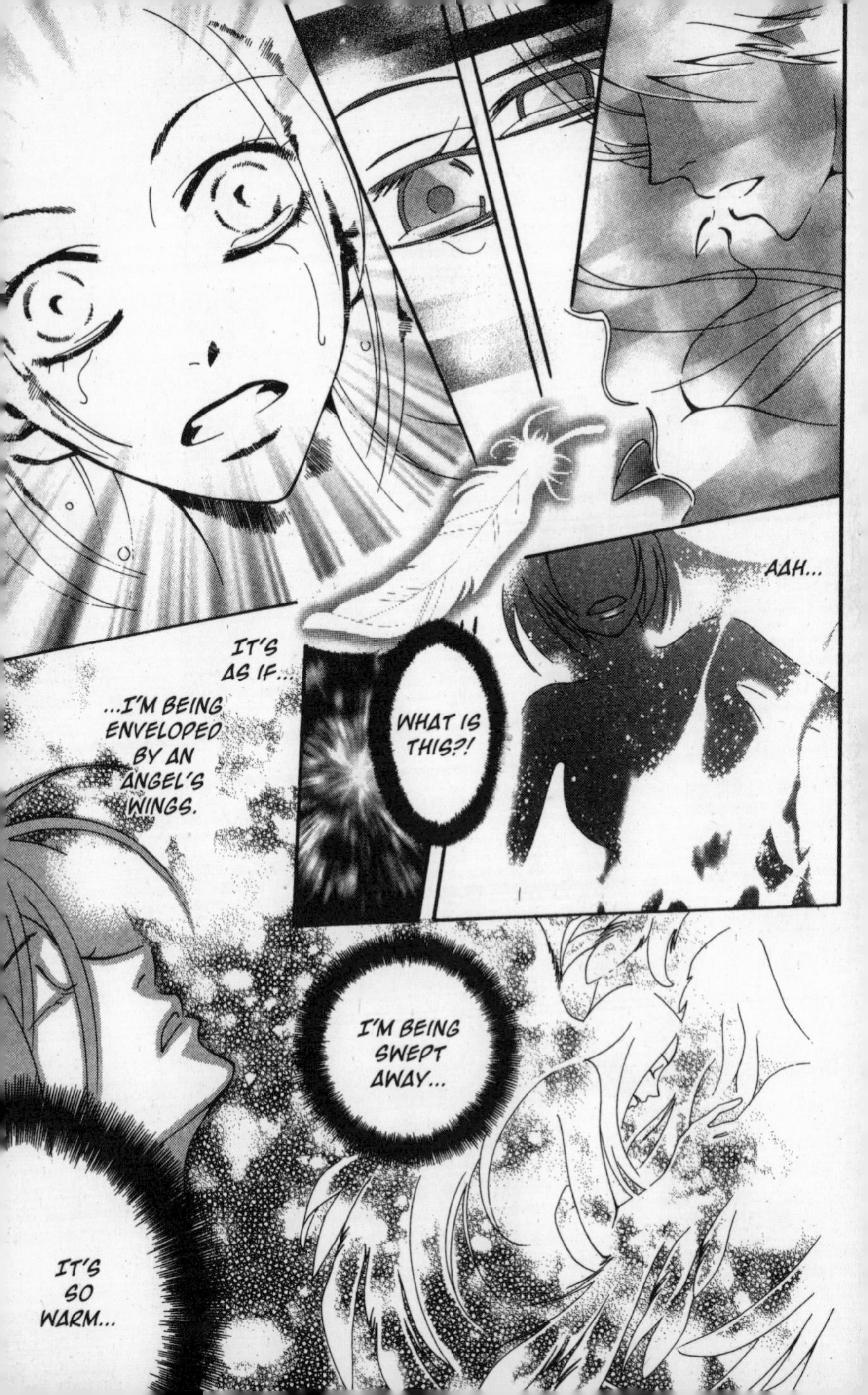
AAH...
WHAT IS THIS?!
IT'S AS IF...
...I'M BEING ENVELOPED BY AN ANGEL'S WINGS.
I'M BEING SWEPT AWAY...
IT'S SO WARM...

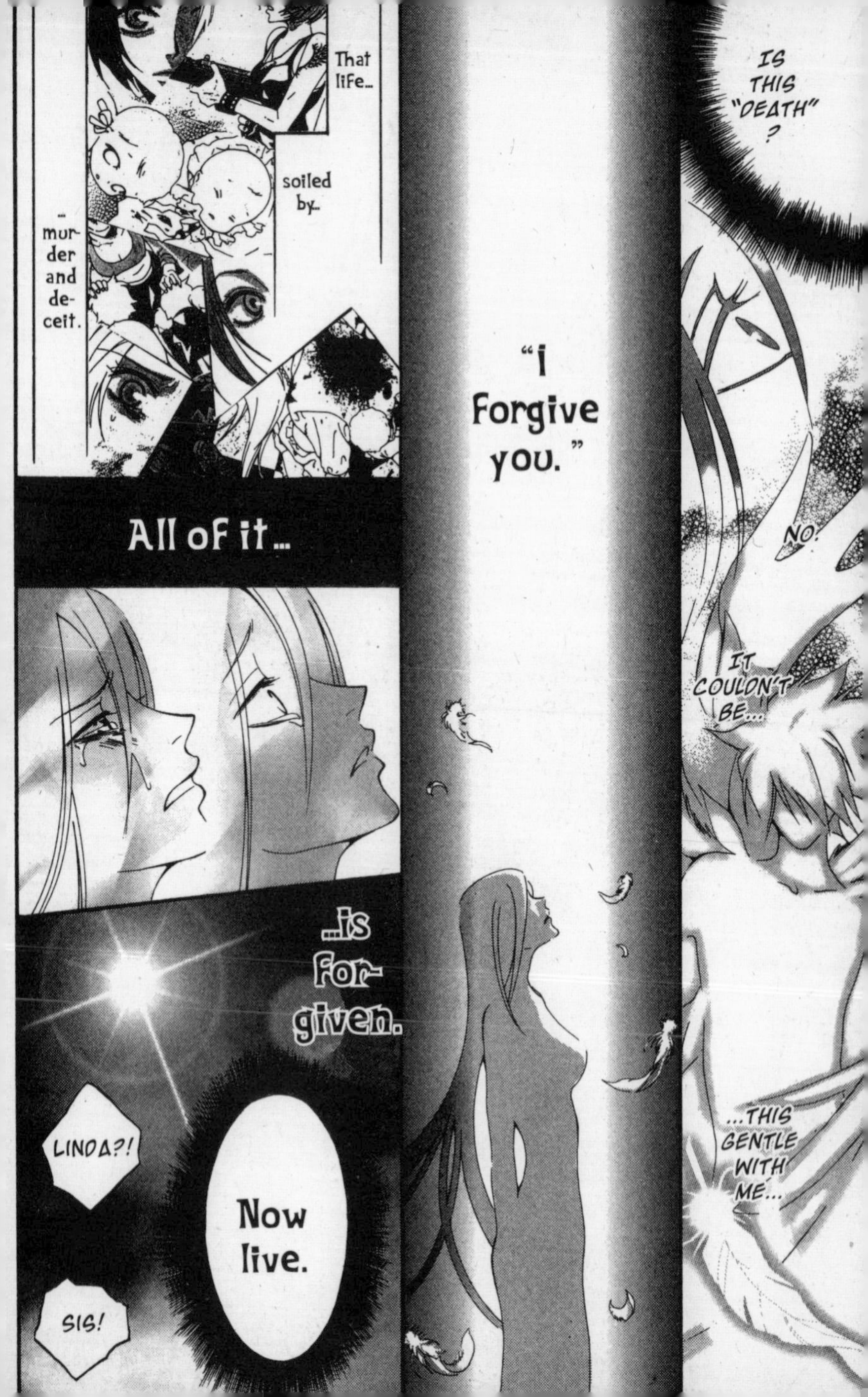
IS THIS "DEATH"?
NO.
IT COULDN'T BE...
...THIS GENTLE WITH ME...
"I Forgive you."
That life...
soiled by...
...murder and deceit.
All of it...
...is forgiven.
Now live.
LINDA?!
SIS!

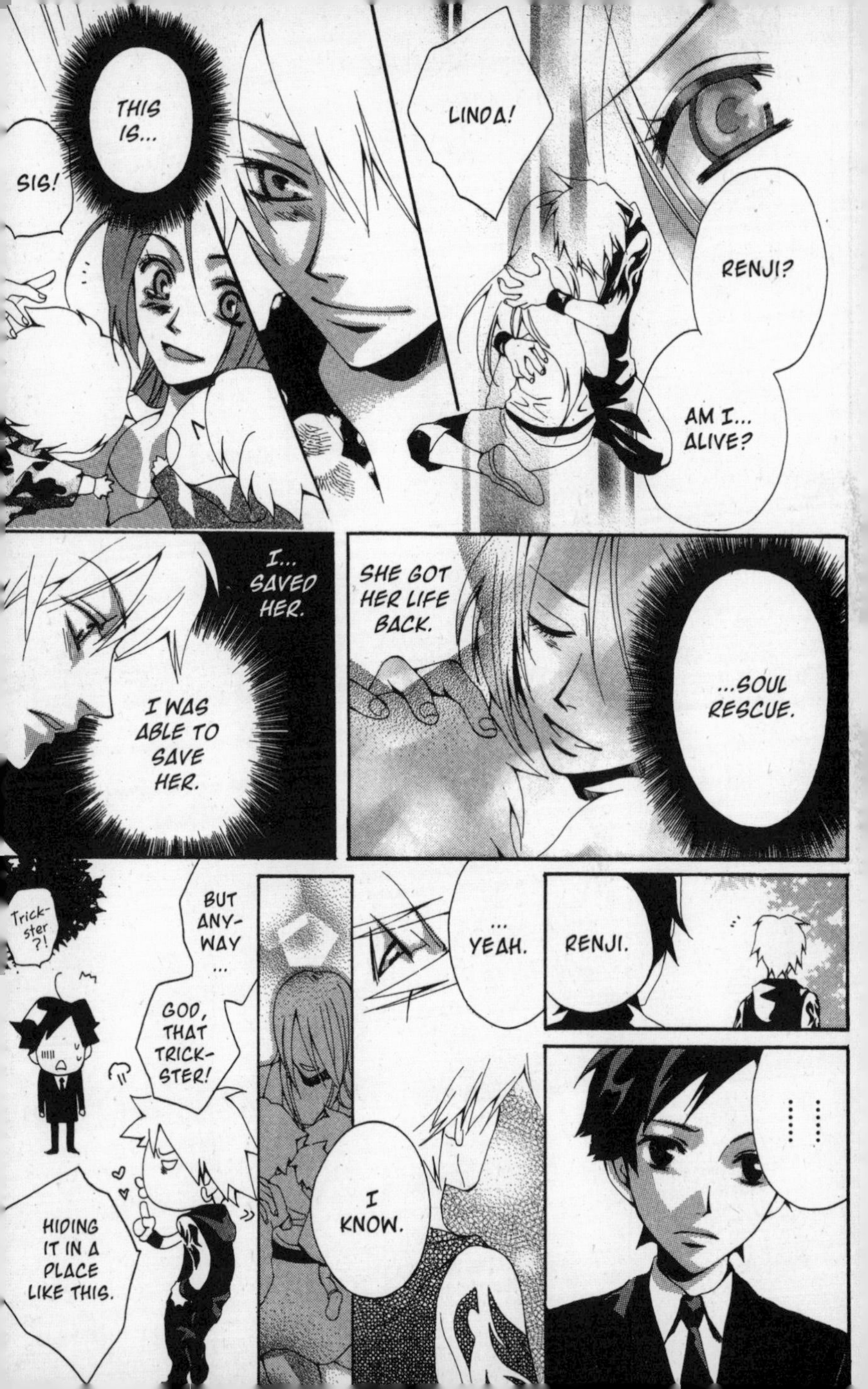
RENJI?
AM I... ALIVE?
LINDA!
THIS IS...
SIS!
...SOUL RESCUE.
SHE GOT HER LIFE BACK.
I... SAVED HER.
I WAS ABLE TO SAVE HER.
RENJI.
......
... YEAH.
I KNOW.
BUT ANY-WAY ...
GOD, THAT TRICK-STER!
Trick-ster ?!
HIDING IT IN A PLACE LIKE THIS.

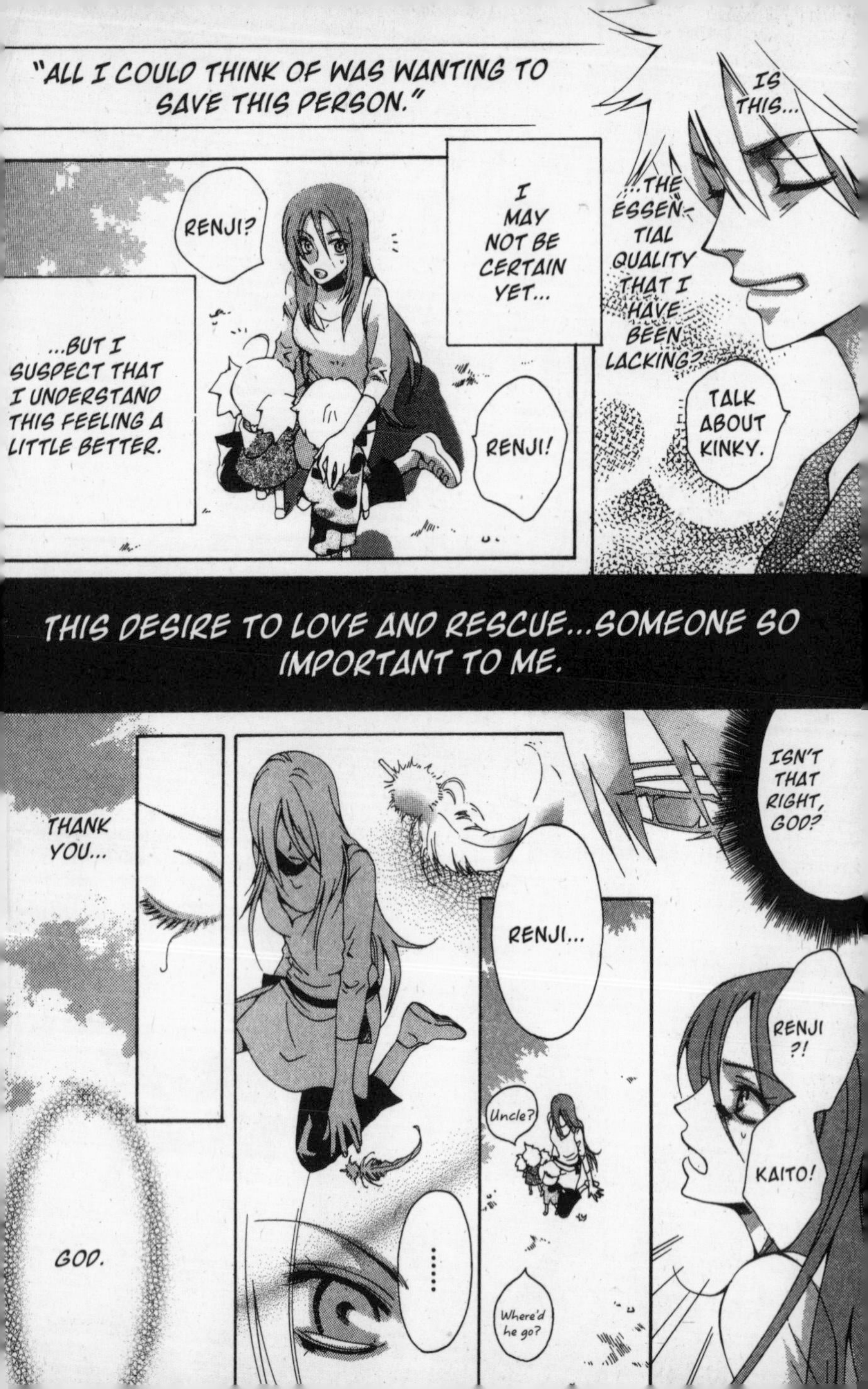
"ALL I COULD THINK OF WAS WANTING TO SAVE THIS PERSON."
IS THIS...
...THE ESSENTIAL QUALITY THAT I HAVE BEEN LACKING?
TALK ABOUT KINKY.
I MAY NOT BE CERTAIN YET...
RENJI?
RENJI!
...BUT I SUSPECT THAT I UNDERSTAND THIS FEELING A LITTLE BETTER.
THIS DESIRE TO LOVE AND RESCUE...SOMEONE SO IMPORTANT TO ME.
ISN'T THAT RIGHT, GOD?
RENJI?!
KAITO!
RENJI...
Uncle?
Where'd he go?
......
THANK YOU...
GOD.

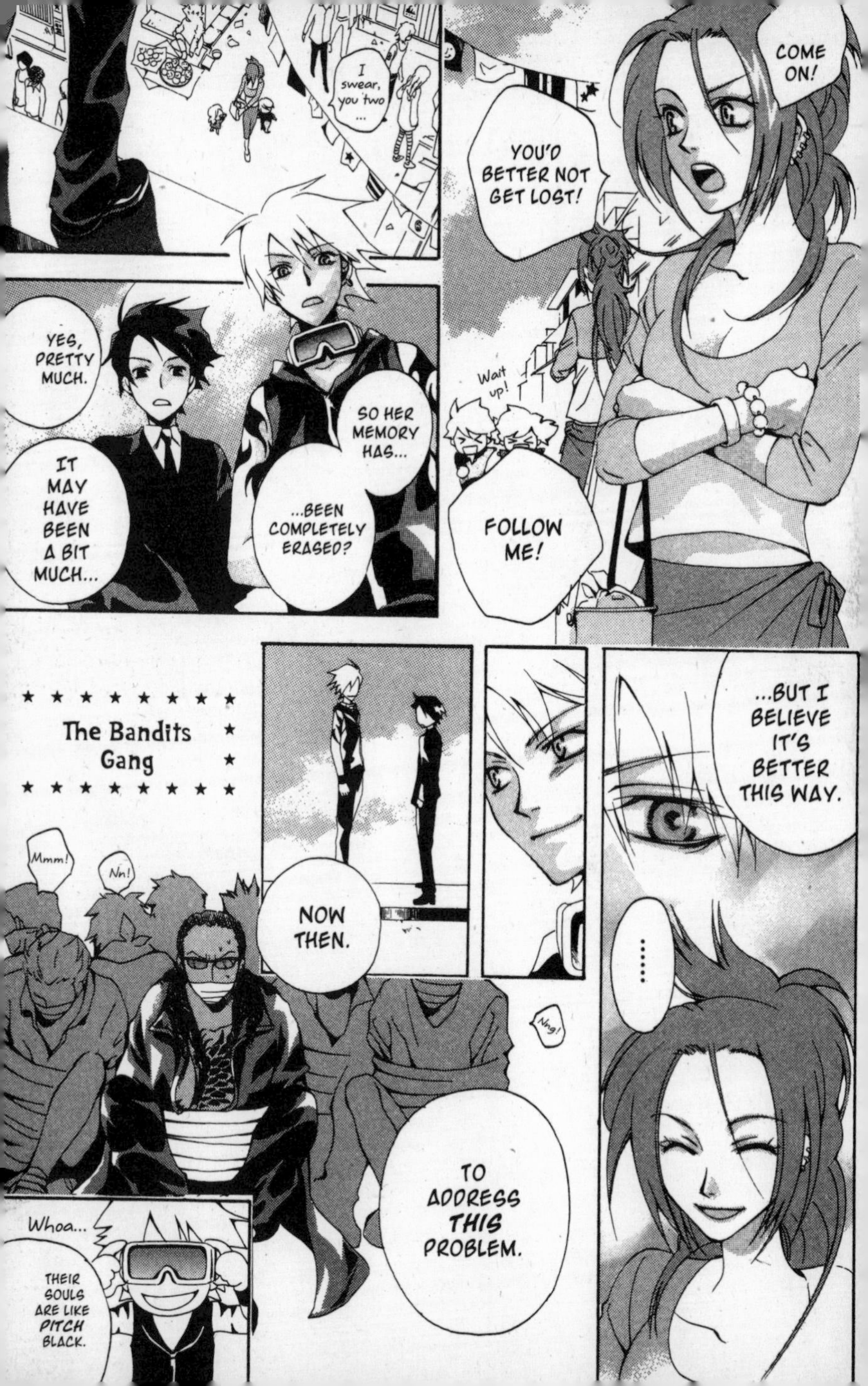
COME ON!
YOU'D BETTER NOT GET LOST!
Wait up!
FOLLOW ME!
I swear, you two ...
SO HER MEMORY HAS...
...BEEN COMPLETELY ERASED?
YES, PRETTY MUCH.
IT MAY HAVE BEEN A BIT MUCH...
...BUT I BELIEVE IT'S BETTER THIS WAY.
......
NOW THEN.
TO ADDRESS **THIS** PROBLEM.
Nng!
The Bandits Gang
Mmm!
Nn!
Whoa...
THEIR SOULS ARE LIKE PITCH BLACK.

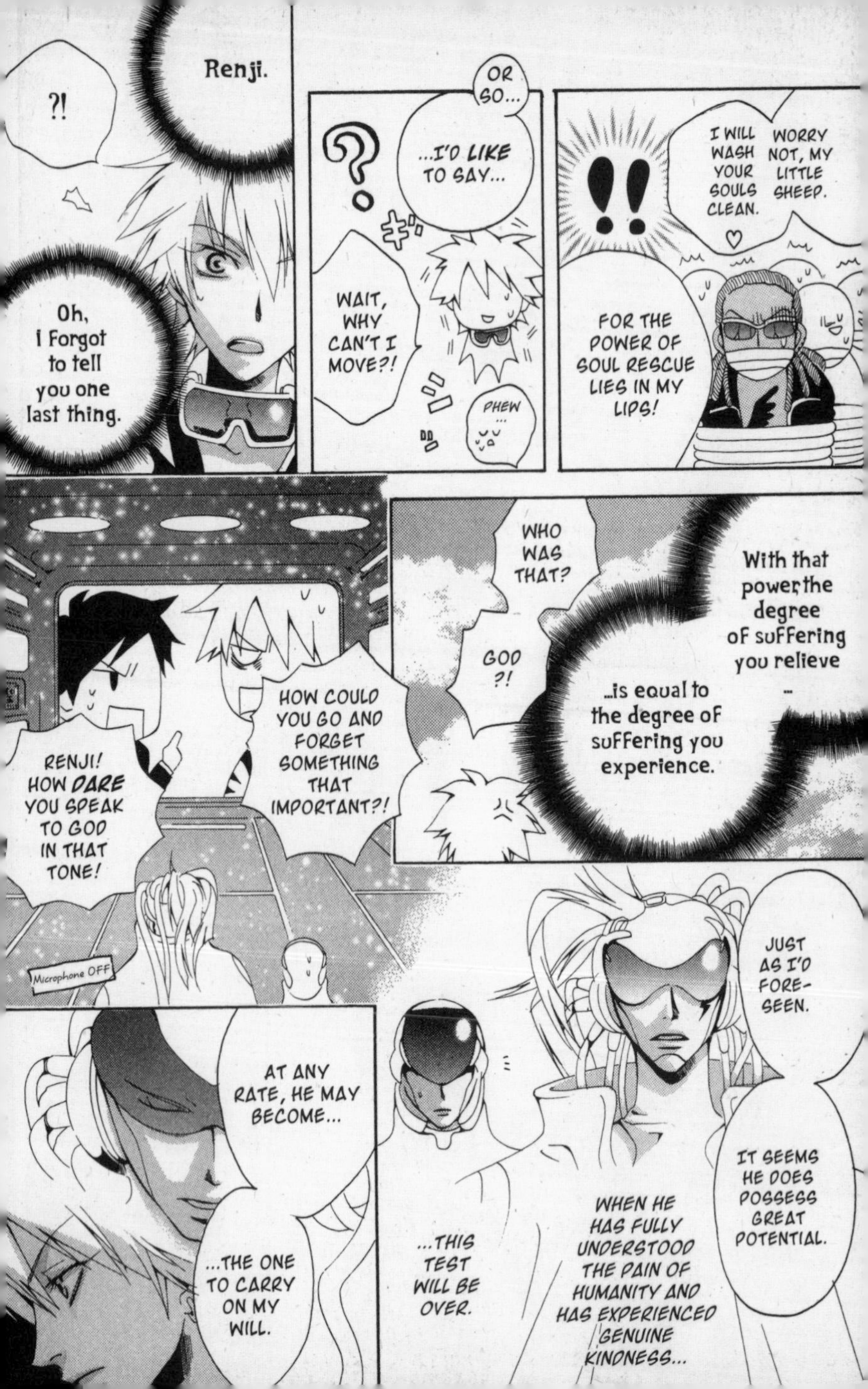
WORRY NOT, MY LITTLE SHEEP. I WILL WASH YOUR SOULS CLEAN.
!!
FOR THE POWER OF SOUL RESCUE LIES IN MY LIPS!
?
...I'D LIKE TO SAY...
OR SO...
WAIT, WHY CAN'T I MOVE?!
PHEW...
Renji.
?!
Oh, I forgot to tell you one last thing.
With that power, the degree of suffering you relieve –
...is equal to the degree of suffering you experience.
WHO WAS THAT?
GOD?!
HOW COULD YOU GO AND FORGET SOMETHING THAT IMPORTANT?!
RENJI! HOW DARE YOU SPEAK TO GOD IN THAT TONE!
Microphone OFF
JUST AS I'D FORESEEN.
IT SEEMS HE DOES POSSESS GREAT POTENTIAL.
WHEN HE HAS FULLY UNDERSTOOD THE PAIN OF HUMANITY AND HAS EXPERIENCED GENUINE KINDNESS...
...THIS TEST WILL BE OVER.
AT ANY RATE, HE MAY BECOME...
...THE ONE TO CARRY ON MY WILL.

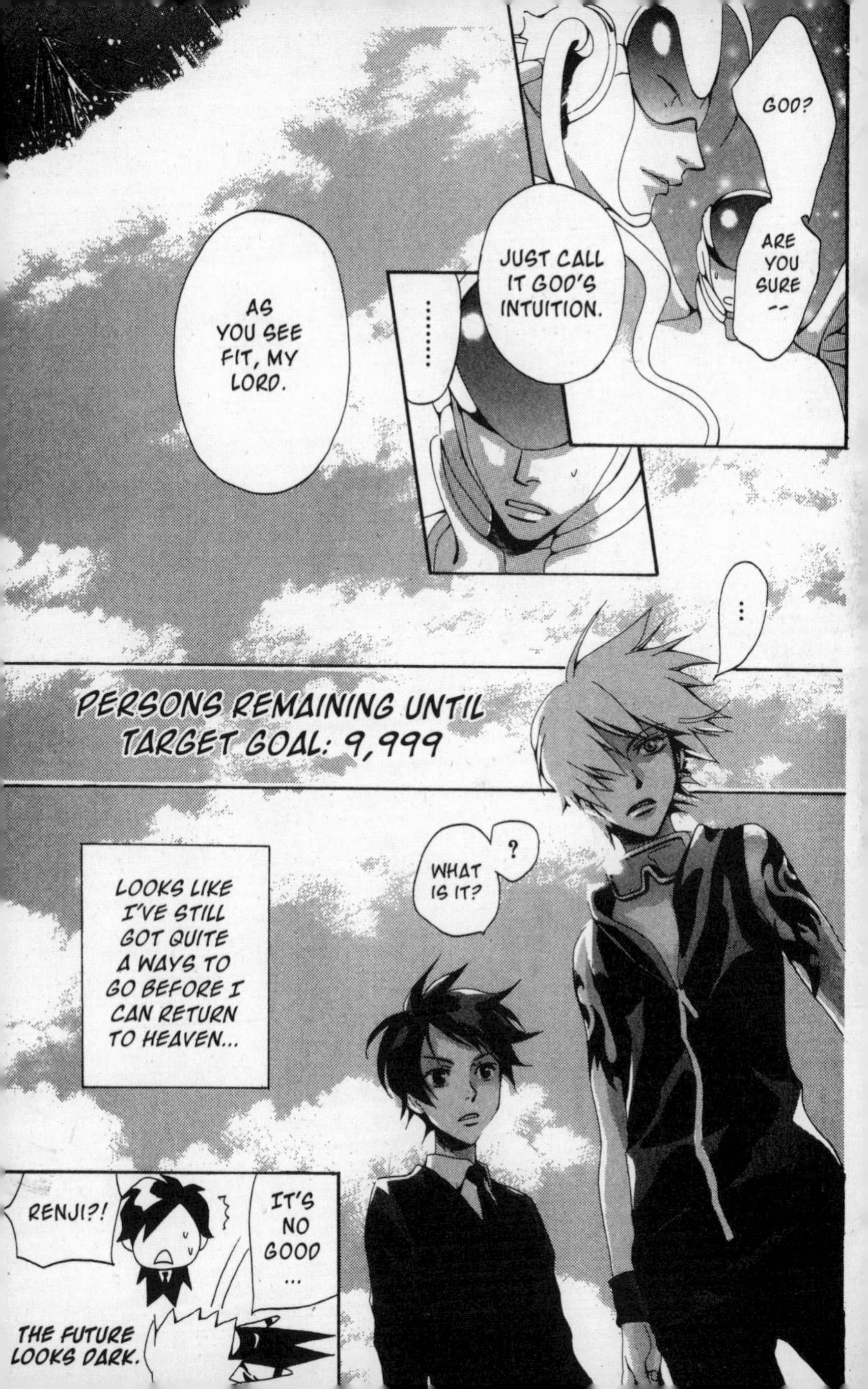
GOD?
ARE YOU SURE --
JUST CALL IT GOD'S INTUITION.
....
AS YOU SEE FIT, MY LORD.
...
PERSONS REMAINING UNTIL TARGET GOAL: 9,999
?
WHAT IS IT?
LOOKS LIKE I'VE STILL GOT QUITE A WAYS TO GO BEFORE I CAN RETURN TO HEAVEN...
IT'S NO GOOD ...
RENJI?!
THE FUTURE LOOKS DARK.

SOUL RESCUE

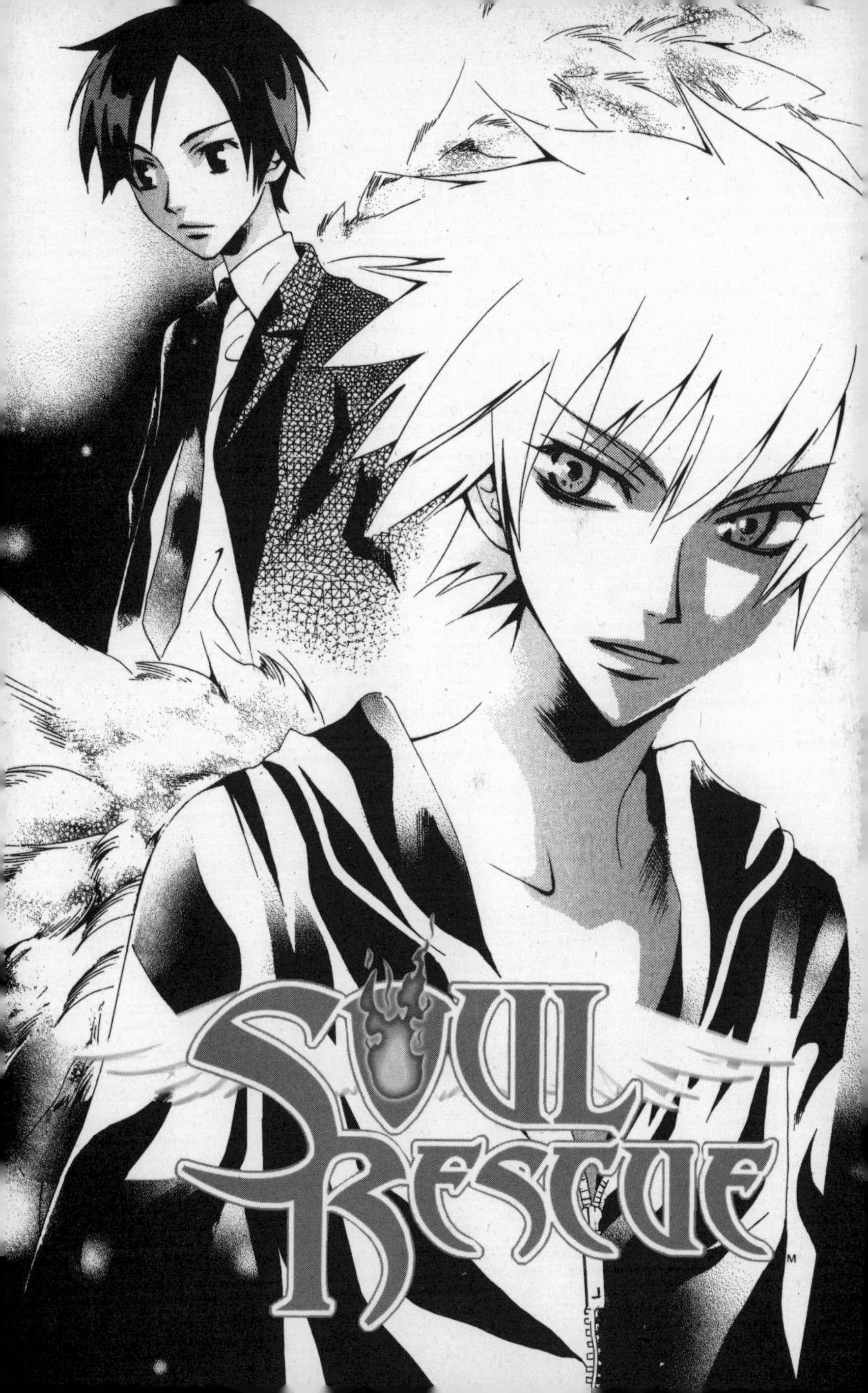
SOUL
RESCUE™

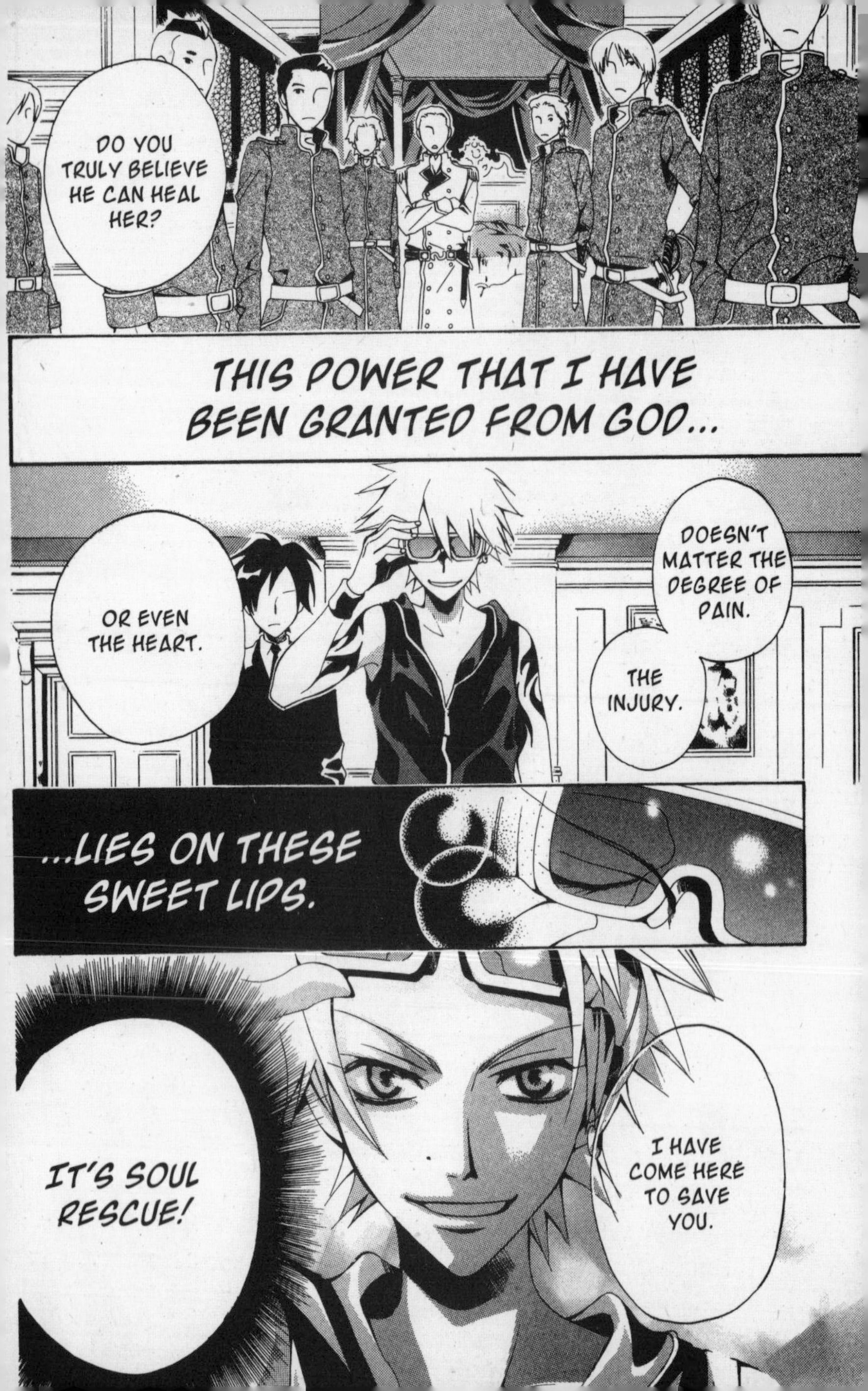
DO YOU TRULY BELIEVE HE CAN HEAL HER?
THIS POWER THAT I HAVE BEEN GRANTED FROM GOD...
DOESN'T MATTER THE DEGREE OF PAIN.
THE INJURY.
OR EVEN THE HEART.
...LIES ON THESE SWEET LIPS.
I HAVE COME HERE TO SAVE YOU.
IT'S SOUL RESCUE!

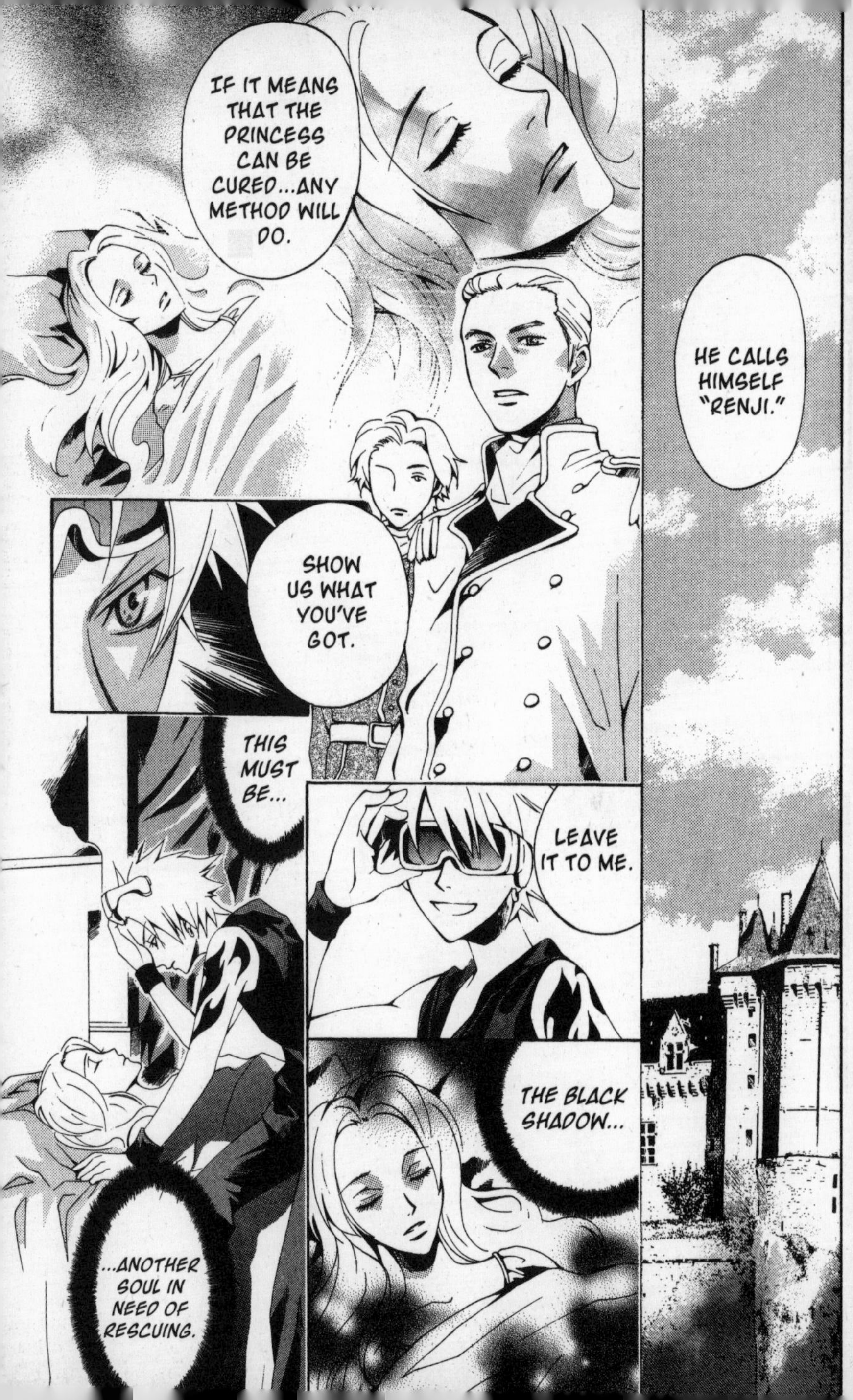
HE CALLS HIMSELF "RENJI."
IF IT MEANS THAT THE PRINCESS CAN BE CURED...ANY METHOD WILL DO.
SHOW US WHAT YOU'VE GOT.
LEAVE IT TO ME.
THE BLACK SHADOW...
THIS MUST BE...
...ANOTHER SOUL IN NEED OF RESCUING.

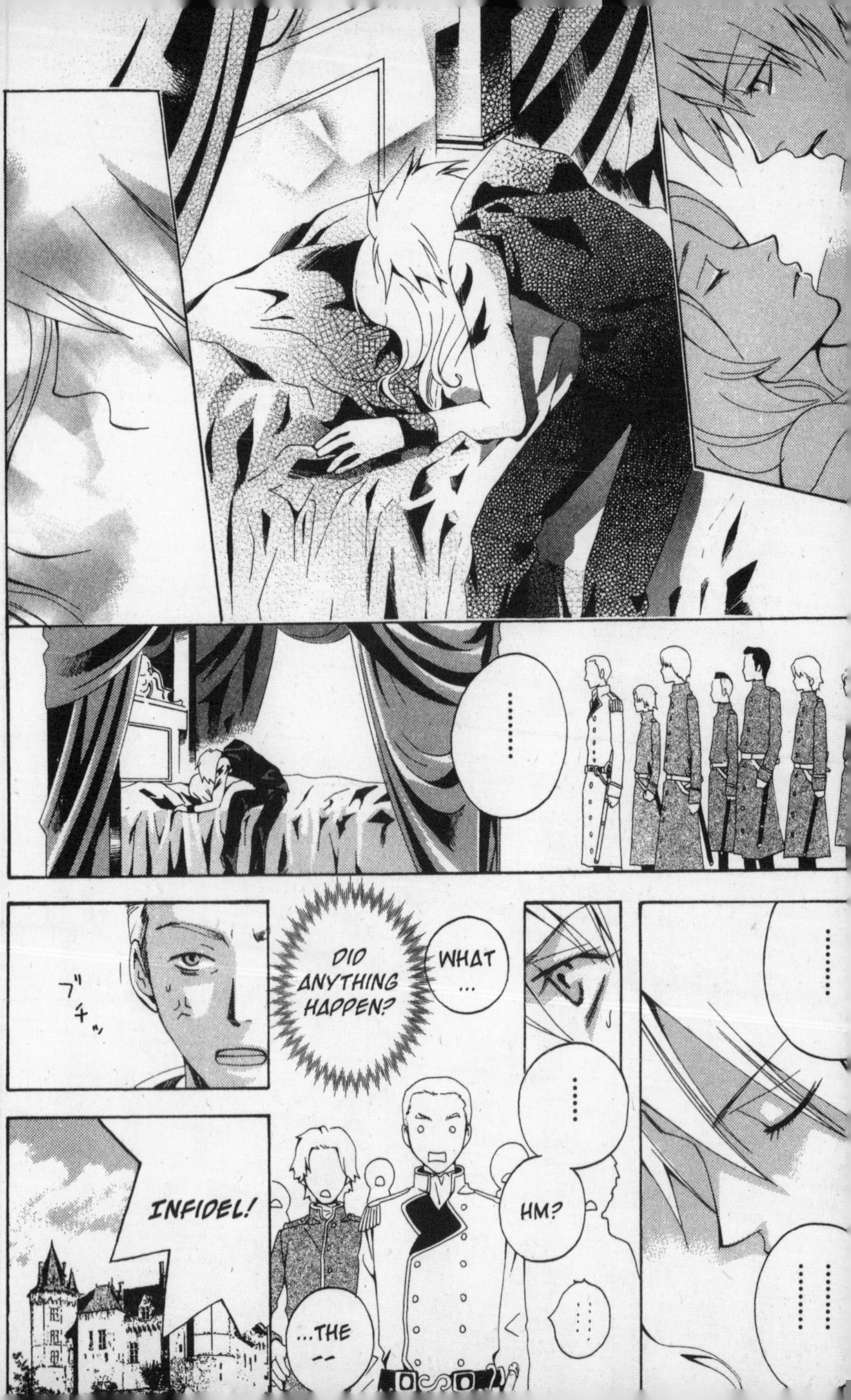

......
......
......
WHAT ...
DID ANYTHING HAPPEN?
ブチッ
......
HM?
......
...THE --
INFIDEL!

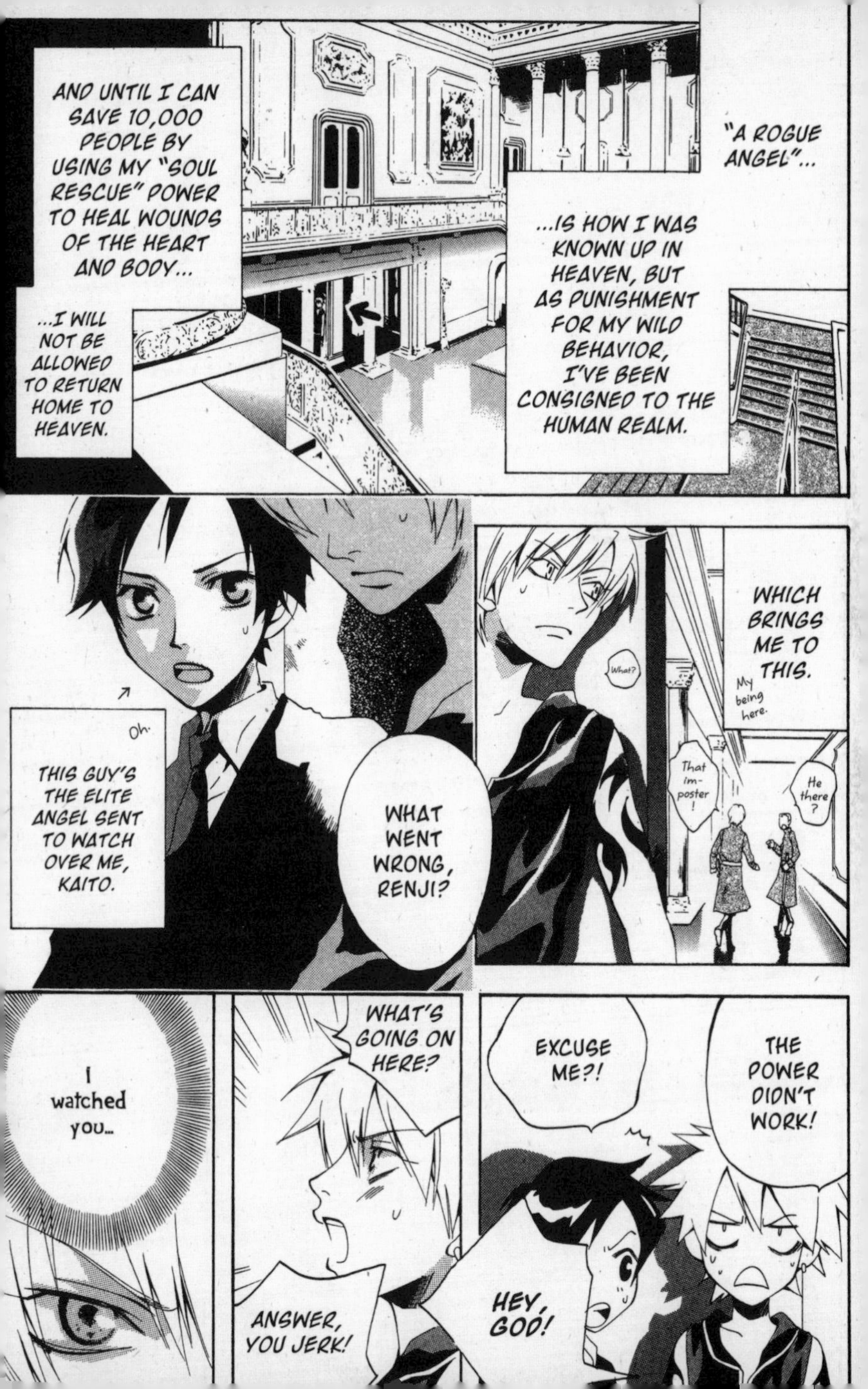
"A ROGUE ANGEL"...
...IS HOW I WAS KNOWN UP IN HEAVEN, BUT AS PUNISHMENT FOR MY WILD BEHAVIOR, I'VE BEEN CONSIGNED TO THE HUMAN REALM.
AND UNTIL I CAN SAVE 10,000 PEOPLE BY USING MY "SOUL RESCUE" POWER TO HEAL WOUNDS OF THE HEART AND BODY...
...I WILL NOT BE ALLOWED TO RETURN HOME TO HEAVEN.
WHICH BRINGS ME TO THIS.
My being here.
He there?
That im-poster!
What?
Oh.
THIS GUY'S THE ELITE ANGEL SENT TO WATCH OVER ME, KAITO.
WHAT WENT WRONG, RENJI?
THE POWER DIDN'T WORK!
EXCUSE ME?!
HEY, GOD!
WHAT'S GOING ON HERE?
ANSWER, YOU JERK!
I watched you...

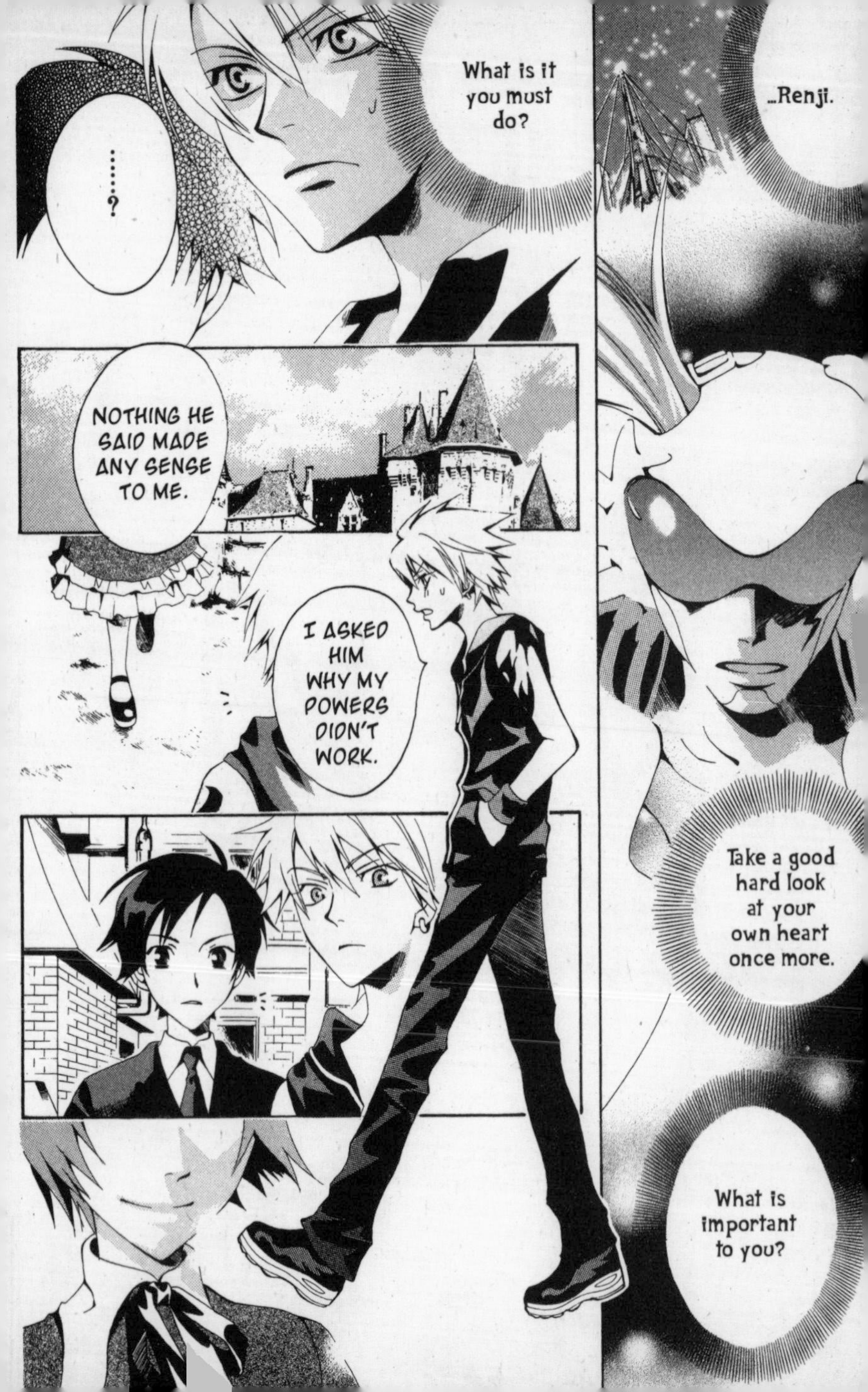
...Renji.
Take a good hard look at your own heart once more.
What is important to you?
What is it you must do?
......?
NOTHING HE SAID MADE ANY SENSE TO ME.
I ASKED HIM WHY MY POWERS DIDN'T WORK.

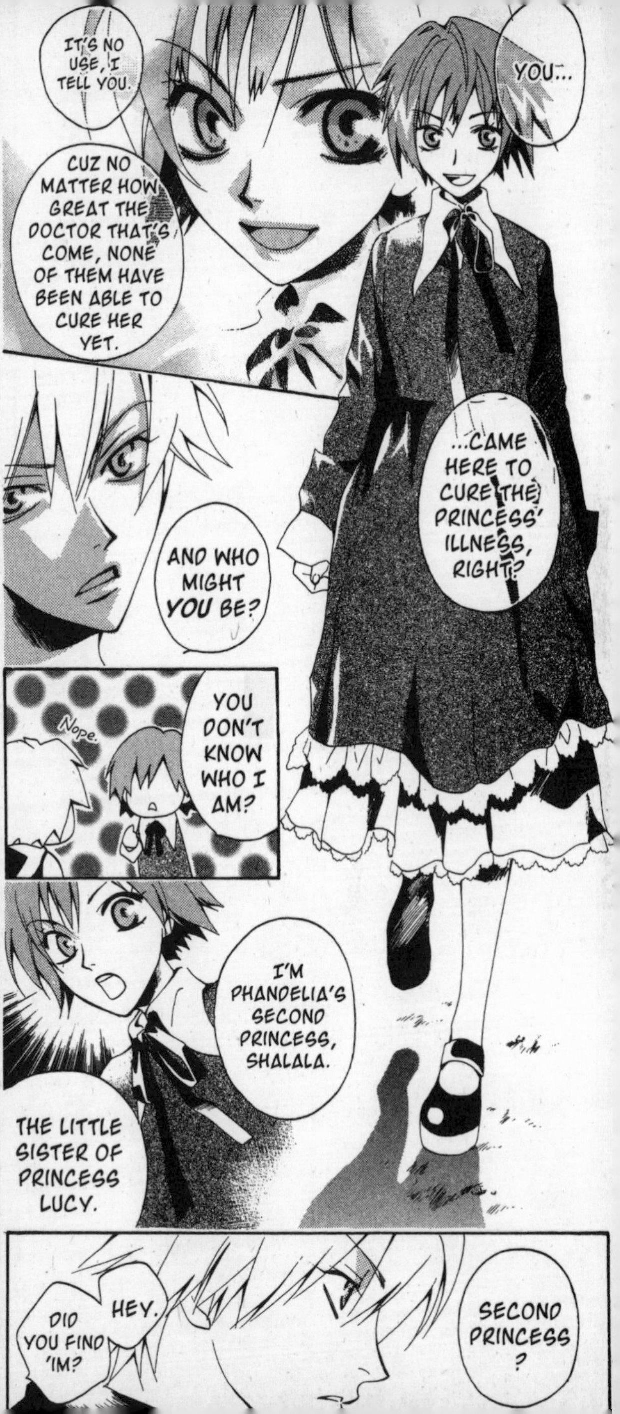
YOU...
...CAME HERE TO CURE THE PRINCESS' ILLNESS, RIGHT?
IT'S NO USE, I TELL YOU.
CUZ NO MATTER HOW GREAT THE DOCTOR THAT'S COME, NONE OF THEM HAVE BEEN ABLE TO CURE HER YET.
AND WHO MIGHT *YOU* BE?
YOU DON'T KNOW WHO I AM?
Nope.
I'M PHANDELIA'S SECOND PRINCESS, SHALALA.
THE LITTLE SISTER OF PRINCESS LUCY.
SECOND PRINCESS?
HEY.
DID YOU FIND 'IM?

SR

The truth is that I originally never drew shoujo manga. When I was in elementary school I drew things all right, but... It was only because of the "Hana to Yume" Big Challenge prize that I was able to debut under this genre. The winning prize was for my first shoujo manga ever. Now, "Soul Rescue" is hardly what I would consider a shoujo manga, but even so, my whim (Ha!) to make the design and scenes "shoujo-manga-esque" has only proven itself to be a fruitless effort... Those sparkly glittery screentones I use embarrass me to this very day... (Heh.)

Persevere!

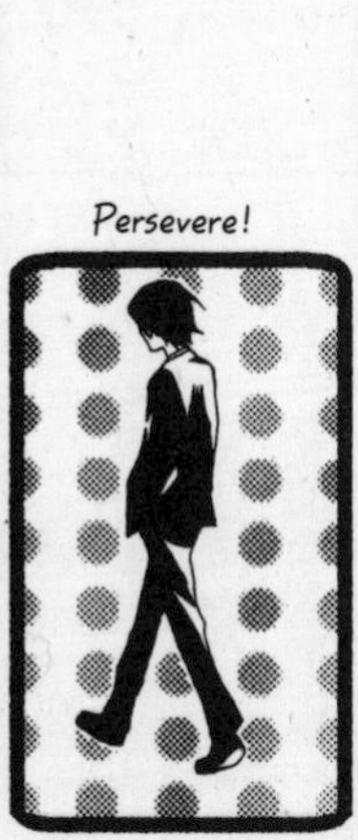

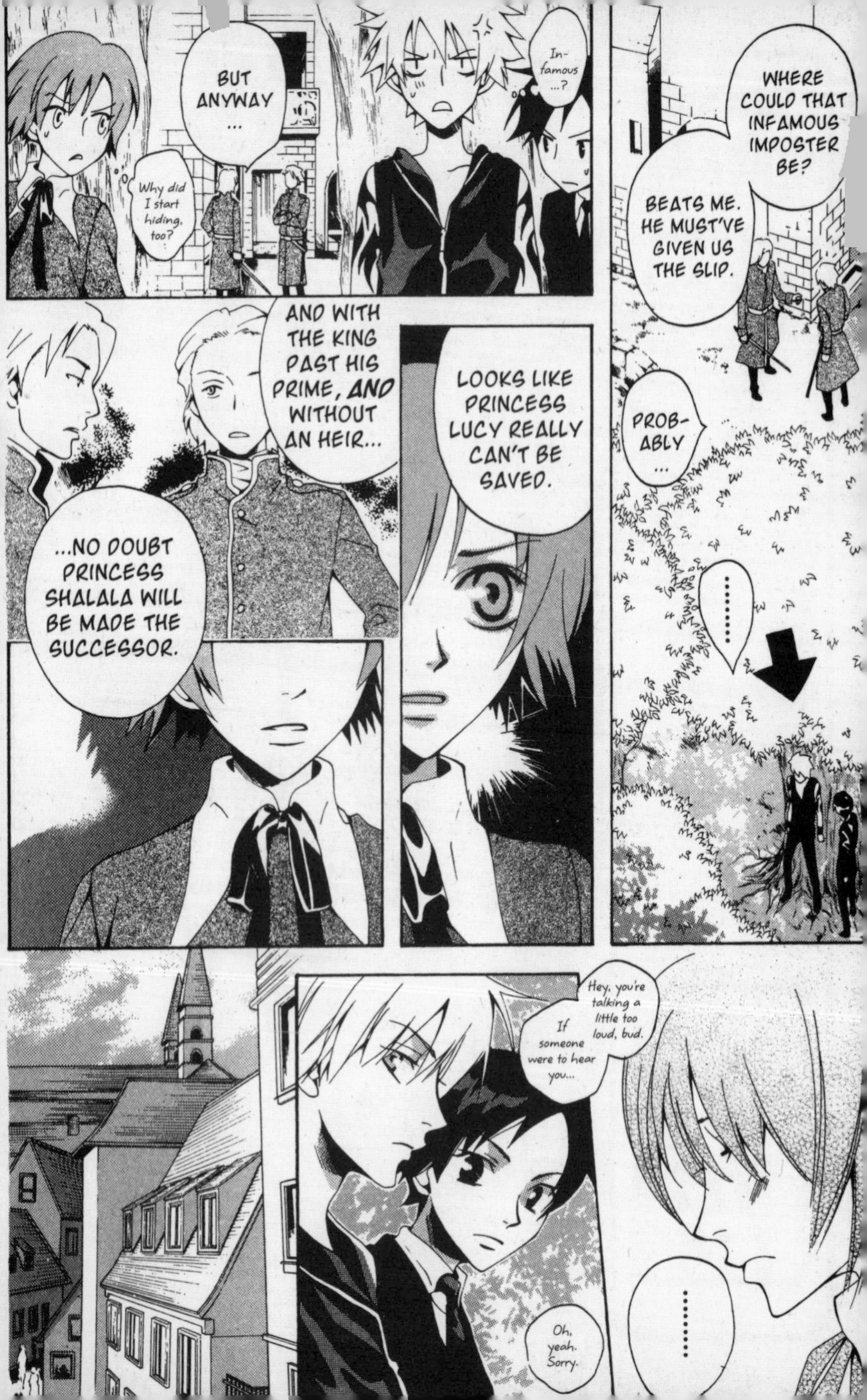

WHERE COULD THAT INFAMOUS IMPOSTER BE?
BEATS ME. HE MUST'VE GIVEN US THE SLIP.
PROBABLY...
......
In-famous...?
BUT ANYWAY...
Why did I start hiding, too?
LOOKS LIKE PRINCESS LUCY REALLY CAN'T BE SAVED.
AND WITH THE KING PAST HIS PRIME, AND WITHOUT AN HEIR...
...NO DOUBT PRINCESS SHALALA WILL BE MADE THE SUCCESSOR.
......
Hey, you're talking a little too loud, bud.
If someone were to hear you...
Oh, yeah. Sorry.

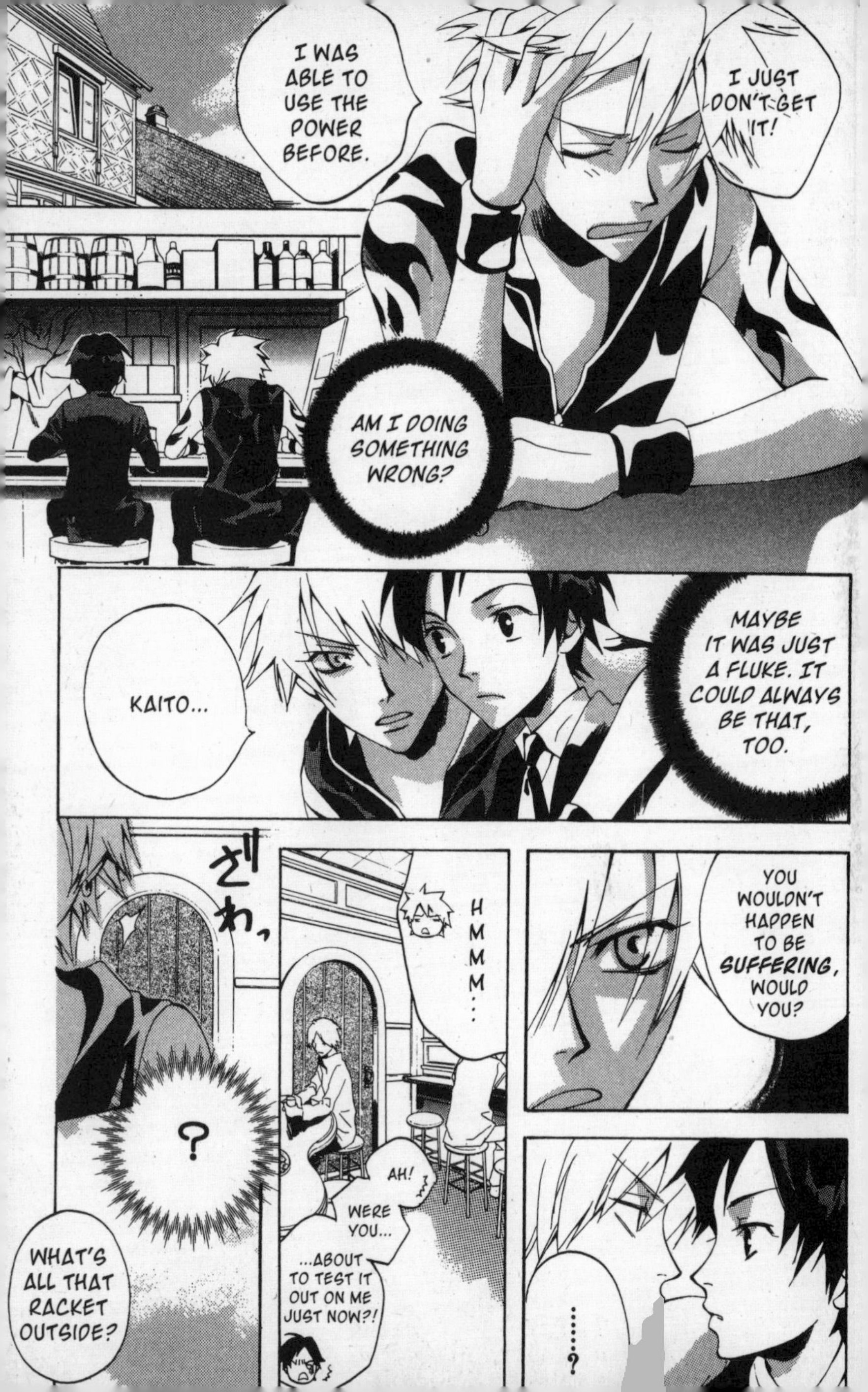
I JUST DON'T GET IT!
I WAS ABLE TO USE THE POWER BEFORE.
AM I DOING SOMETHING WRONG?
MAYBE IT WAS JUST A FLUKE. IT COULD ALWAYS BE THAT, TOO.
KAITO...
YOU WOULDN'T HAPPEN TO BE SUFFERING, WOULD YOU?
......?
HMMM...
AH!
WERE YOU...
...ABOUT TO TEST IT OUT ON ME JUST NOW?!
ざわっ
?
WHAT'S ALL THAT RACKET OUTSIDE?

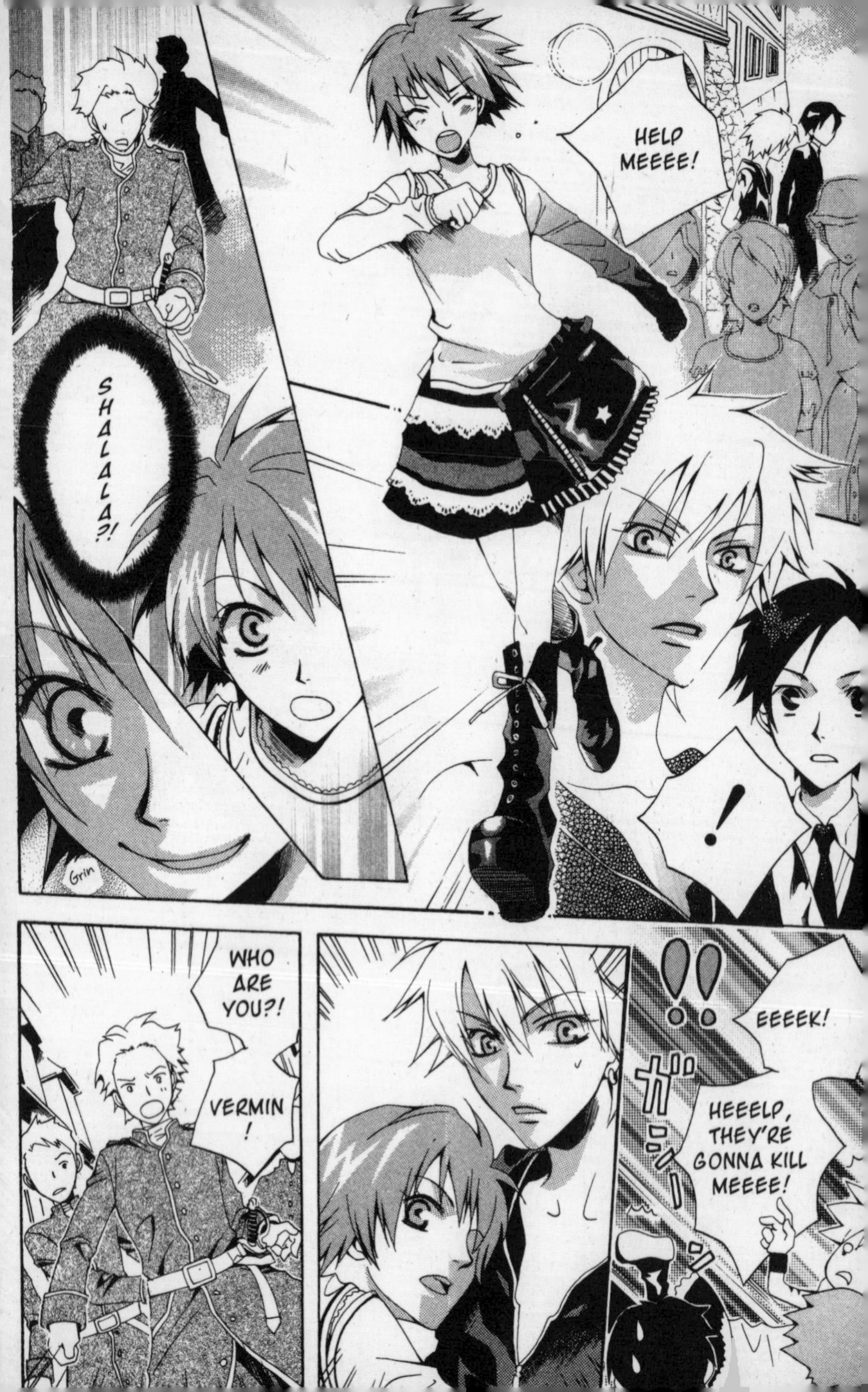
HELP MEEEE!
!
SHALALA?!
Grin
EEEEK!
HEEELP, THEY'RE GONNA KILL MEEEE!
WHO ARE YOU?!
VERMIN!

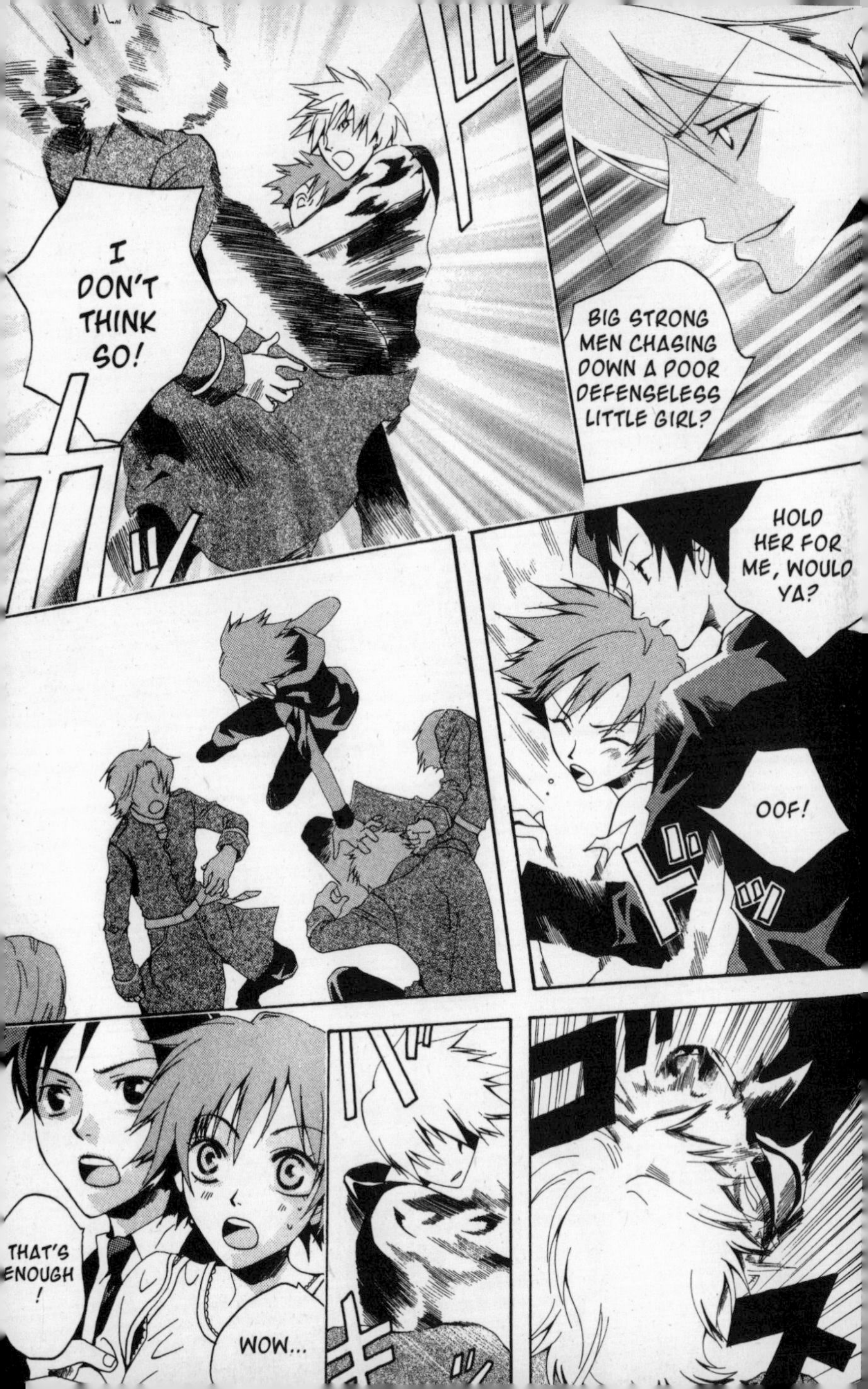
BIG STRONG MEN CHASING DOWN A POOR DEFENSELESS LITTLE GIRL?
I DON'T THINK SO!
HOLD HER FOR ME, WOULD YA?
OOF!
THAT'S ENOUGH!
WOW...

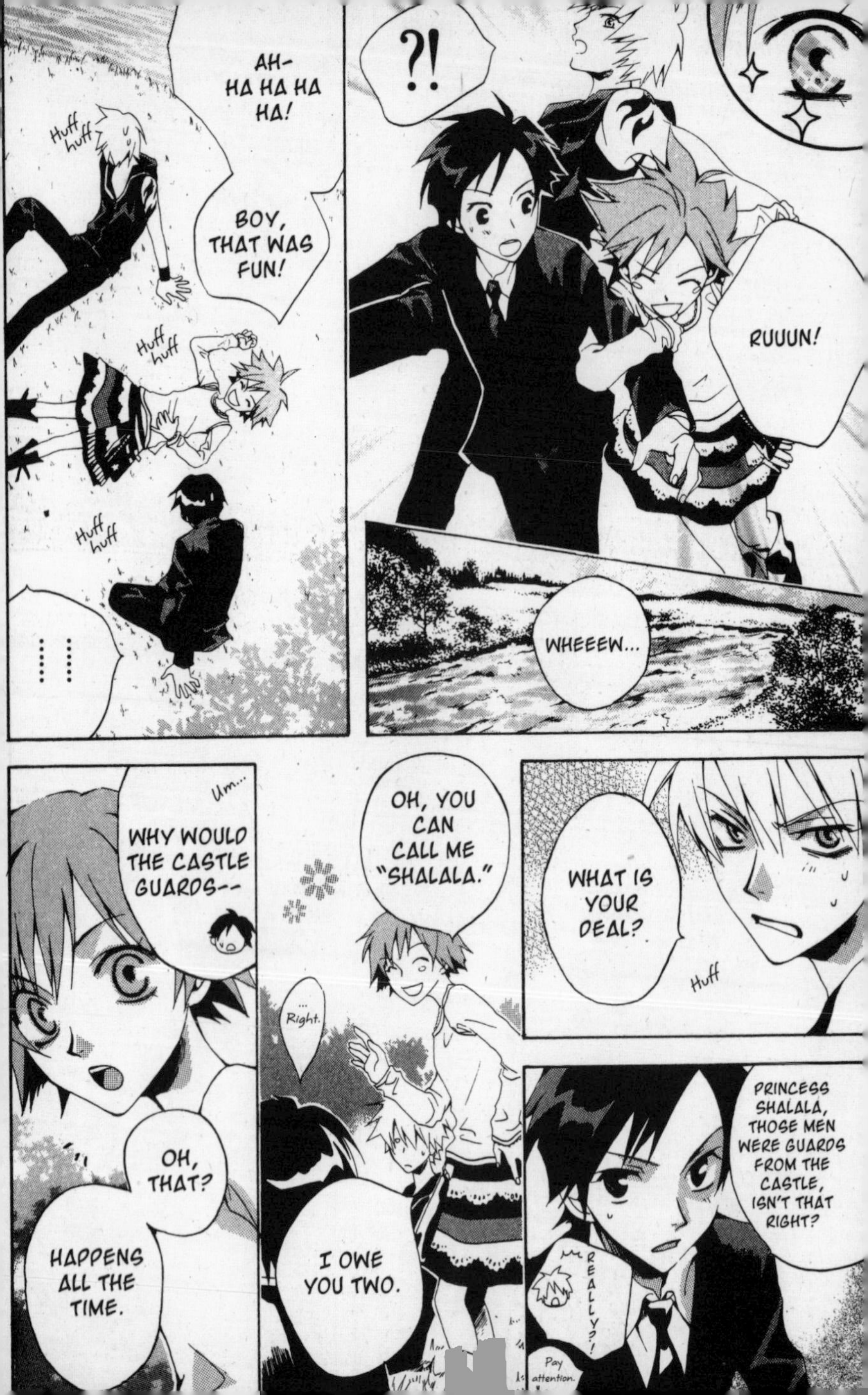
RUUUN!
?!
WHEEEW...
AH- HA HA HA HA!
BOY, THAT WAS FUN!
Huff huff
Huff huff
Huff huff
......
WHAT IS YOUR DEAL?
Huff
PRINCESS SHALALA, THOSE MEN WERE GUARDS FROM THE CASTLE, ISN'T THAT RIGHT?
REALLY?!
Pay attention.
OH, YOU CAN CALL ME "SHALALA."
... Right.
I OWE YOU TWO.
Um...
WHY WOULD THE CASTLE GUARDS--
OH, THAT?
HAPPENS ALL THE TIME.

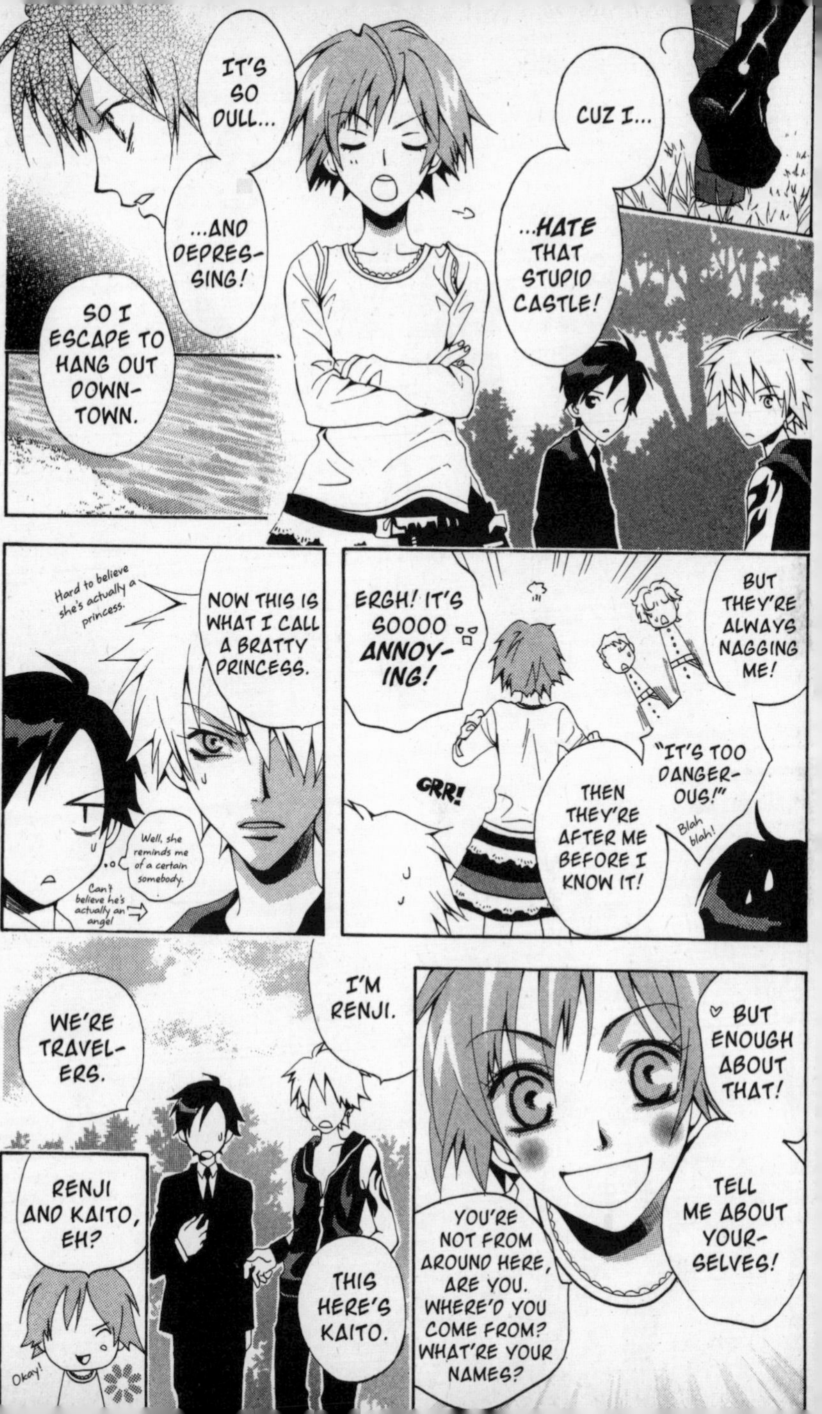
CUZ I...
...HATE THAT STUPID CASTLE!
IT'S SO DULL...
...AND DEPRES-SING!
SO I ESCAPE TO HANG OUT DOWN-TOWN.
BUT THEY'RE ALWAYS NAGGING ME!
"IT'S TOO DANGER-OUS!"
Blah blah!
THEN THEY'RE AFTER ME BEFORE I KNOW IT!
ERGH! IT'S SOOOO ANNOY-ING!
GRR!
NOW THIS IS WHAT I CALL A BRATTY PRINCESS.
Hard to believe she's actually a princess.
Well, she reminds me of a certain somebody.
Can't believe he's actually an angel
BUT ENOUGH ABOUT THAT!
TELL ME ABOUT YOUR-SELVES!
YOU'RE NOT FROM AROUND HERE, ARE YOU. WHERE'D YOU COME FROM? WHAT'RE YOUR NAMES?
I'M RENJI.
WE'RE TRAVEL-ERS.
THIS HERE'S KAITO.
RENJI AND KAITO, EH?
Okay!

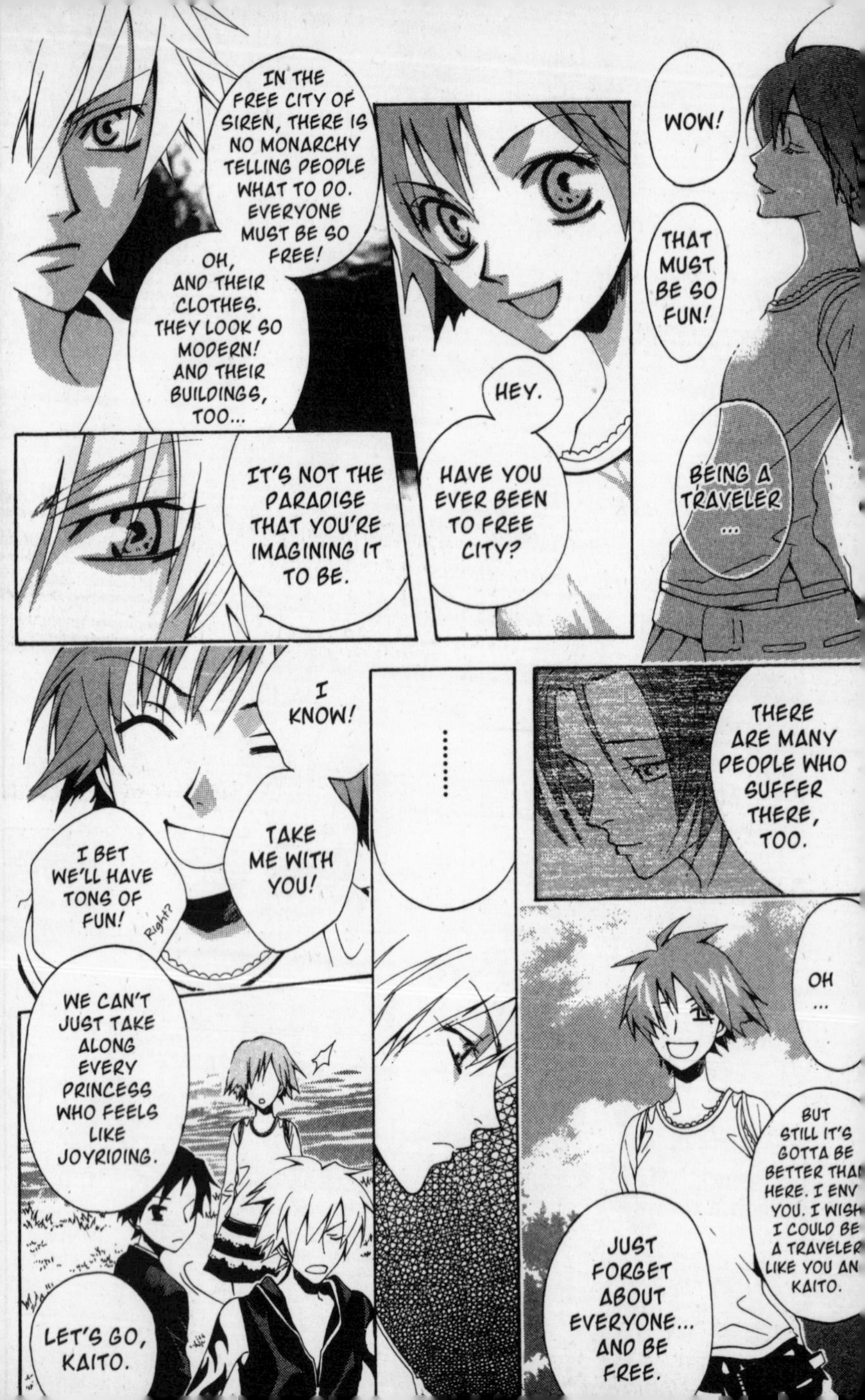
WOW!
THAT MUST BE SO FUN!
BEING A TRAVELER ...
IN THE FREE CITY OF SIREN, THERE IS NO MONARCHY TELLING PEOPLE WHAT TO DO. EVERYONE MUST BE SO FREE!
OH, AND THEIR CLOTHES. THEY LOOK SO MODERN! AND THEIR BUILDINGS, TOO...
HEY.
HAVE YOU EVER BEEN TO FREE CITY?
IT'S NOT THE PARADISE THAT YOU'RE IMAGINING IT TO BE.
THERE ARE MANY PEOPLE WHO SUFFER THERE, TOO.
OH ...
BUT STILL IT'S GOTTA BE BETTER THA HERE. I ENV YOU. I WISH I COULD BE A TRAVELER LIKE YOU AN KAITO.
JUST FORGET ABOUT EVERYONE... AND BE FREE.
....
I KNOW!
TAKE ME WITH YOU!
I BET WE'LL HAVE TONS OF FUN!
Right?
WE CAN'T JUST TAKE ALONG EVERY PRINCESS WHO FEELS LIKE JOYRIDING.
LET'S GO, KAITO.

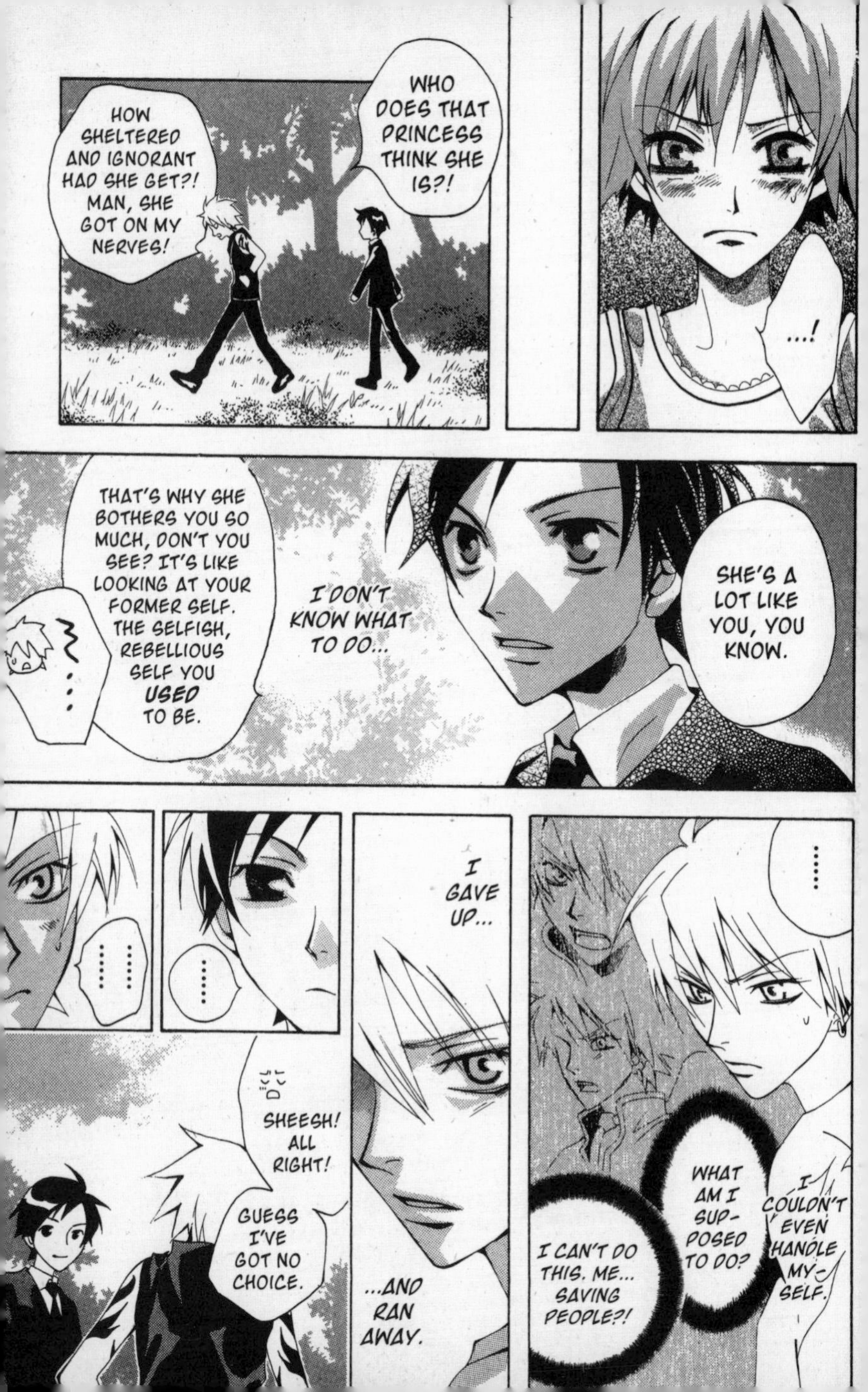
...!
WHO DOES THAT PRINCESS THINK SHE IS?!
HOW SHELTERED AND IGNORANT HAD SHE GET?! MAN, SHE GOT ON MY NERVES!
SHE'S A LOT LIKE YOU, YOU KNOW.
I DON'T KNOW WHAT TO DO...
THAT'S WHY SHE BOTHERS YOU SO MUCH, DON'T YOU SEE? IT'S LIKE LOOKING AT YOUR FORMER SELF. THE SELFISH, REBELLIOUS SELF YOU **USED** TO BE.
...
......
I- COULDN'T EVEN HANDLE MY-SELF.
WHAT AM I SUP-POSED TO DO?
I CAN'T DO THIS. ME... SAVING PEOPLE?!
I GAVE UP...
...AND RAN AWAY.
......
......
SHEESH! ALL RIGHT!
GUESS I'VE GOT NO CHOICE.

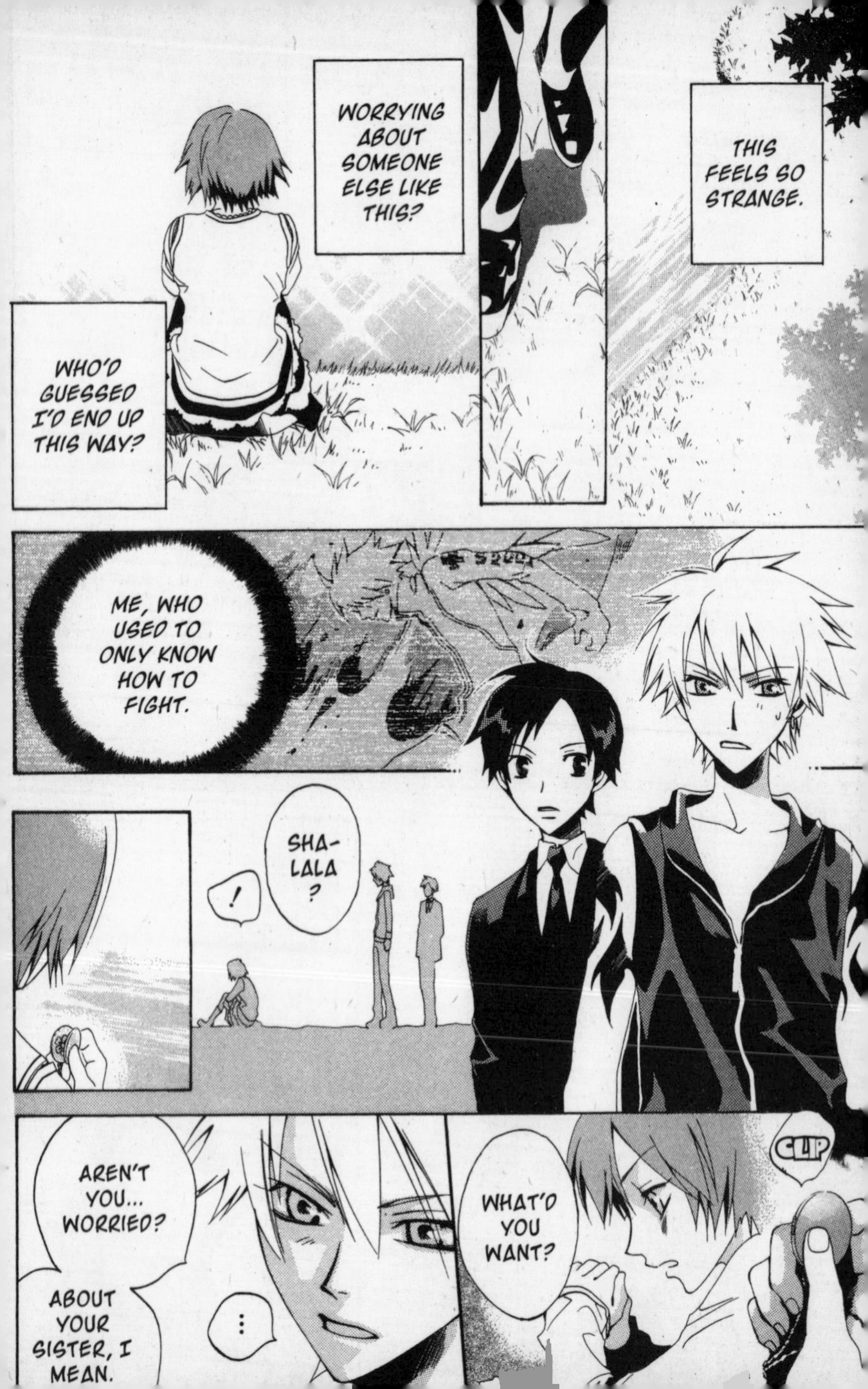
THIS FEELS SO STRANGE.
WORRYING ABOUT SOMEONE ELSE LIKE THIS?
WHO'D GUESSED I'D END UP THIS WAY?
ME, WHO USED TO ONLY KNOW HOW TO FIGHT.
SHA-LALA?
!
CLIP
WHAT'D YOU WANT?
AREN'T YOU... WORRIED?
...
ABOUT YOUR SISTER, I MEAN.

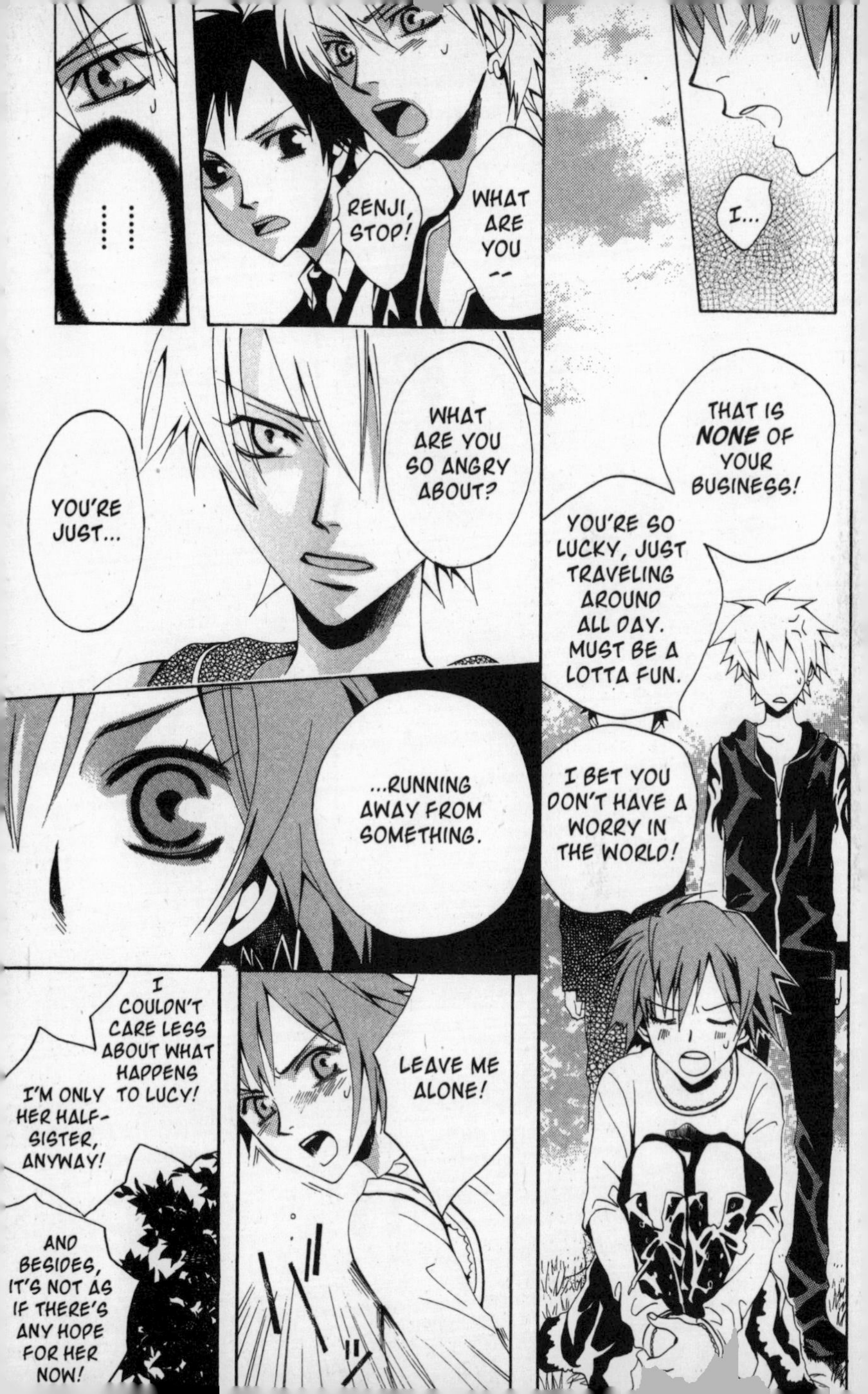

I...
THAT IS **NONE** OF YOUR BUSINESS!
YOU'RE SO LUCKY, JUST TRAVELING AROUND ALL DAY. MUST BE A LOTTA FUN.
I BET YOU DON'T HAVE A WORRY IN THE WORLD!
WHAT ARE YOU --
RENJI, STOP!
......
WHAT ARE YOU SO ANGRY ABOUT?
YOU'RE JUST...
...RUNNING AWAY FROM SOMETHING.
LEAVE ME ALONE!
I COULDN'T CARE LESS ABOUT WHAT HAPPENS TO LUCY!
I'M ONLY HER HALF-SISTER, ANYWAY!
AND BESIDES, IT'S NOT AS IF THERE'S ANY HOPE FOR HER NOW!

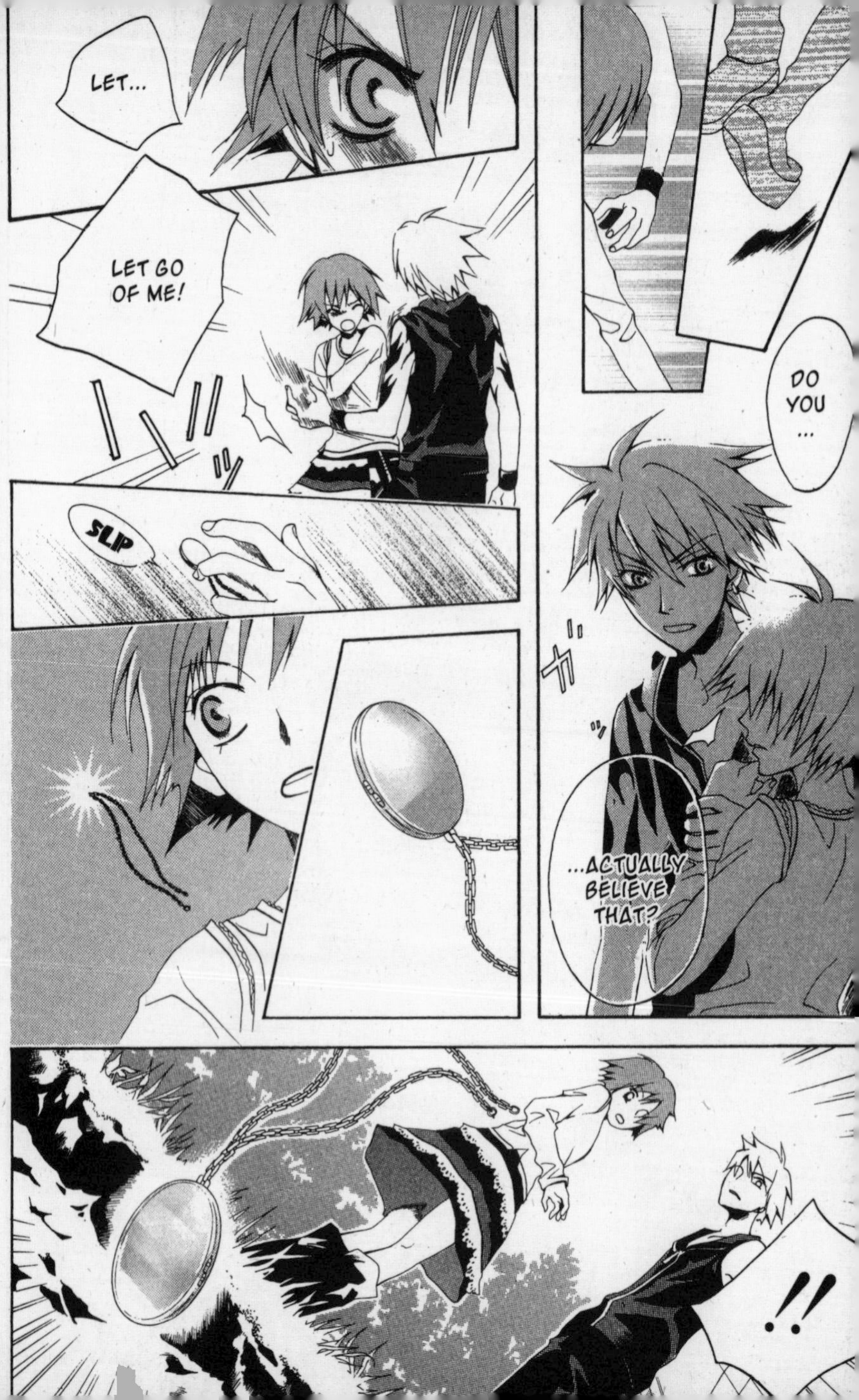
DO YOU ...
...ACTUALLY BELIEVE THAT?
LET...
LET GO OF ME!
SLIP
!!

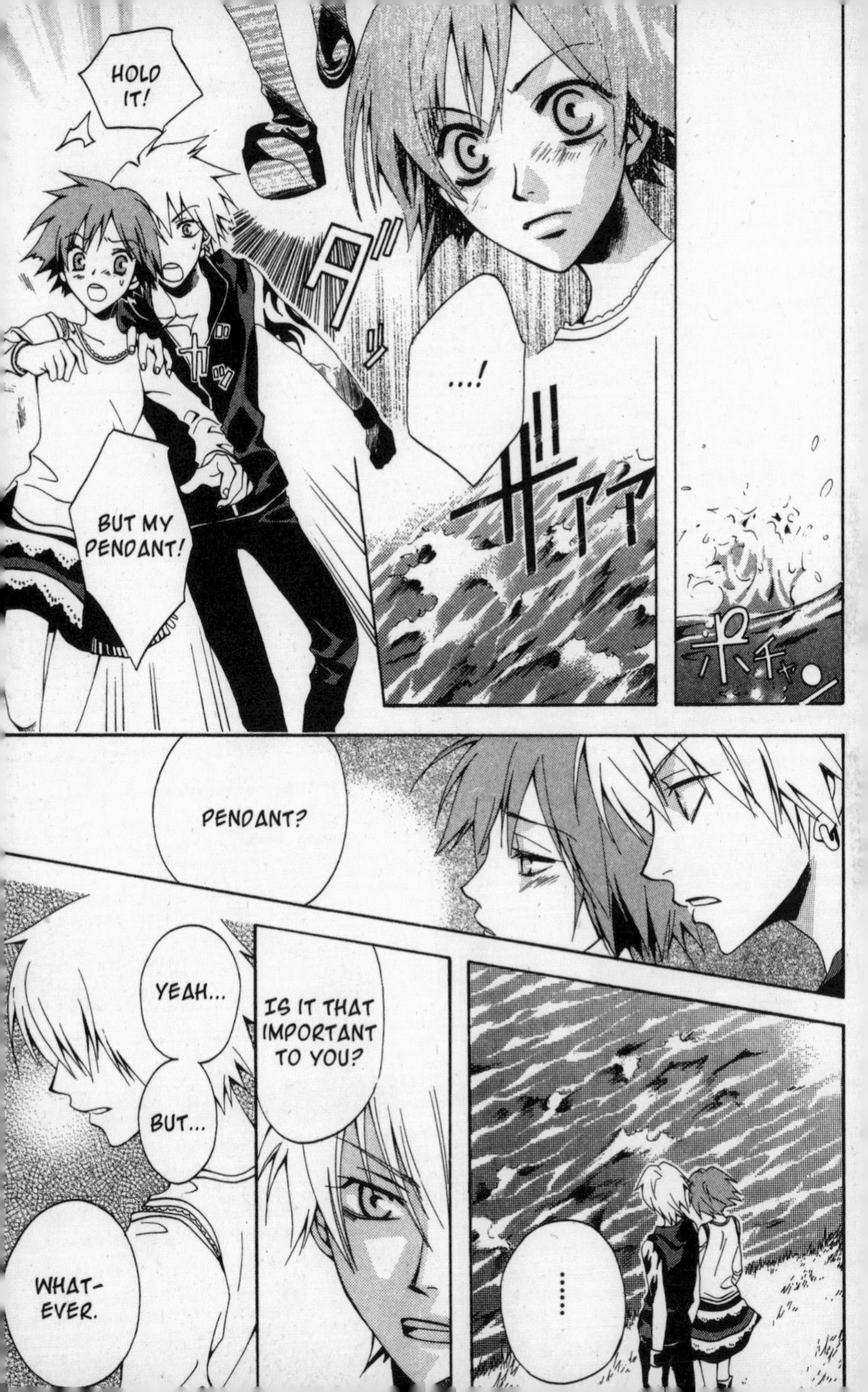

...!
ザァア
ポチャ
HOLD IT!
ダッ
BUT MY PENDANT!
PENDANT?
......
IS IT THAT IMPORTANT TO YOU?
YEAH...
BUT...
WHAT-EVER.

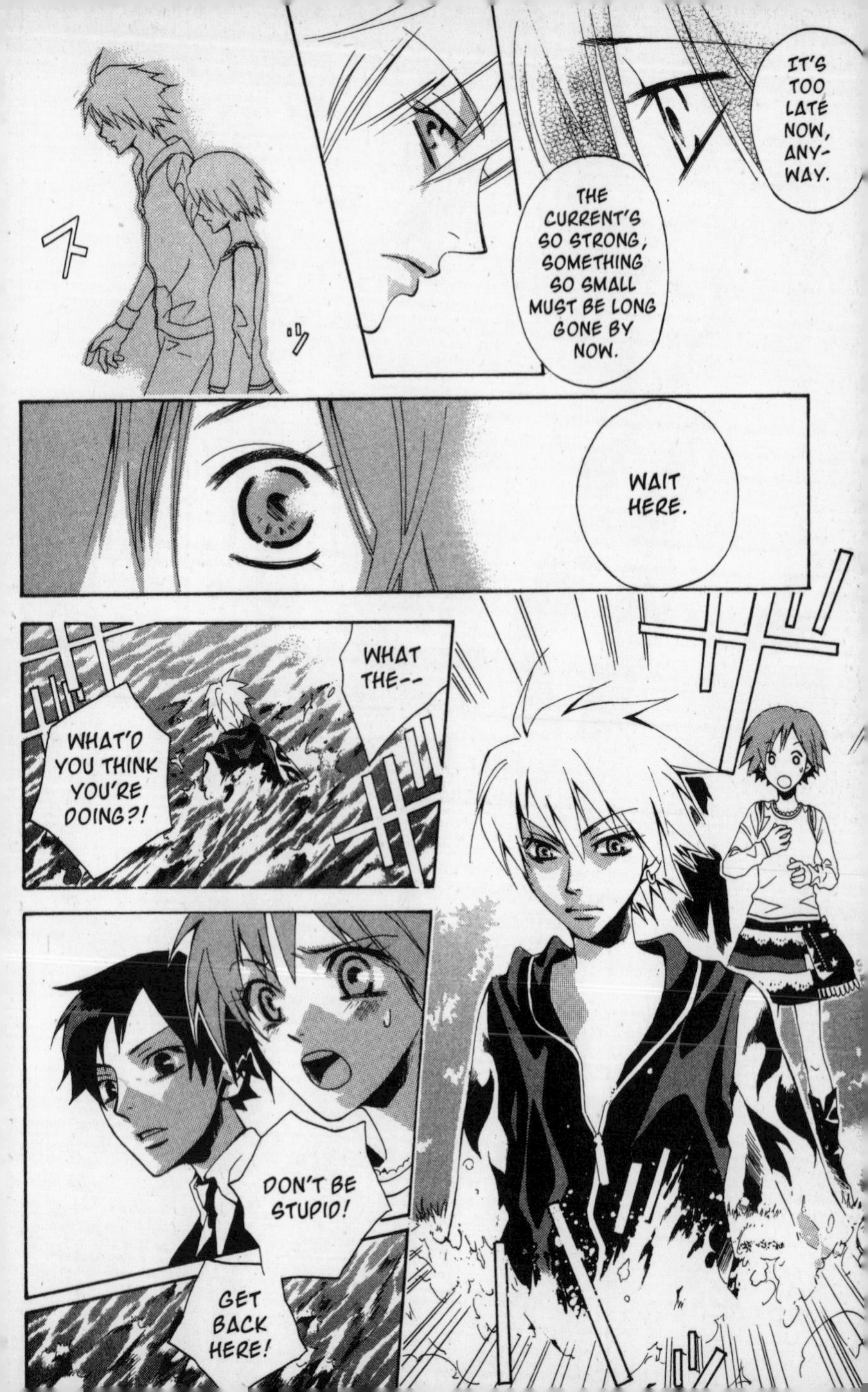
IT'S TOO LATE NOW, ANY-WAY.
THE CURRENT'S SO STRONG, SOMETHING SO SMALL MUST BE LONG GONE BY NOW.
WAIT HERE.
WHAT THE--
WHAT'D YOU THINK YOU'RE DOING?!
DON'T BE STUPID!
GET BACK HERE!

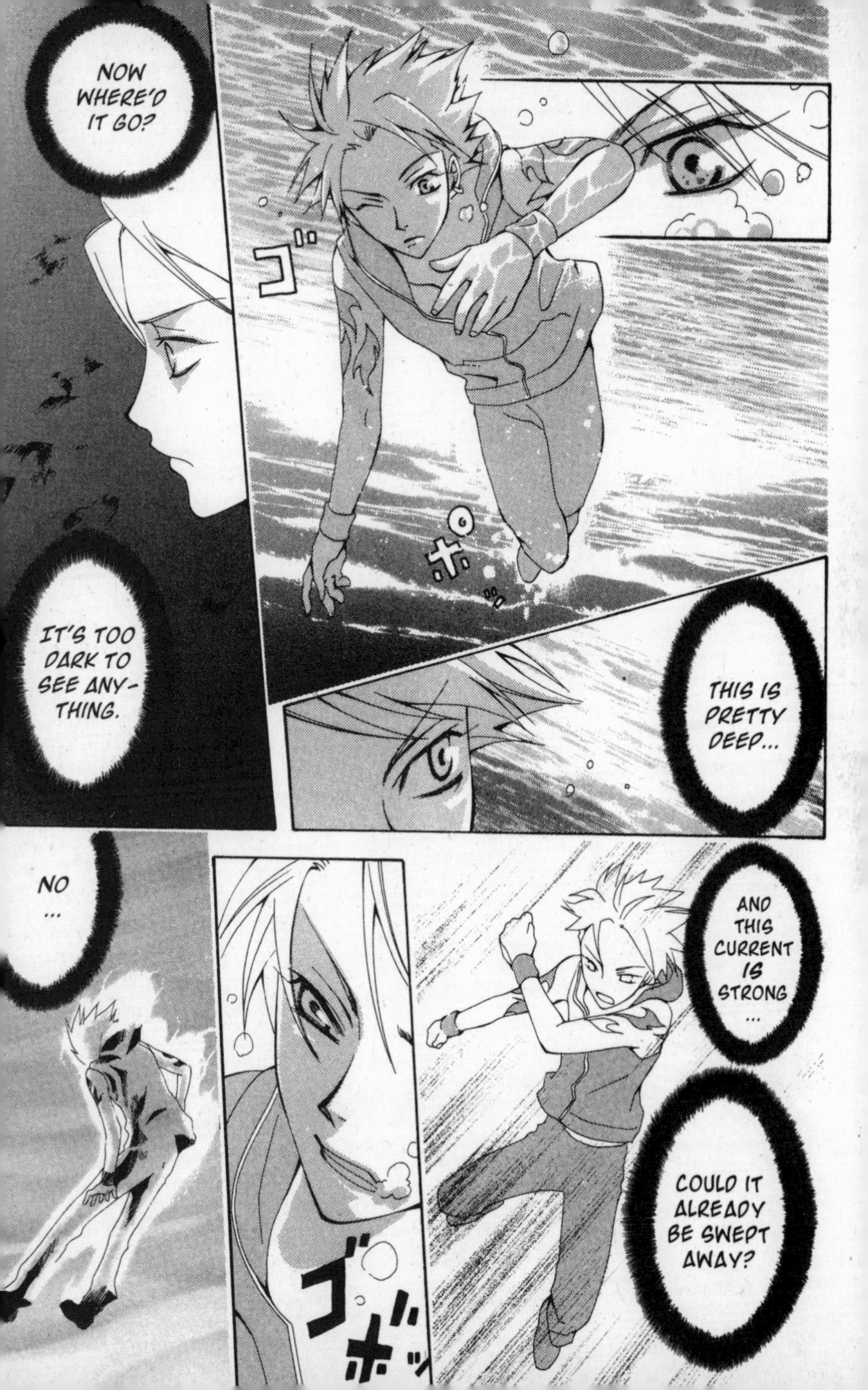
THIS IS PRETTY DEEP...
NOW WHERE'D IT GO?
IT'S TOO DARK TO SEE ANY-THING.
AND THIS CURRENT IS STRONG ...
COULD IT ALREADY BE SWEPT AWAY?
ゴボッ
NO ...

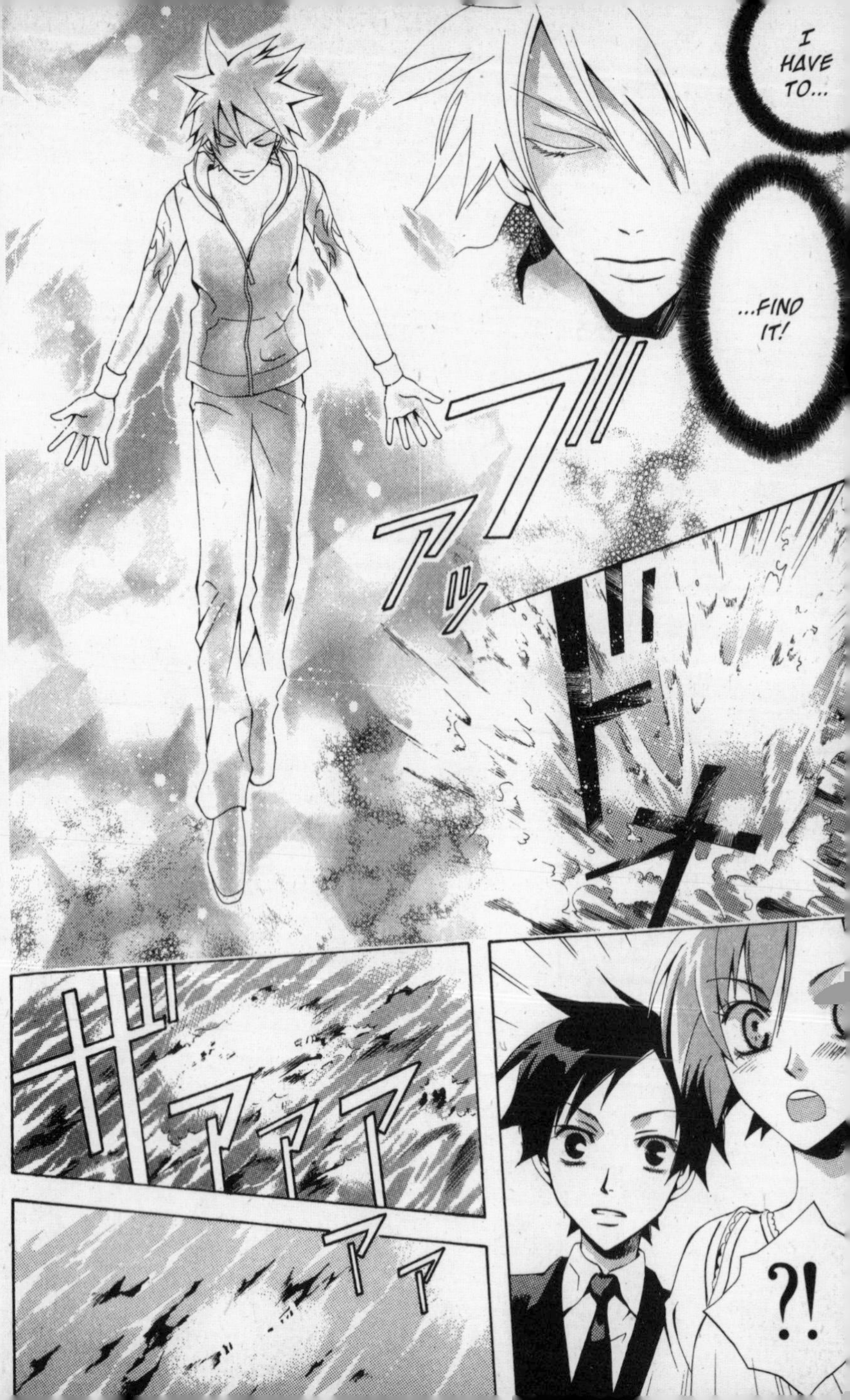
I HAVE TO...
...FIND IT!
?!

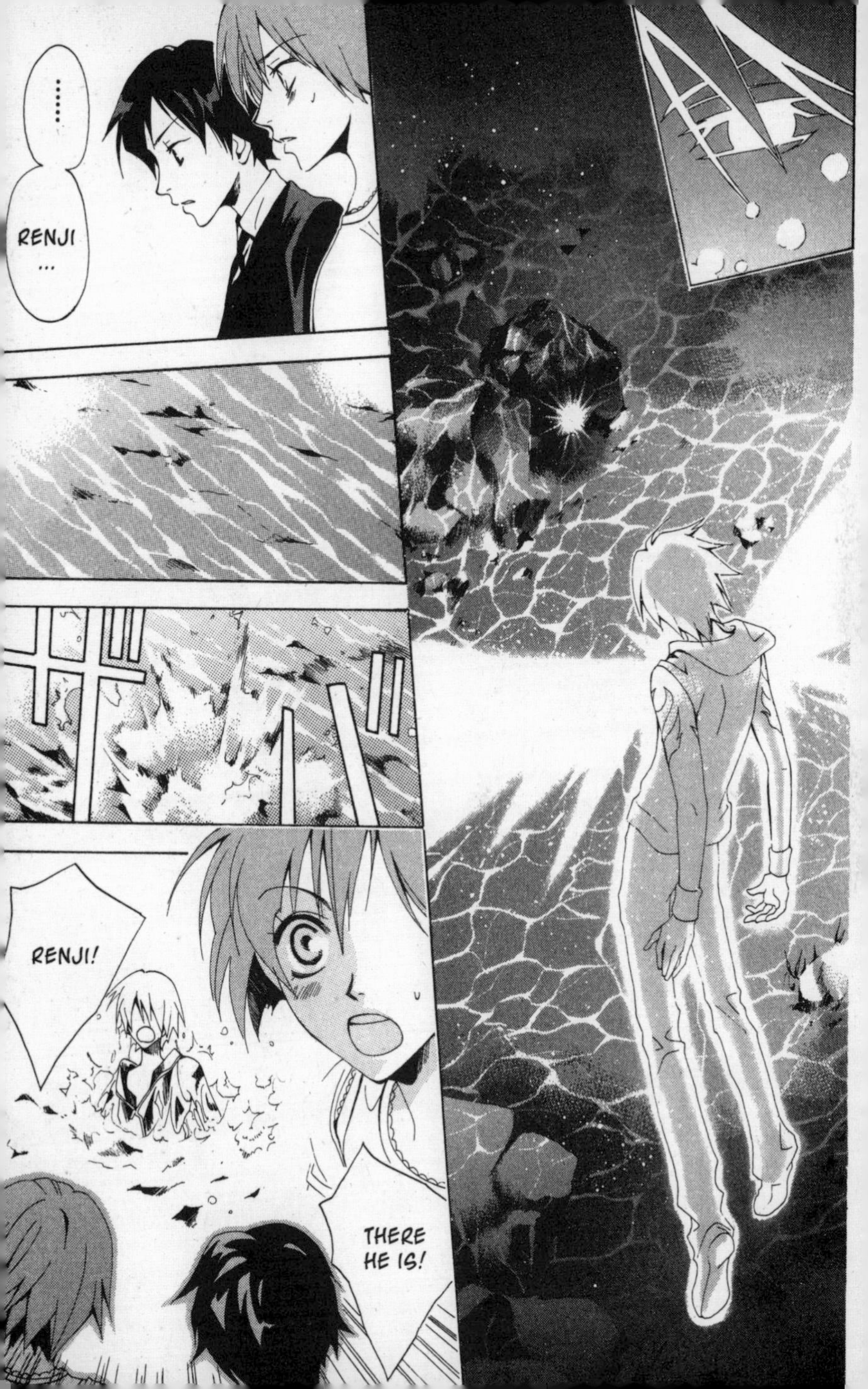
......
RENJI ...
RENJI!
THERE HE IS!

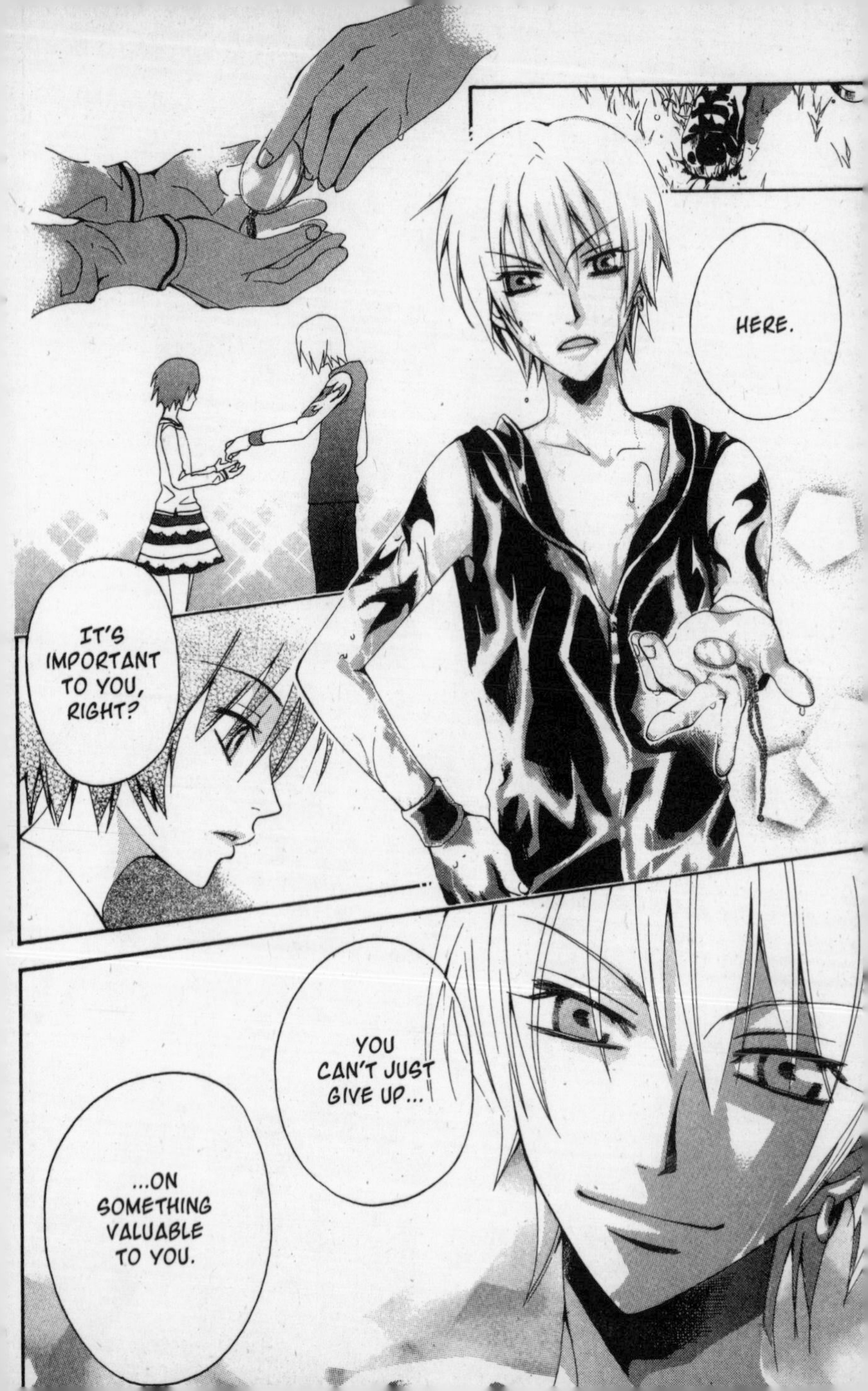
HERE.
IT'S IMPORTANT TO YOU, RIGHT?
YOU CAN'T JUST GIVE UP...
...ON SOMETHING VALUABLE TO YOU.

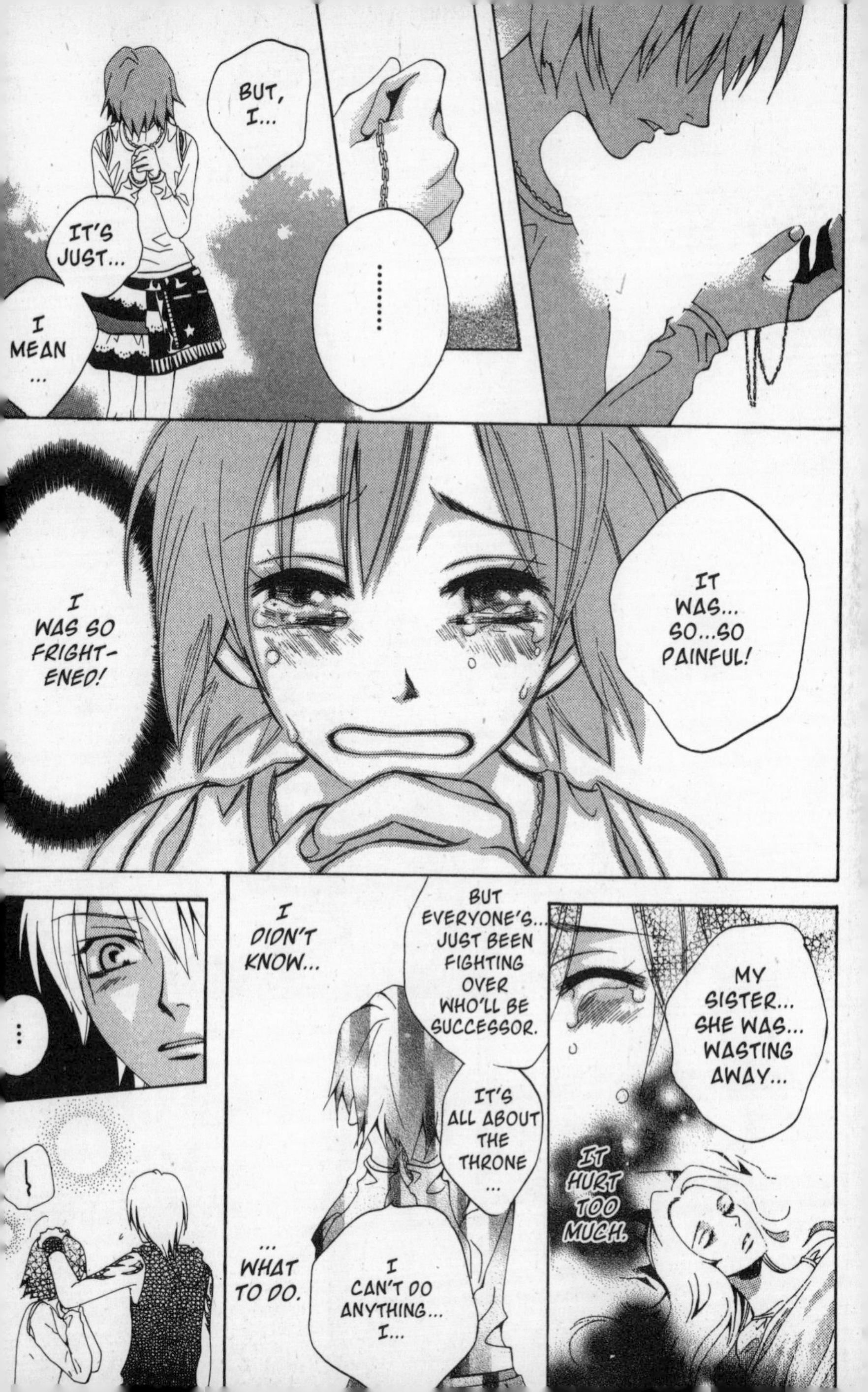
......
BUT, I...
IT'S JUST...
I MEAN ...
IT WAS... SO...SO PAINFUL!
I WAS SO FRIGHT-ENED!
MY SISTER... SHE WAS... WASTING AWAY...
IT HURT TOO MUCH.
BUT EVERYONE'S... JUST BEEN FIGHTING OVER WHO'LL BE SUCCESSOR.
IT'S ALL ABOUT THE THRONE ...
I DIDN'T KNOW...
... WHAT TO DO.
I CAN'T DO ANYTHING... I...
...
!

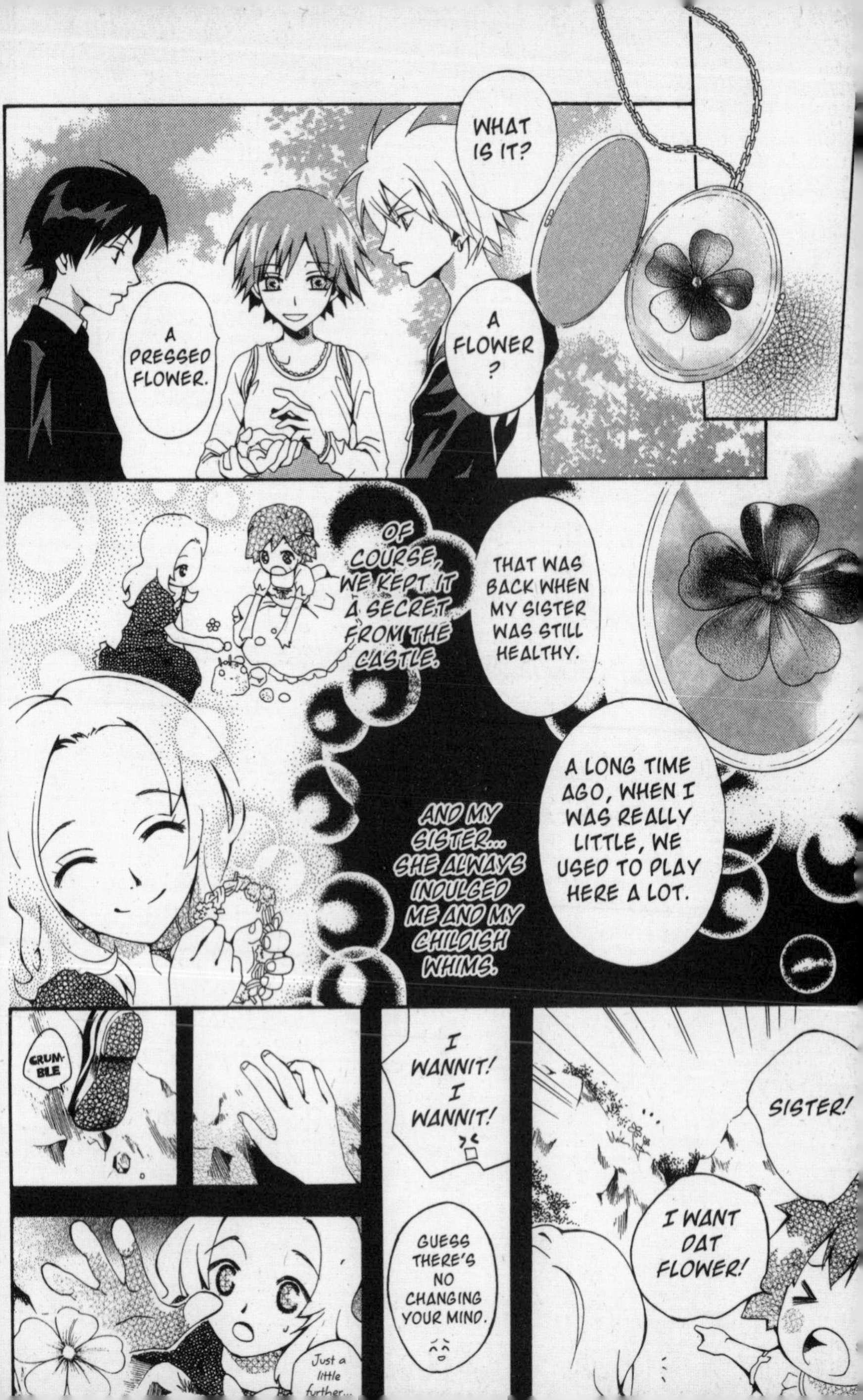
WHAT IS IT?
A FLOWER ?
A PRESSED FLOWER.
THAT WAS BACK WHEN MY SISTER WAS STILL HEALTHY.
OF COURSE, WE KEPT IT A SECRET FROM THE CASTLE.
A LONG TIME AGO, WHEN I WAS REALLY LITTLE, WE USED TO PLAY HERE A LOT.
AND MY SISTER... SHE ALWAYS INDULGED ME AND MY CHILDISH WHIMS.
SISTER!
I WANT DAT FLOWER!
I WANNIT! I WANNIT!
GRUMBLE
GUESS THERE'S NO CHANGING YOUR MIND.
Just a little further...

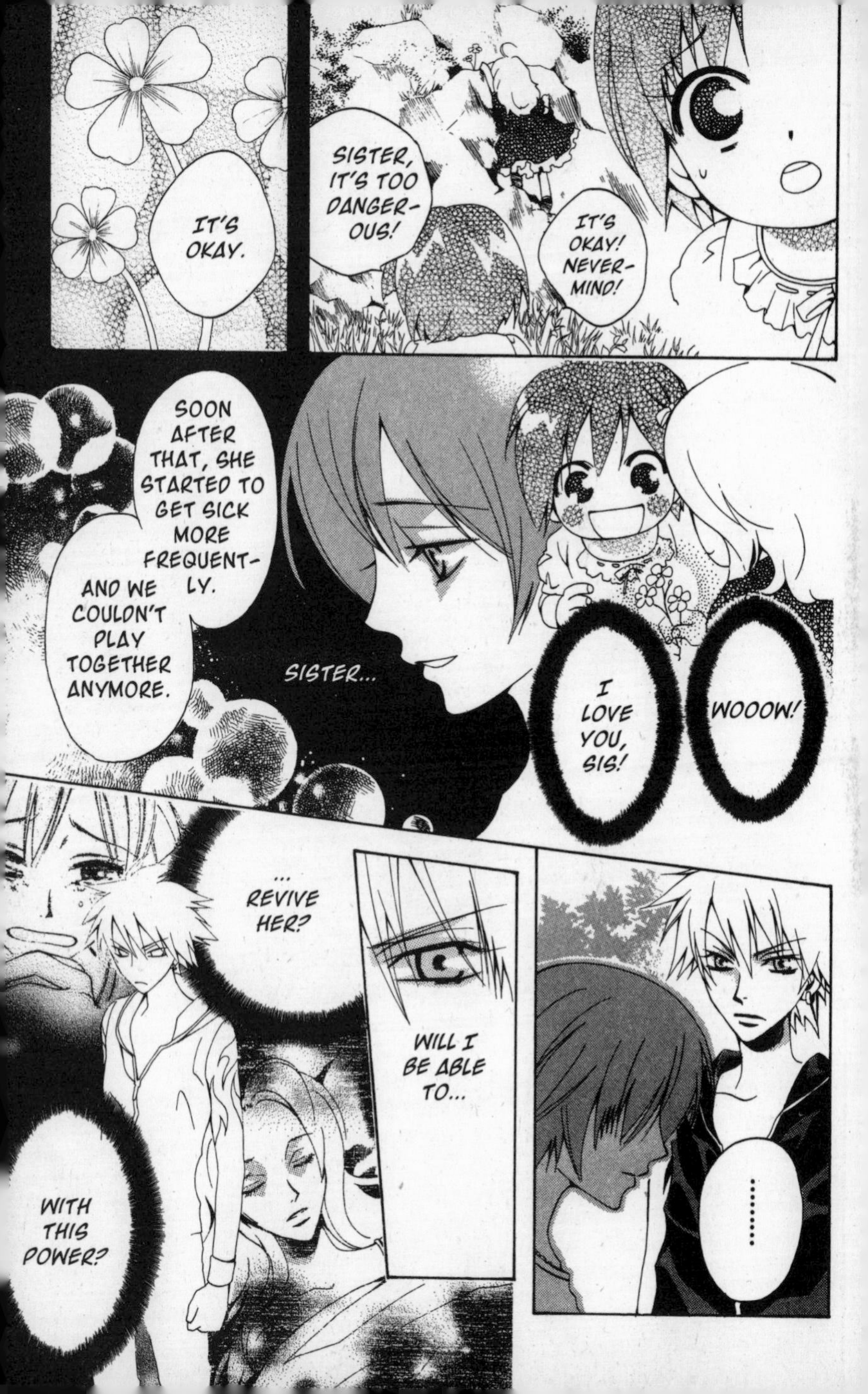
SISTER, IT'S TOO DANGER-OUS!
IT'S OKAY! NEVER-MIND!
IT'S OKAY.
WOOOW!
I LOVE YOU, SIS!
SISTER...
SOON AFTER THAT, SHE STARTED TO GET SICK MORE FREQUENT-LY.
AND WE COULDN'T PLAY TOGETHER ANYMORE.
......
WILL I BE ABLE TO...
... REVIVE HER?
WITH THIS POWER?

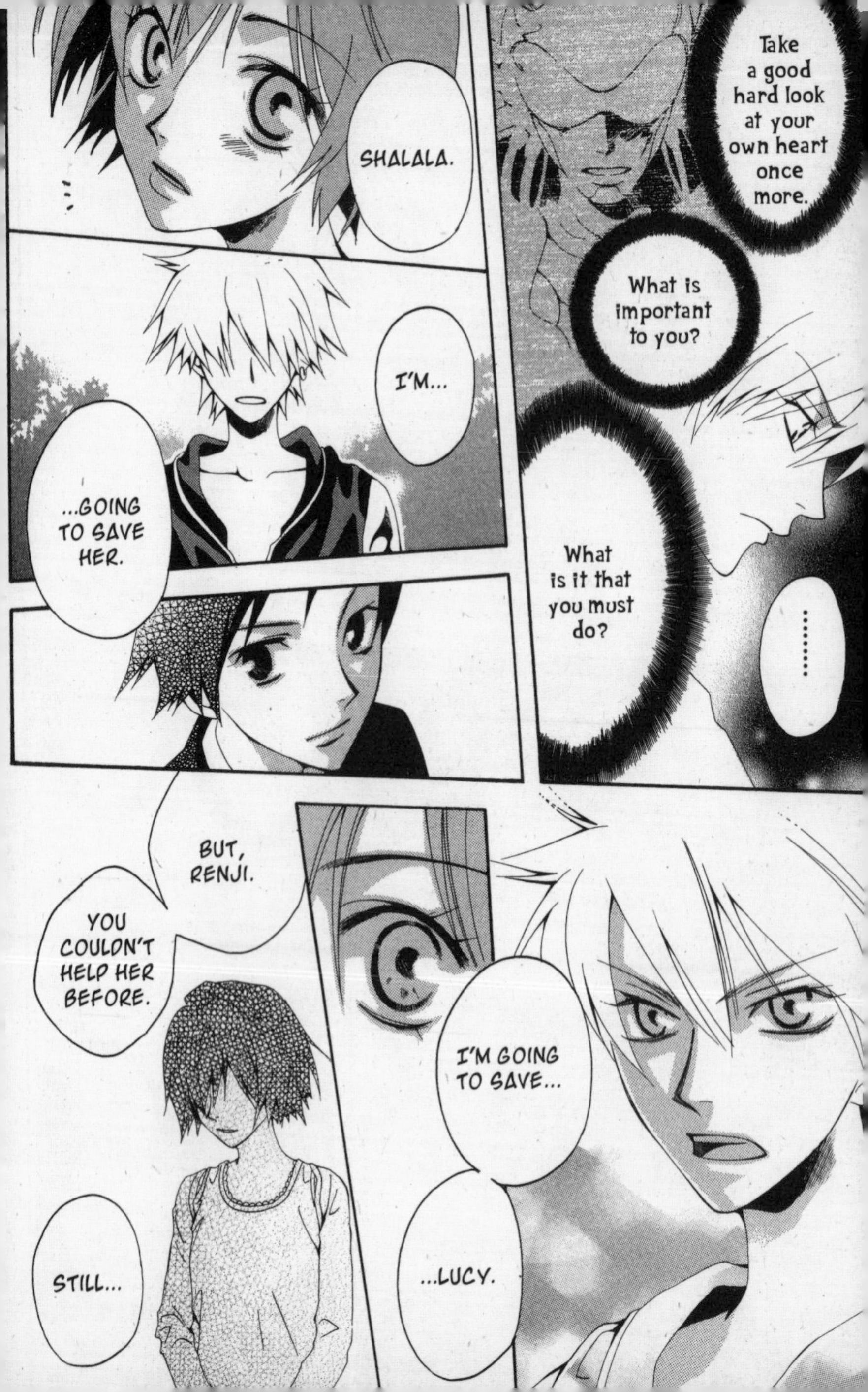

Take a good hard look at your own heart once more.
What is important to you?
What is it that you must do?
....
SHALALA.
I'M...
...GOING TO SAVE HER.
I'M GOING TO SAVE...
...LUCY.
BUT, RENJI.
YOU COULDN'T HELP HER BEFORE.
STILL...

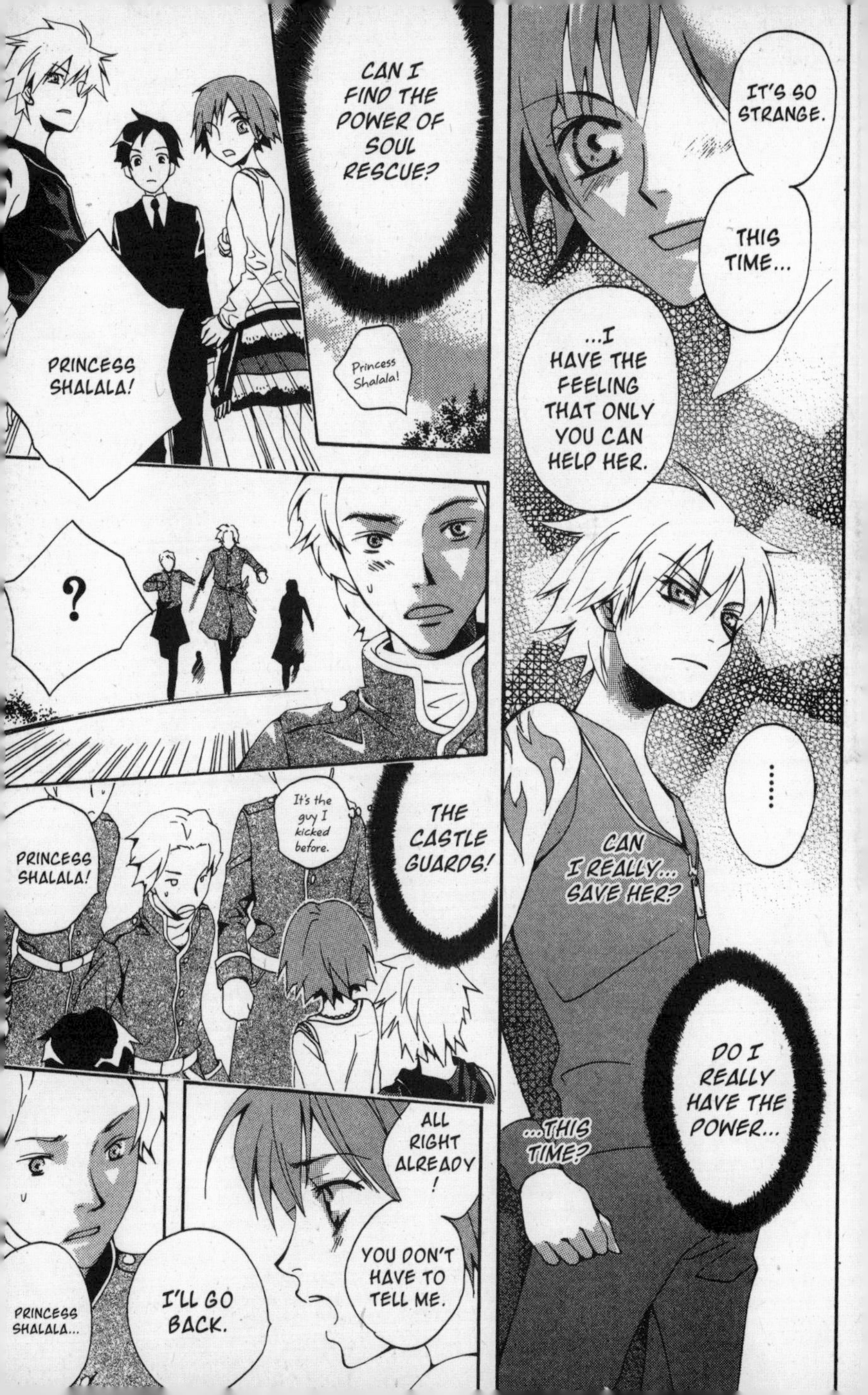
IT'S SO STRANGE.
THIS TIME...
...I HAVE THE FEELING THAT ONLY YOU CAN HELP HER.
......
CAN I REALLY... SAVE HER?
DO I REALLY HAVE THE POWER...
...THIS TIME?
CAN I FIND THE POWER OF SOUL RESCUE?
Princess Shalala!
PRINCESS SHALALA!
?
THE CASTLE GUARDS!
It's the guy I kicked before.
PRINCESS SHALALA!
ALL RIGHT ALREADY!
YOU DON'T HAVE TO TELL ME.
I'LL GO BACK.
PRINCESS SHALALA...

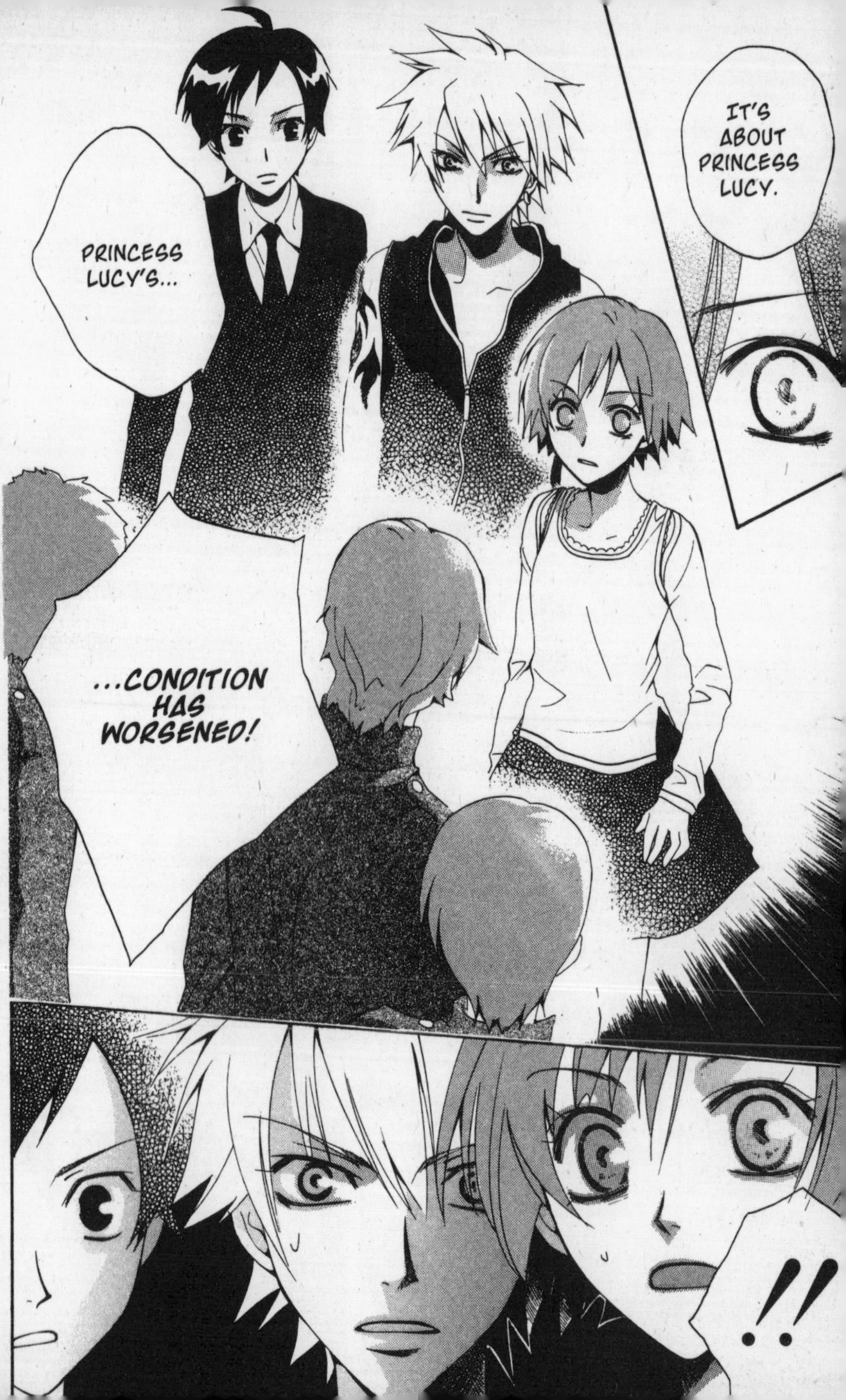
IT'S ABOUT PRINCESS LUCY.
PRINCESS LUCY'S...
...CONDITION HAS WORSENED!
!!

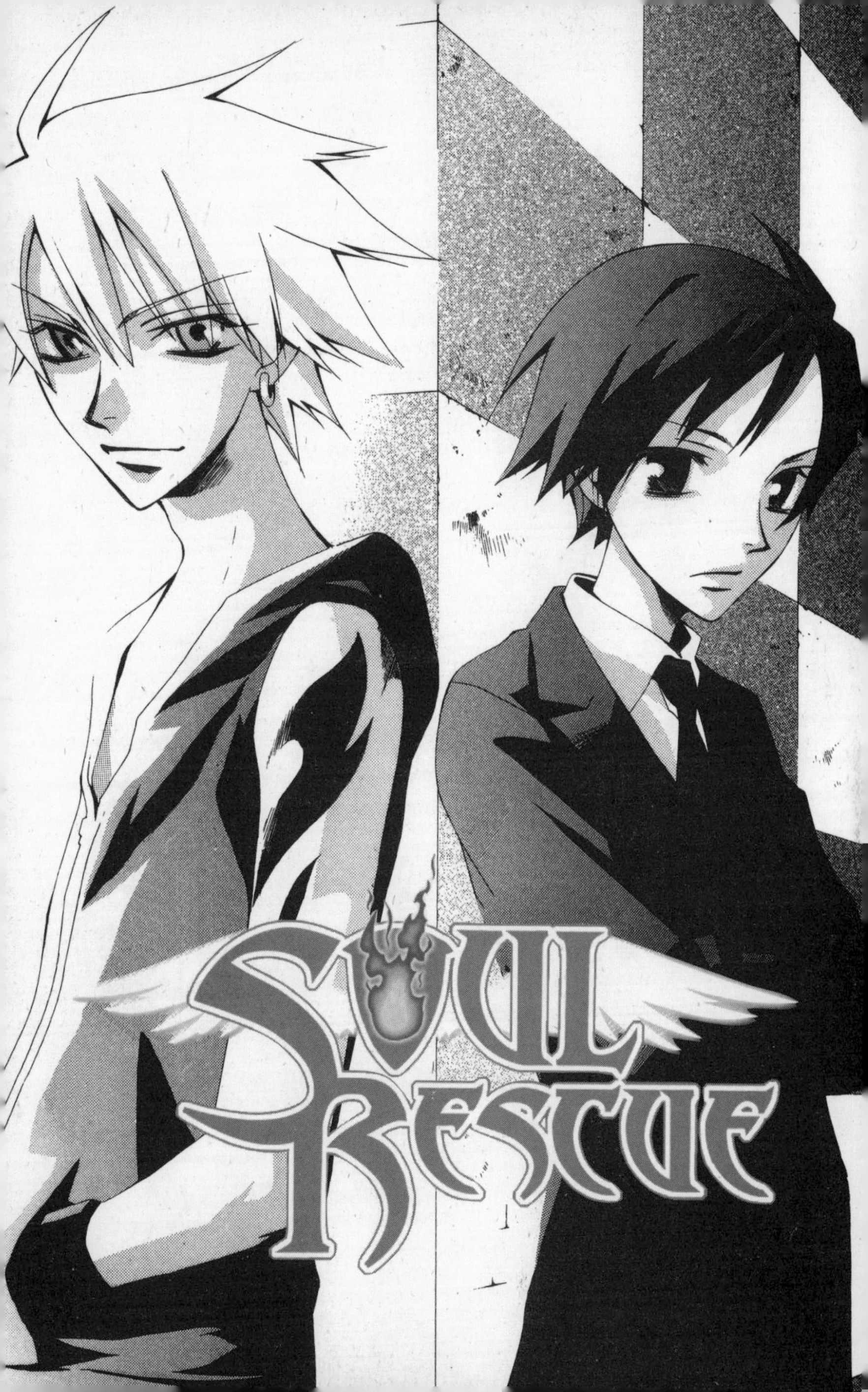
SOUL
RESCUE

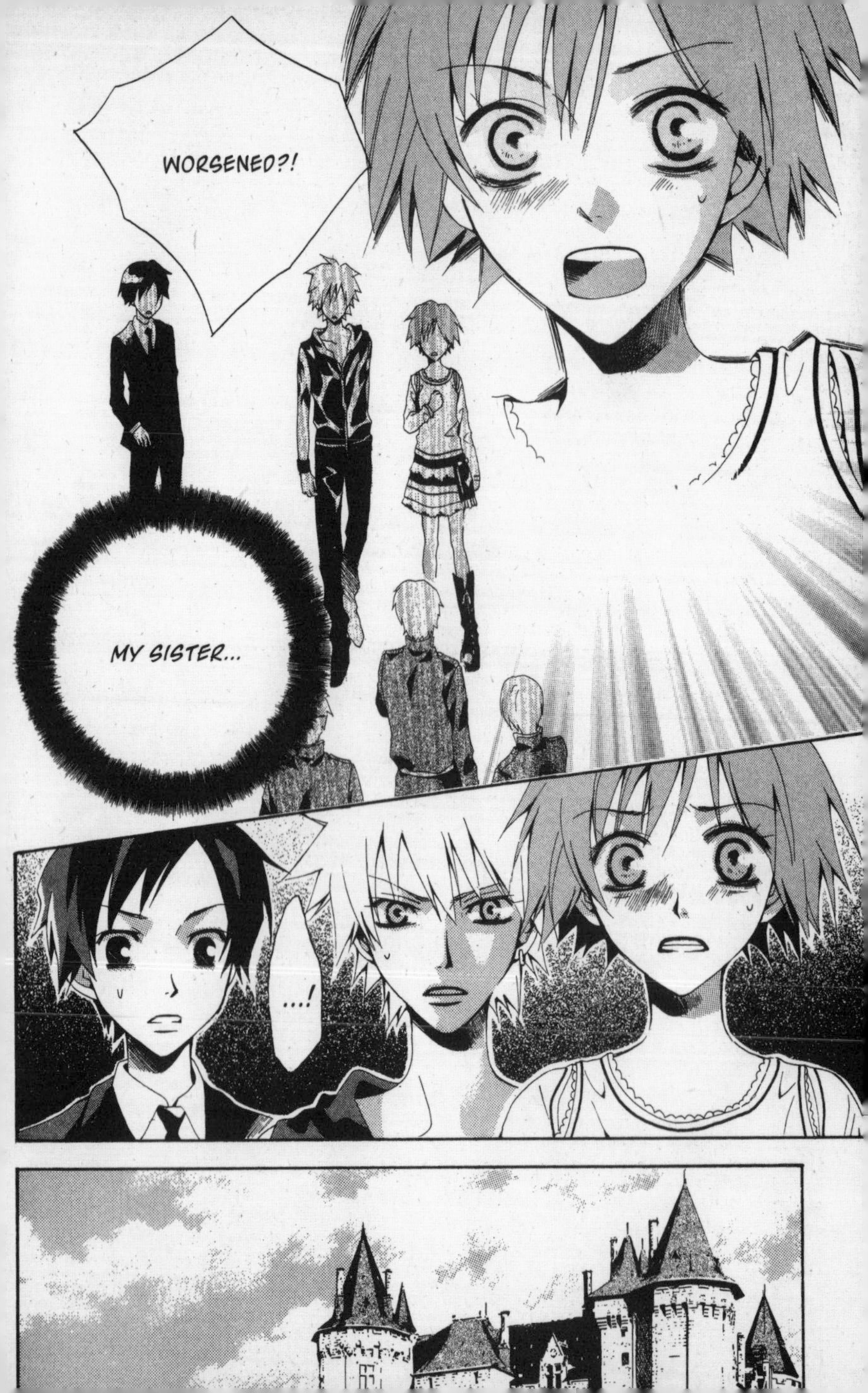
WORSENED?!
MY SISTER...
...!

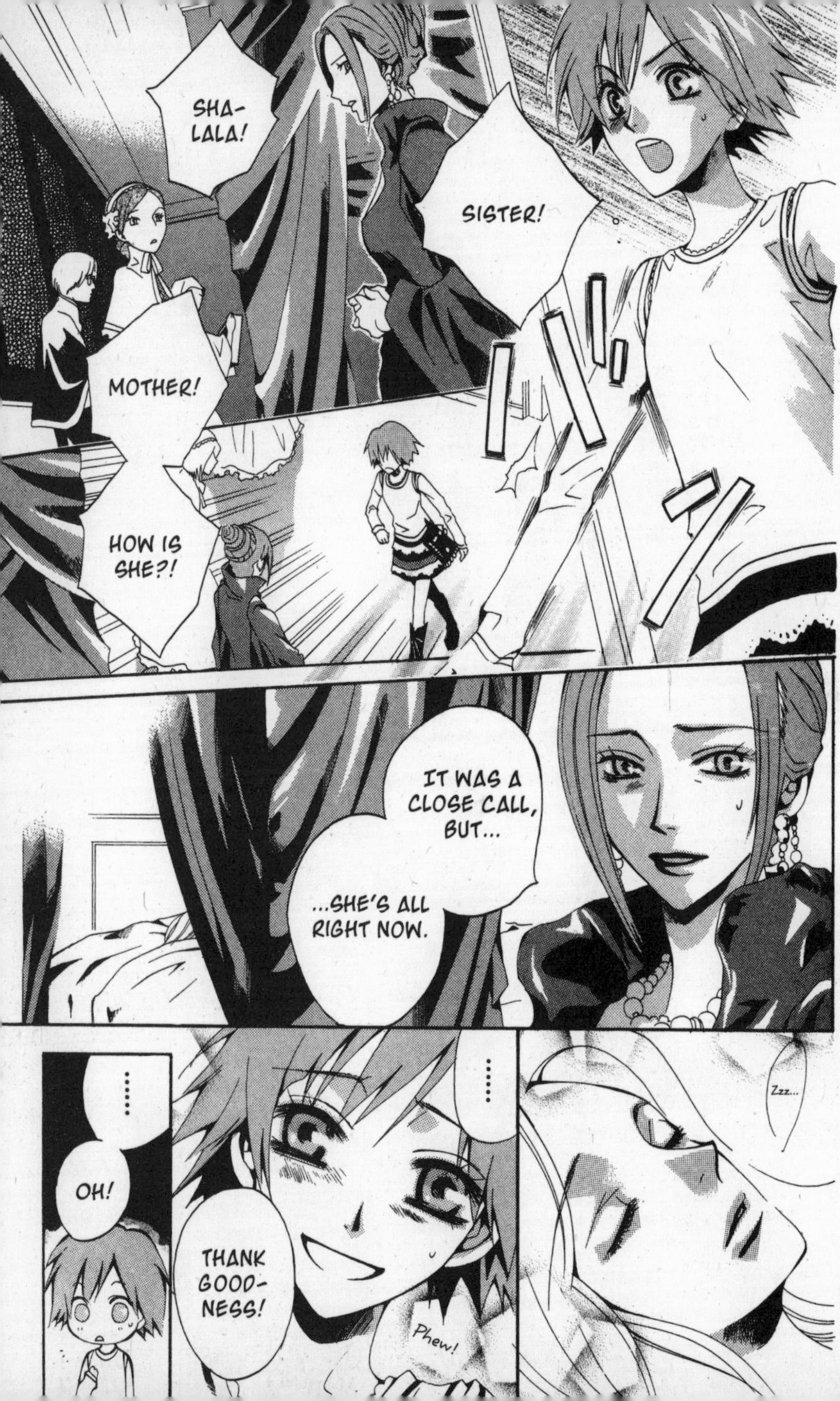
SISTER!
SHA-LALA!
MOTHER!
HOW IS SHE?!
IT WAS A CLOSE CALL, BUT...
...SHE'S ALL RIGHT NOW.
Zzz...
......
THANK GOODNESS!
Phew!
......
OH!

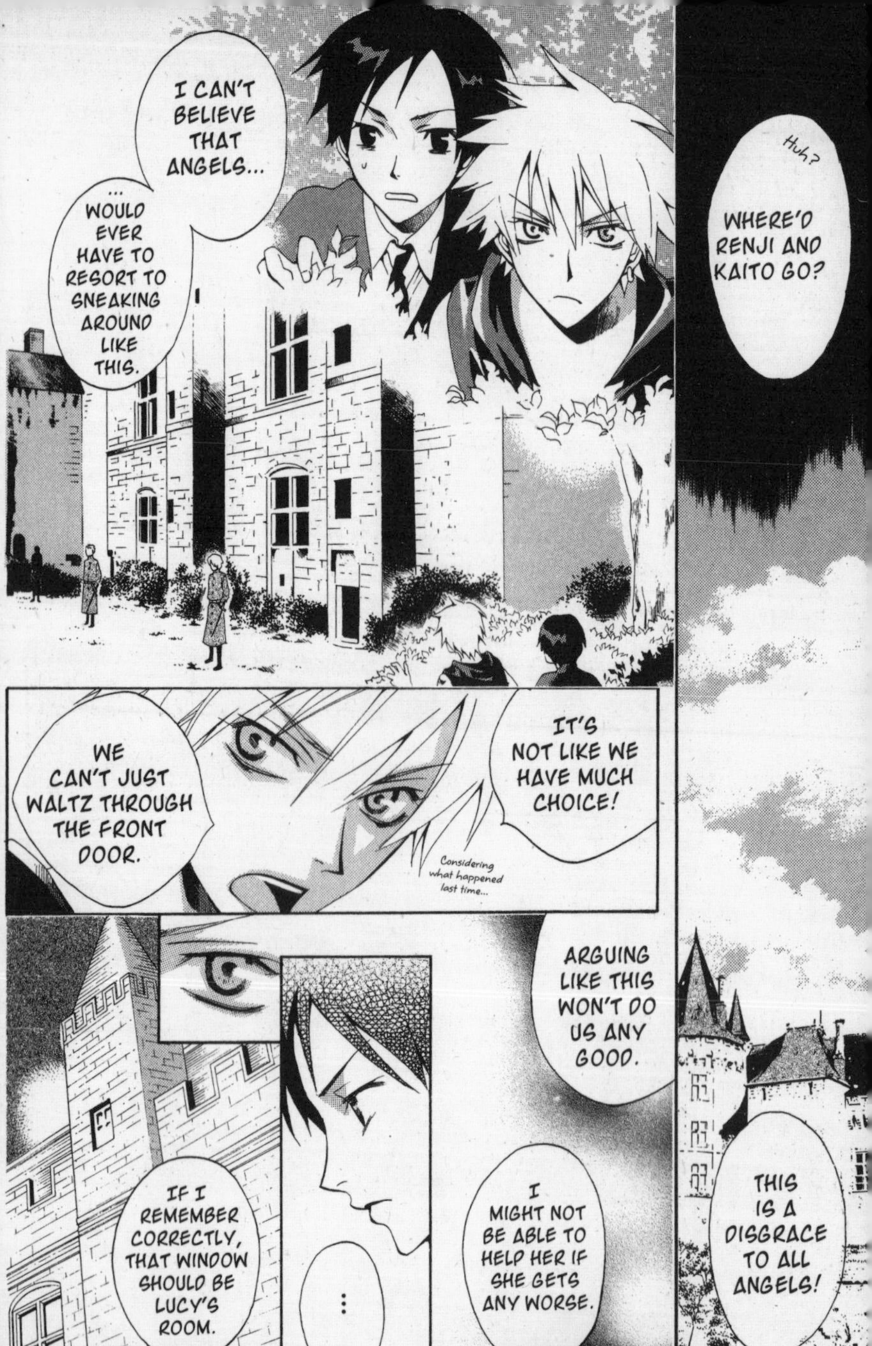
Huh?
WHERE'D RENJI AND KAITO GO?
THIS IS A DISGRACE TO ALL ANGELS!
I CAN'T BELIEVE THAT ANGELS...
... WOULD EVER HAVE TO RESORT TO SNEAKING AROUND LIKE THIS.
IT'S NOT LIKE WE HAVE MUCH CHOICE!
Considering what happened last time...
WE CAN'T JUST WALTZ THROUGH THE FRONT DOOR.
ARGUING LIKE THIS WON'T DO US ANY GOOD.
I MIGHT NOT BE ABLE TO HELP HER IF SHE GETS ANY WORSE.
...
IF I REMEMBER CORRECTLY, THAT WINDOW SHOULD BE LUCY'S ROOM.

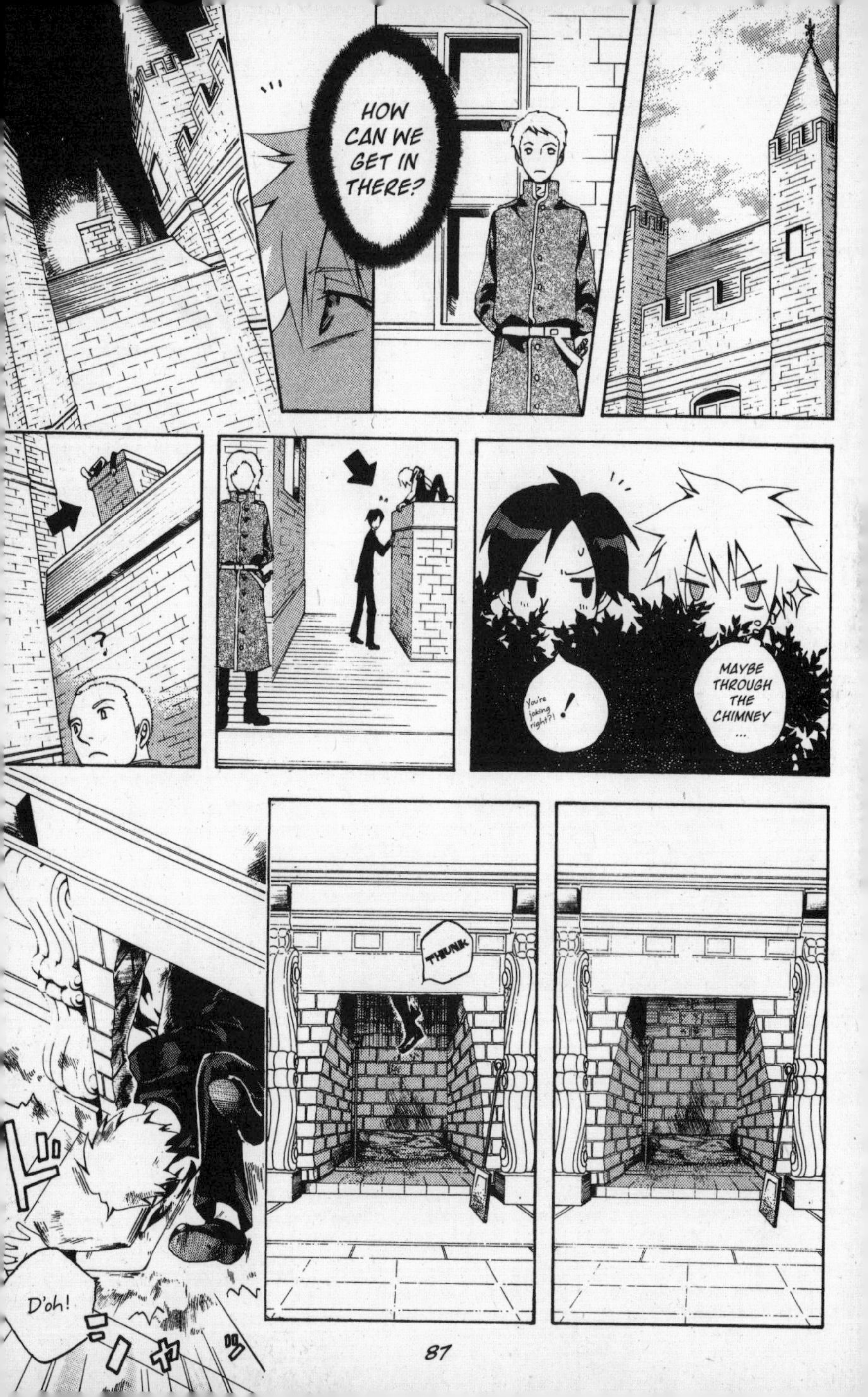
HOW CAN WE GET IN THERE?
MAYBE THROUGH THE CHIMNEY ...
You're joking right?!
THUNK
D'oh!

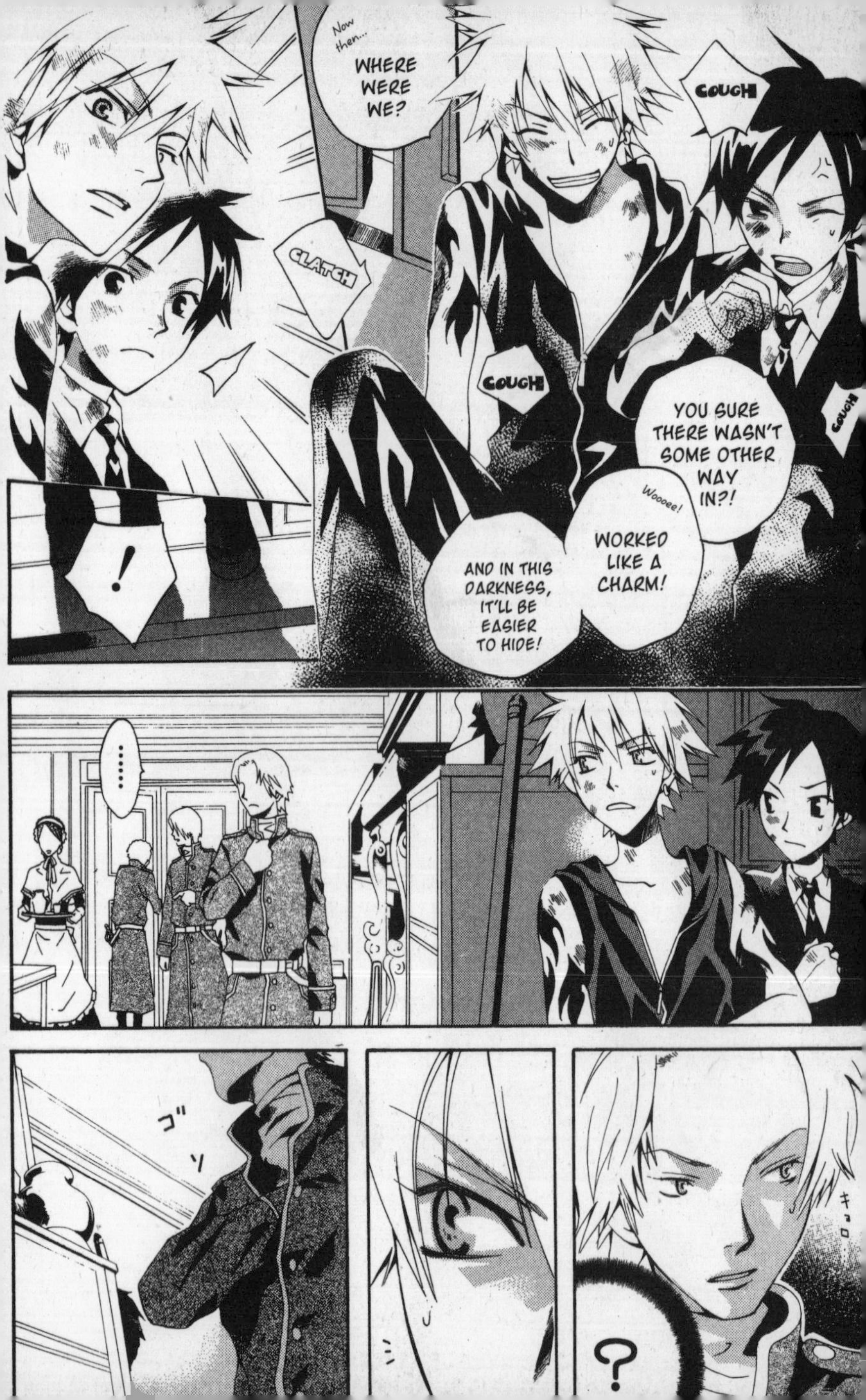
COUGH
Now then... WHERE WERE WE?
COUGH
YOU SURE THERE WASN'T SOME OTHER WAY IN?!
Woooee!
WORKED LIKE A CHARM!
COUGH
AND IN THIS DARKNESS, IT'LL BE EASIER TO HIDE!
CLATCH
!
......
キョロ
?
ゴソ

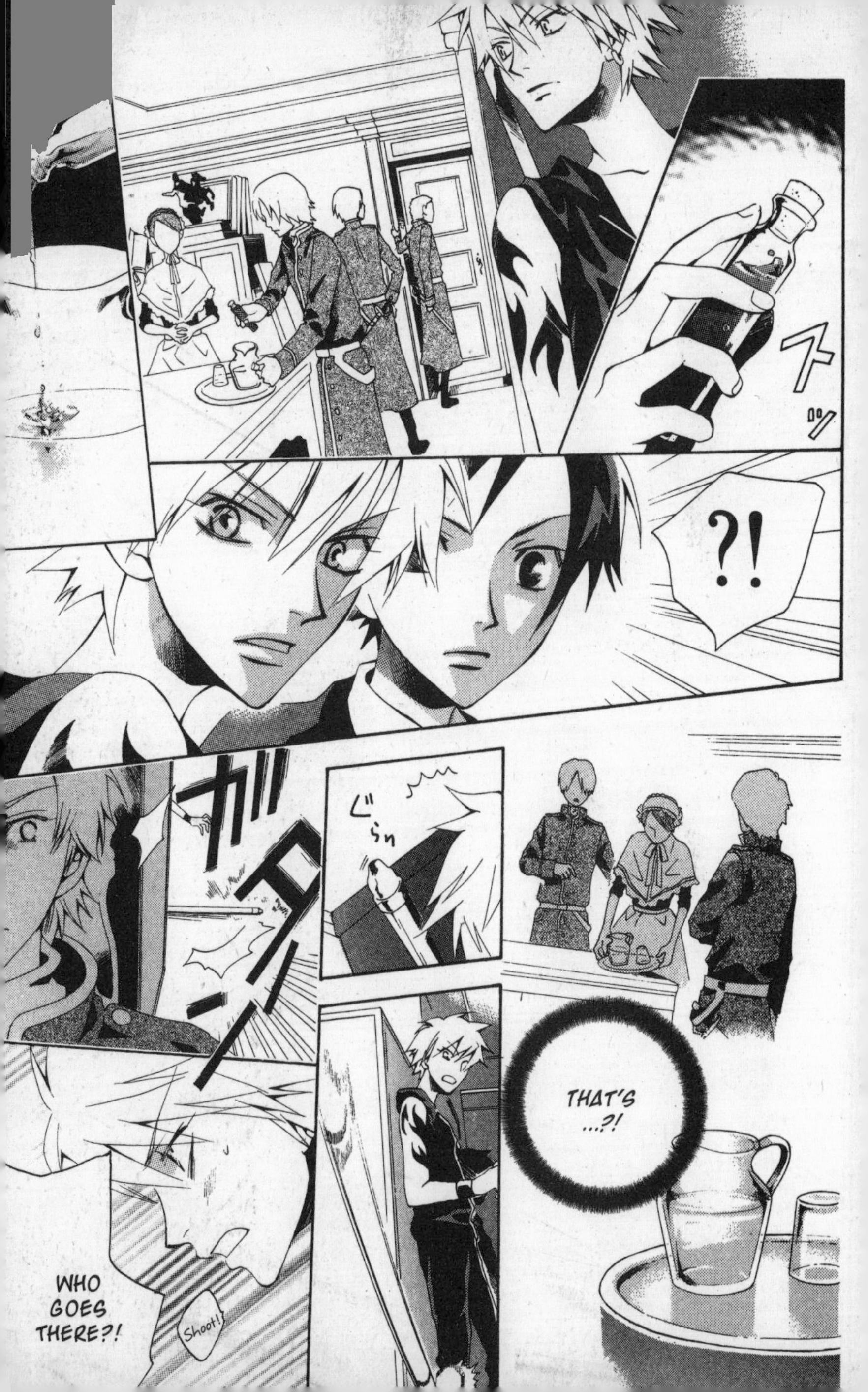
?!
THAT'S ...?!
WHO GOES THERE?!
Shoot!

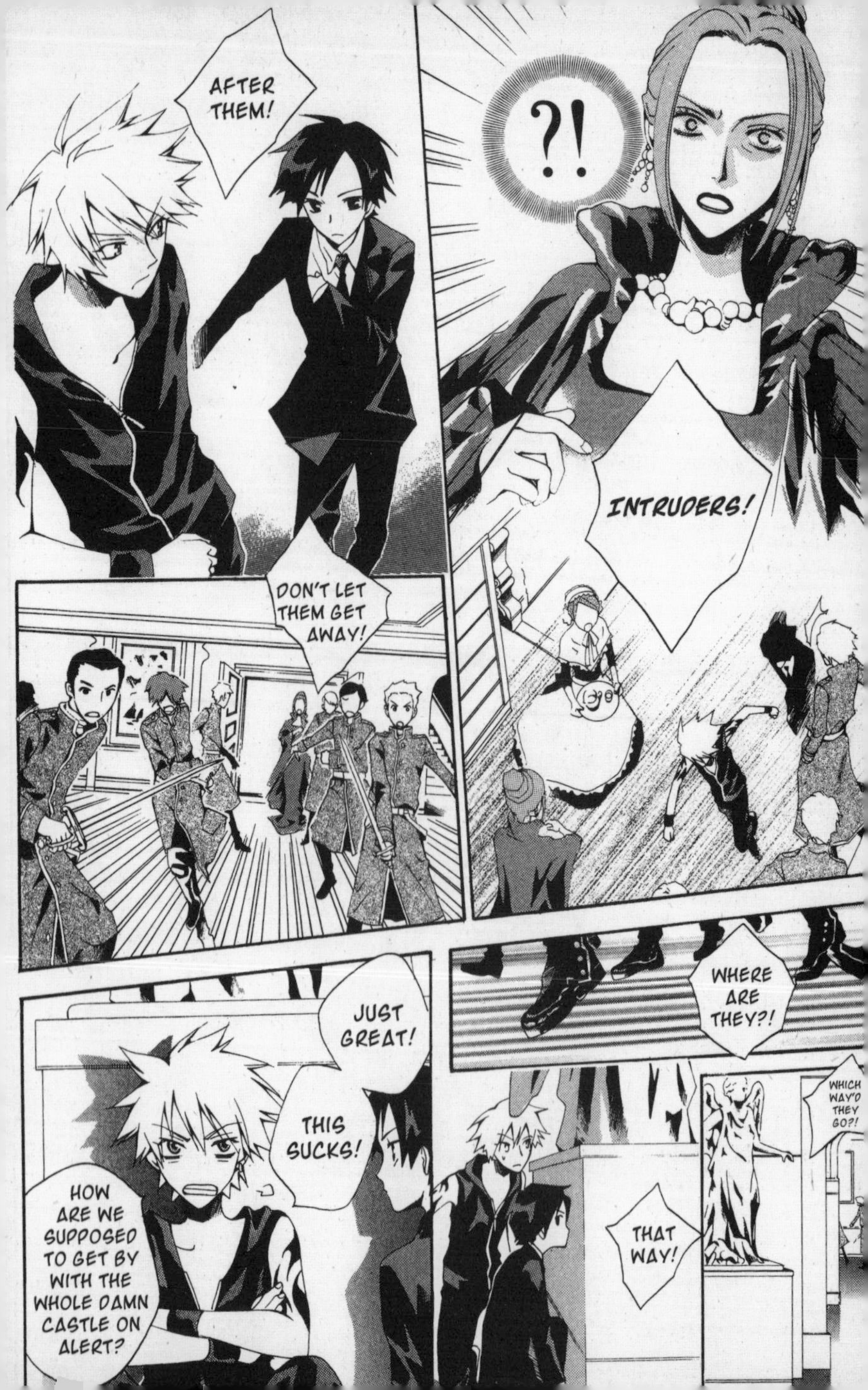
?!
INTRUDERS!
AFTER THEM!
DON'T LET THEM GET AWAY!
WHERE ARE THEY?!
WHICH WAY'D THEY GO?!
THAT WAY!
JUST GREAT!
THIS SUCKS!
HOW ARE WE SUPPOSED TO GET BY WITH THE WHOLE DAMN CASTLE ON ALERT?

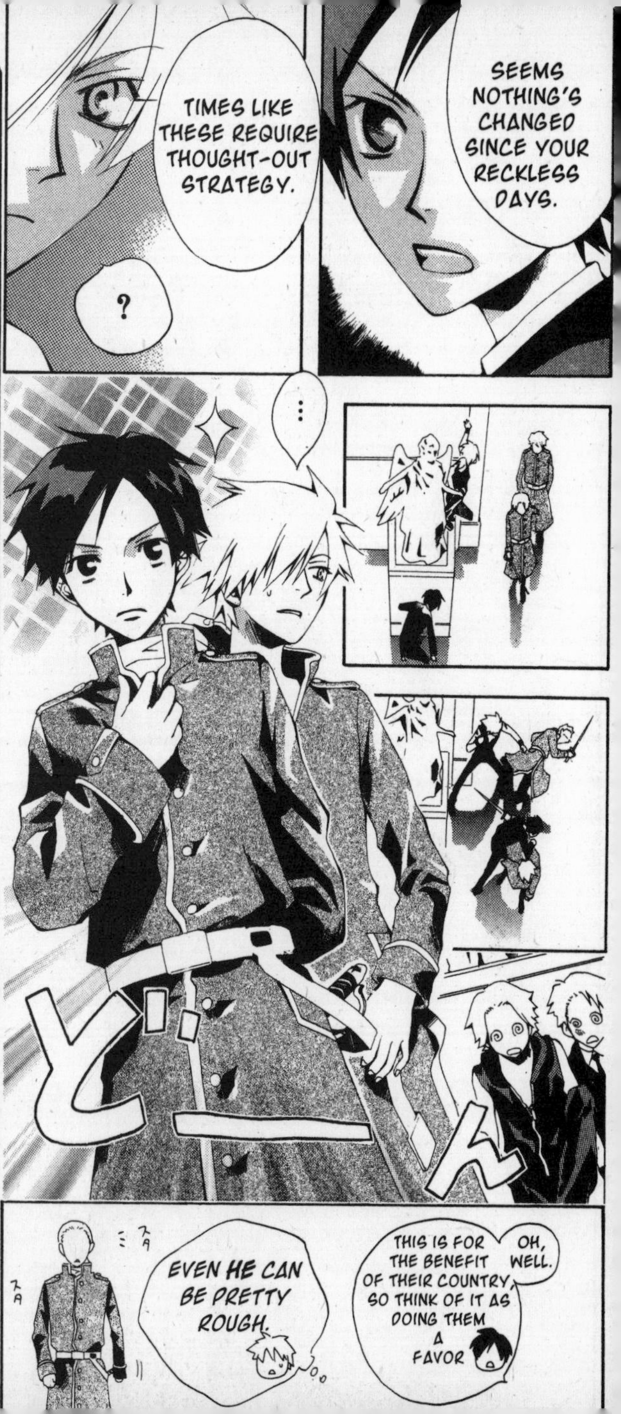
SEEMS NOTHING'S CHANGED SINCE YOUR RECKLESS DAYS.
TIMES LIKE THESE REQUIRE THOUGHT-OUT STRATEGY.
?
...
OH, WELL.
THIS IS FOR THE BENEFIT OF THEIR COUNTRY, SO THINK OF IT AS DOING THEM A FAVOR
EVEN HE CAN BE PRETTY ROUGH.

SR

It's chapter two and three! Aaah! Believe it or not, "Aaah!" is the only feeling I have about that. I love the character of Shalala. Generally speaking, I have a soft spot for all strong and go-getter kinds of girls. Yup.

While I was working on the first part of chapter two, two days before the deadline for it, I went to a rock concert (Ha!). And on my way home, it rained a little and was a cold, miserable day... so of course I caught a fever. Reeaaal good memory there. Right.

As for whether or not going to concerts is a past-time of mine: well, I love music. I never fail to put on background music while I'm working. Lately, I've been listening to a lot of Eastern Youth and Kingbrothers... But I love Thee Michelle Gun Elephant, Elephant Kashimashi, and Buck-tick. Oh, and BJC.

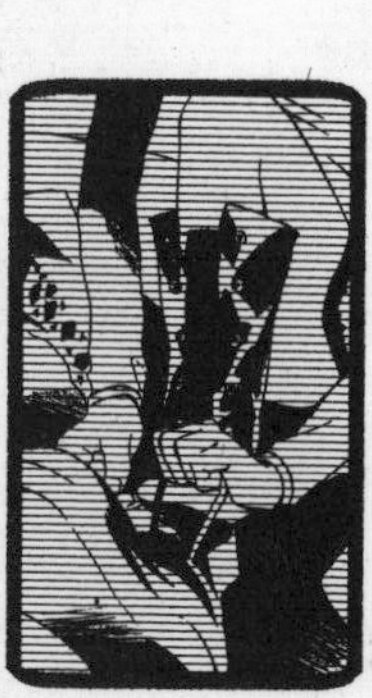

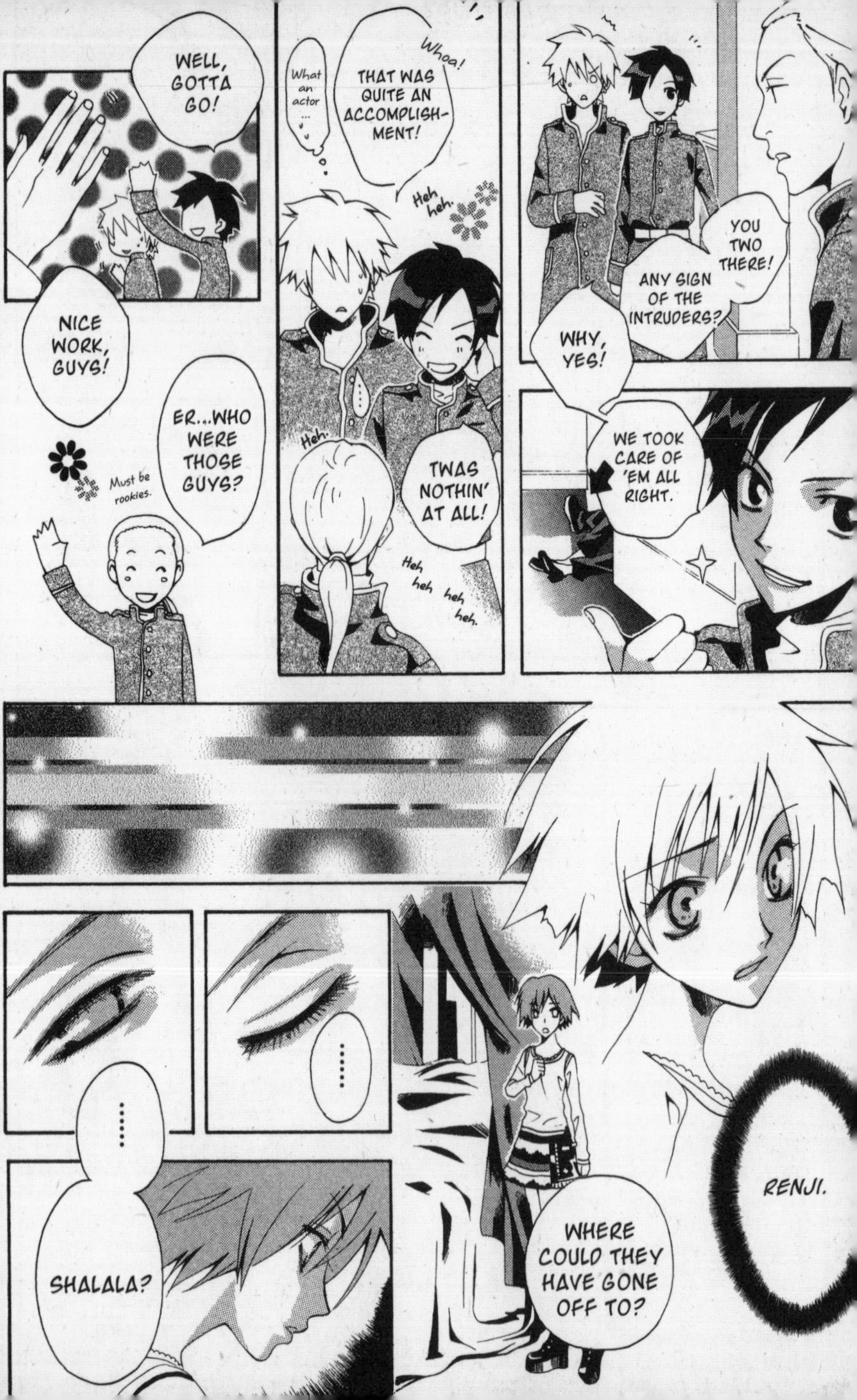
YOU TWO THERE!
ANY SIGN OF THE INTRUDERS?
WHY, YES!
WE TOOK CARE OF 'EM ALL RIGHT.
Whoa!
THAT WAS QUITE AN ACCOMPLISH-MENT!
What an actor ...
Heh heh.
....
TWAS NOTHIN' AT ALL!
Heh.
Heh heh heh heh.
WELL, GOTTA GO!
NICE WORK, GUYS!
ER...WHO WERE THOSE GUYS?
Must be rookies.
RENJI.
WHERE COULD THEY HAVE GONE OFF TO?
......
......
SHALALA?

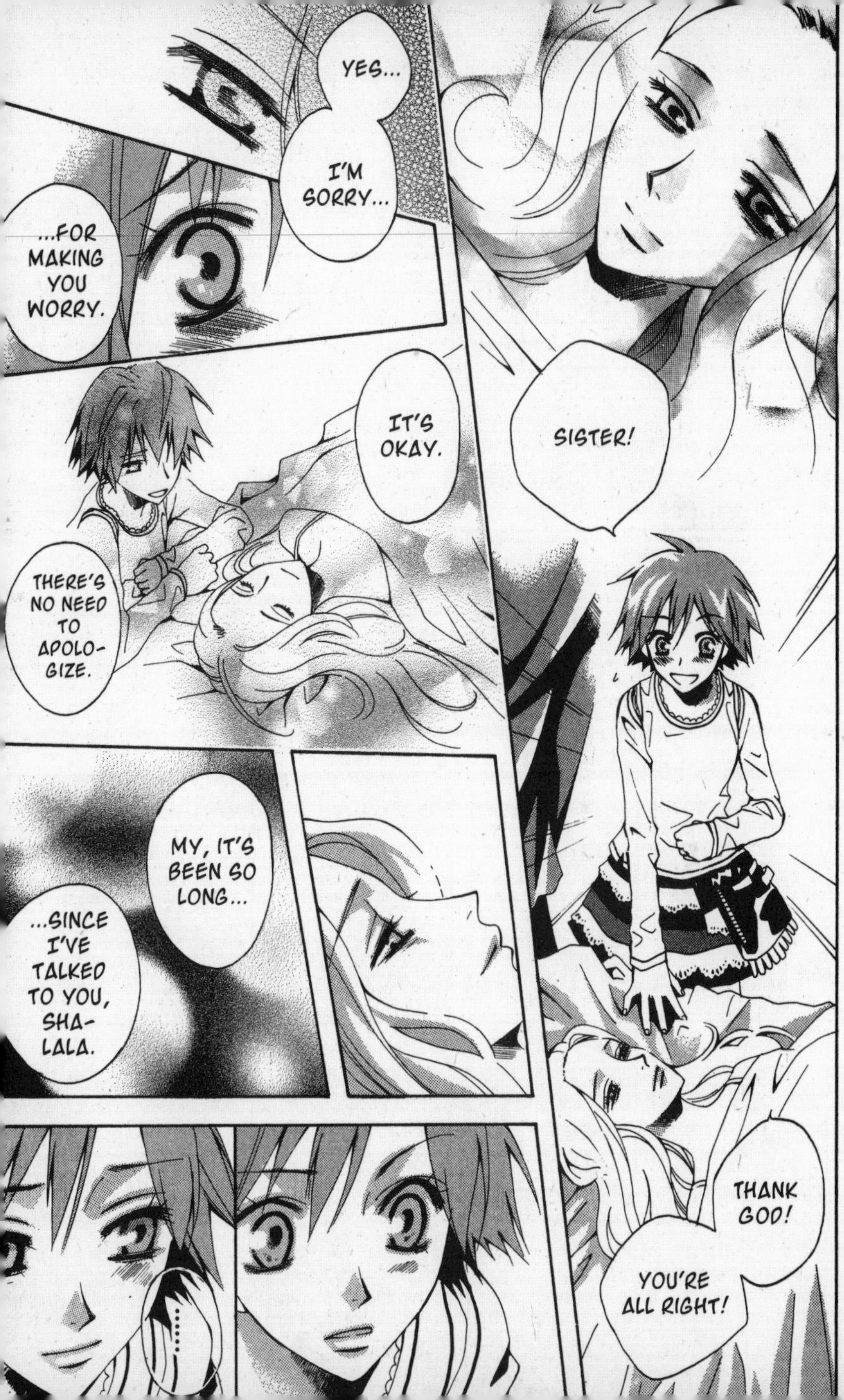
SISTER!
THANK GOD!
YOU'RE ALL RIGHT!
YES...
I'M SORRY...
...FOR MAKING YOU WORRY.
IT'S OKAY.
THERE'S NO NEED TO APOLOGIZE.
MY, IT'S BEEN SO LONG...
...SINCE I'VE TALKED TO YOU, SHALALA.
......

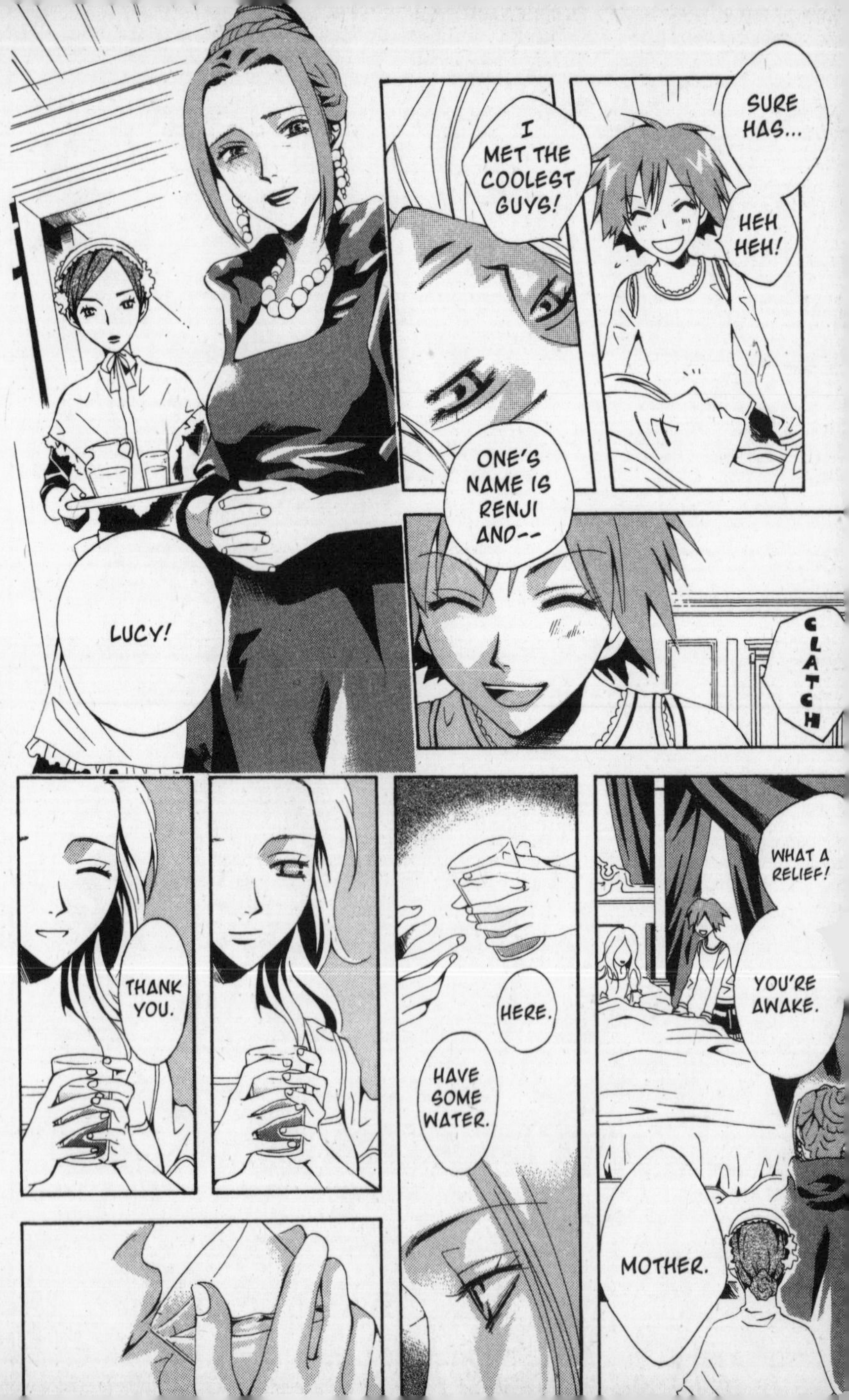
SURE HAS...
HEH HEH!
I MET THE COOLEST GUYS!
ONE'S NAME IS RENJI AND--
CLATCH
LUCY!
WHAT A RELIEF!
YOU'RE AWAKE.
MOTHER.
HERE.
HAVE SOME WATER.
THANK YOU.

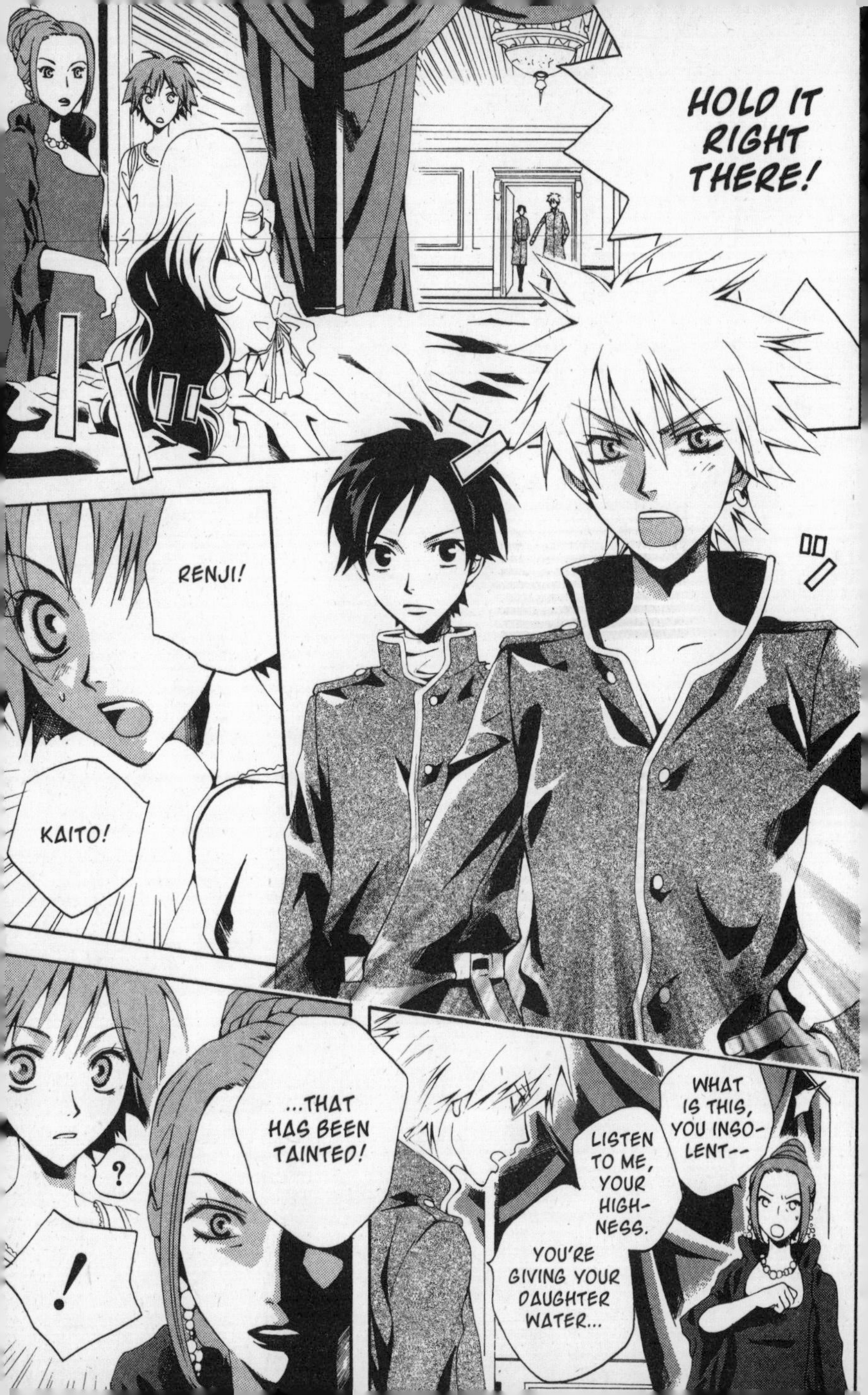
HOLD IT RIGHT THERE!
RENJI!
KAITO!
WHAT IS THIS, YOU INSO-LENT--
LISTEN TO ME, YOUR HIGH-NESS.
YOU'RE GIVING YOUR DAUGHTER WATER...
...THAT HAS BEEN TAINTED!
?
!

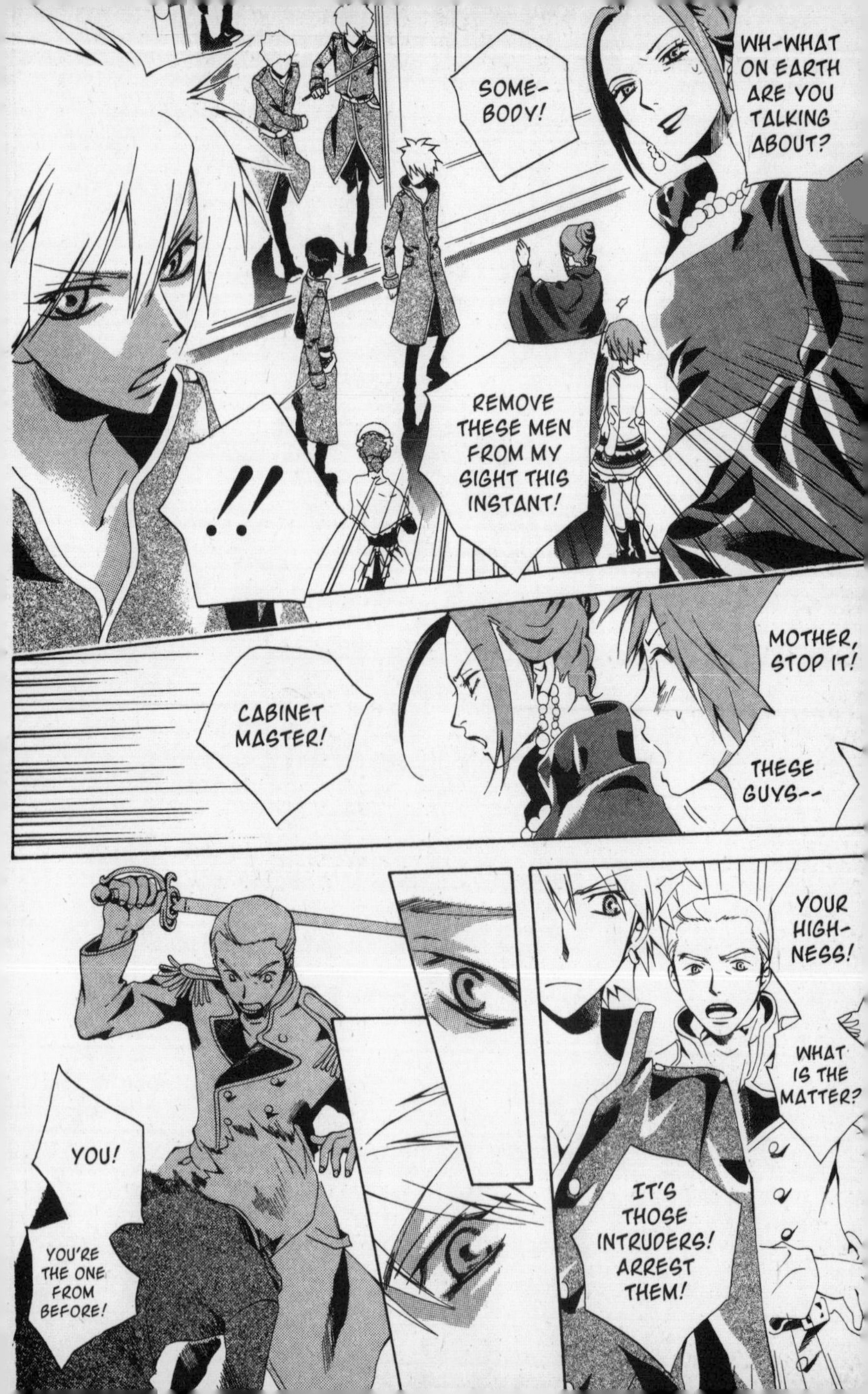
WH-WHAT ON EARTH ARE YOU TALKING ABOUT?
SOME-BODY!
REMOVE THESE MEN FROM MY SIGHT THIS INSTANT!
!!
MOTHER, STOP IT!
THESE GUYS--
CABINET MASTER!
YOUR HIGH-NESS!
WHAT IS THE MATTER?
IT'S THOSE INTRUDERS! ARREST THEM!
YOU!
YOU'RE THE ONE FROM BEFORE!

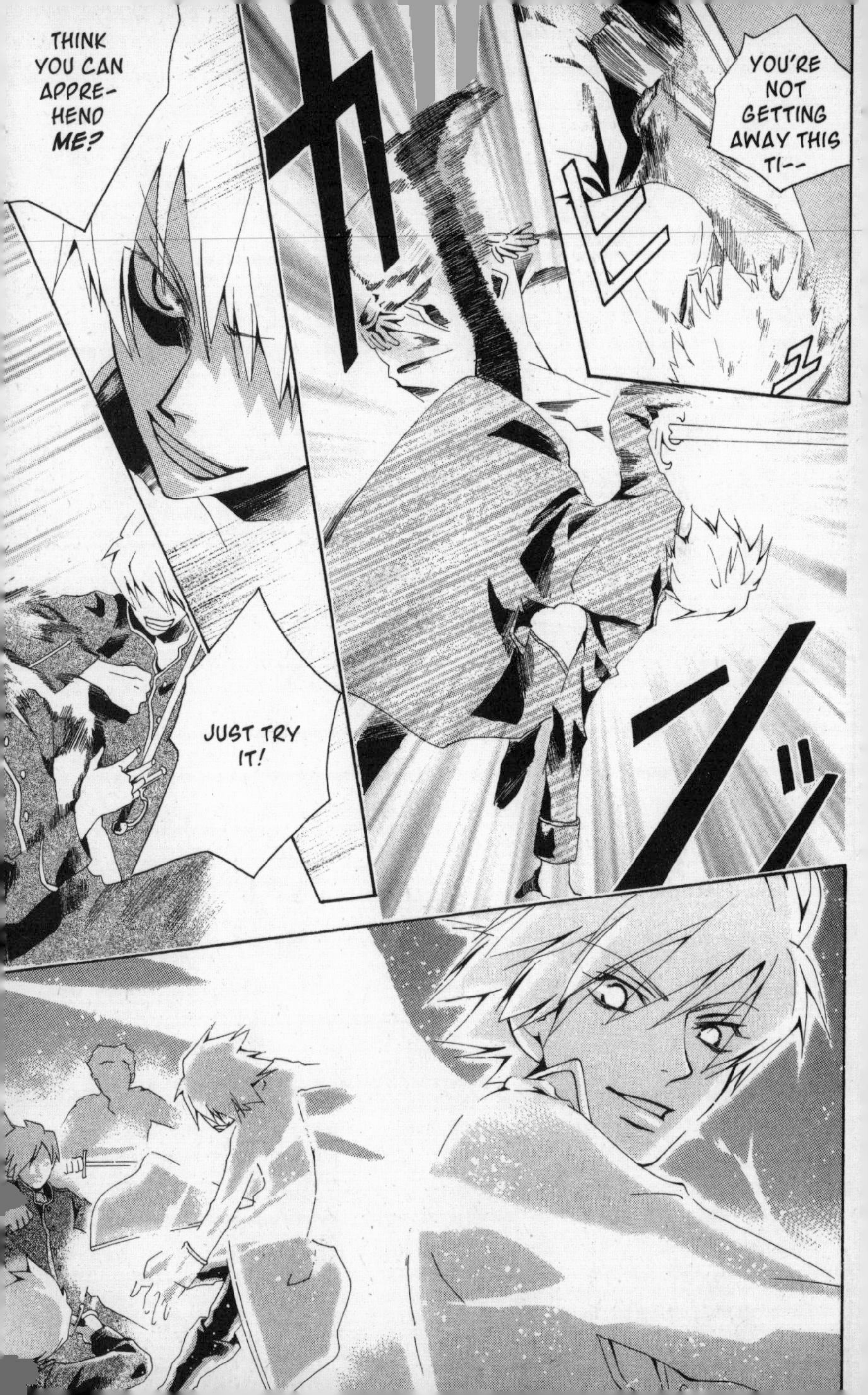
YOU'RE NOT GETTING AWAY THIS TI--
THINK YOU CAN APPRE-HEND ME?
JUST TRY IT!

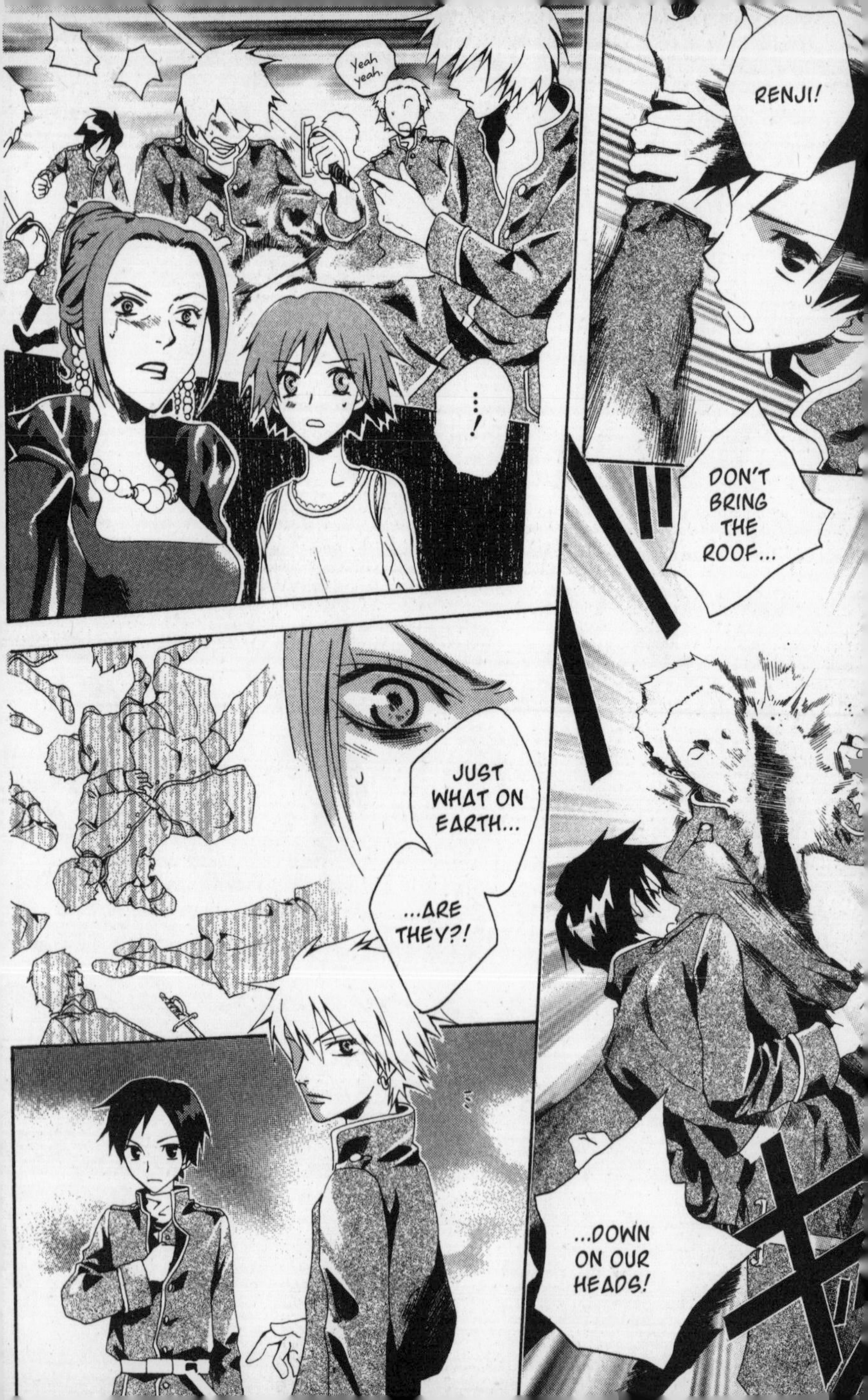
RENJI!
Yeah yeah.
...!
DON'T BRING THE ROOF...
...DOWN ON OUR HEADS!
JUST WHAT ON EARTH...
...ARE THEY?!

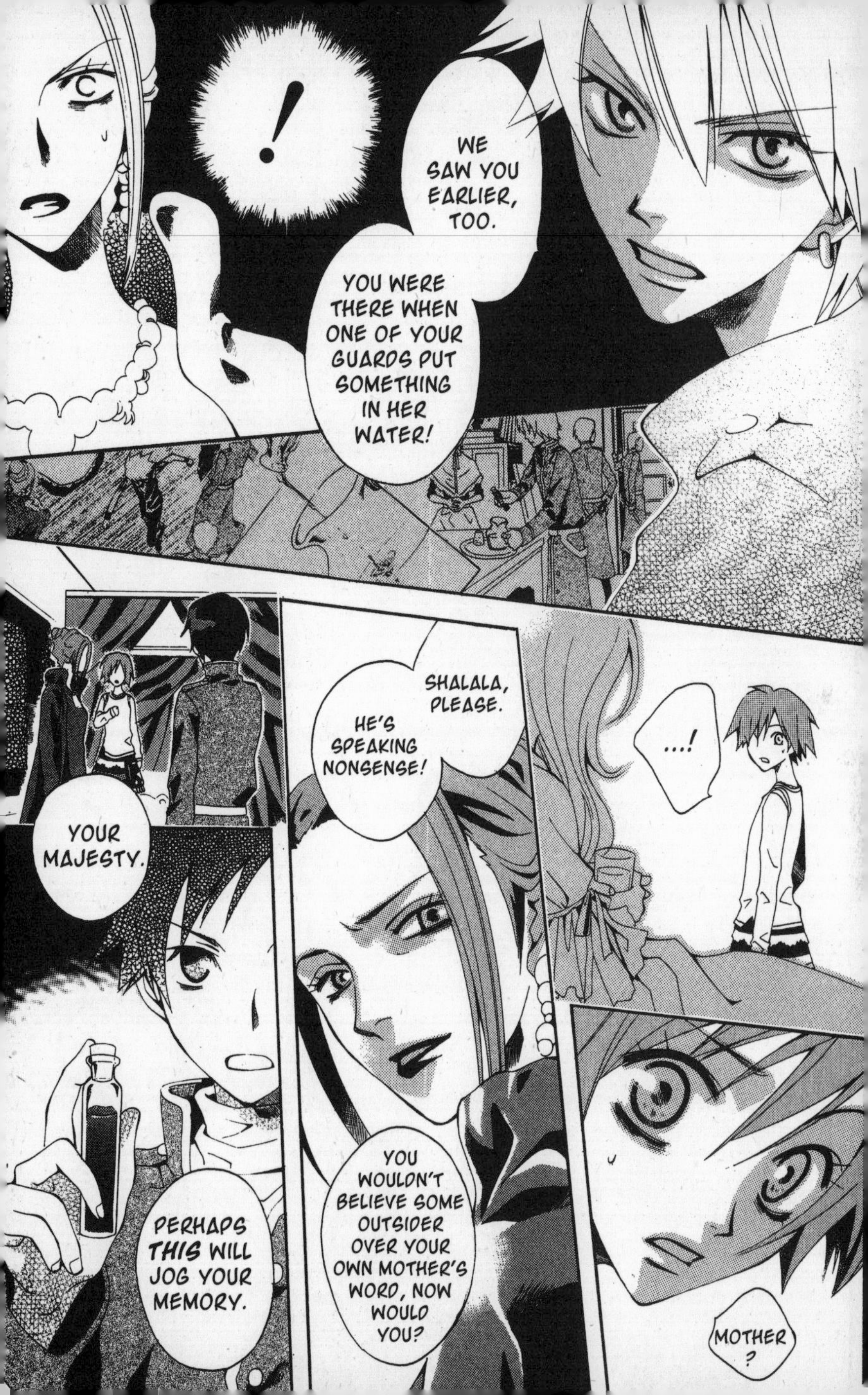
WE SAW YOU EARLIER, TOO.
YOU WERE THERE WHEN ONE OF YOUR GUARDS PUT SOMETHING IN HER WATER!
!
...!
MOTHER?
SHALALA, PLEASE.
HE'S SPEAKING NONSENSE!
YOU WOULDN'T BELIEVE SOME OUTSIDER OVER YOUR OWN MOTHER'S WORD, NOW WOULD YOU?
YOUR MAJESTY.
PERHAPS THIS WILL JOG YOUR MEMORY.

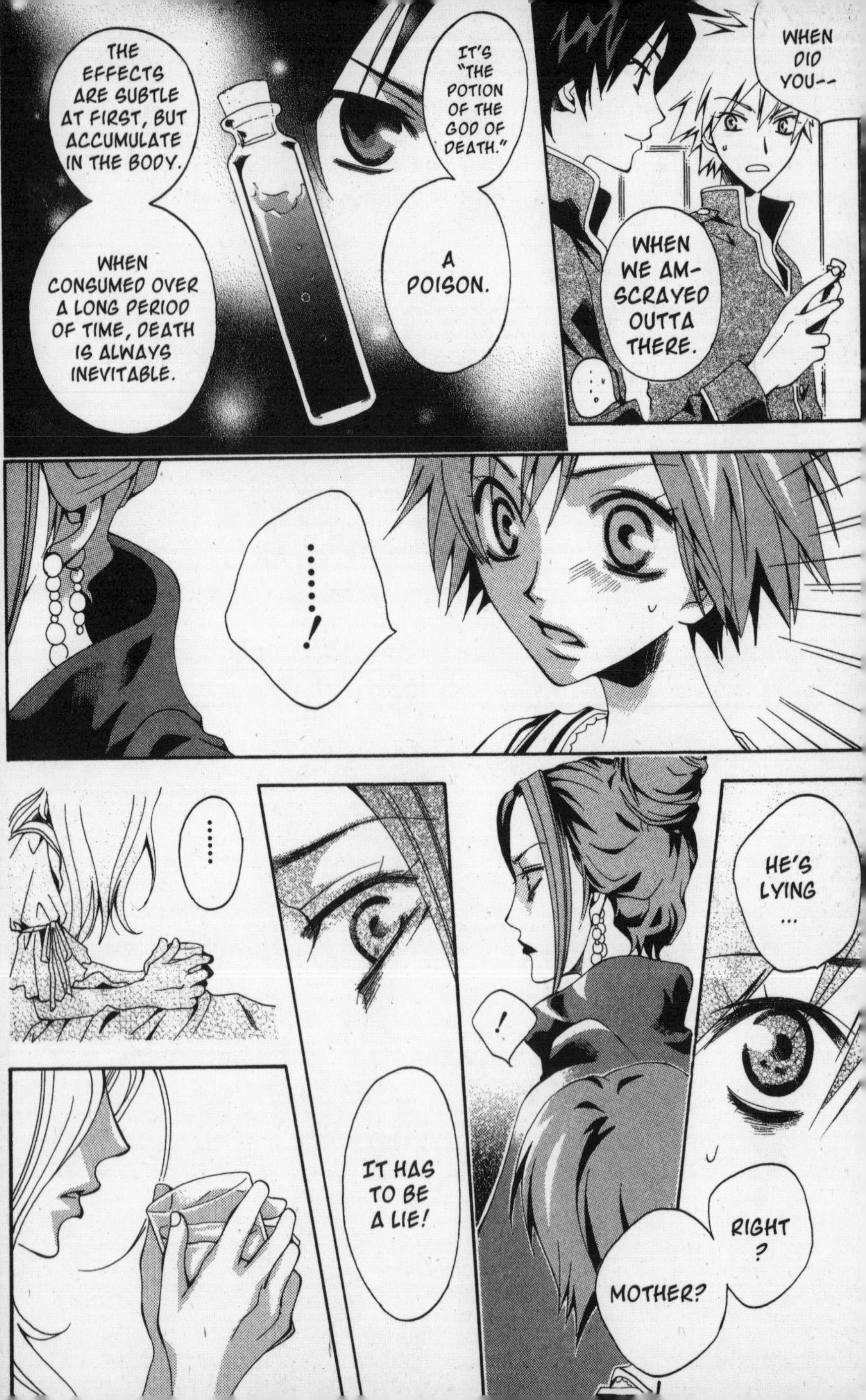
WHEN DID YOU--
WHEN WE AMSCRAYED OUTTA THERE.
...
IT'S "THE POTION OF THE GOD OF DEATH."
A POISON.
THE EFFECTS ARE SUBTLE AT FIRST, BUT ACCUMULATE IN THE BODY.
WHEN CONSUMED OVER A LONG PERIOD OF TIME, DEATH IS ALWAYS INEVITABLE.
......!
HE'S LYING ...
RIGHT ?
MOTHER?
!
IT HAS TO BE A LIE!
......

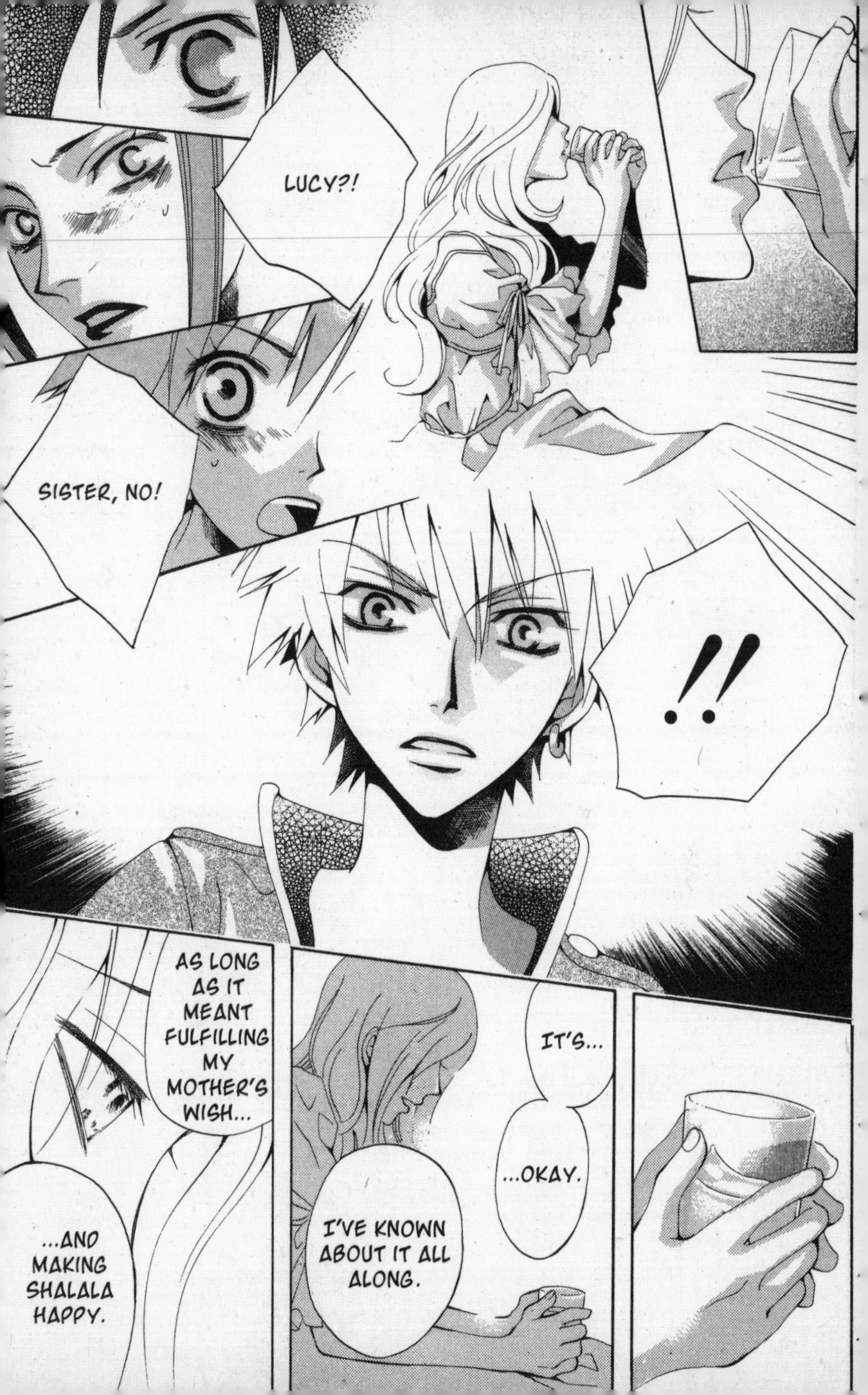
LUCY?!
SISTER, NO!
!!
IT'S...
...OKAY.
I'VE KNOWN ABOUT IT ALL ALONG.
AS LONG AS IT MEANT FULFILLING MY MOTHER'S WISH...
...AND MAKING SHALALA HAPPY.

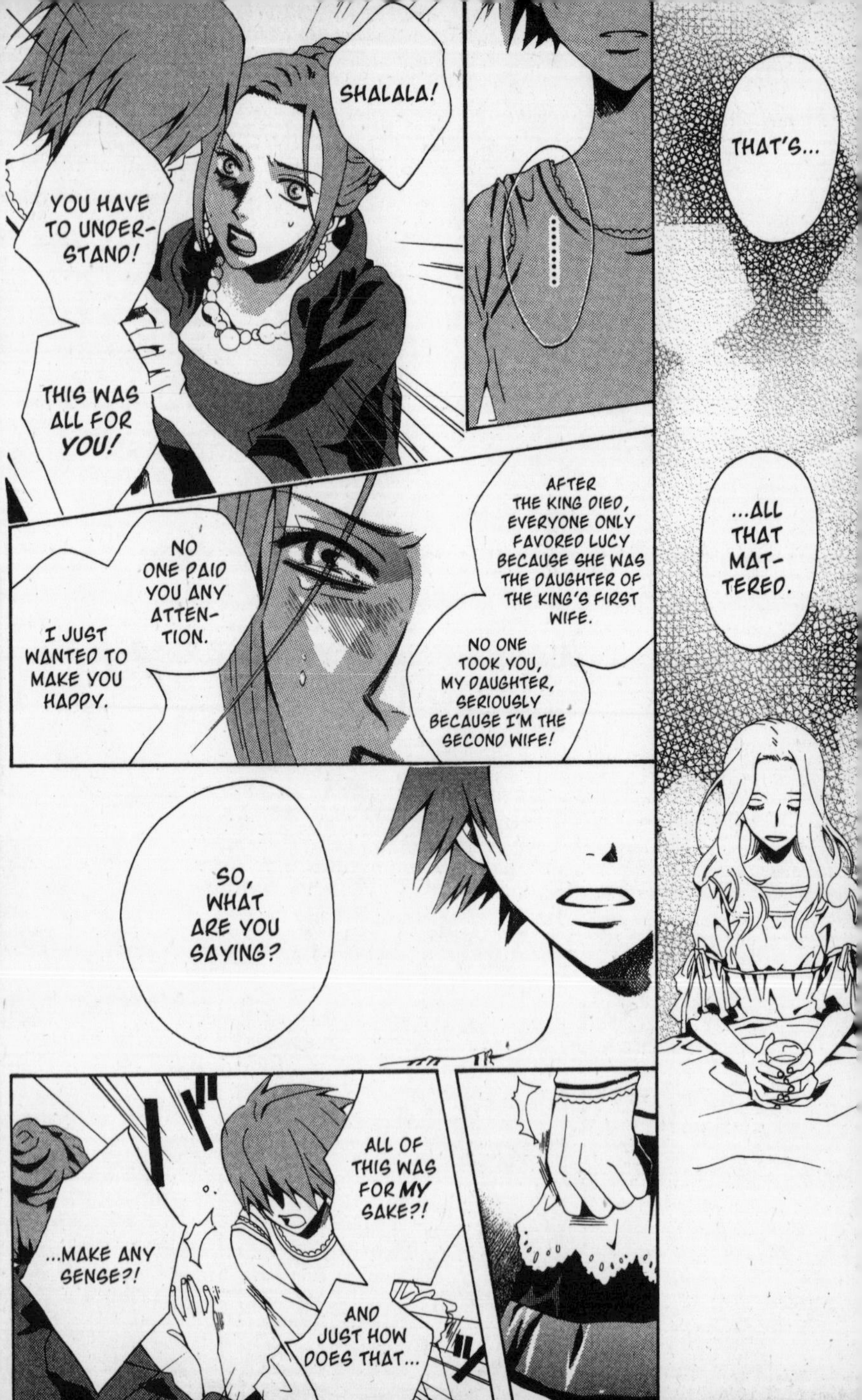
THAT'S...
...ALL THAT MATTERED.
......
SHALALA!
YOU HAVE TO UNDERSTAND!
THIS WAS ALL FOR YOU!
AFTER THE KING DIED, EVERYONE ONLY FAVORED LUCY BECAUSE SHE WAS THE DAUGHTER OF THE KING'S FIRST WIFE.
NO ONE TOOK YOU, MY DAUGHTER, SERIOUSLY BECAUSE I'M THE SECOND WIFE!
NO ONE PAID YOU ANY ATTENTION.
I JUST WANTED TO MAKE YOU HAPPY.
SO, WHAT ARE YOU SAYING?
ALL OF THIS WAS FOR MY SAKE?!
AND JUST HOW DOES THAT...
...MAKE ANY SENSE?!

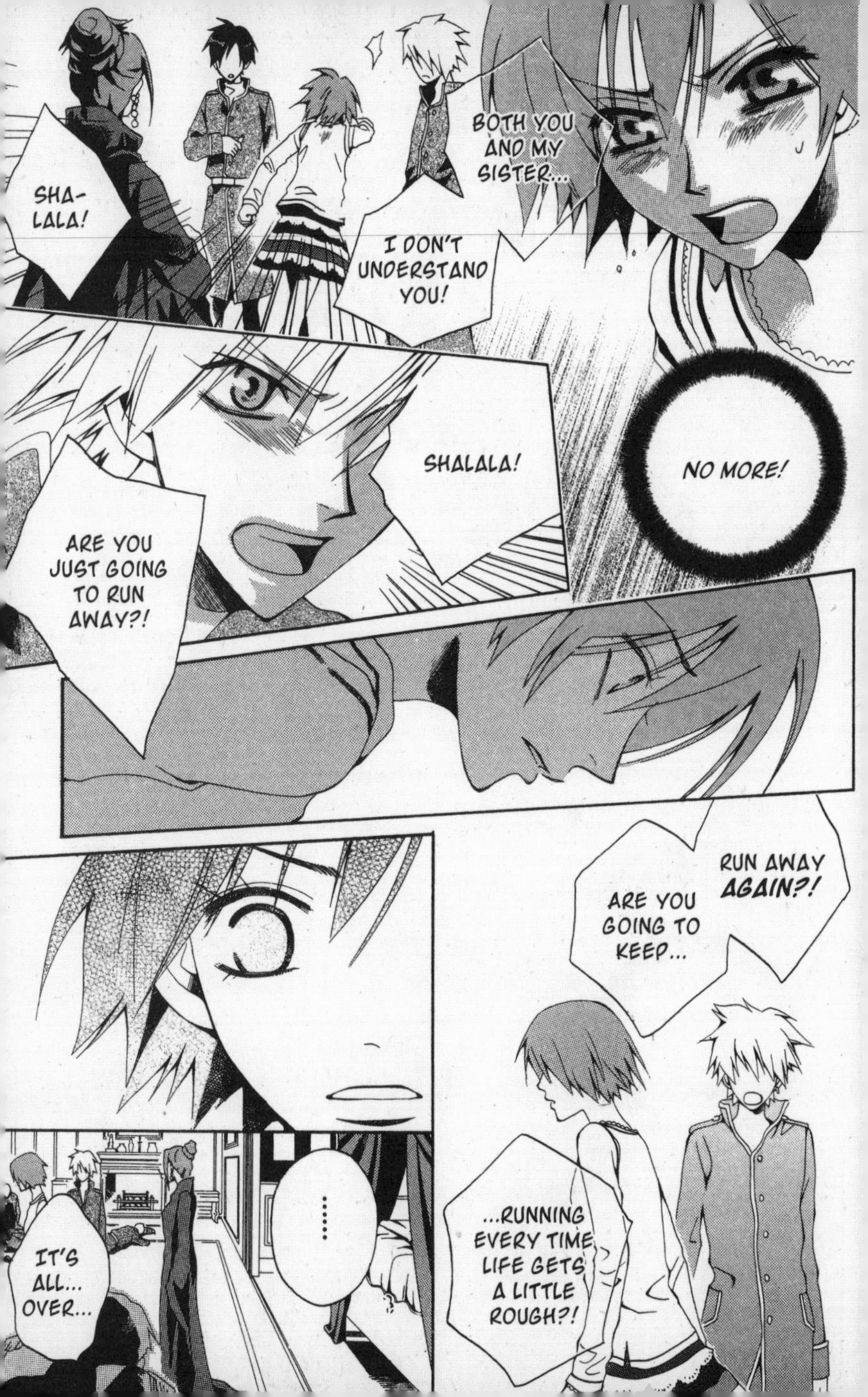
BOTH YOU AND MY SISTER...
I DON'T UNDERSTAND YOU!
SHA-LALA!
NO MORE!
SHALALA!
ARE YOU JUST GOING TO RUN AWAY?!
RUN AWAY **AGAIN?!**
ARE YOU GOING TO KEEP...
...RUNNING EVERY TIME LIFE GETS A LITTLE ROUGH?!
......
IT'S ALL... OVER...

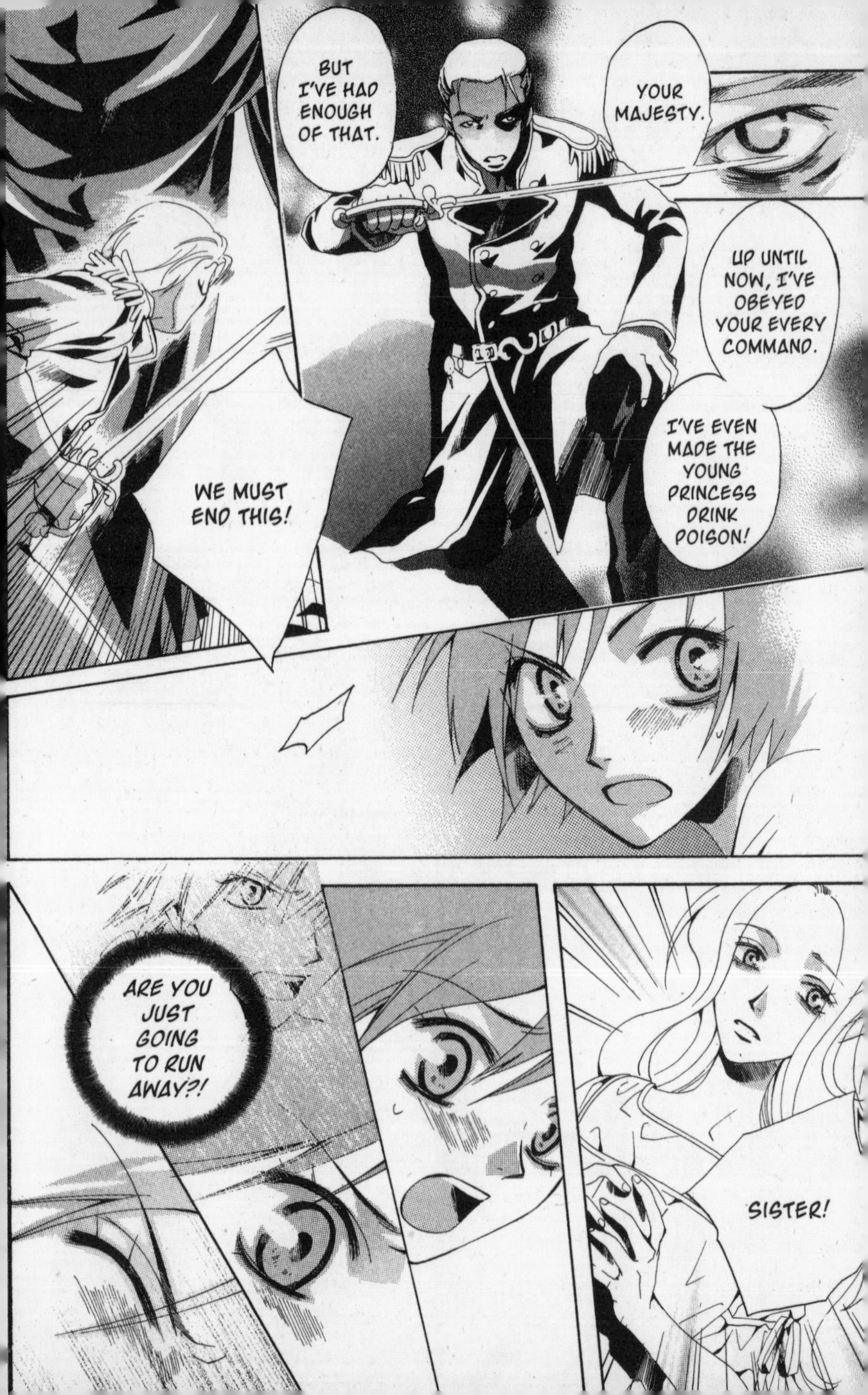
YOUR MAJESTY.
UP UNTIL NOW, I'VE OBEYED YOUR EVERY COMMAND.
I'VE EVEN MADE THE YOUNG PRINCESS DRINK POISON!
BUT I'VE HAD ENOUGH OF THAT.
WE MUST END THIS!
SISTER!
ARE YOU JUST GOING TO RUN AWAY?!

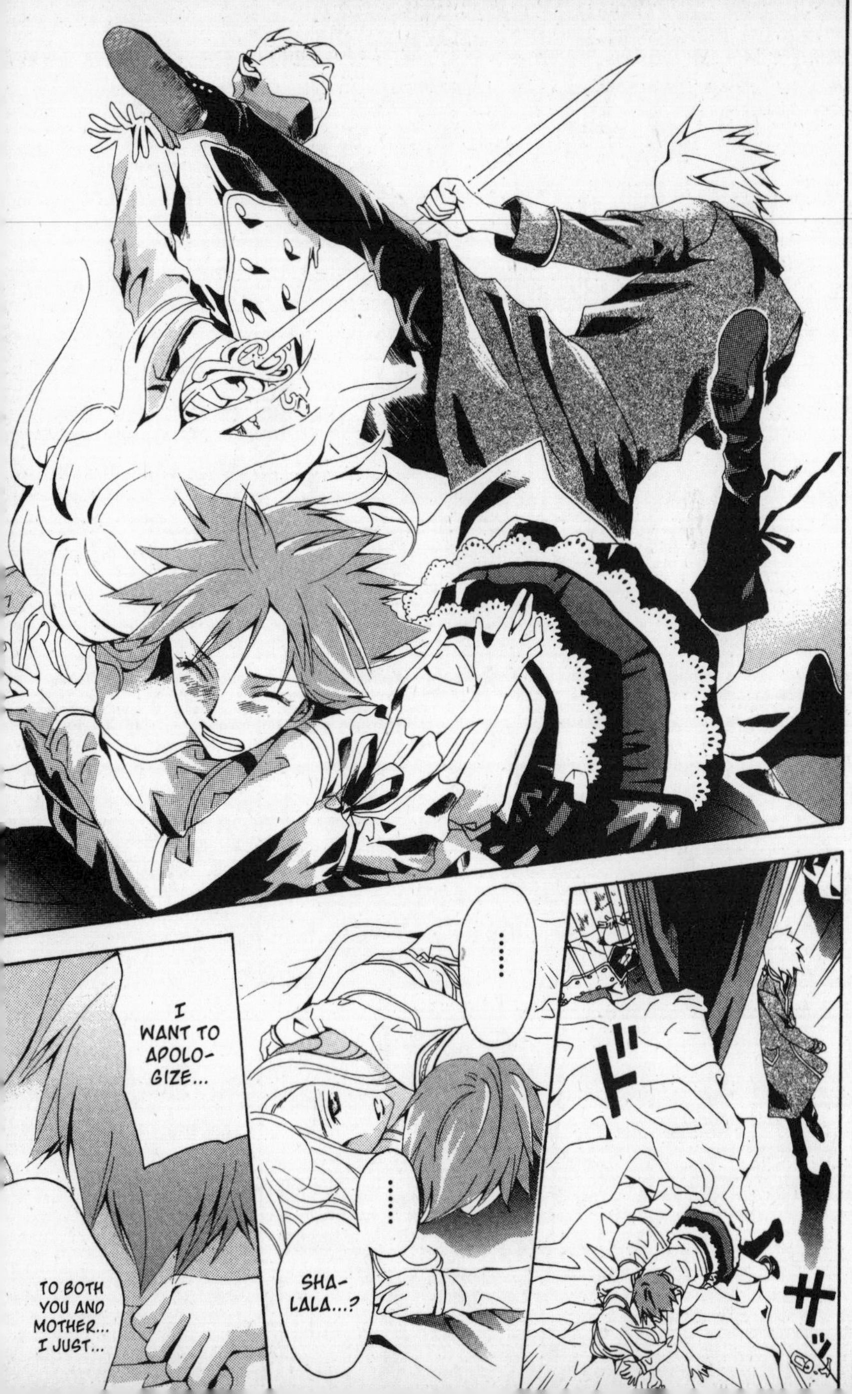
ド
サッ
......
......
SHA-LALA...?
I WANT TO APOLOGIZE...
TO BOTH YOU AND MOTHER... I JUST...

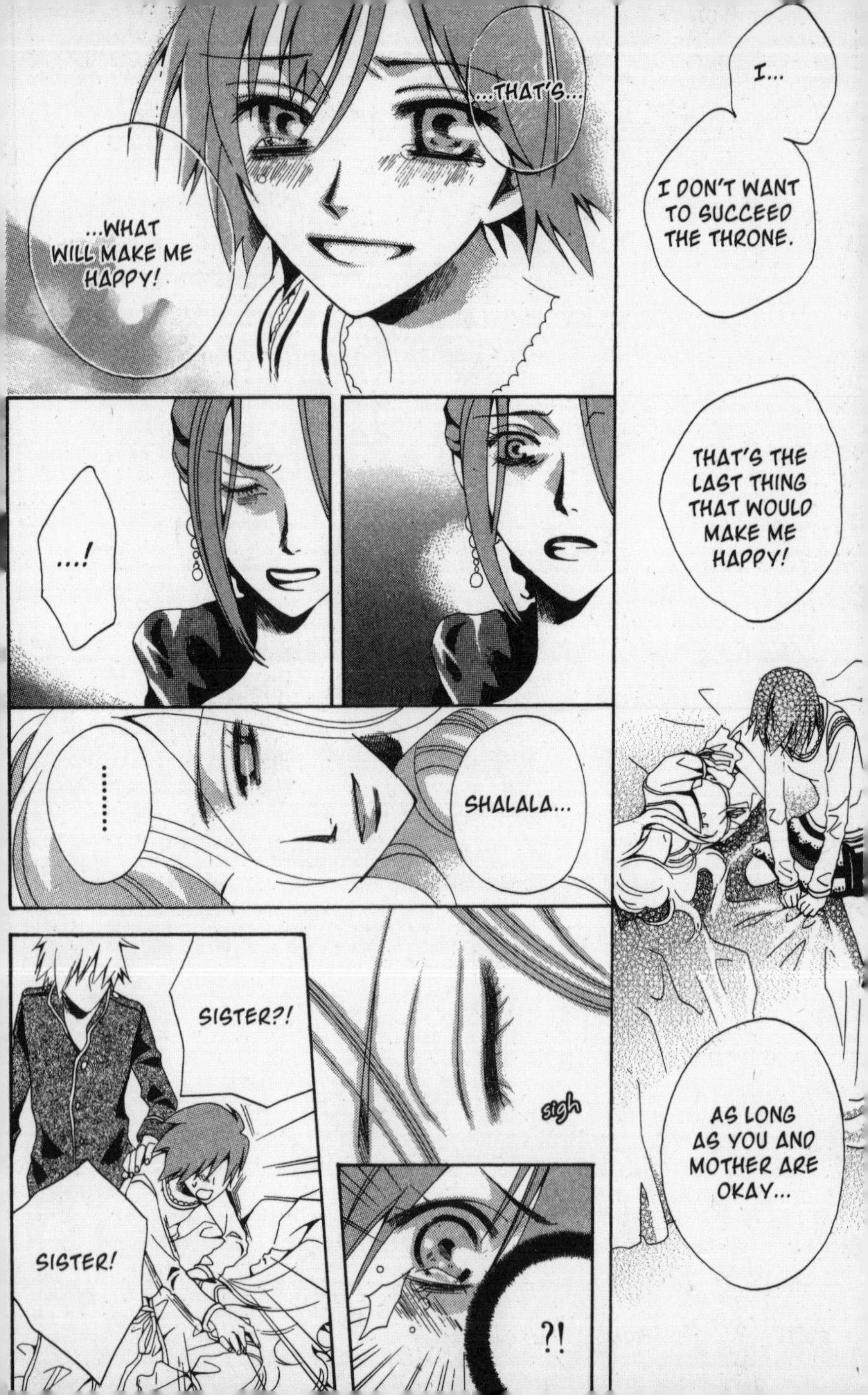
I...
I DON'T WANT TO SUCCEED THE THRONE.
THAT'S THE LAST THING THAT WOULD MAKE ME HAPPY!
AS LONG AS YOU AND MOTHER ARE OKAY...
...THAT'S...
...WHAT WILL MAKE ME HAPPY!
...!
SHALALA...
......
sigh
?!
SISTER?!
SISTER!

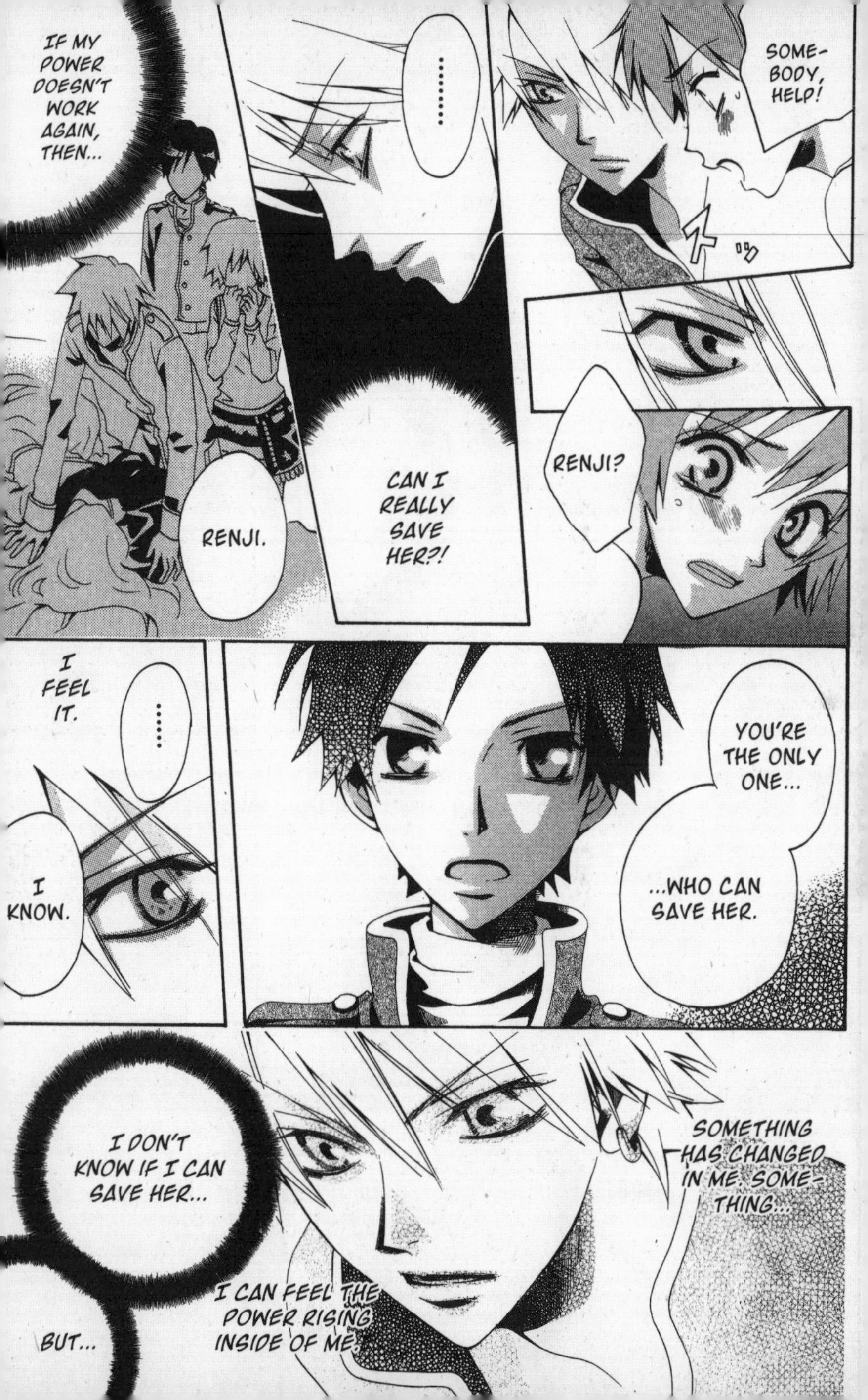
SOME-BODY, HELP!
RENJI?
......
CAN I REALLY SAVE HER?!
IF MY POWER DOESN'T WORK AGAIN, THEN...
RENJI.
YOU'RE THE ONLY ONE...
...WHO CAN SAVE HER.
I FEEL IT.
......
I KNOW.
SOMETHING HAS CHANGED IN ME. SOME-THING...
I DON'T KNOW IF I CAN SAVE HER...
I CAN FEEL THE POWER RISING INSIDE OF ME.
BUT...

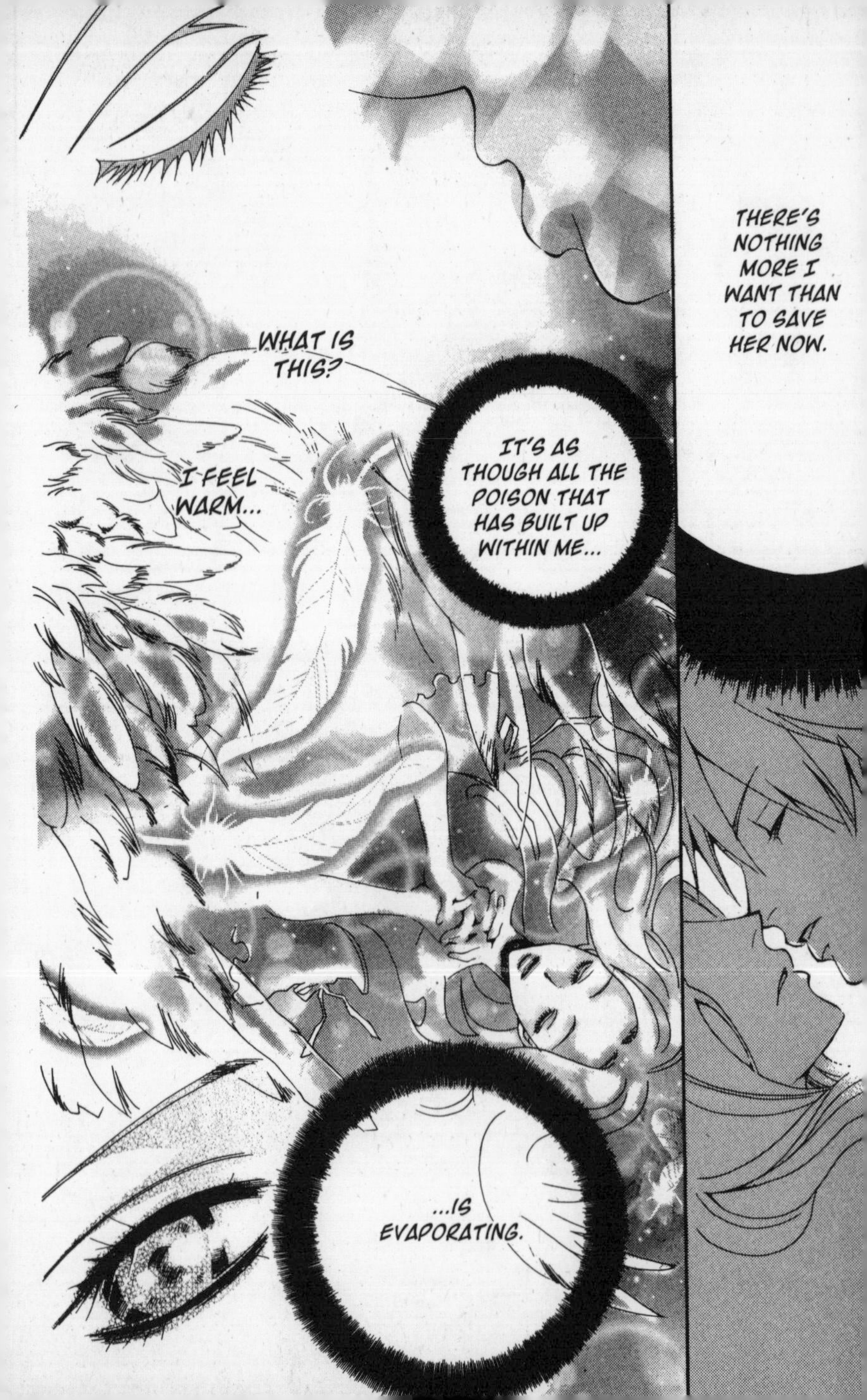
THERE'S NOTHING MORE I WANT THAN TO SAVE HER NOW.
WHAT IS THIS?
I FEEL WARM...
IT'S AS THOUGH ALL THE POISON THAT HAS BUILT UP WITHIN ME...
...IS EVAPORATING.

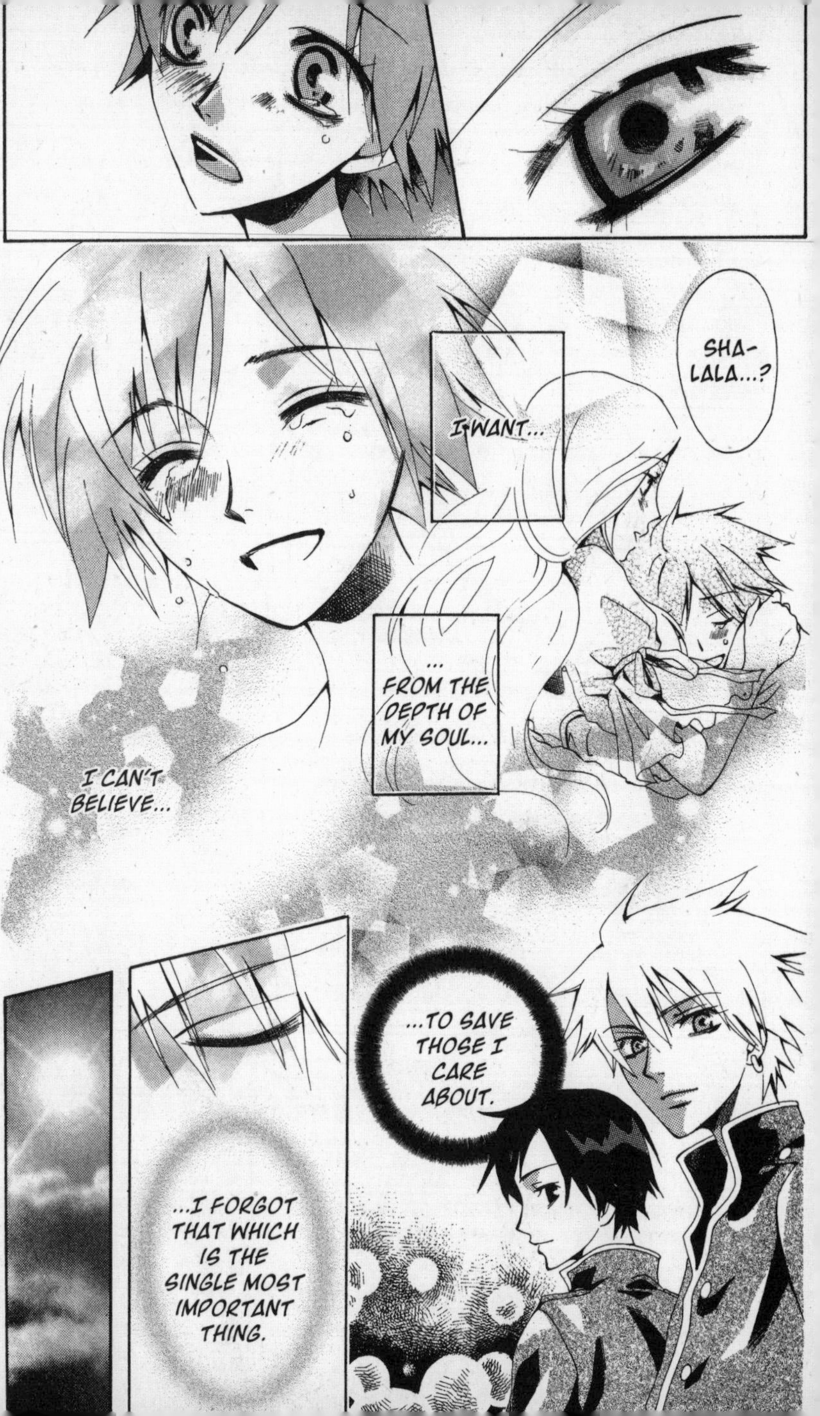
SHA-LALA...?
I WANT...
...FROM THE DEPTH OF MY SOUL...
I CAN'T BELIEVE...
...TO SAVE THOSE I CARE ABOUT.
...I FORGOT THAT WHICH IS THE SINGLE MOST IMPORTANT THING.

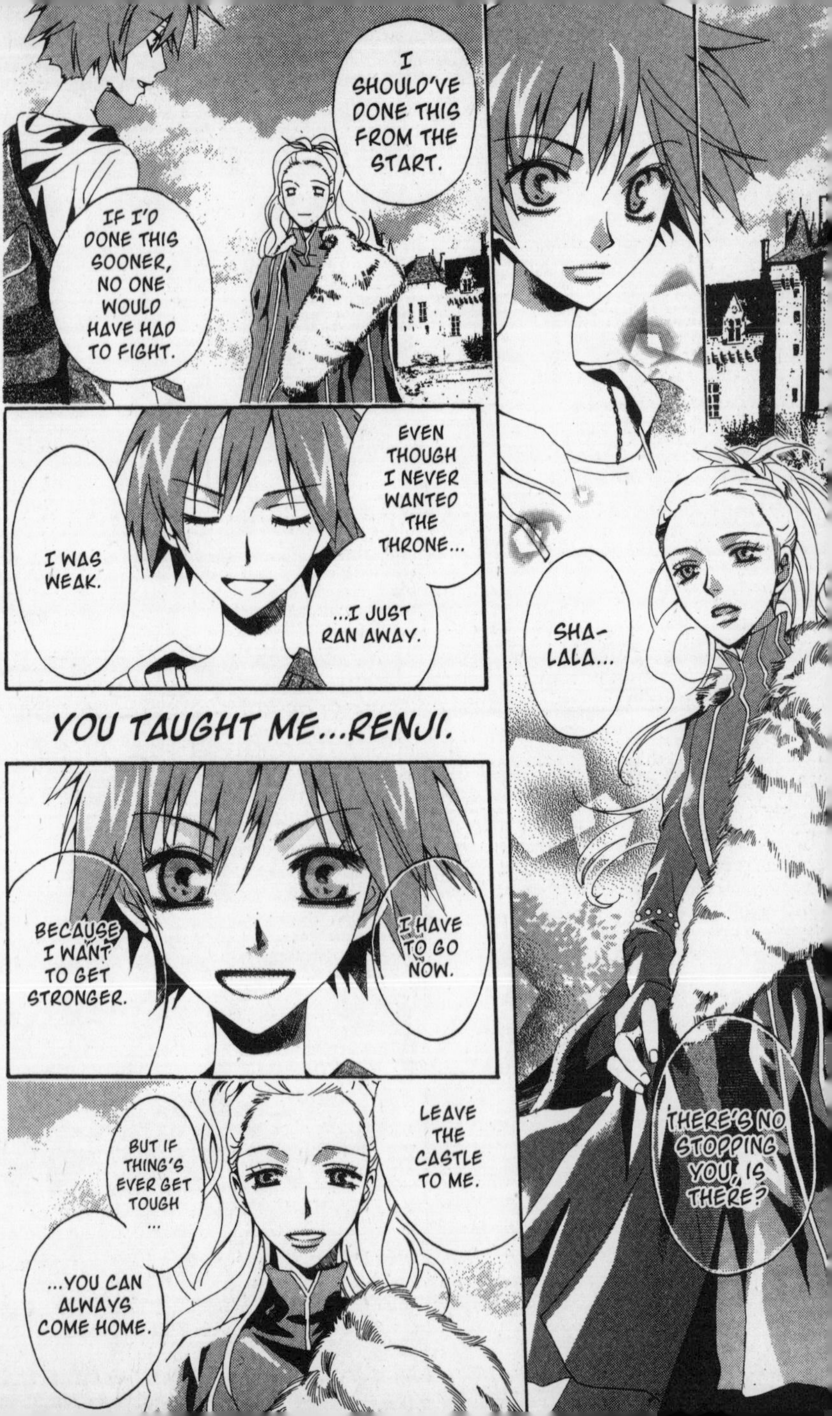
SHA-LALA...
THERE'S NO STOPPING YOU, IS THERE?
I SHOULD'VE DONE THIS FROM THE START.
IF I'D DONE THIS SOONER, NO ONE WOULD HAVE HAD TO FIGHT.
EVEN THOUGH I NEVER WANTED THE THRONE...
...I JUST RAN AWAY.
I WAS WEAK.
YOU TAUGHT ME...RENJI.
I HAVE TO GO NOW.
BECAUSE I WANT TO GET STRONGER.
LEAVE THE CASTLE TO ME.
BUT IF THING'S EVER GET TOUGH ...
...YOU CAN ALWAYS COME HOME.

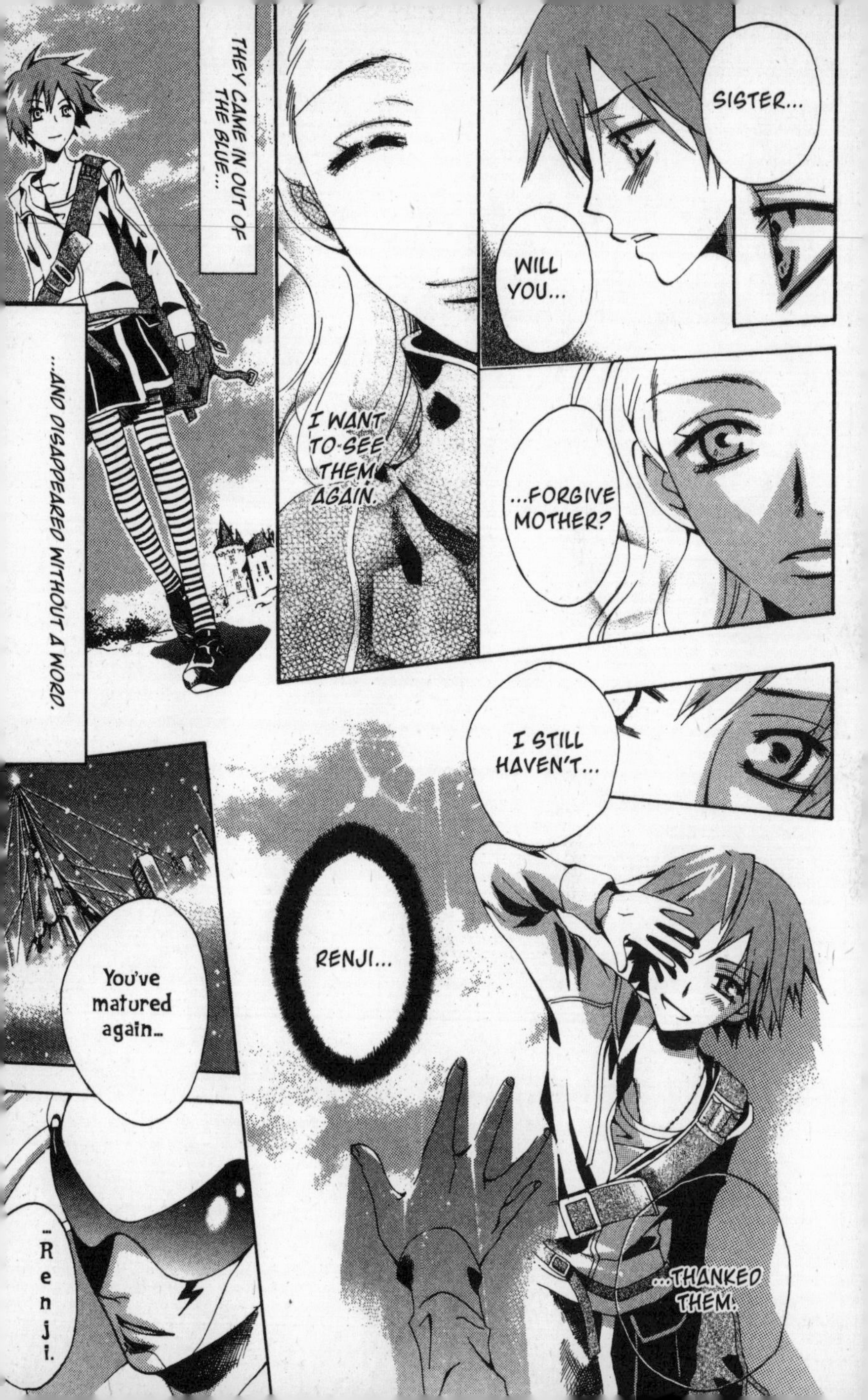
SISTER...
WILL YOU...
...FORGIVE MOTHER?
I WANT TO SEE THEM AGAIN.
THEY CAME IN OUT OF THE BLUE...
...AND DISAPPEARED WITHOUT A WORD.
I STILL HAVEN'T...
RENJI...
...THANKED THEM.
You've matured again...
...Renji.

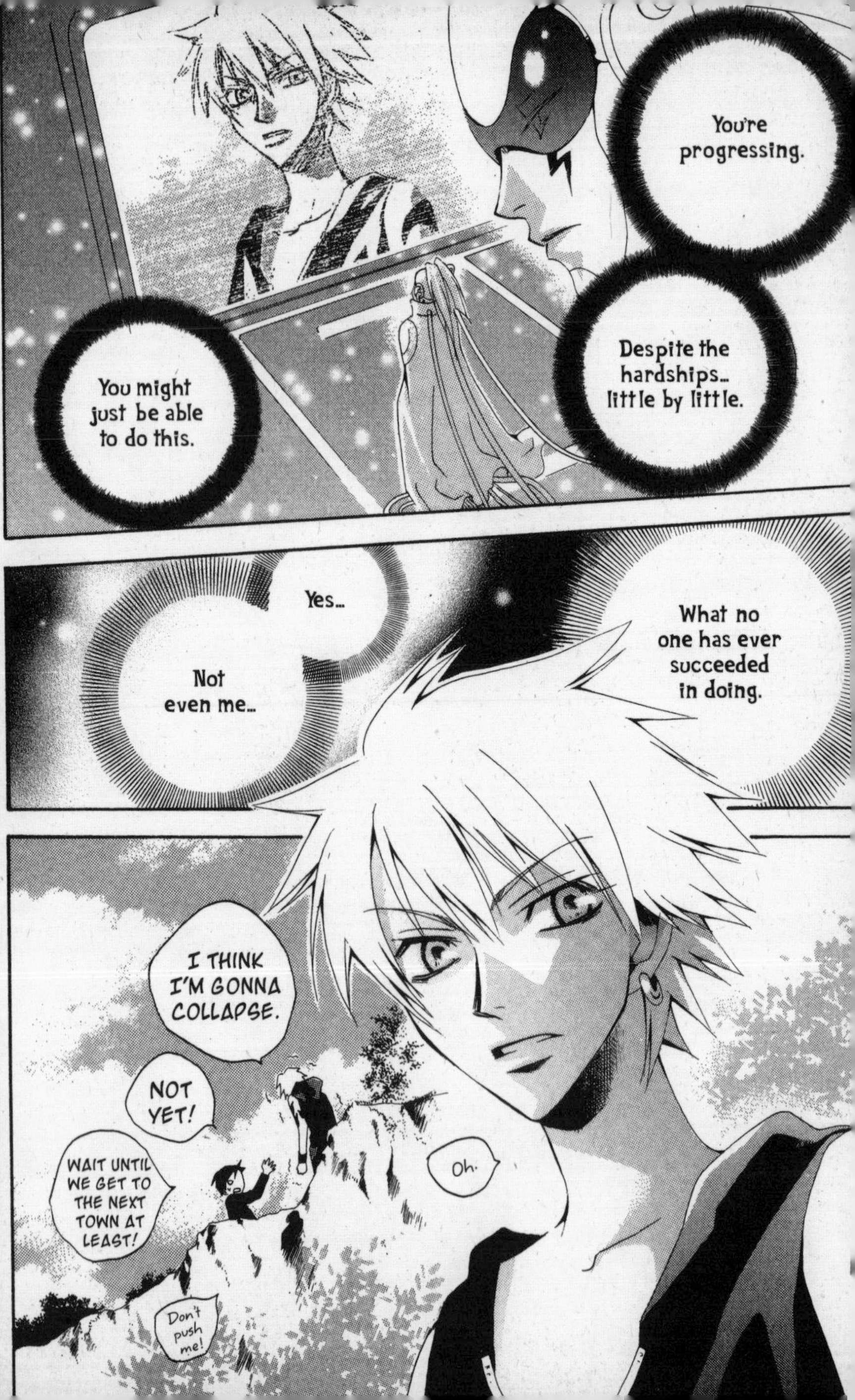
You're progressing.
Despite the hardships... little by little.
You might just be able to do this.
What no one has ever succeeded in doing.
Yes...
Not even me...
I THINK I'M GONNA COLLAPSE.
NOT YET!
WAIT UNTIL WE GET TO THE NEXT TOWN AT LEAST!
Don't push me!
Oh.

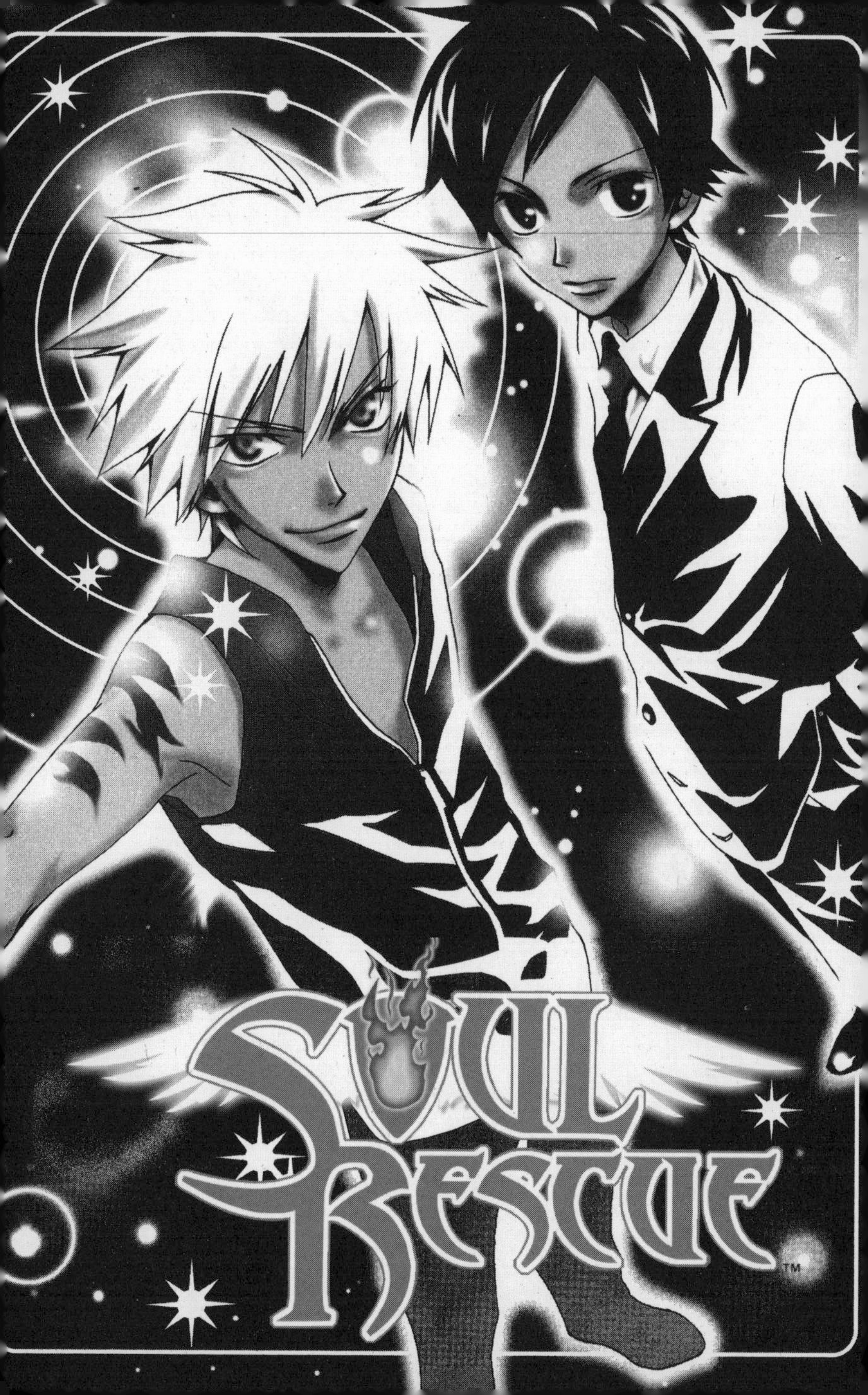
SOUL
RESCUE
™

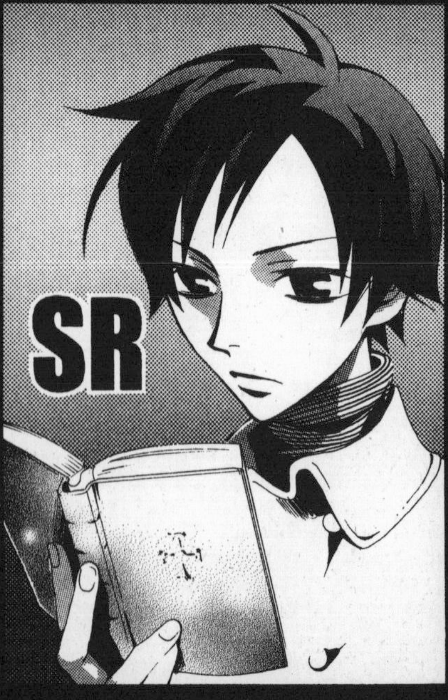
SR

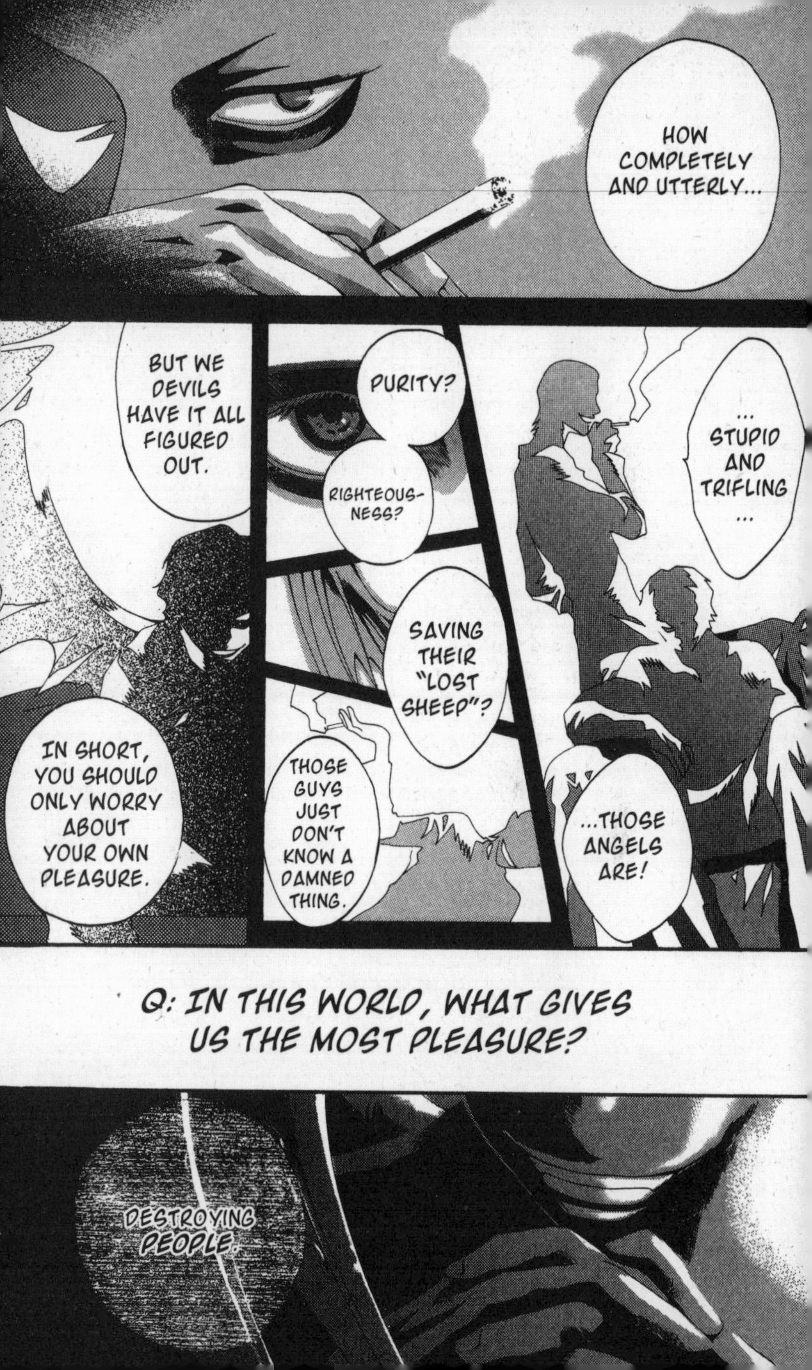
HOW COMPLETELY AND UTTERLY...
... STUPID AND TRIFLING ...
...THOSE ANGELS ARE!
PURITY?
RIGHTEOUS-NESS?
SAVING THEIR "LOST SHEEP"?
THOSE GUYS JUST DON'T KNOW A DAMNED THING.
BUT WE DEVILS HAVE IT ALL FIGURED OUT.
IN SHORT, YOU SHOULD ONLY WORRY ABOUT YOUR OWN PLEASURE.
Q: IN THIS WORLD, WHAT GIVES US THE MOST PLEASURE?
DESTROYING PEOPLE.

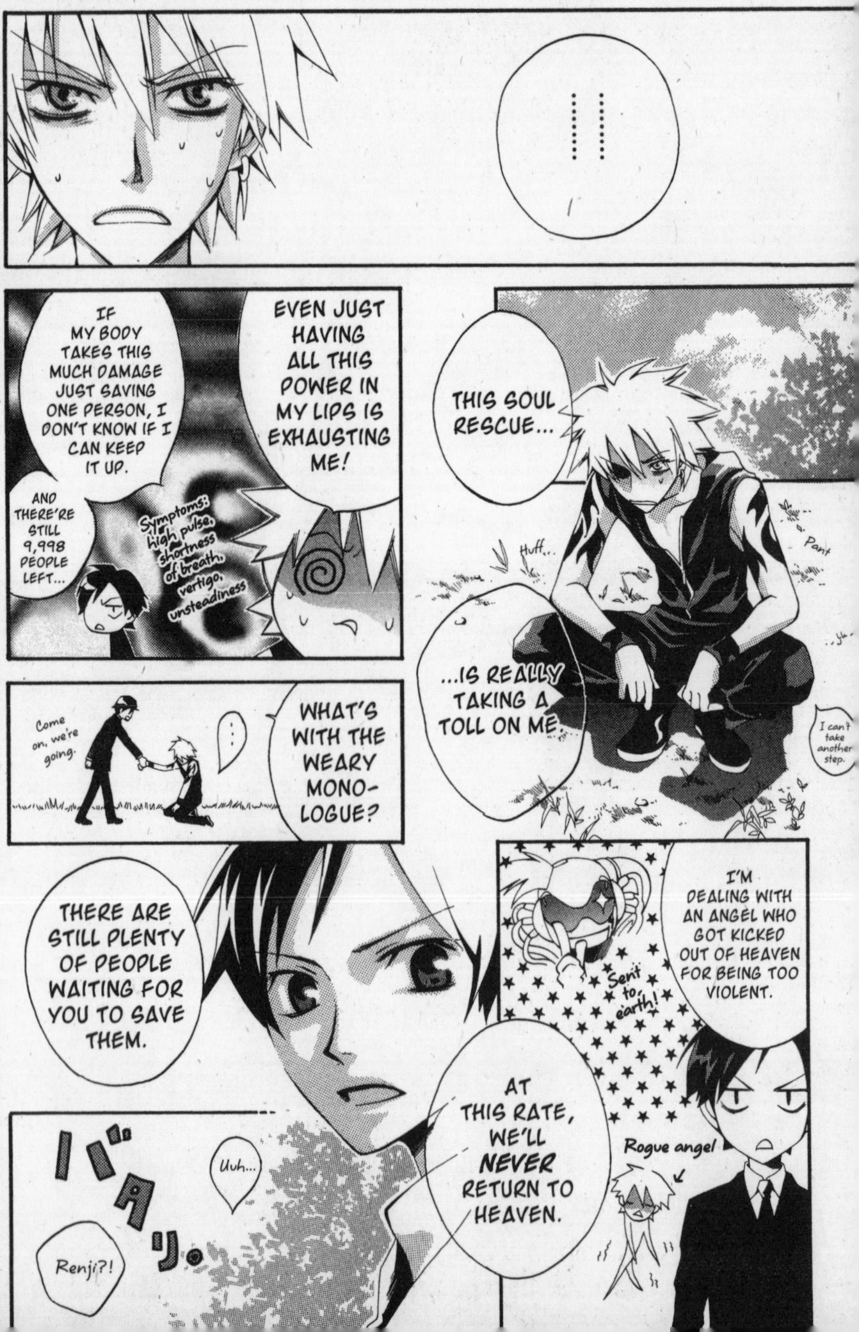
......
THIS SOUL RESCUE...
...IS REALLY TAKING A TOLL ON ME.
Huff...
Pant
I can't take another step.
EVEN JUST HAVING ALL THIS POWER IN MY LIPS IS EXHAUSTING ME!
IF MY BODY TAKES THIS MUCH DAMAGE JUST SAVING ONE PERSON, I DON'T KNOW IF I CAN KEEP IT UP.
Symptoms: high pulse, shortness of breath, vertigo, unsteadiness
AND THERE'RE STILL 9,998 PEOPLE LEFT...
WHAT'S WITH THE WEARY MONOLOGUE?
...
Come on, we're going.
I'M DEALING WITH AN ANGEL WHO GOT KICKED OUT OF HEAVEN FOR BEING TOO VIOLENT.
Sent to earth!
AT THIS RATE, WE'LL NEVER RETURN TO HEAVEN.
Rogue angel
THERE ARE STILL PLENTY OF PEOPLE WAITING FOR YOU TO SAVE THEM.
Uuh...
バタリ。
Renji?!

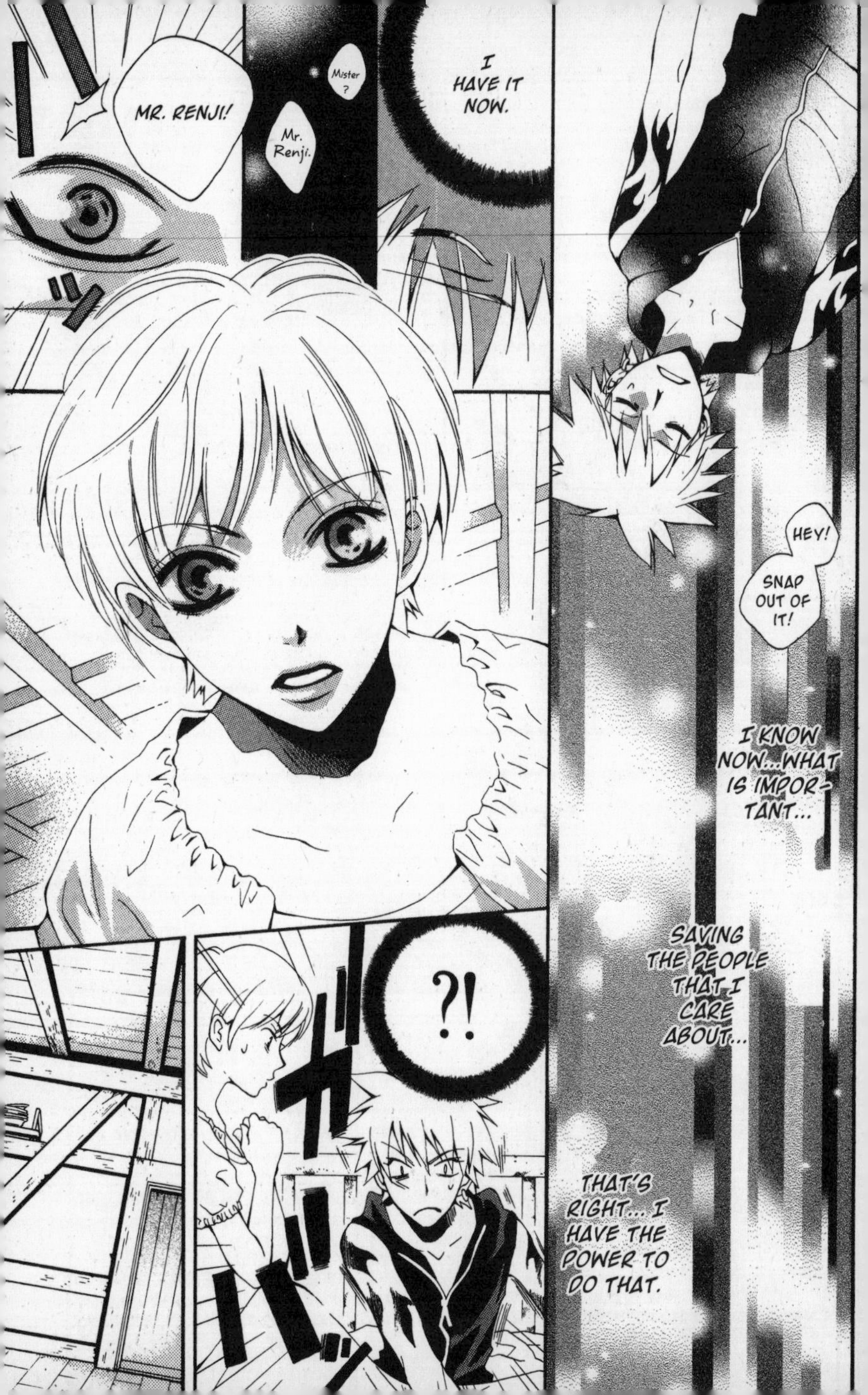
HEY!
SNAP OUT OF IT!
I KNOW NOW...WHAT IS IMPOR-TANT...
SAVING THE PEOPLE THAT I CARE ABOUT...
THAT'S RIGHT... I HAVE THE POWER TO DO THAT.
I HAVE IT NOW.
Mister?
Mr. Renji.
MR. RENJI!
?!

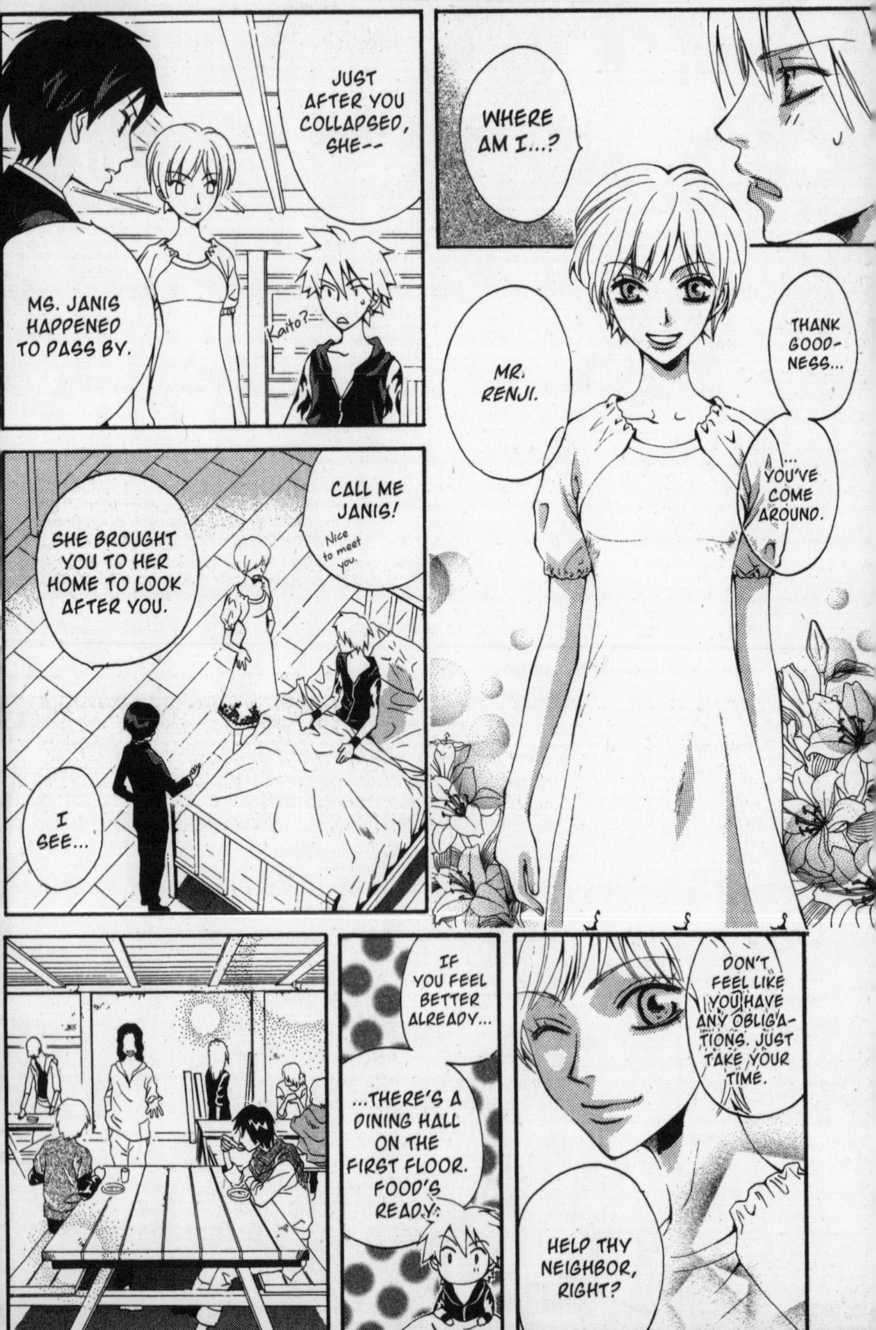
WHERE AM I...?
THANK GOODNESS...
...YOU'VE COME AROUND.
MR. RENJI.
JUST AFTER YOU COLLAPSED, SHE--
Kaito?
MS. JANIS HAPPENED TO PASS BY.
CALL ME JANIS!
Nice to meet you.
SHE BROUGHT YOU TO HER HOME TO LOOK AFTER YOU.
I SEE...
DON'T FEEL LIKE YOU HAVE ANY OBLIGATIONS. JUST TAKE YOUR TIME.
HELP THY NEIGHBOR, RIGHT?
IF YOU FEEL BETTER ALREADY...
...THERE'S A DINING HALL ON THE FIRST FLOOR. FOOD'S READY.

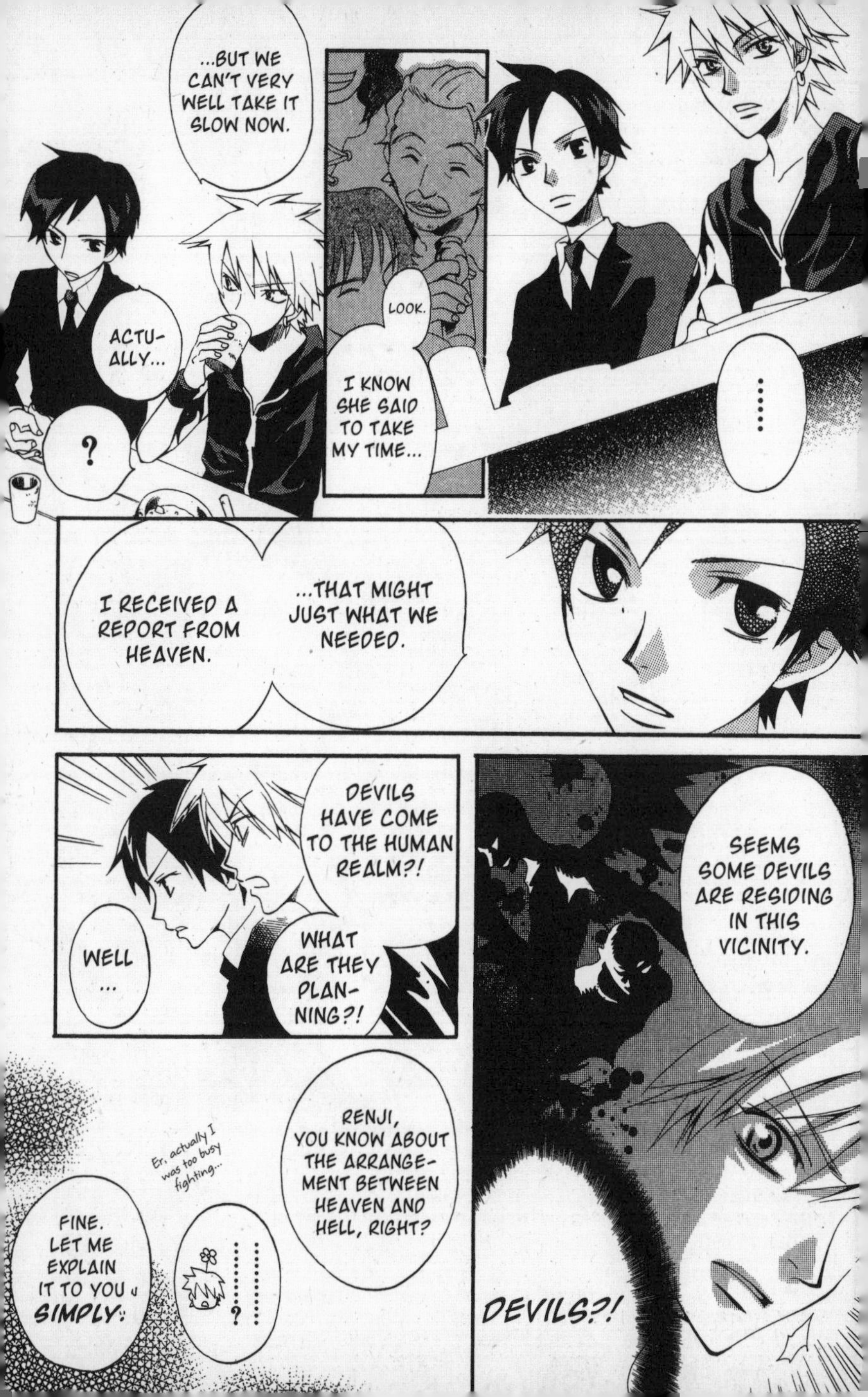

......
LOOK.
I KNOW SHE SAID TO TAKE MY TIME...
...BUT WE CAN'T VERY WELL TAKE IT SLOW NOW.
ACTU-ALLY...
?
...THAT MIGHT JUST WHAT WE NEEDED.
I RECEIVED A REPORT FROM HEAVEN.
SEEMS SOME DEVILS ARE RESIDING IN THIS VICINITY.
DEVILS?!
DEVILS HAVE COME TO THE HUMAN REALM?!
WHAT ARE THEY PLAN-NING?!
WELL...
RENJI, YOU KNOW ABOUT THE ARRANGE-MENT BETWEEN HEAVEN AND HELL, RIGHT?
......?
Er, actually I was too busy fighting...
FINE. LET ME EXPLAIN IT TO YOU SIMPLY.

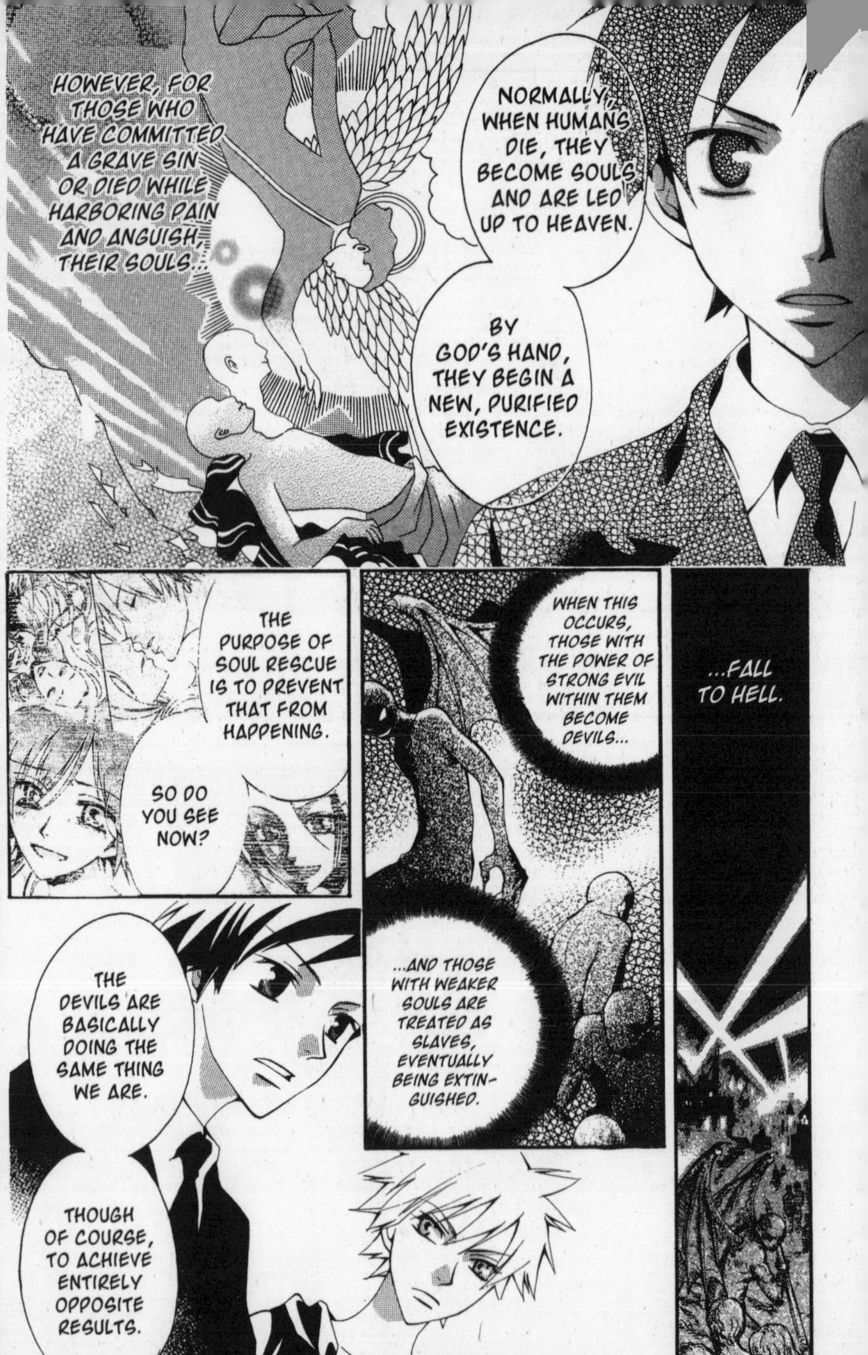

NORMALLY, WHEN HUMANS DIE, THEY BECOME SOULS AND ARE LED UP TO HEAVEN.
BY GOD'S HAND, THEY BEGIN A NEW, PURIFIED EXISTENCE.
HOWEVER, FOR THOSE WHO HAVE COMMITTED A GRAVE SIN OR DIED WHILE HARBORING PAIN AND ANGUISH, THEIR SOULS...
...FALL TO HELL.
WHEN THIS OCCURS, THOSE WITH THE POWER OF STRONG EVIL WITHIN THEM BECOME DEVILS...
...AND THOSE WITH WEAKER SOULS ARE TREATED AS SLAVES, EVENTUALLY BEING EXTIN-GUISHED.
THE PURPOSE OF SOUL RESCUE IS TO PREVENT THAT FROM HAPPENING.
SO DO YOU SEE NOW?
THE DEVILS ARE BASICALLY DOING THE SAME THING WE ARE.
THOUGH OF COURSE, TO ACHIEVE ENTIRELY OPPOSITE RESULTS.

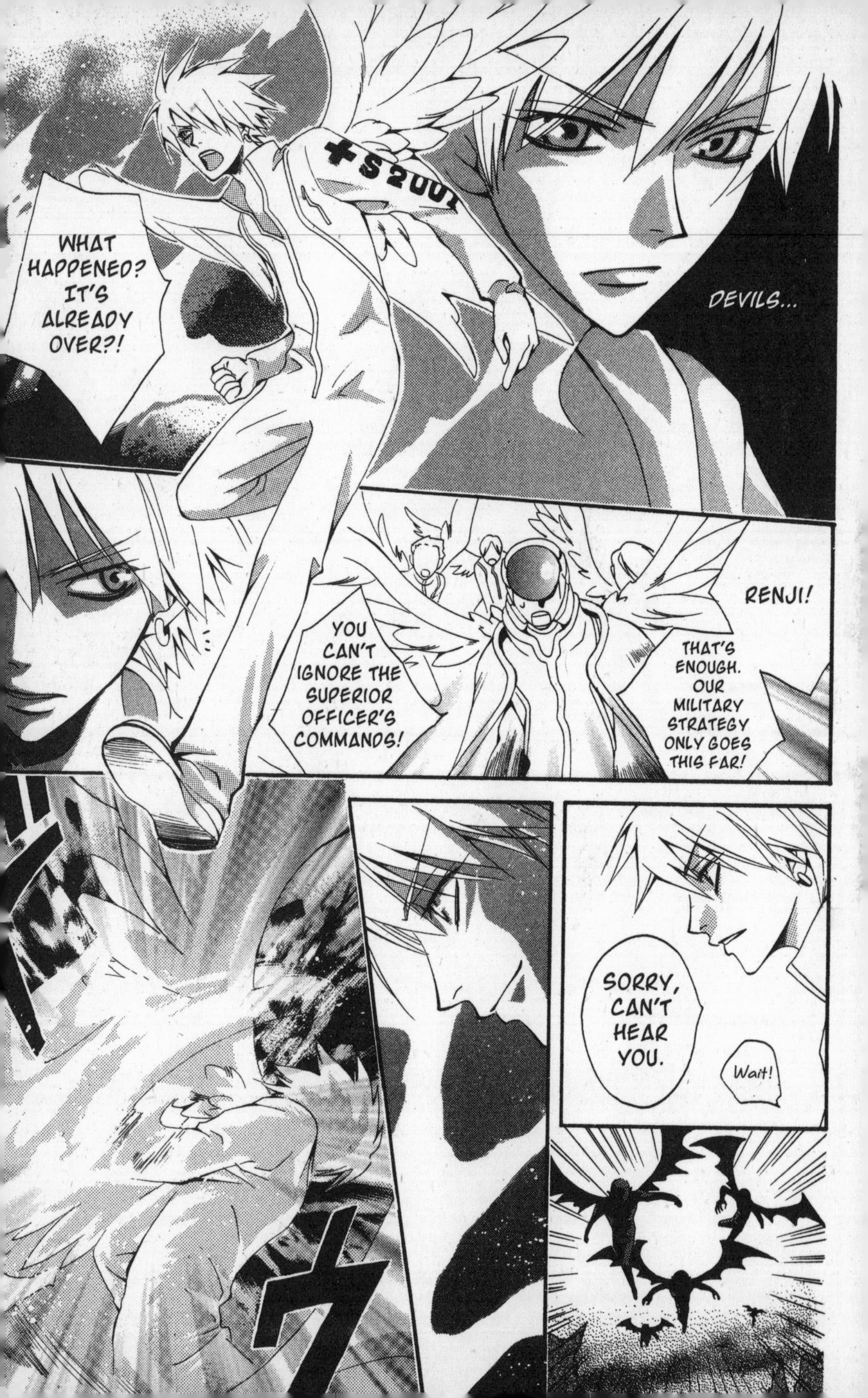
DEVILS...
WHAT HAPPENED? IT'S ALREADY OVER?!
RENJI!
THAT'S ENOUGH. OUR MILITARY STRATEGY ONLY GOES THIS FAR!
YOU CAN'T IGNORE THE SUPERIOR OFFICER'S COMMANDS!
SORRY, CAN'T HEAR YOU.
Wait!

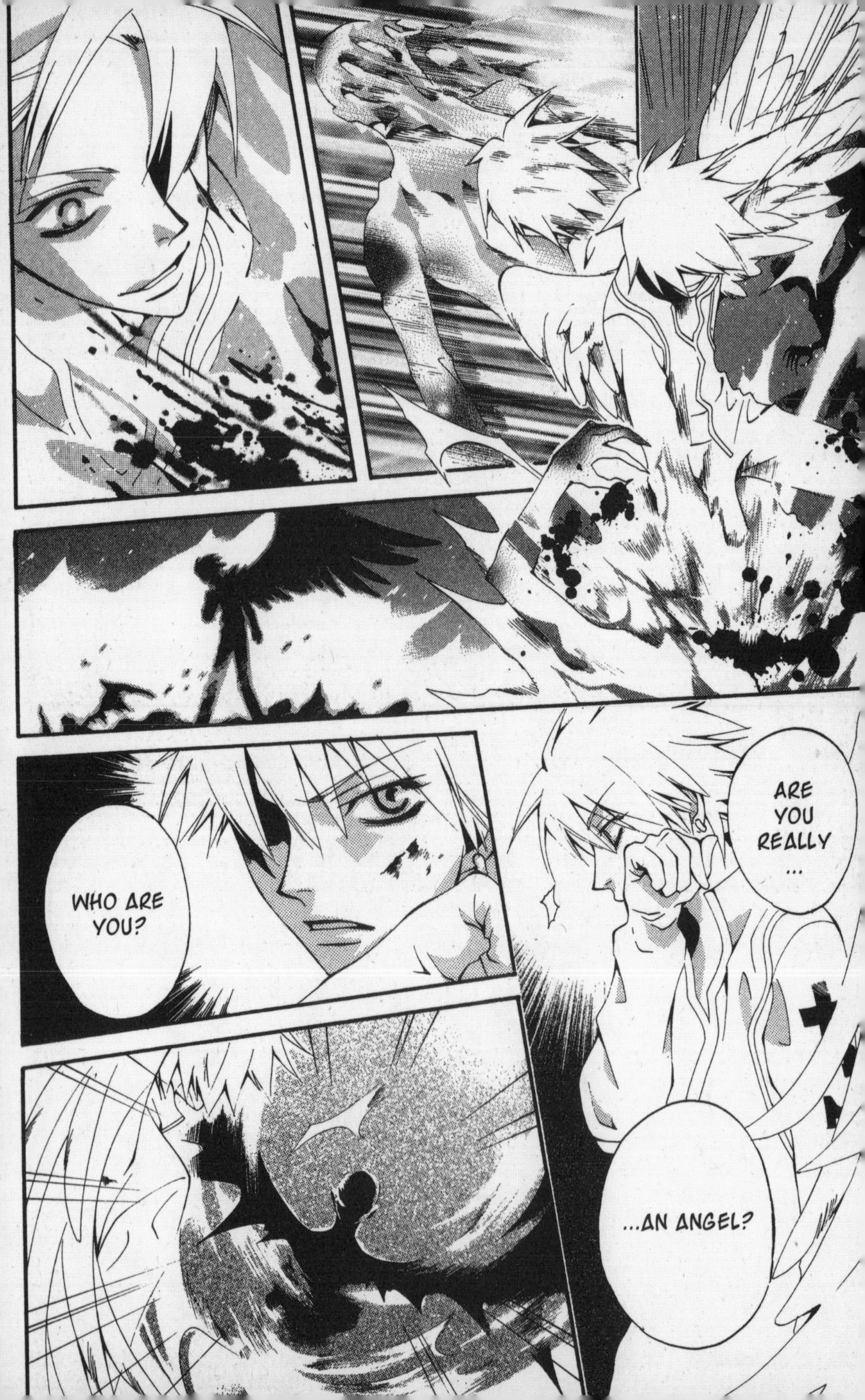
ARE YOU REALLY ...
...AN ANGEL?
WHO ARE YOU?

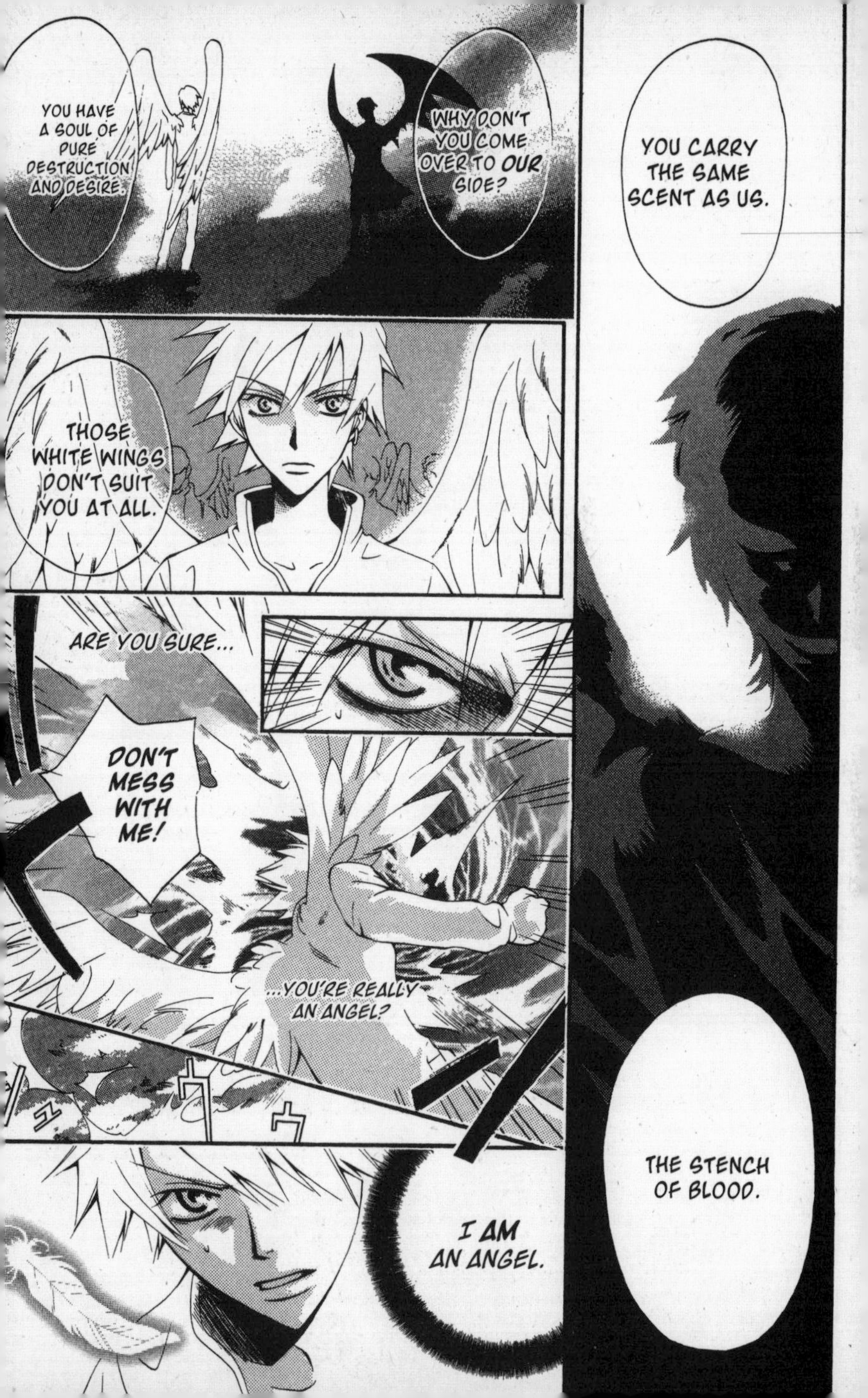
YOU CARRY THE SAME SCENT AS US.
THE STENCH OF BLOOD.
WHY DON'T YOU COME OVER TO OUR SIDE?
YOU HAVE A SOUL OF PURE DESTRUCTION AND DESIRE.
THOSE WHITE WINGS DON'T SUIT YOU AT ALL.
ARE YOU SURE...
DON'T MESS WITH ME!
...YOU'RE REALLY AN ANGEL?
I AM AN ANGEL.

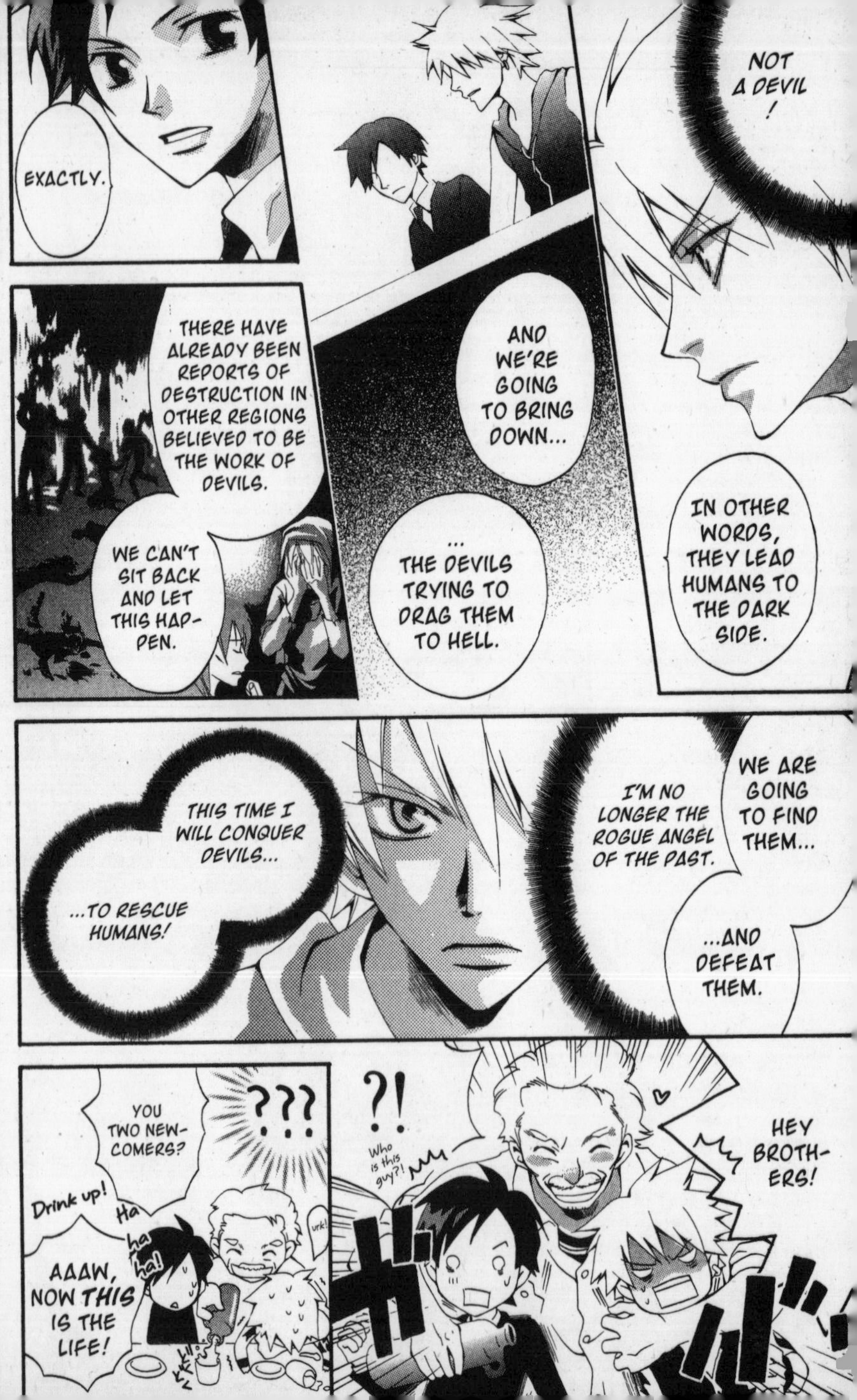
NOT A DEVIL!
IN OTHER WORDS, THEY LEAD HUMANS TO THE DARK SIDE.
EXACTLY.
THERE HAVE ALREADY BEEN REPORTS OF DESTRUCTION IN OTHER REGIONS BELIEVED TO BE THE WORK OF DEVILS.
WE CAN'T SIT BACK AND LET THIS HAP-PEN.
AND WE'RE GOING TO BRING DOWN...
...THE DEVILS TRYING TO DRAG THEM TO HELL.
WE ARE GOING TO FIND THEM...
I'M NO LONGER THE ROGUE ANGEL OF THE PAST.
...AND DEFEAT THEM.
THIS TIME I WILL CONQUER DEVILS...
...TO RESCUE HUMANS!
HEY BROTH-ERS!
?!
Who is this guy?!
YOU TWO NEW-COMERS?
???
Drink up!
Ha ha ha!
urk!
AAAW, NOW **THIS** IS THE LIFE!

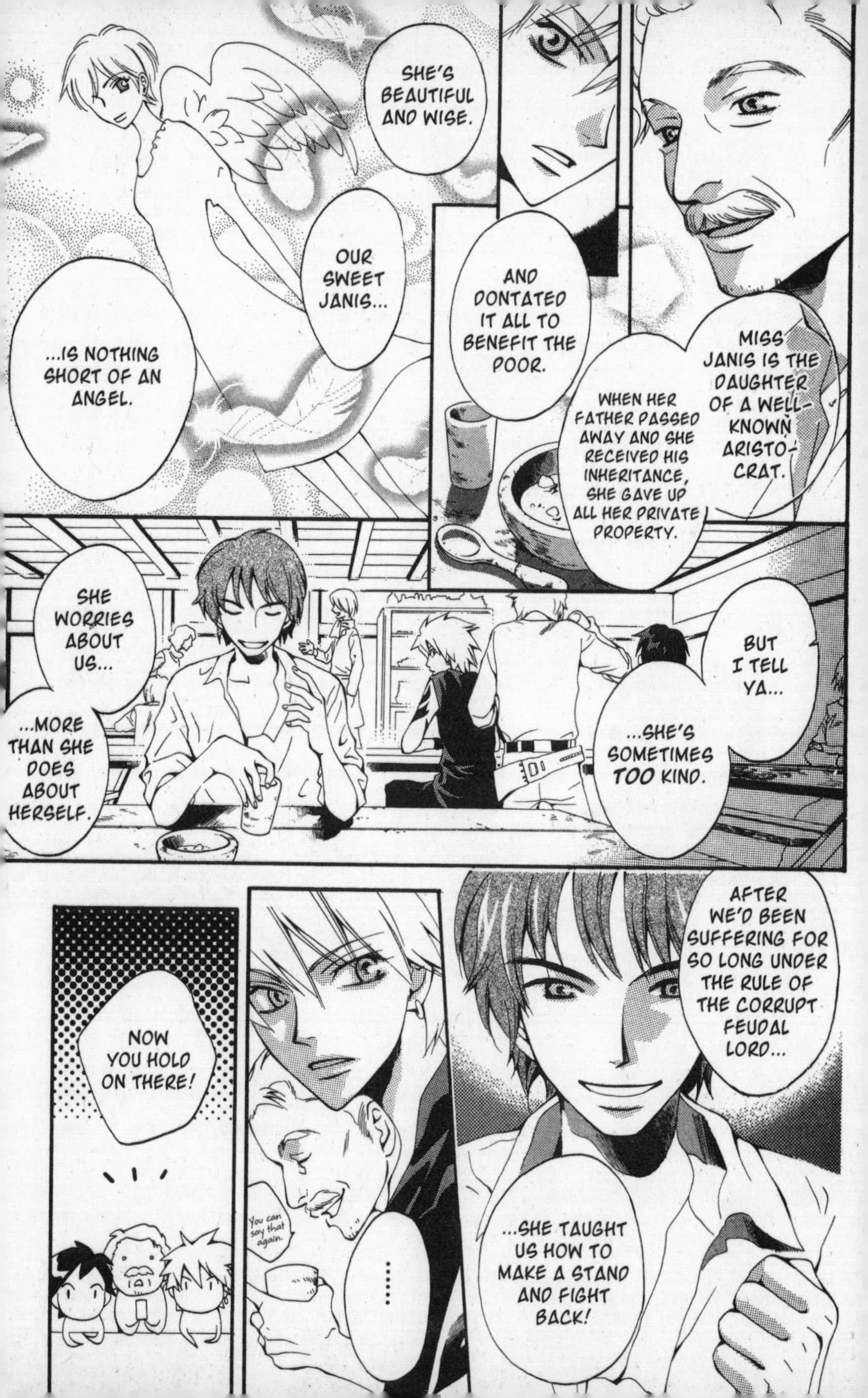
MISS JANIS IS THE DAUGHTER OF A WELL-KNOWN ARISTOCRAT.
WHEN HER FATHER PASSED AWAY AND SHE RECEIVED HIS INHERITANCE, SHE GAVE UP ALL HER PRIVATE PROPERTY.
AND DONTATED IT ALL TO BENEFIT THE POOR.
SHE'S BEAUTIFUL AND WISE.
OUR SWEET JANIS...
...IS NOTHING SHORT OF AN ANGEL.
BUT I TELL YA...
...SHE'S SOMETIMES *TOO* KIND.
SHE WORRIES ABOUT US...
...MORE THAN SHE DOES ABOUT HERSELF.
AFTER WE'D BEEN SUFFERING FOR SO LONG UNDER THE RULE OF THE CORRUPT FEUDAL LORD...
...SHE TAUGHT US HOW TO MAKE A STAND AND FIGHT BACK!
......
You can say that again.
NOW YOU HOLD ON THERE!

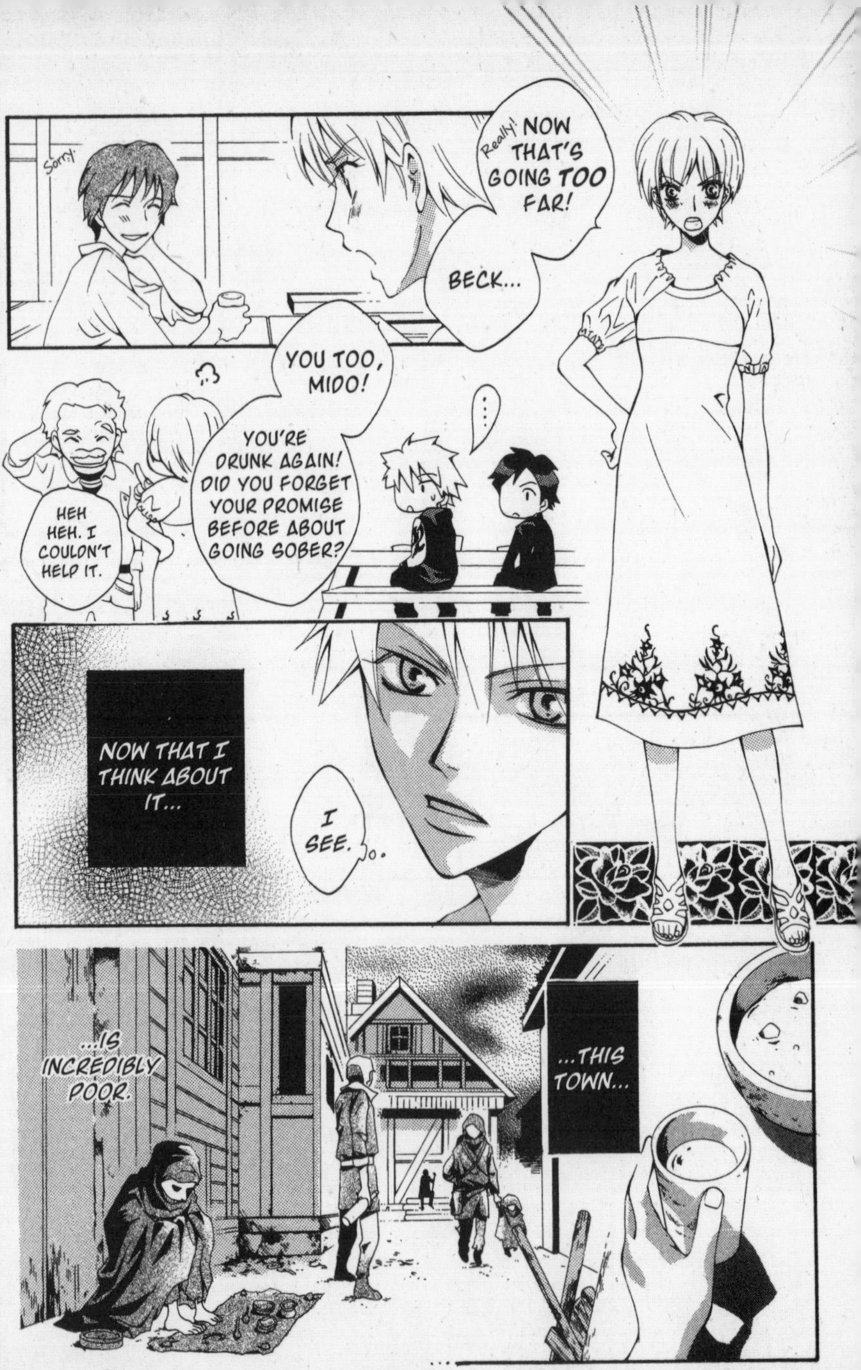
Really! NOW THAT'S GOING TOO FAR!
BECK...
Sorry.
YOU TOO, MIDO!
YOU'RE DRUNK AGAIN! DID YOU FORGET YOUR PROMISE BEFORE ABOUT GOING SOBER?
...
HEH HEH. I COULDN'T HELP IT.
I SEE.
NOW THAT I THINK ABOUT IT...
...THIS TOWN...
...IS INCREDIBLY POOR.
...

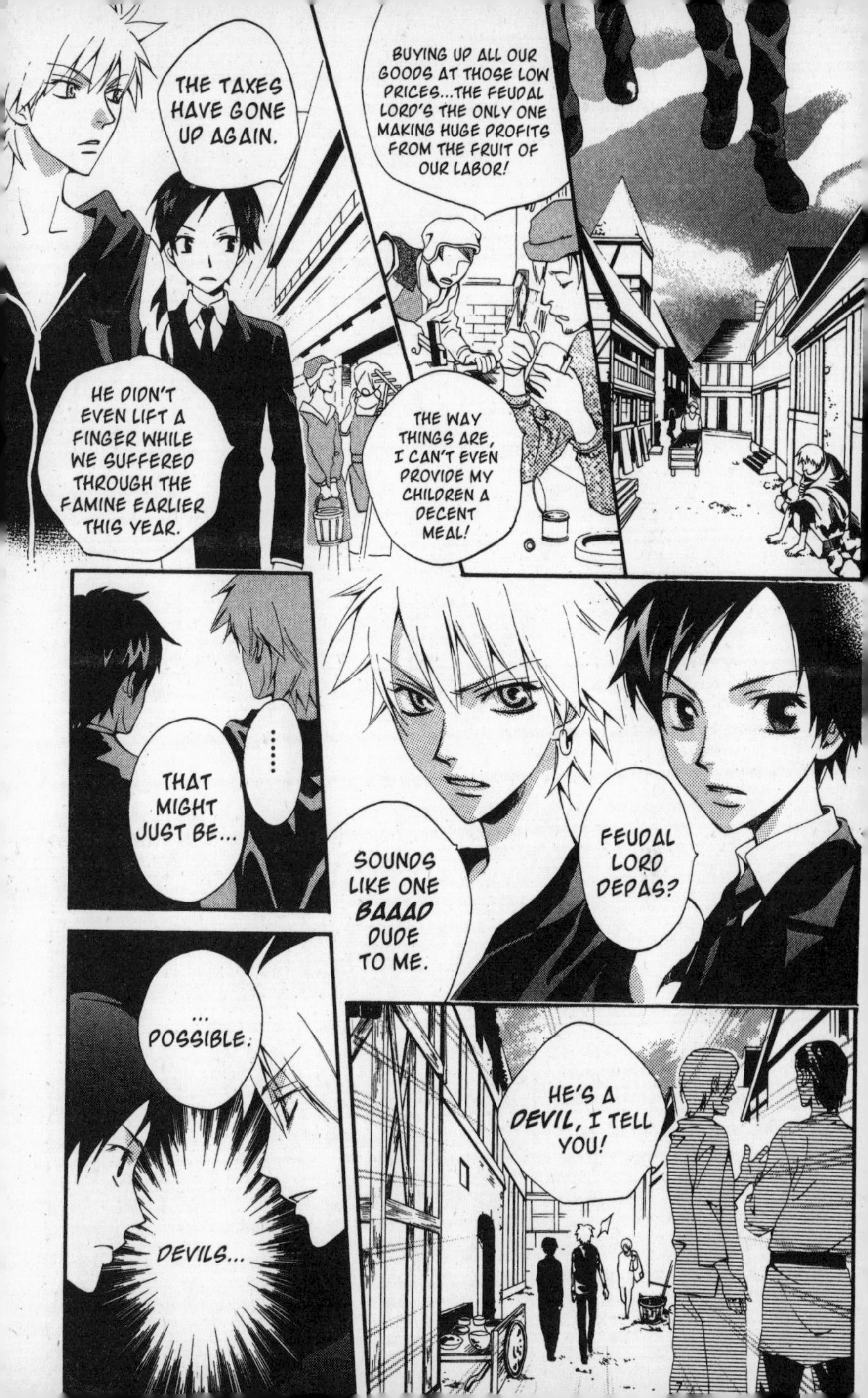
BUYING UP ALL OUR GOODS AT THOSE LOW PRICES...THE FEUDAL LORD'S THE ONLY ONE MAKING HUGE PROFITS FROM THE FRUIT OF OUR LABOR!
THE WAY THINGS ARE, I CAN'T EVEN PROVIDE MY CHILDREN A DECENT MEAL!
THE TAXES HAVE GONE UP AGAIN.
HE DIDN'T EVEN LIFT A FINGER WHILE WE SUFFERED THROUGH THE FAMINE EARLIER THIS YEAR.
FEUDAL LORD DEPAS?
SOUNDS LIKE ONE BAAAD DUDE TO ME.
......
THAT MIGHT JUST BE...
HE'S A DEVIL, I TELL YOU!
... POSSIBLE.
DEVILS...

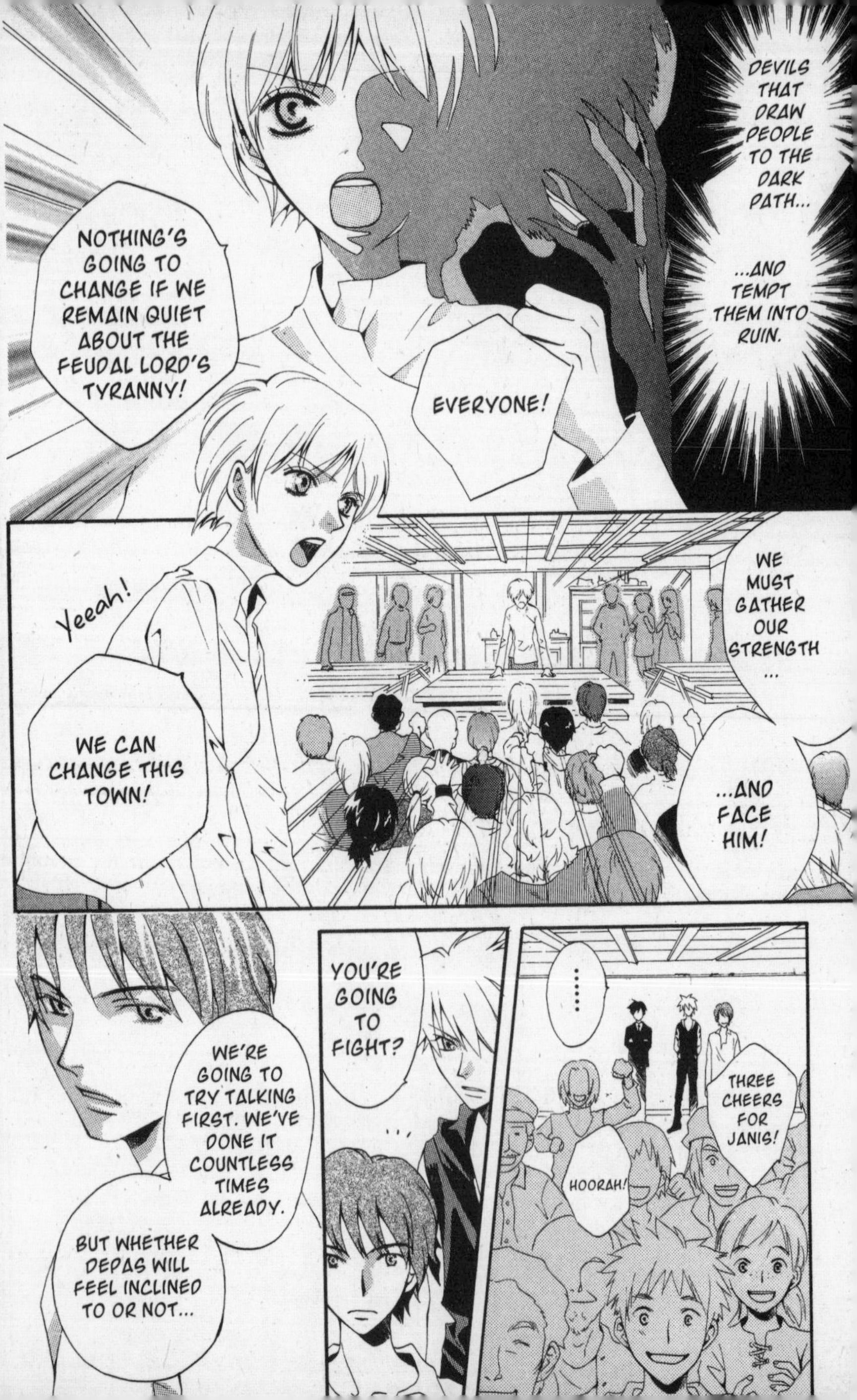
DEVILS THAT DRAW PEOPLE TO THE DARK PATH...
...AND TEMPT THEM INTO RUIN.
EVERYONE!
NOTHING'S GOING TO CHANGE IF WE REMAIN QUIET ABOUT THE FEUDAL LORD'S TYRANNY!
WE MUST GATHER OUR STRENGTH...
...AND FACE HIM!
Yeeah!
WE CAN CHANGE THIS TOWN!
......
THREE CHEERS FOR JANIS!
HOORAH!
YOU'RE GOING TO FIGHT?
...
WE'RE GOING TO TRY TALKING FIRST. WE'VE DONE IT COUNTLESS TIMES ALREADY.
BUT WHETHER DEPAS WILL FEEL INCLINED TO OR NOT...

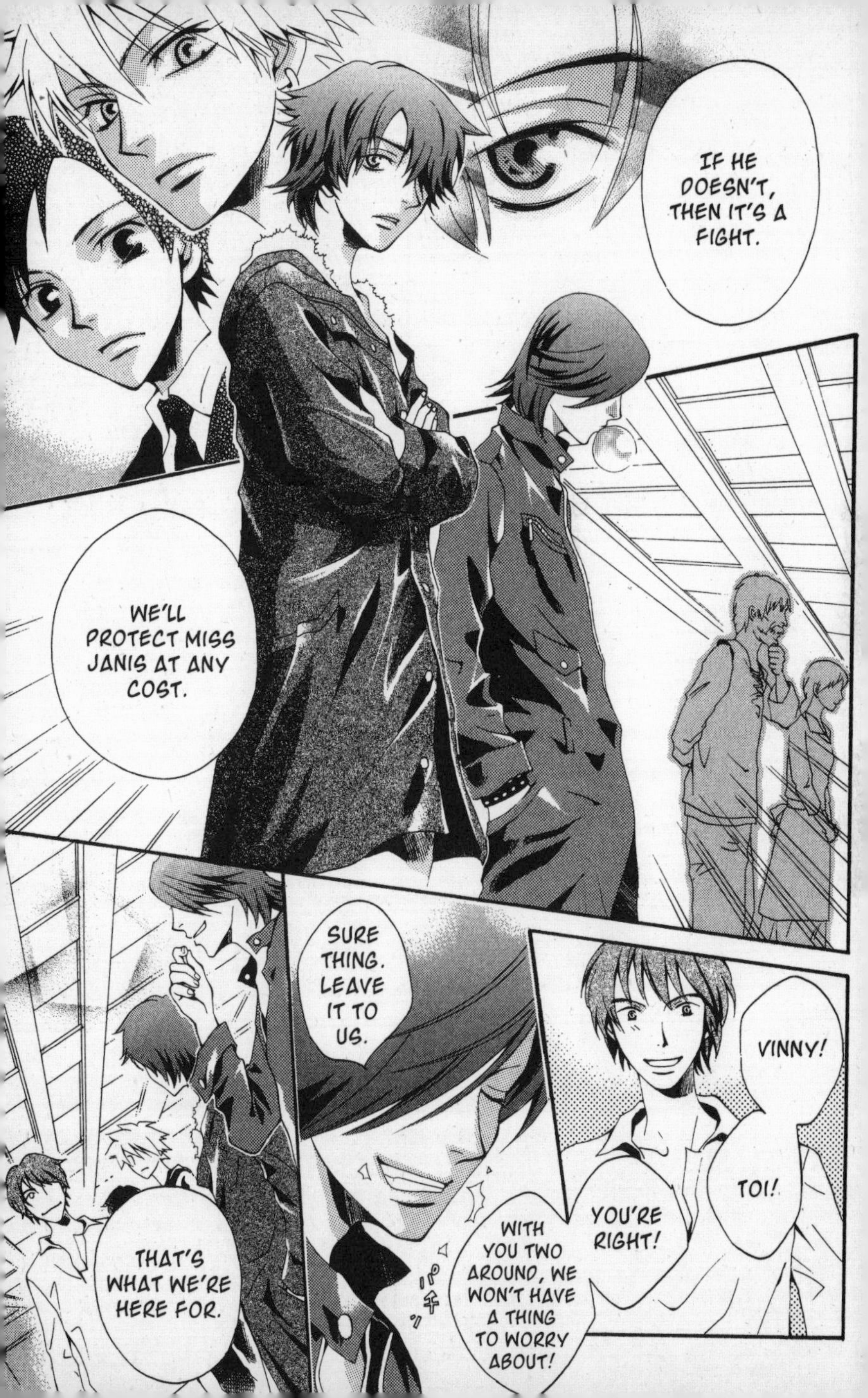
IF HE DOESN'T, THEN IT'S A FIGHT.
WE'LL PROTECT MISS JANIS AT ANY COST.
VINNY!
TOI!
YOU'RE RIGHT!
WITH YOU TWO AROUND, WE WON'T HAVE A THING TO WORRY ABOUT!
SURE THING. LEAVE IT TO US.
THAT'S WHAT WE'RE HERE FOR.

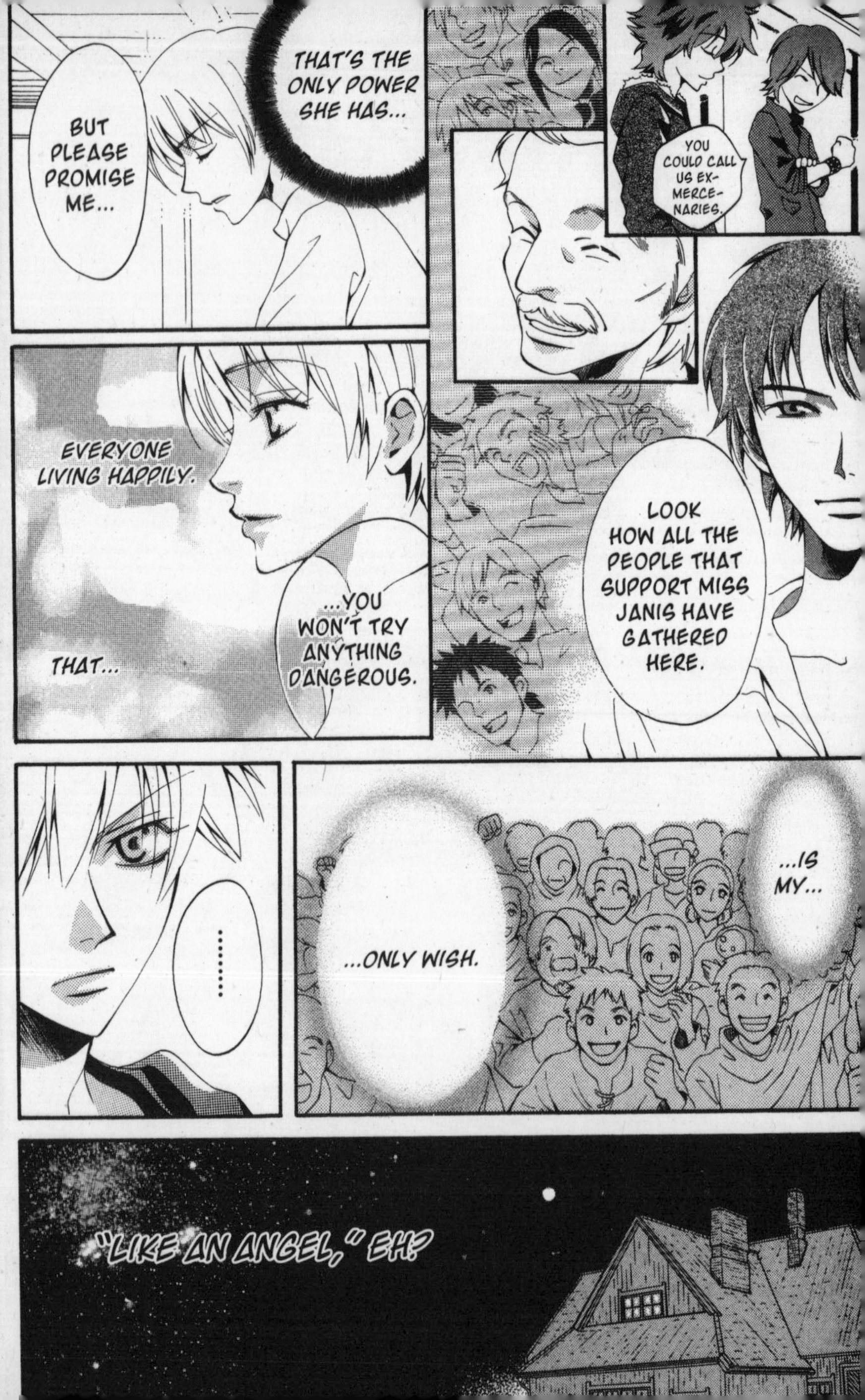
YOU COULD CALL US EX-MERCENARIES.
THAT'S THE ONLY POWER SHE HAS...
BUT PLEASE PROMISE ME...
LOOK HOW ALL THE PEOPLE THAT SUPPORT MISS JANIS HAVE GATHERED HERE.
EVERYONE LIVING HAPPILY.
...YOU WON'T TRY ANYTHING DANGEROUS.
THAT...
...IS MY...
...ONLY WISH.
....
"LIKE AN ANGEL," EH?

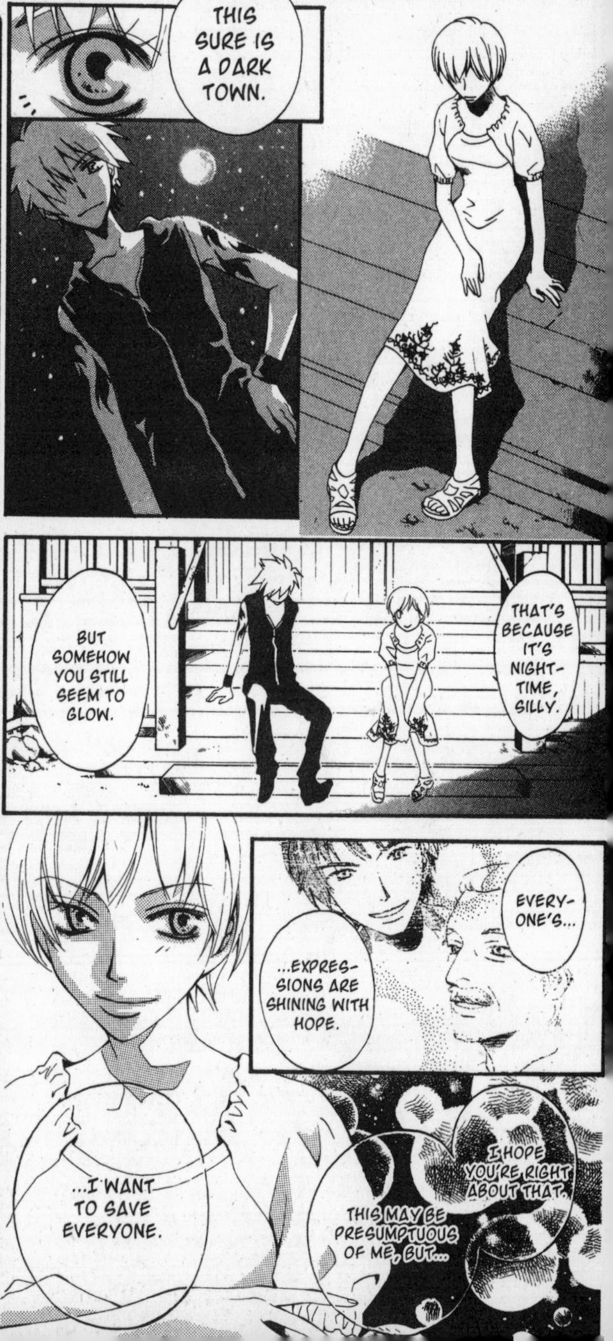
THIS SURE IS A DARK TOWN.
THAT'S BECAUSE IT'S NIGHT-TIME, SILLY.
BUT SOMEHOW YOU STILL SEEM TO GLOW.
EVERY-ONE'S...
...EXPRES-SIONS ARE SHINING WITH HOPE.
I HOPE YOU'RE RIGHT ABOUT THAT.
THIS MAY BE PRESUMPTUOUS OF ME, BUT...
...I WANT TO SAVE EVERYONE.

SR

Okay!
The devils have made their appearance!
You can't have angels without devils, right?
It's fun to draw devils. The reason I'm better at drawing bad guys than good guys is because my personality's evil. Believe it or not, I enjoy the color black.

Oh, but aren't the two angels in this story black, too...?

At any rate, just wanted to say having this one-fourth page space in my own tankobon to write comments has been my dream for a long time.

But I just can't ever get my true feelings out here.
It really seems that all I end up doing is write boring stuff... Aaww...

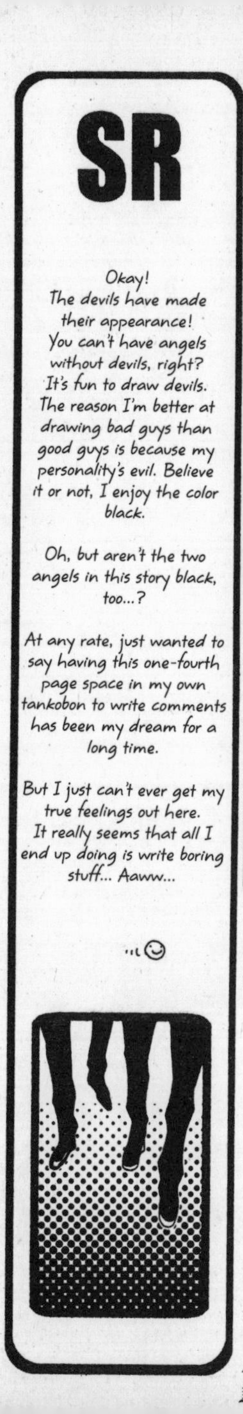

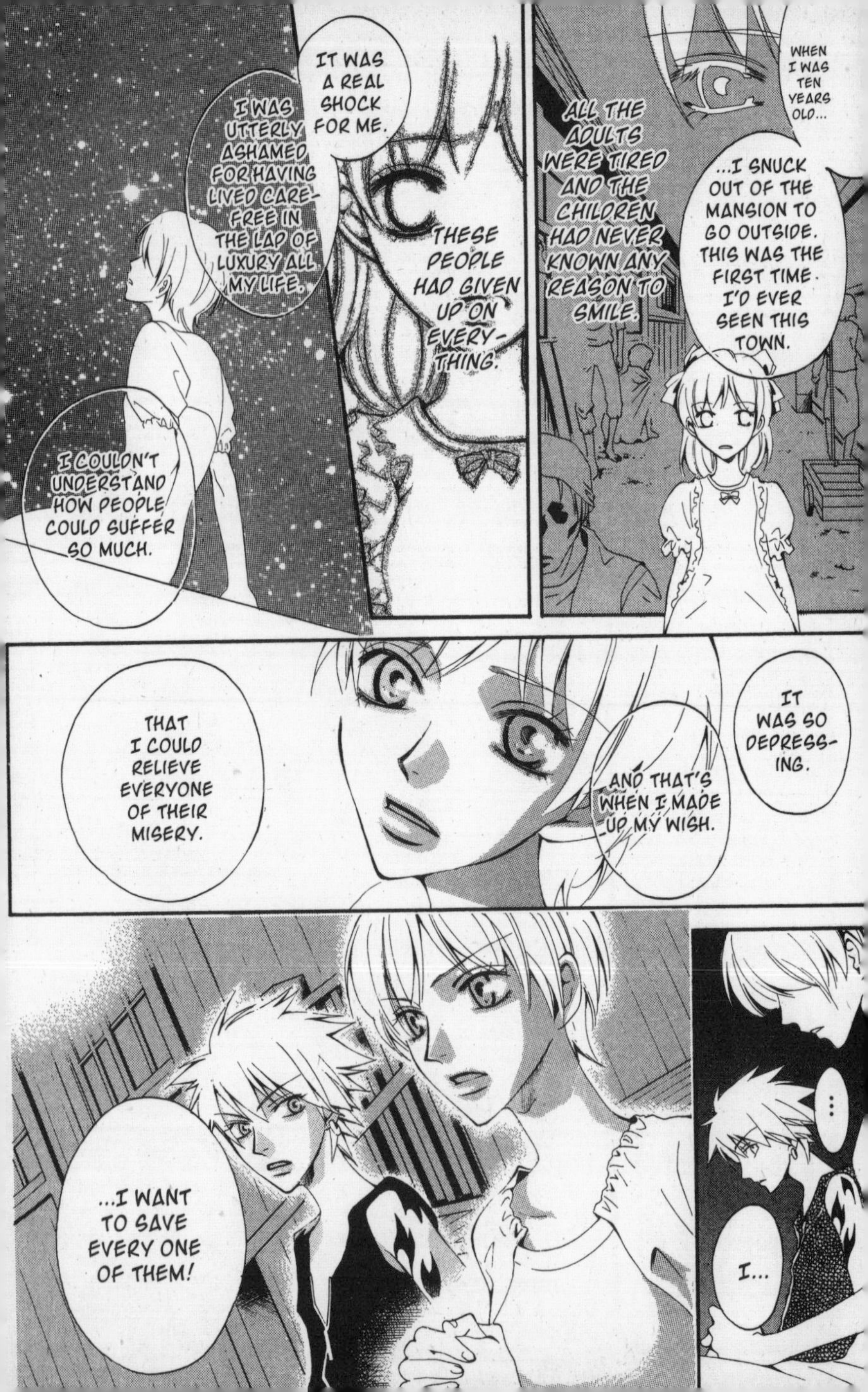
WHEN I WAS TEN YEARS OLD...
...I SNUCK OUT OF THE MANSION TO GO OUTSIDE. THIS WAS THE FIRST TIME I'D EVER SEEN THIS TOWN.
ALL THE ADULTS WERE TIRED AND THE CHILDREN HAD NEVER KNOWN ANY REASON TO SMILE.
IT WAS A REAL SHOCK FOR ME.
THESE PEOPLE HAD GIVEN UP ON EVERYTHING.
I WAS UTTERLY ASHAMED FOR HAVING LIVED CAREFREE IN THE LAP OF LUXURY ALL MY LIFE.
I COULDN'T UNDERSTAND HOW PEOPLE COULD SUFFER SO MUCH.
IT WAS SO DEPRESSING.
AND THAT'S WHEN I MADE UP MY WISH.
THAT I COULD RELIEVE EVERYONE OF THEIR MISERY.
...
I...
...I WANT TO SAVE EVERY ONE OF THEM!

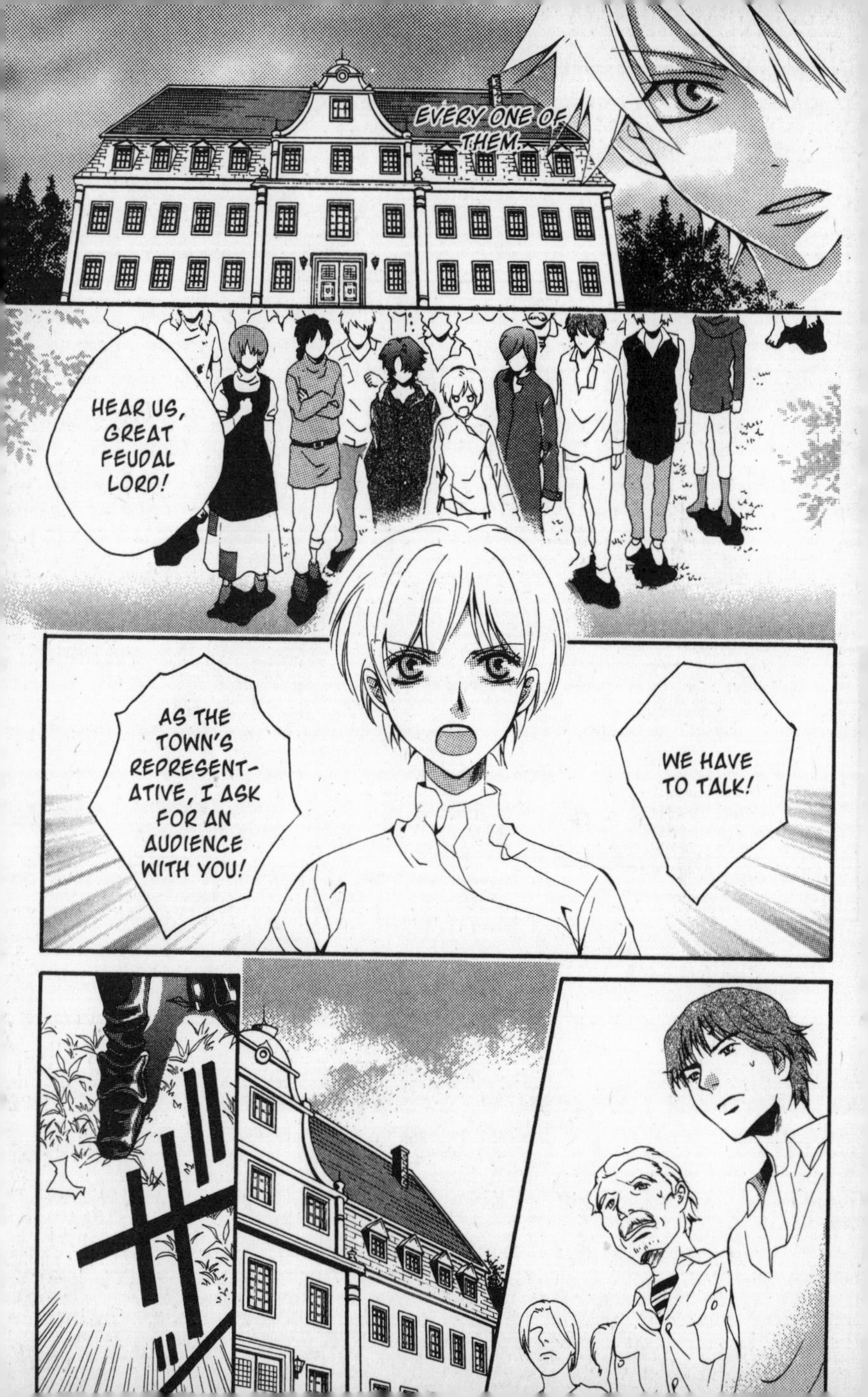
EVERY ONE OF THEM.
HEAR US, GREAT FEUDAL LORD!
WE HAVE TO TALK!
AS THE TOWN'S REPRESENT-ATIVE, I ASK FOR AN AUDIENCE WITH YOU!

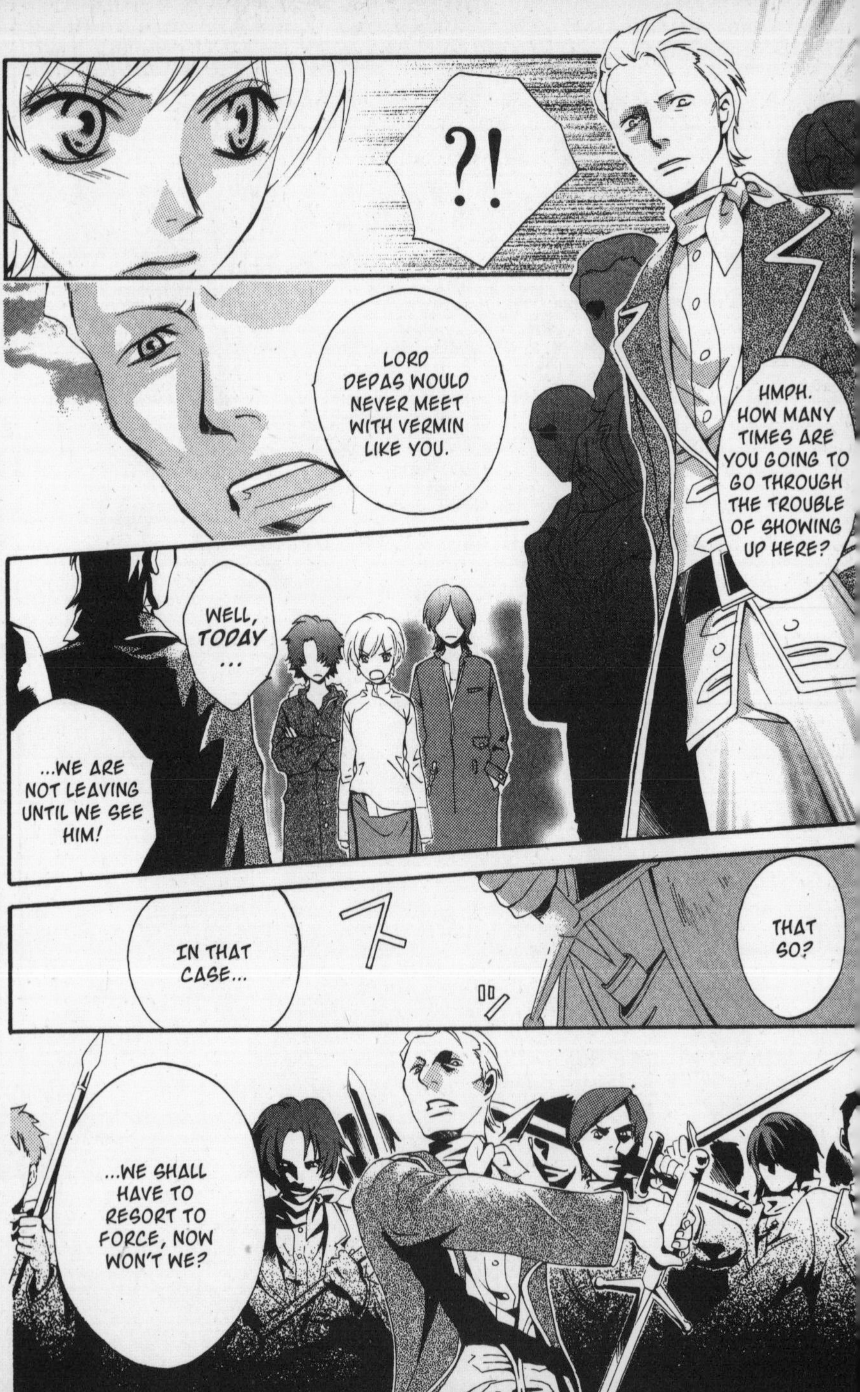
HMPH. HOW MANY TIMES ARE YOU GOING TO GO THROUGH THE TROUBLE OF SHOWING UP HERE?
?!
LORD DEPAS WOULD NEVER MEET WITH VERMIN LIKE YOU.
WELL, TODAY ...
...WE ARE NOT LEAVING UNTIL WE SEE HIM!
THAT SO?
ス
IN THAT CASE...
...WE SHALL HAVE TO RESORT TO FORCE, NOW WON'T WE?

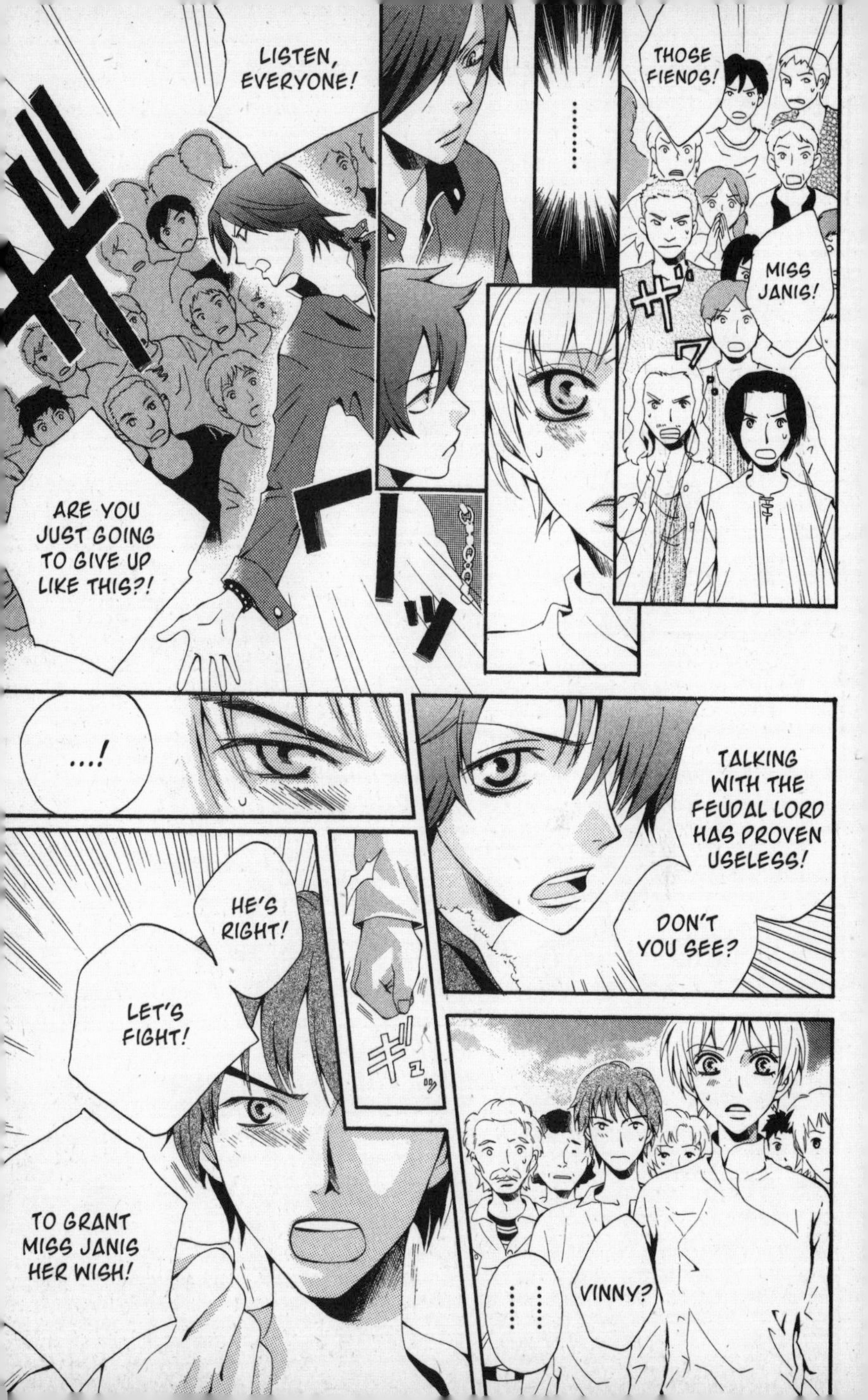
THOSE FIENDS!
MISS JANIS!
……
LISTEN, EVERYONE!
ARE YOU JUST GOING TO GIVE UP LIKE THIS?!
TALKING WITH THE FEUDAL LORD HAS PROVEN USELESS!
DON'T YOU SEE?
VINNY?
……
…!
HE'S RIGHT!
LET'S FIGHT!
TO GRANT MISS JANIS HER WISH!

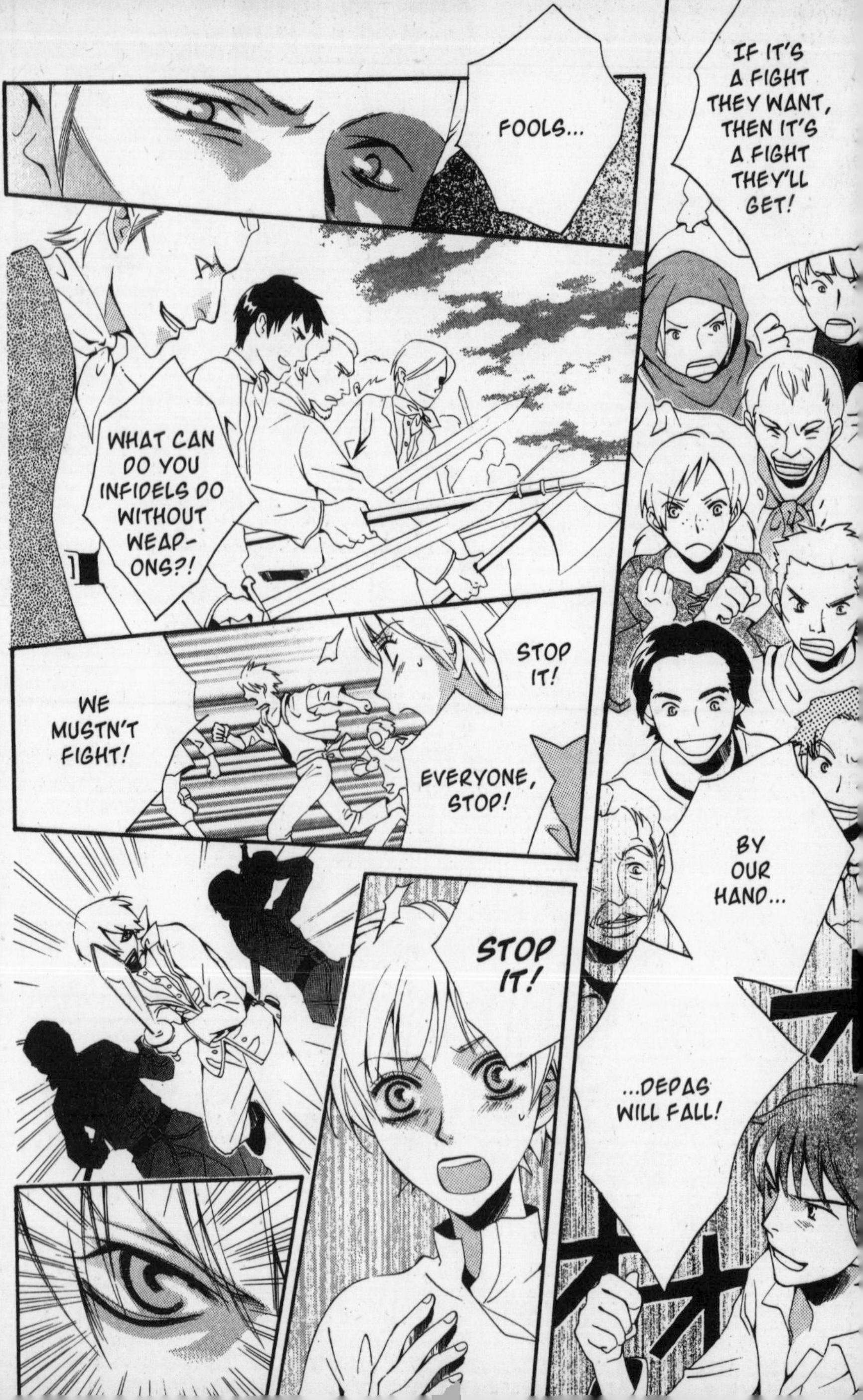
IF IT'S A FIGHT THEY WANT, THEN IT'S A FIGHT THEY'LL GET!
BY OUR HAND...
...DEPAS WILL FALL!
FOOLS...
WHAT CAN DO YOU INFIDELS DO WITHOUT WEAPONS?!
STOP IT!
EVERYONE, STOP!
WE MUSTN'T FIGHT!
STOP IT!

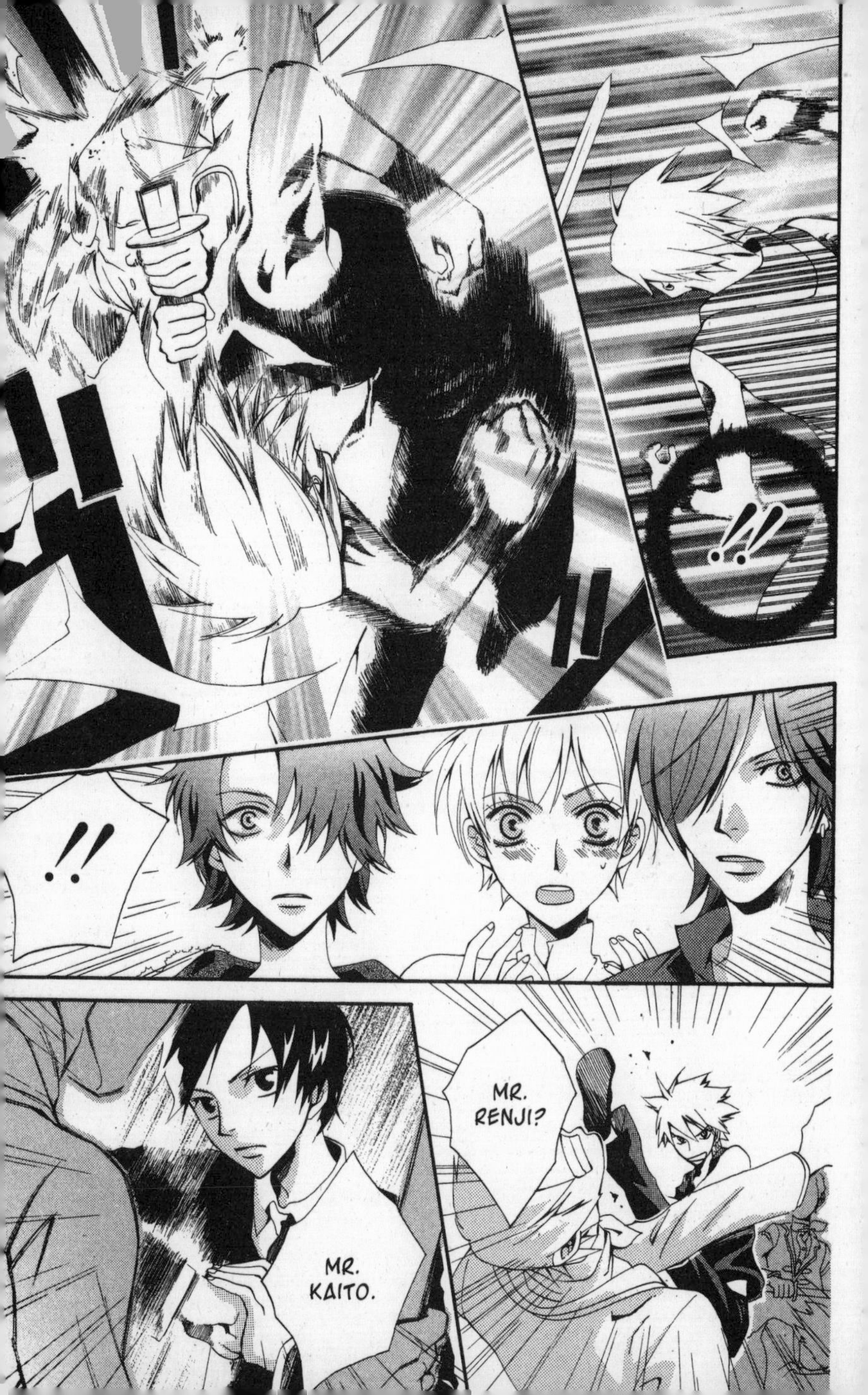
!!
!!
MR. RENJI?
MR. KAITO.

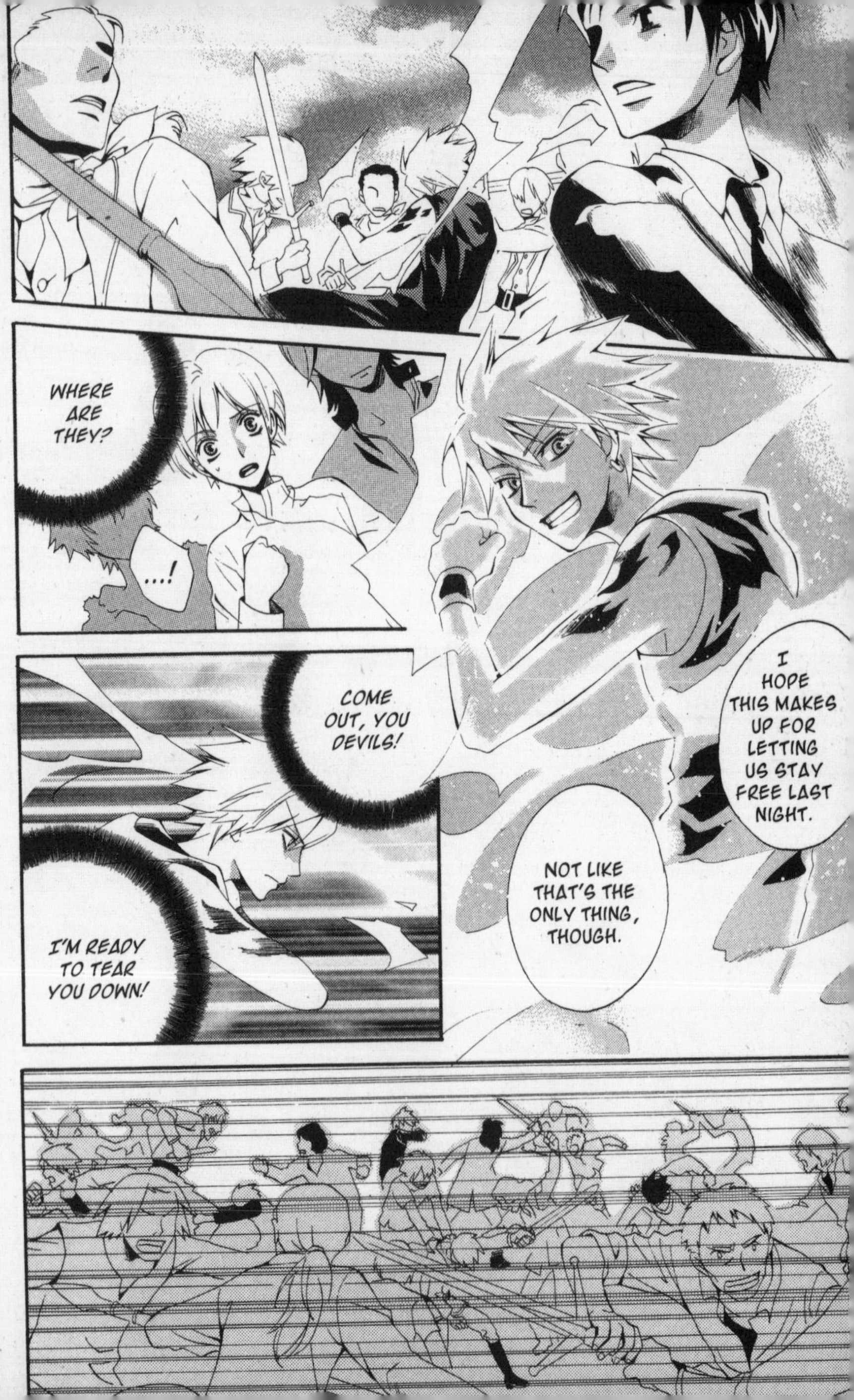
I HOPE THIS MAKES UP FOR LETTING US STAY FREE LAST NIGHT.
NOT LIKE THAT'S THE ONLY THING, THOUGH.
WHERE ARE THEY?
...!
COME OUT, YOU DEVILS!
I'M READY TO TEAR YOU DOWN!

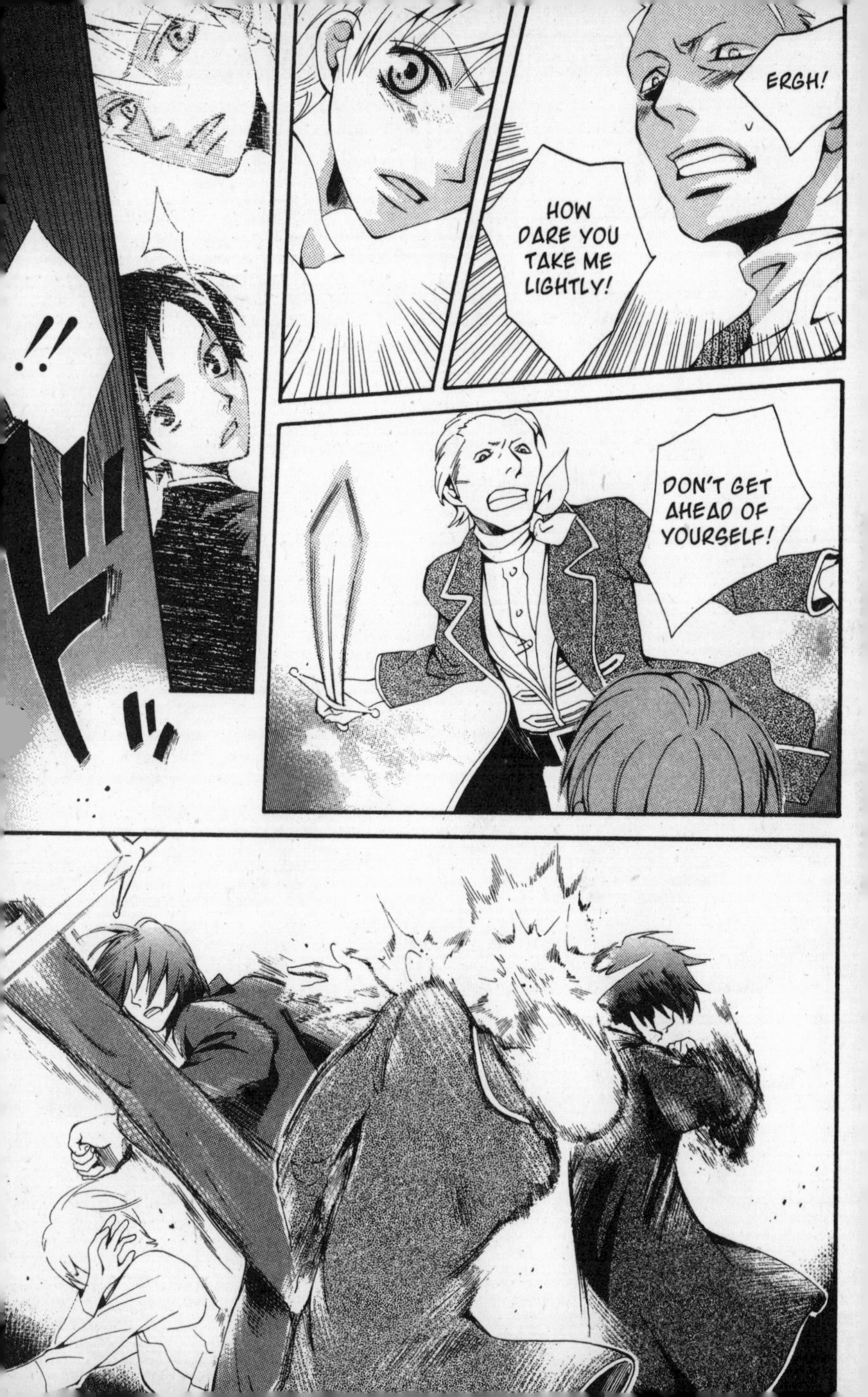
ERGH!
HOW DARE YOU TAKE ME LIGHTLY!
DON'T GET AHEAD OF YOURSELF!
!!
..

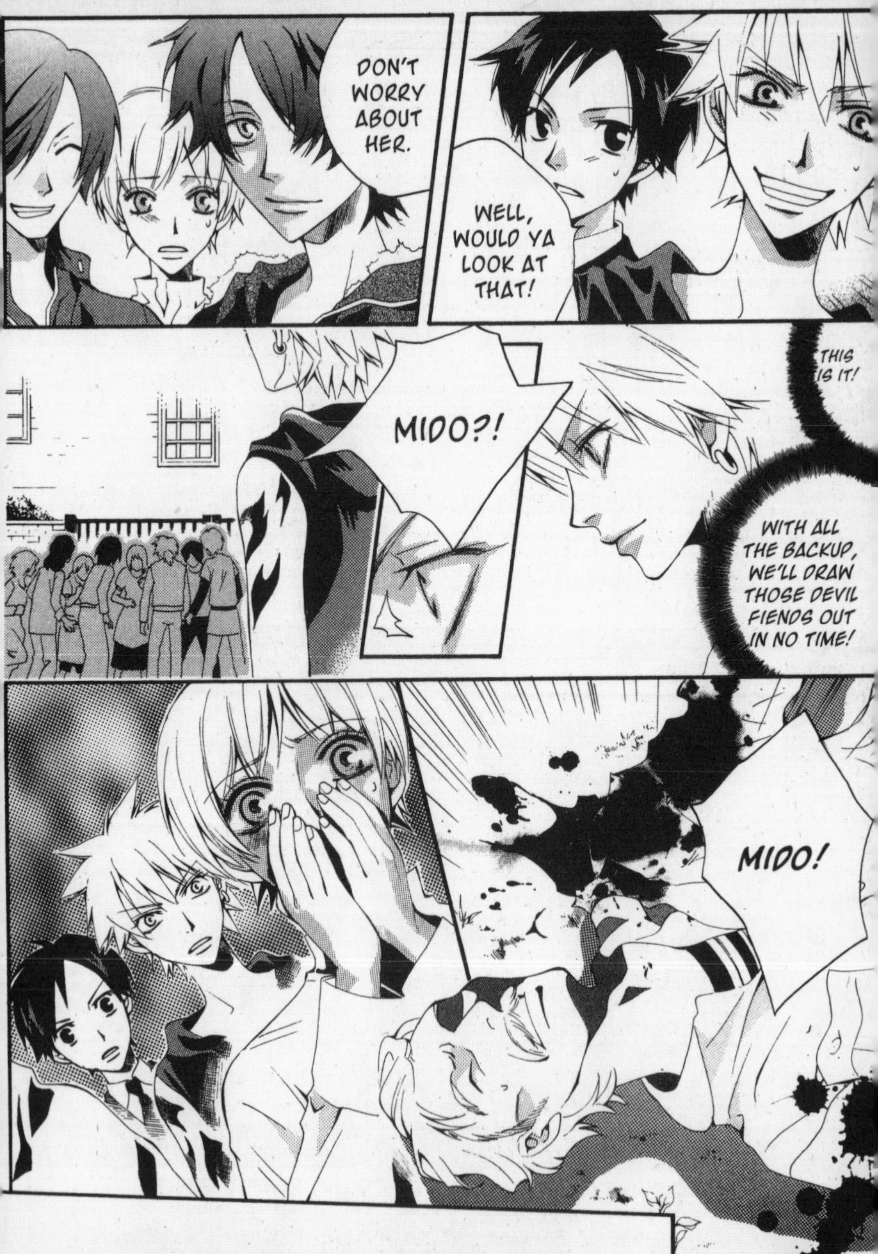
WELL, WOULD YA LOOK AT THAT!
DON'T WORRY ABOUT HER.
THIS IS IT!
WITH ALL THE BACKUP, WE'LL DRAW THOSE DEVIL FIENDS OUT IN NO TIME!
MIDO?!
MIDO!

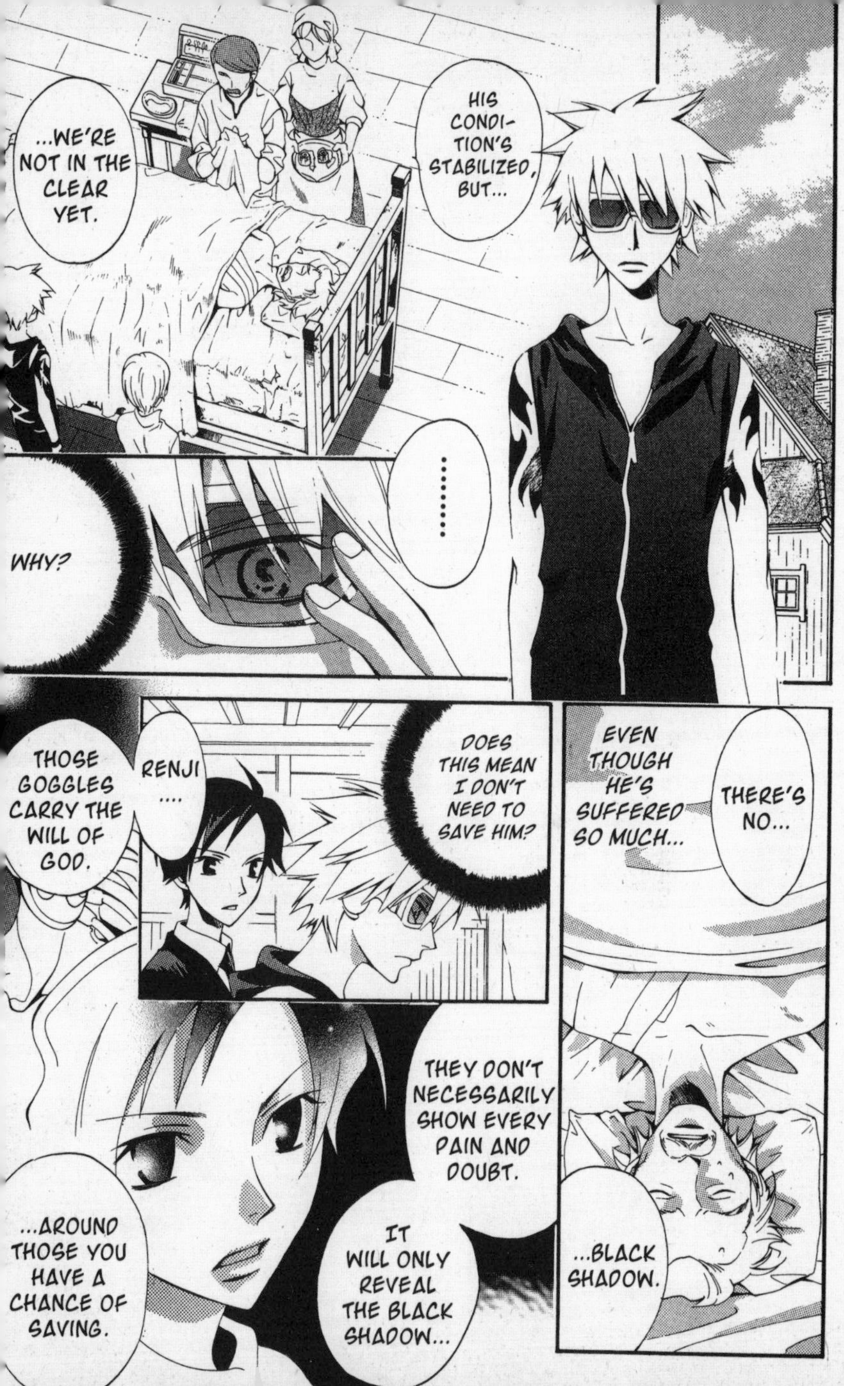

HIS CONDITION'S STABILIZED, BUT...
...WE'RE NOT IN THE CLEAR YET.
......
WHY?
THERE'S NO...
EVEN THOUGH HE'S SUFFERED SO MUCH...
...BLACK SHADOW.
DOES THIS MEAN I DON'T NEED TO SAVE HIM?
RENJI....
THOSE GOGGLES CARRY THE WILL OF GOD.
THEY DON'T NECESSARILY SHOW EVERY PAIN AND DOUBT.
IT WILL ONLY REVEAL THE BLACK SHADOW...
...AROUND THOSE YOU HAVE A CHANCE OF SAVING.

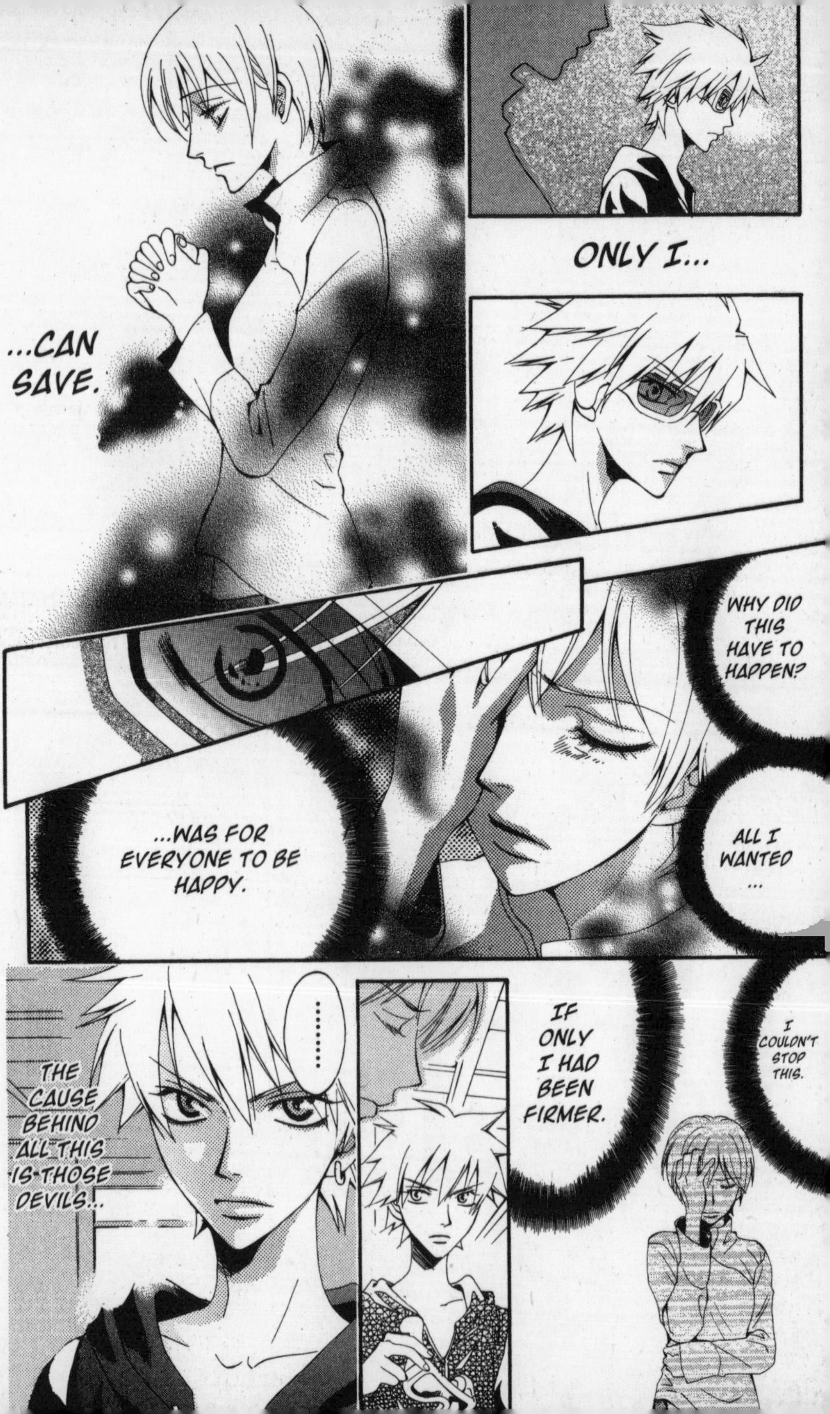

ONLY I...
...CAN SAVE.
WHY DID THIS HAVE TO HAPPEN?
ALL I WANTED ...
...WAS FOR EVERYONE TO BE HAPPY.
I COULDN'T STOP THIS.
IF ONLY I HAD BEEN FIRMER.
......
THE CAUSE BEHIND ALL THIS IS THOSE DEVILS...

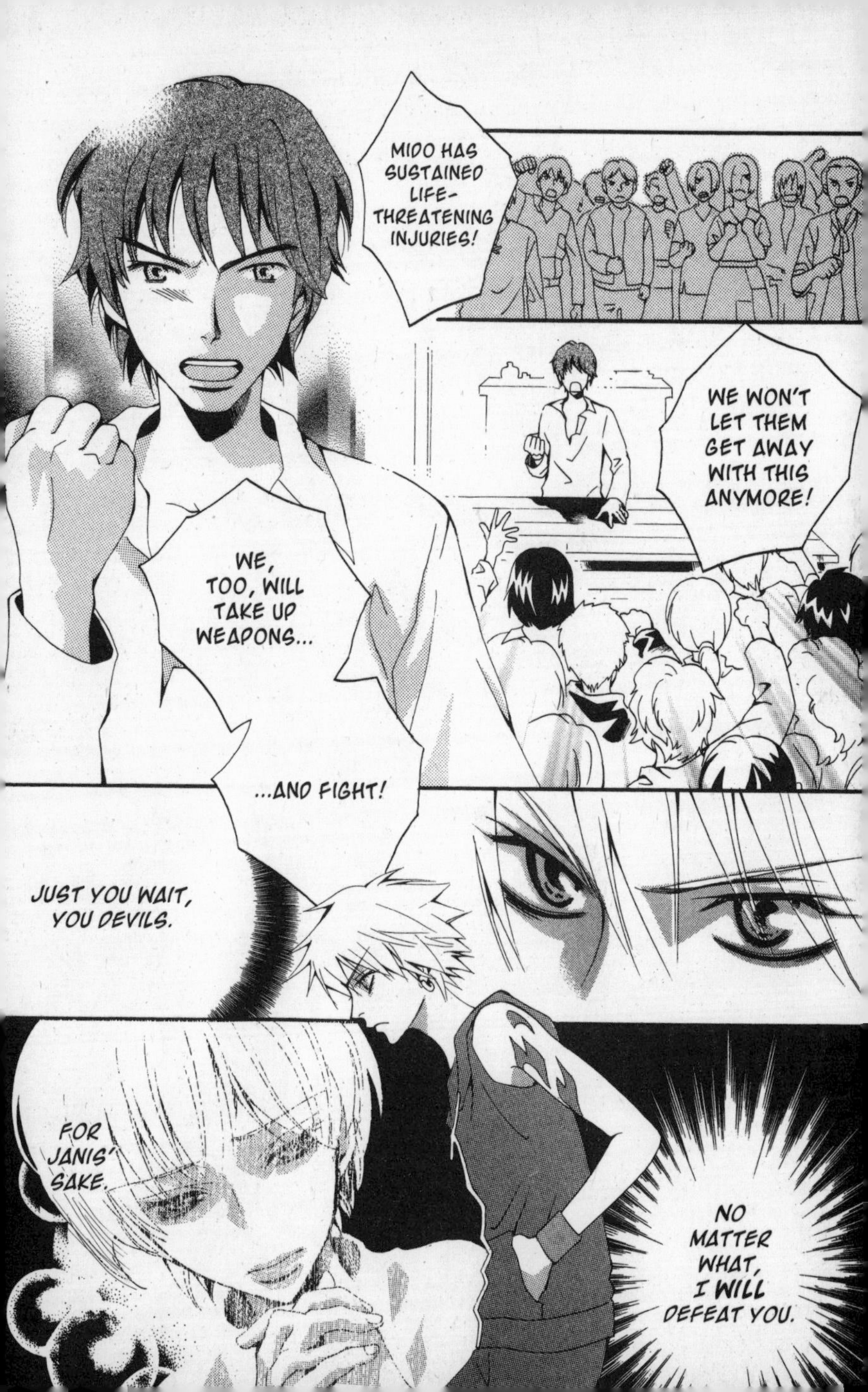
MIDO HAS SUSTAINED LIFE-THREATENING INJURIES!
WE WON'T LET THEM GET AWAY WITH THIS ANYMORE!
WE, TOO, WILL TAKE UP WEAPONS...
...AND FIGHT!
JUST YOU WAIT, YOU DEVILS.
NO MATTER WHAT, I WILL DEFEAT YOU.
FOR JANIS' SAKE.

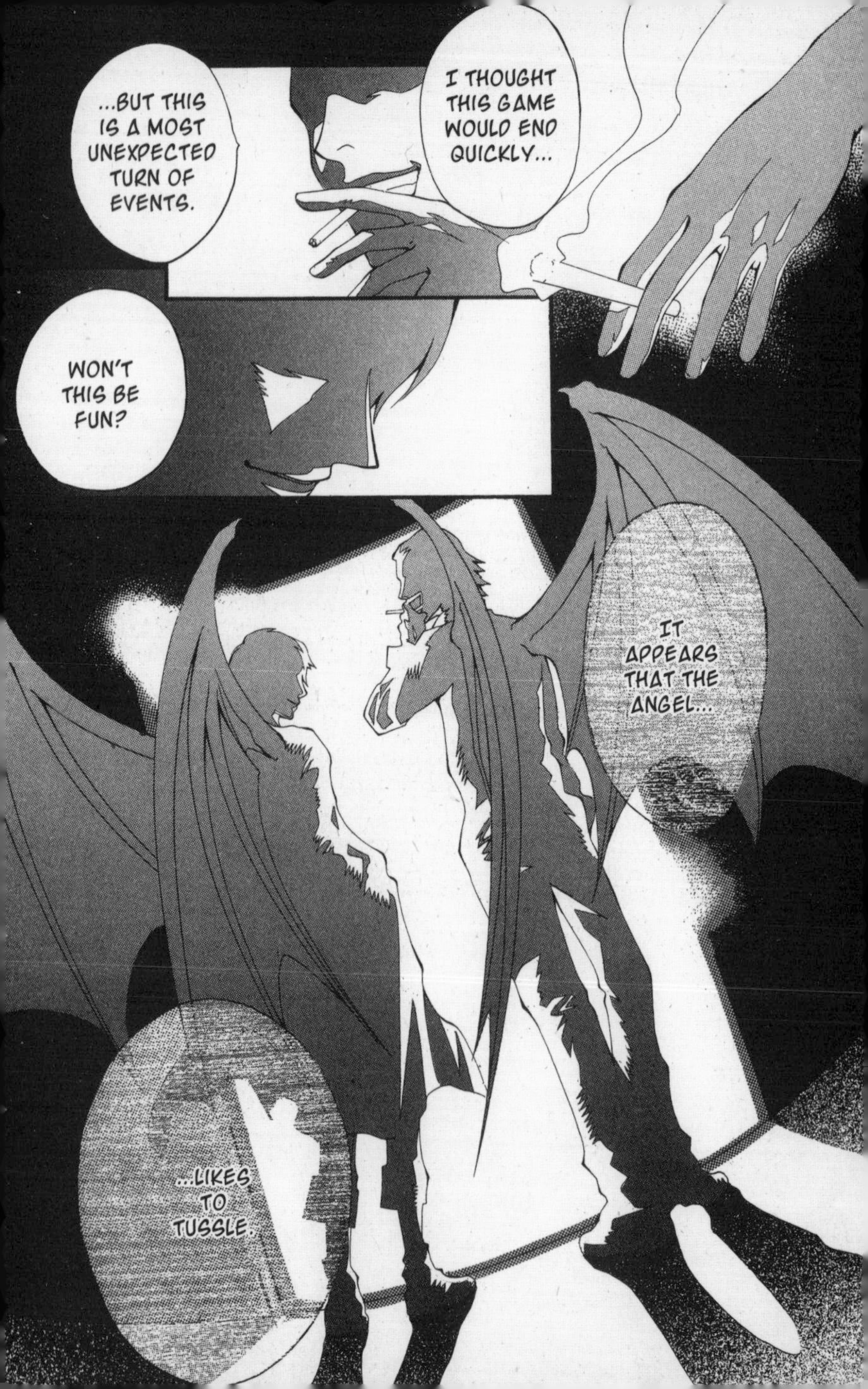
I THOUGHT THIS GAME WOULD END QUICKLY...
...BUT THIS IS A MOST UNEXPECTED TURN OF EVENTS.
WON'T THIS BE FUN?
IT APPEARS THAT THE ANGEL...
...LIKES TO TUSSLE.

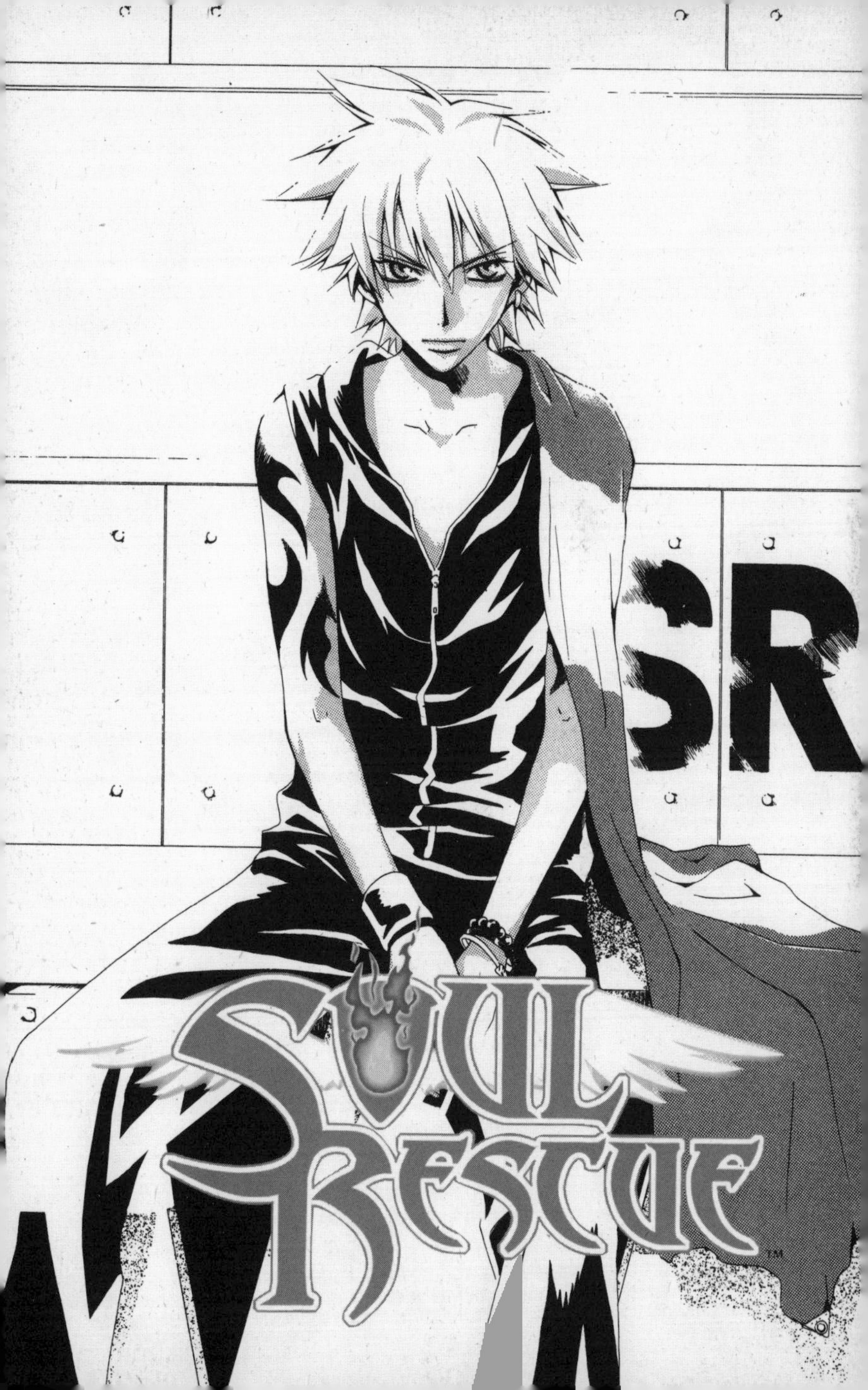
SR
Soul Rescue™

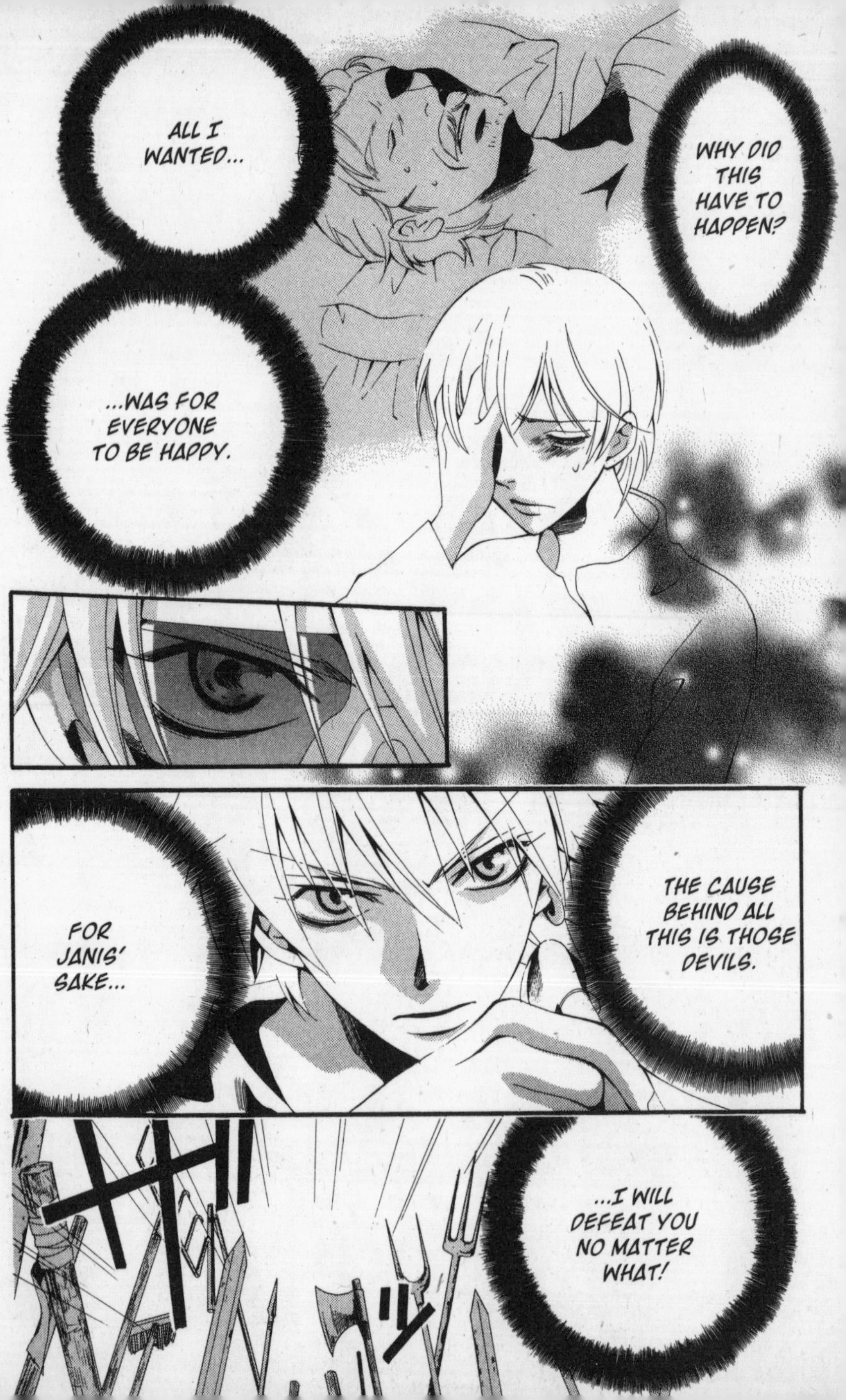
WHY DID THIS HAVE TO HAPPEN?
ALL I WANTED...
...WAS FOR EVERYONE TO BE HAPPY.
THE CAUSE BEHIND ALL THIS IS THOSE DEVILS.
FOR JANIS' SAKE...
...I WILL DEFEAT YOU NO MATTER WHAT!

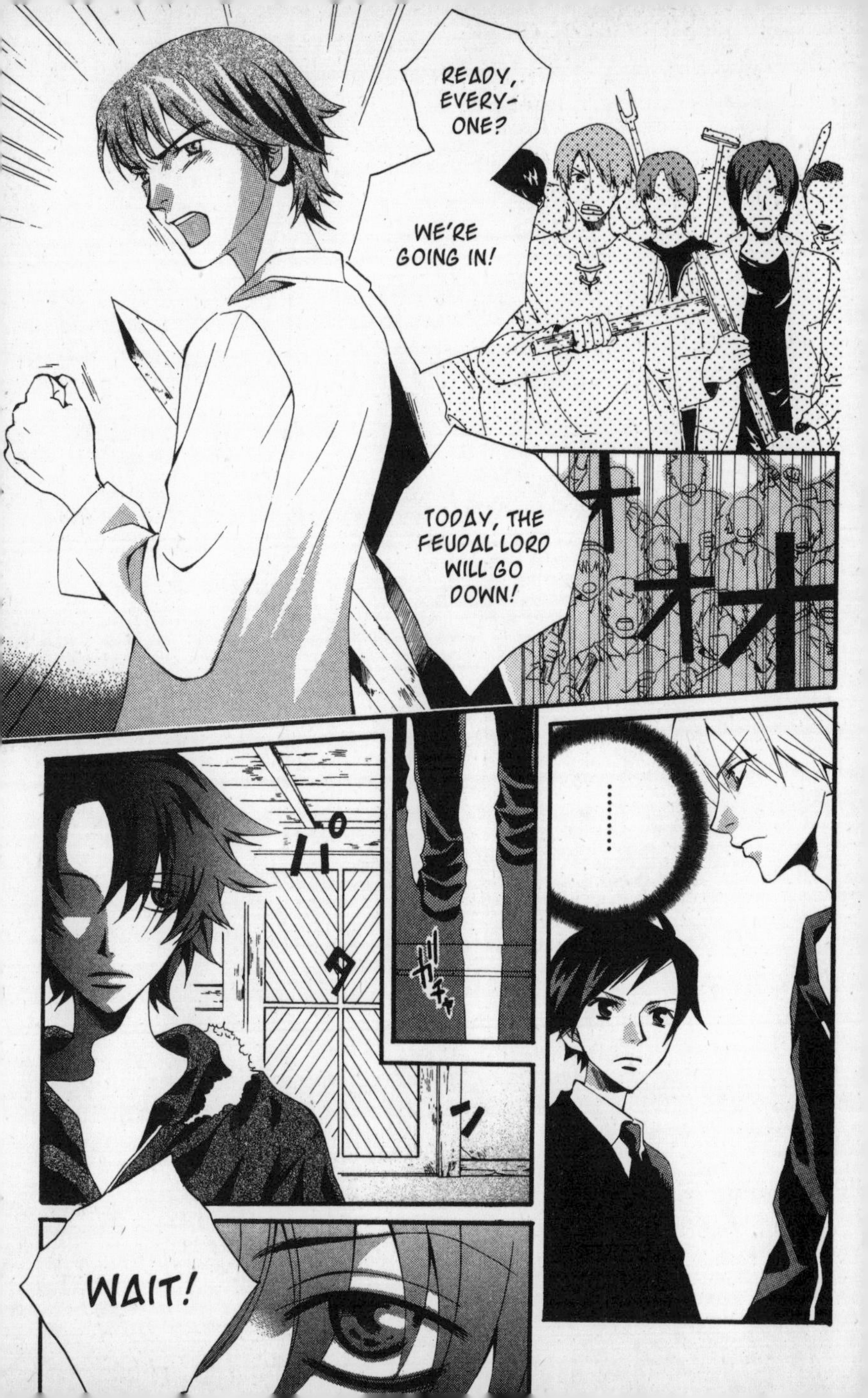
READY, EVERYONE?
WE'RE GOING IN!
オオオ
TODAY, THE FEUDAL LORD WILL GO DOWN!
……
ガチャ
パタン
WAIT!

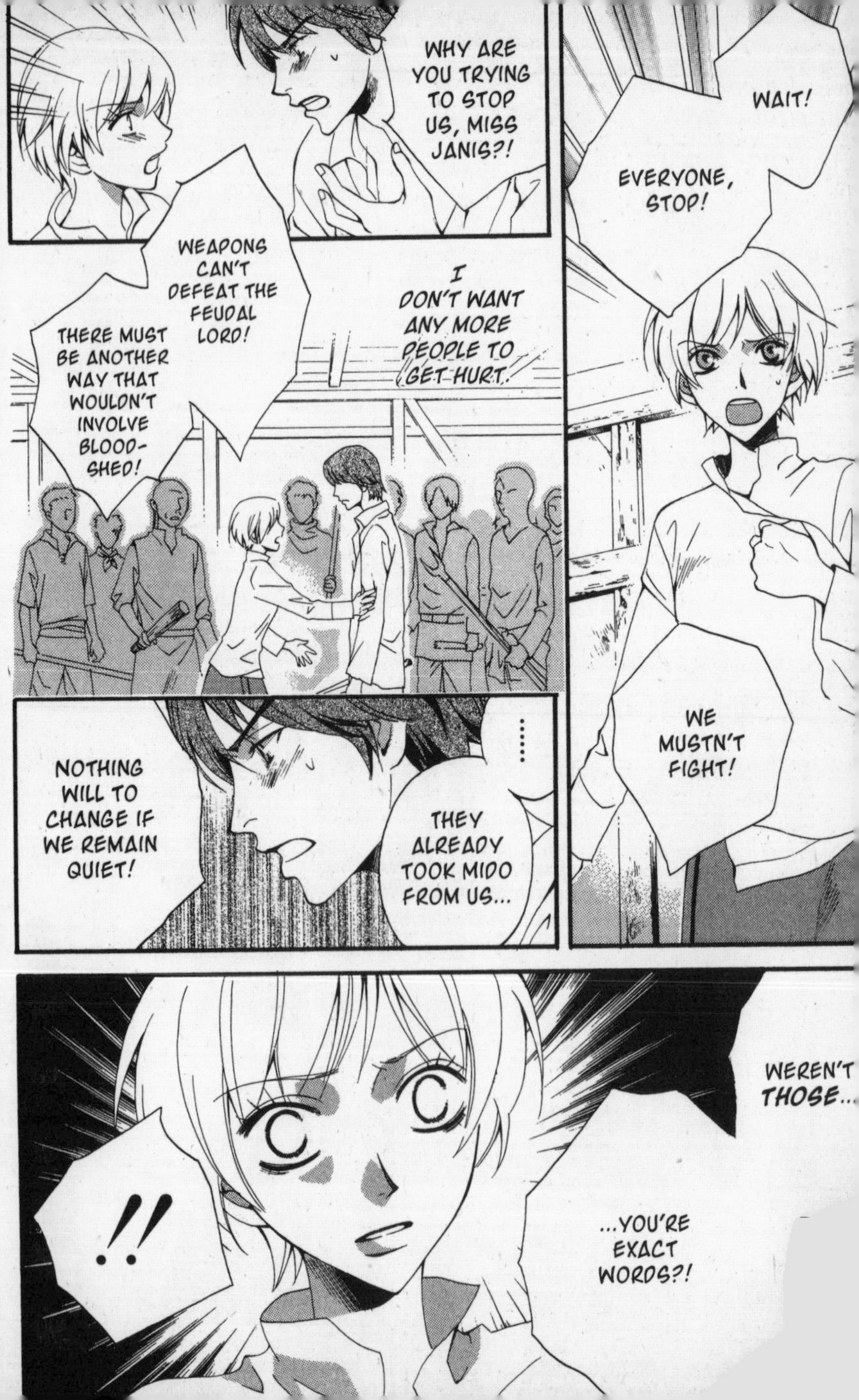
WAIT!
EVERYONE, STOP!
WE MUSTN'T FIGHT!
WHY ARE YOU TRYING TO STOP US, MISS JANIS?!
I DON'T WANT ANY MORE PEOPLE TO GET HURT.
WEAPONS CAN'T DEFEAT THE FEUDAL LORD!
THERE MUST BE ANOTHER WAY THAT WOULDN'T INVOLVE BLOOD-SHED!
......
THEY ALREADY TOOK MIDO FROM US...
NOTHING WILL TO CHANGE IF WE REMAIN QUIET!
WEREN'T THOSE...
...YOU'RE EXACT WORDS?!
!!

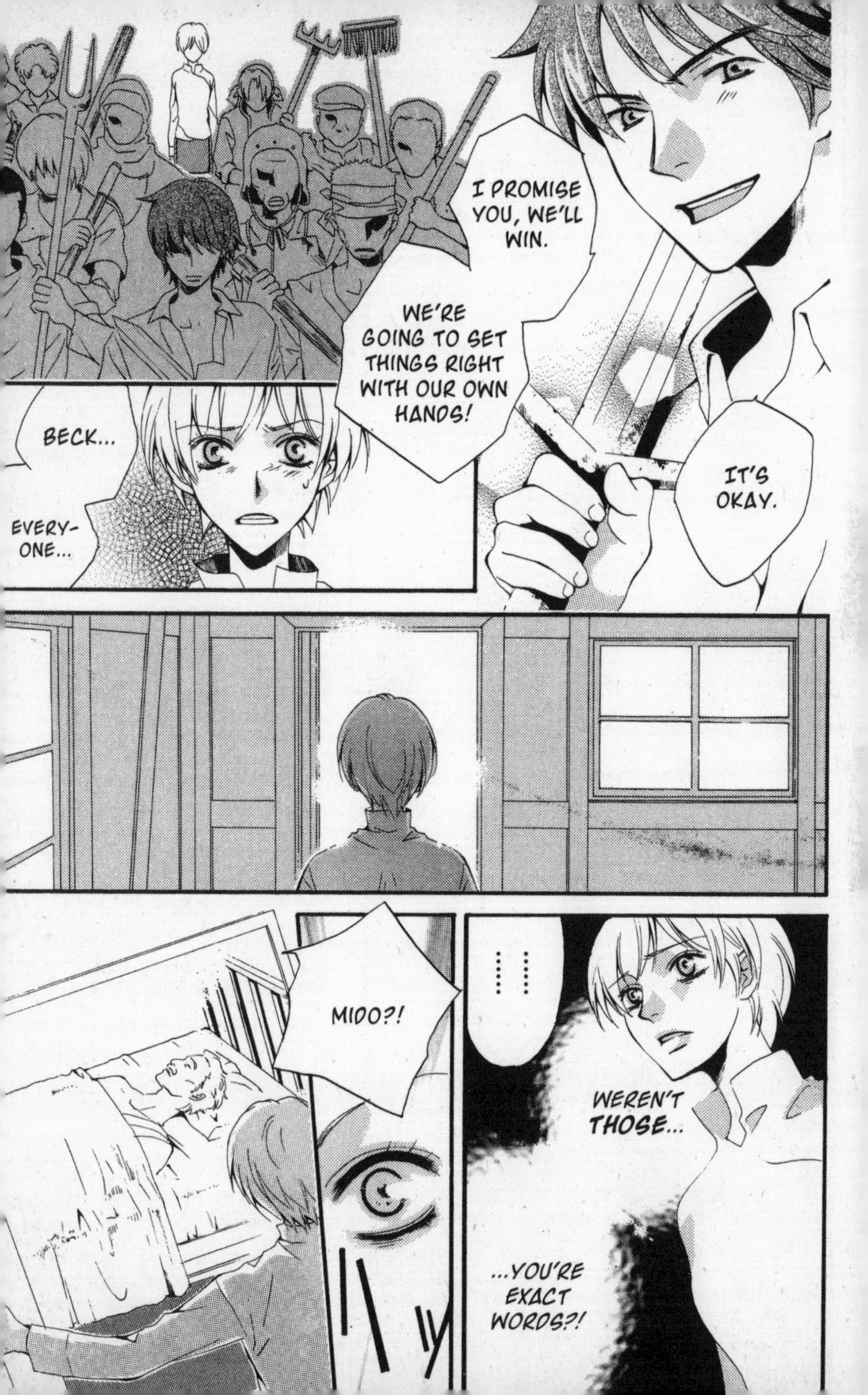

I PROMISE YOU, WE'LL WIN.
WE'RE GOING TO SET THINGS RIGHT WITH OUR OWN HANDS!
IT'S OKAY.
BECK...
EVERY-ONE...
......
WEREN'T THOSE...
...YOU'RE EXACT WORDS?!
MIDO?!

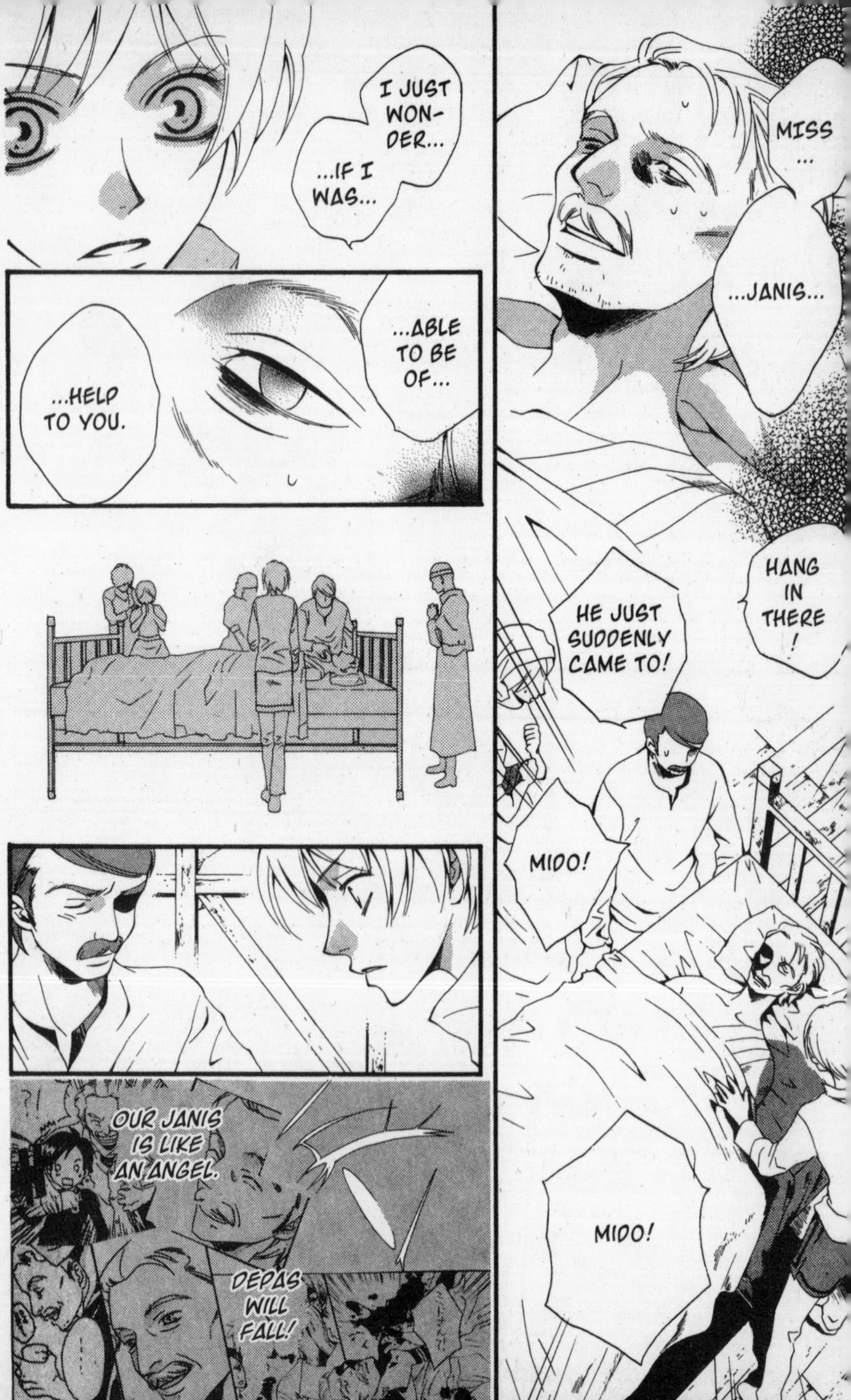
MISS...
...JANIS...
HANG IN THERE!
HE JUST SUDDENLY CAME TO!
MIDO!
MIDO!
I JUST WONDER...
...IF I WAS...
...ABLE TO BE OF...
...HELP TO YOU.
OUR JANIS IS LIKE AN ANGEL.
DEPAS WILL FALL!
?!

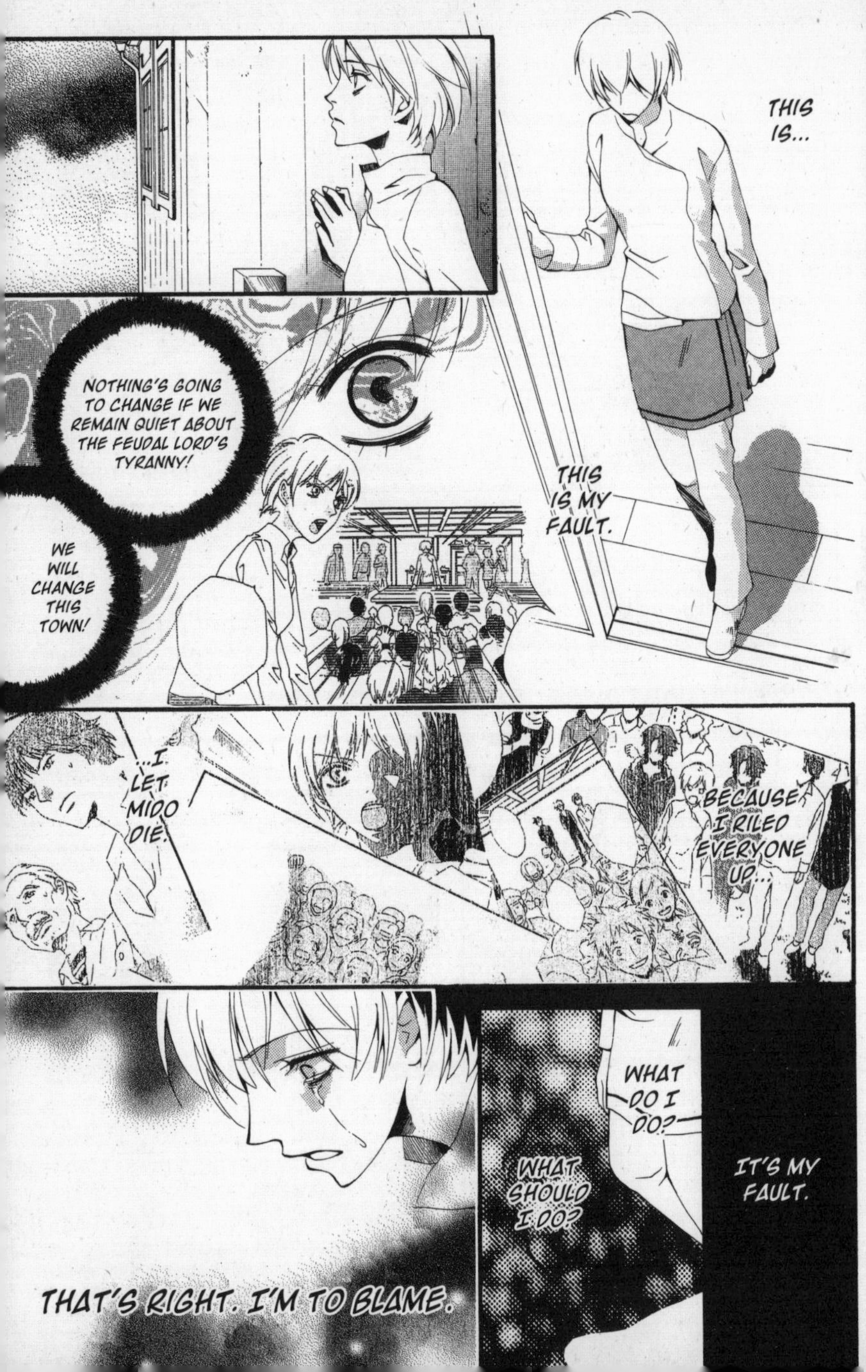
THIS IS...
THIS IS MY FAULT.
NOTHING'S GOING TO CHANGE IF WE REMAIN QUIET ABOUT THE FEUDAL LORD'S TYRANNY!
WE WILL CHANGE THIS TOWN!
BECAUSE I RILED EVERYONE UP...
...I LET MIDO DIE.
IT'S MY FAULT.
WHAT DO I DO?
WHAT SHOULD I DO?
THAT'S RIGHT. I'M TO BLAME.

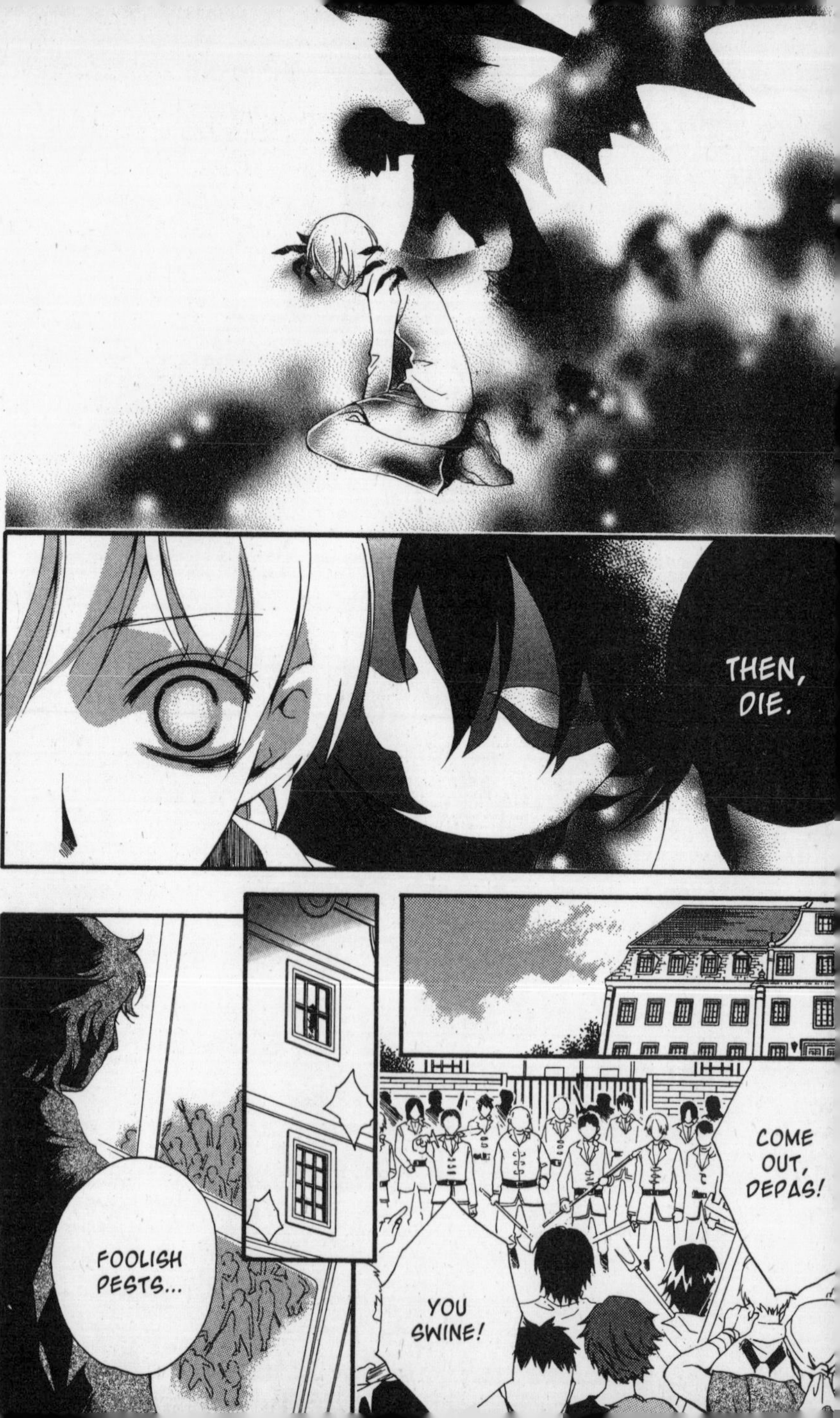
THEN, DIE.
COME OUT, DEPAS!
YOU SWINE!
FOOLISH PESTS...

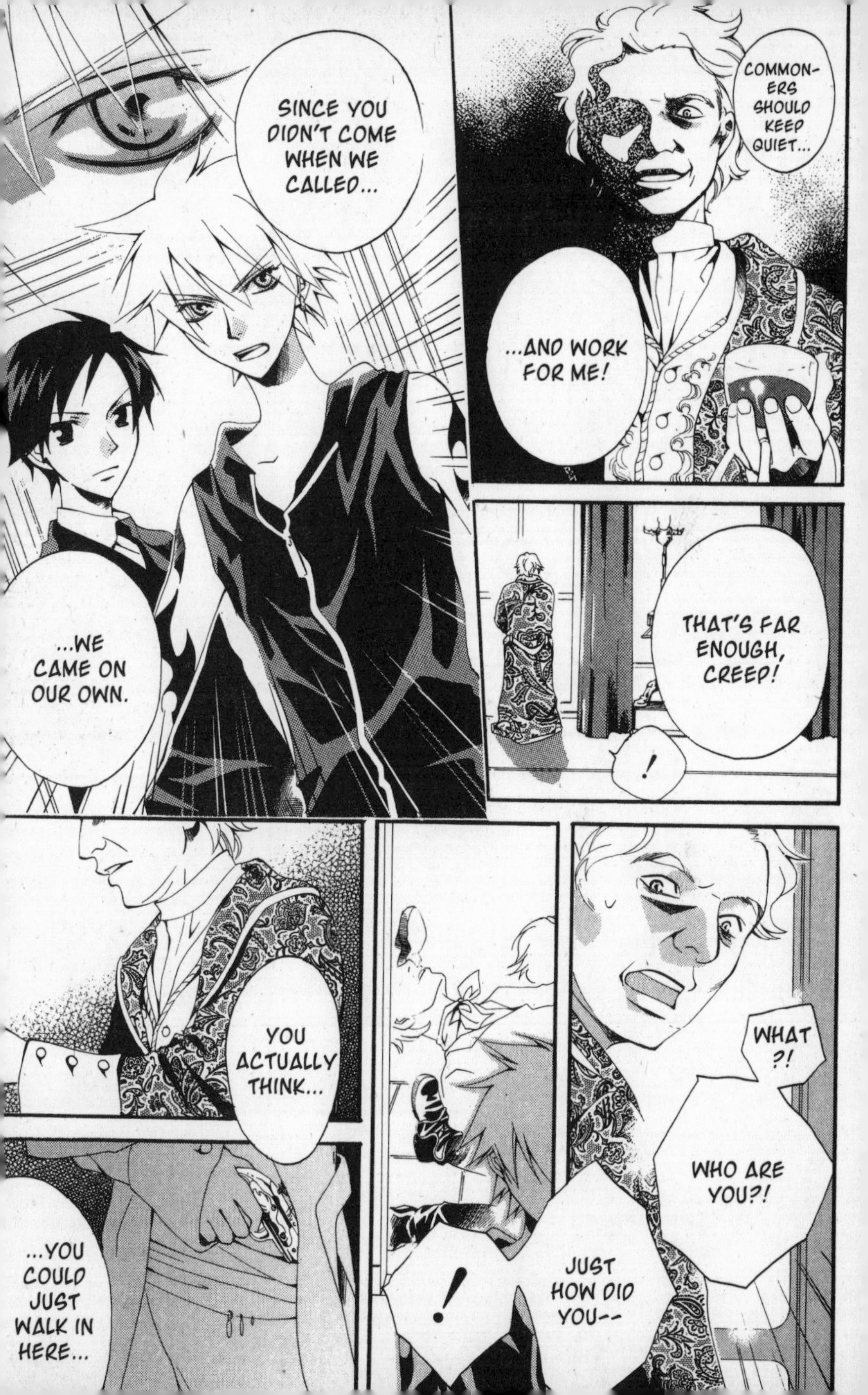
COMMONERS SHOULD KEEP QUIET...
...AND WORK FOR ME!
THAT'S FAR ENOUGH, CREEP!
!
SINCE YOU DIDN'T COME WHEN WE CALLED...
...WE CAME ON OUR OWN.
WHAT?!
WHO ARE YOU?!
JUST HOW DID YOU--
!
YOU ACTUALLY THINK...
...YOU COULD JUST WALK IN HERE...

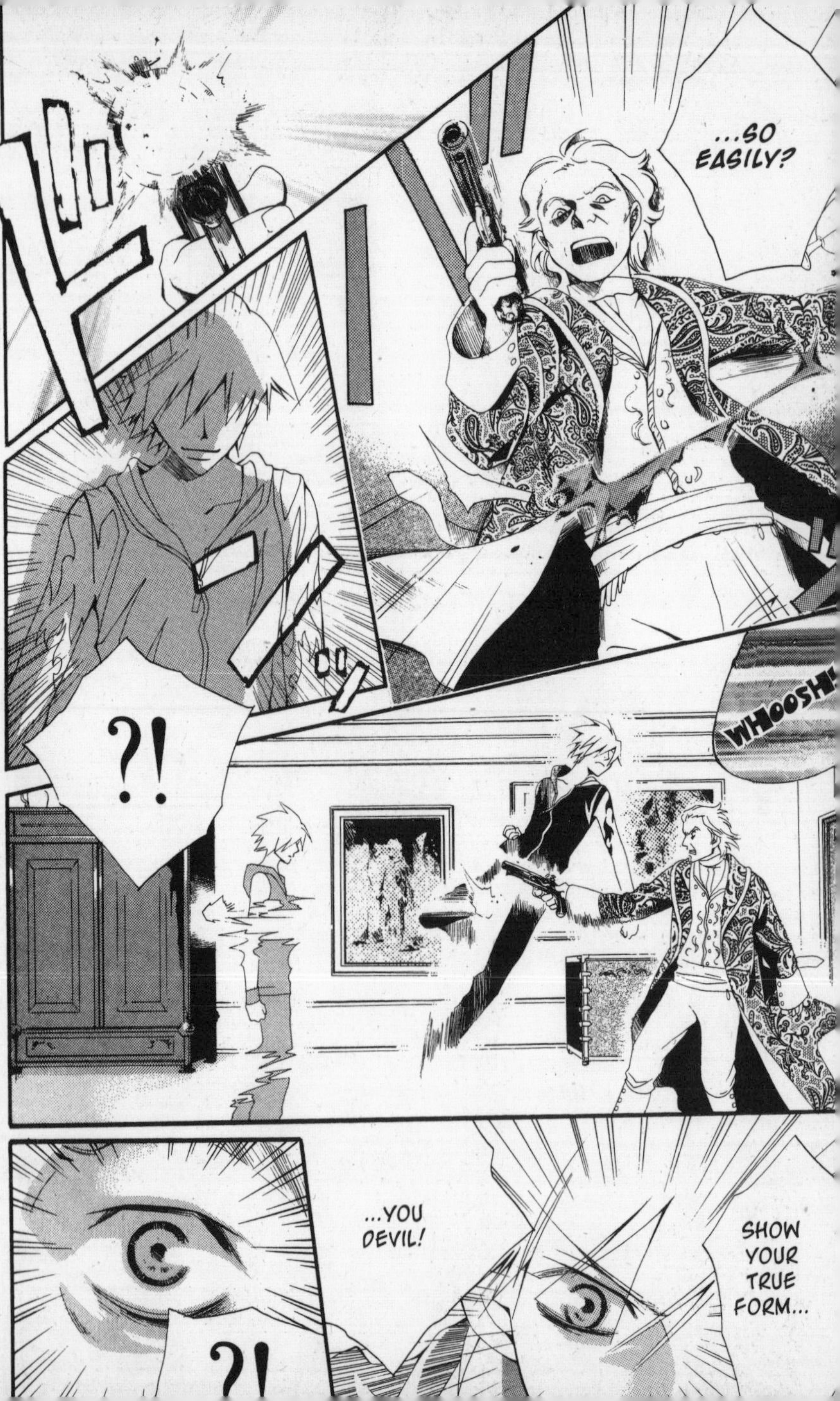
...SO EASILY?
?!
WHOOSH!
SHOW YOUR TRUE FORM...
...YOU DEVIL!
?!

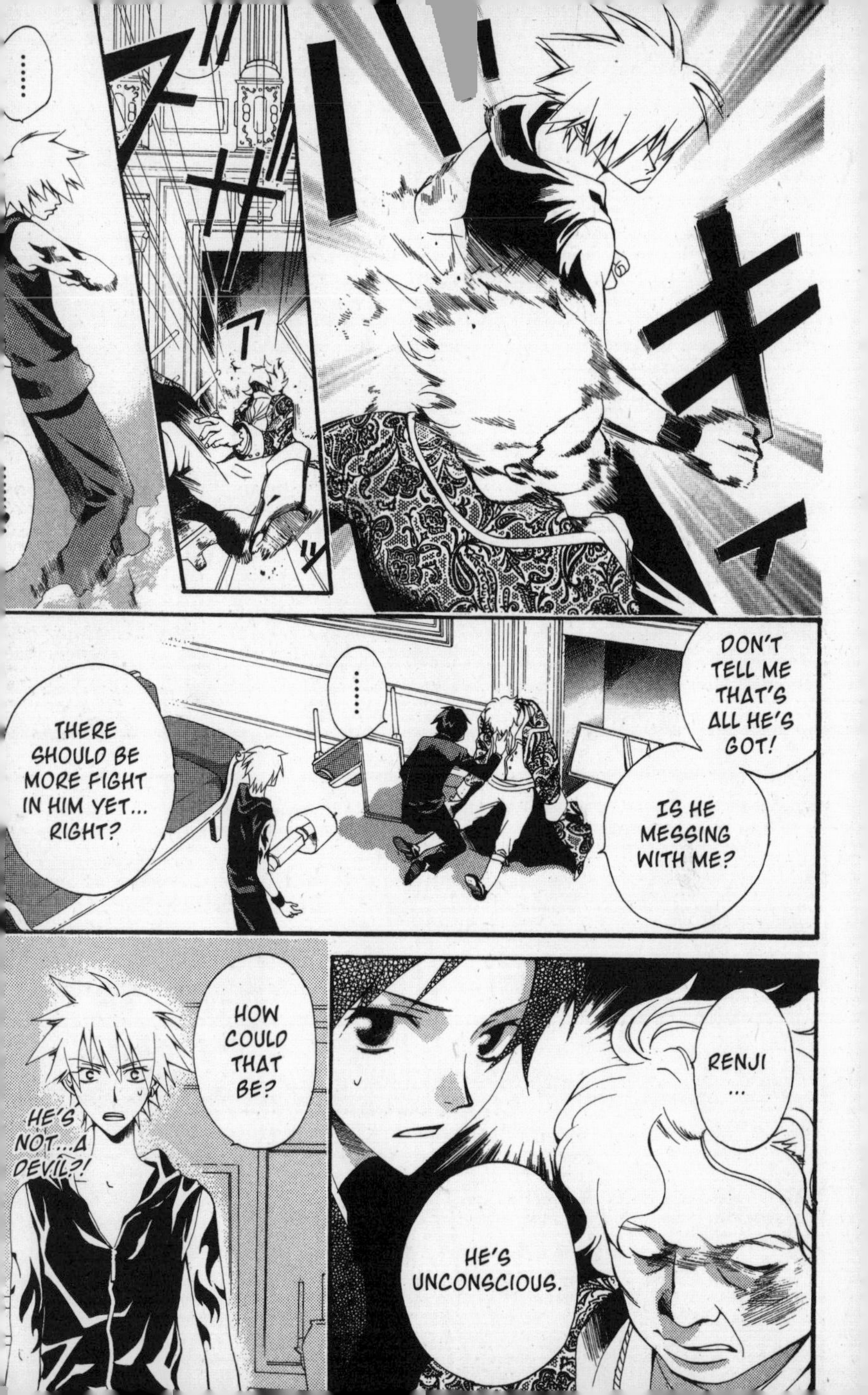

......
DON'T TELL ME THAT'S ALL HE'S GOT!
IS HE MESSING WITH ME?
......
THERE SHOULD BE MORE FIGHT IN HIM YET... RIGHT?
RENJI ...
HE'S UNCONSCIOUS.
HOW COULD THAT BE?
HE'S NOT...A DEVIL?!

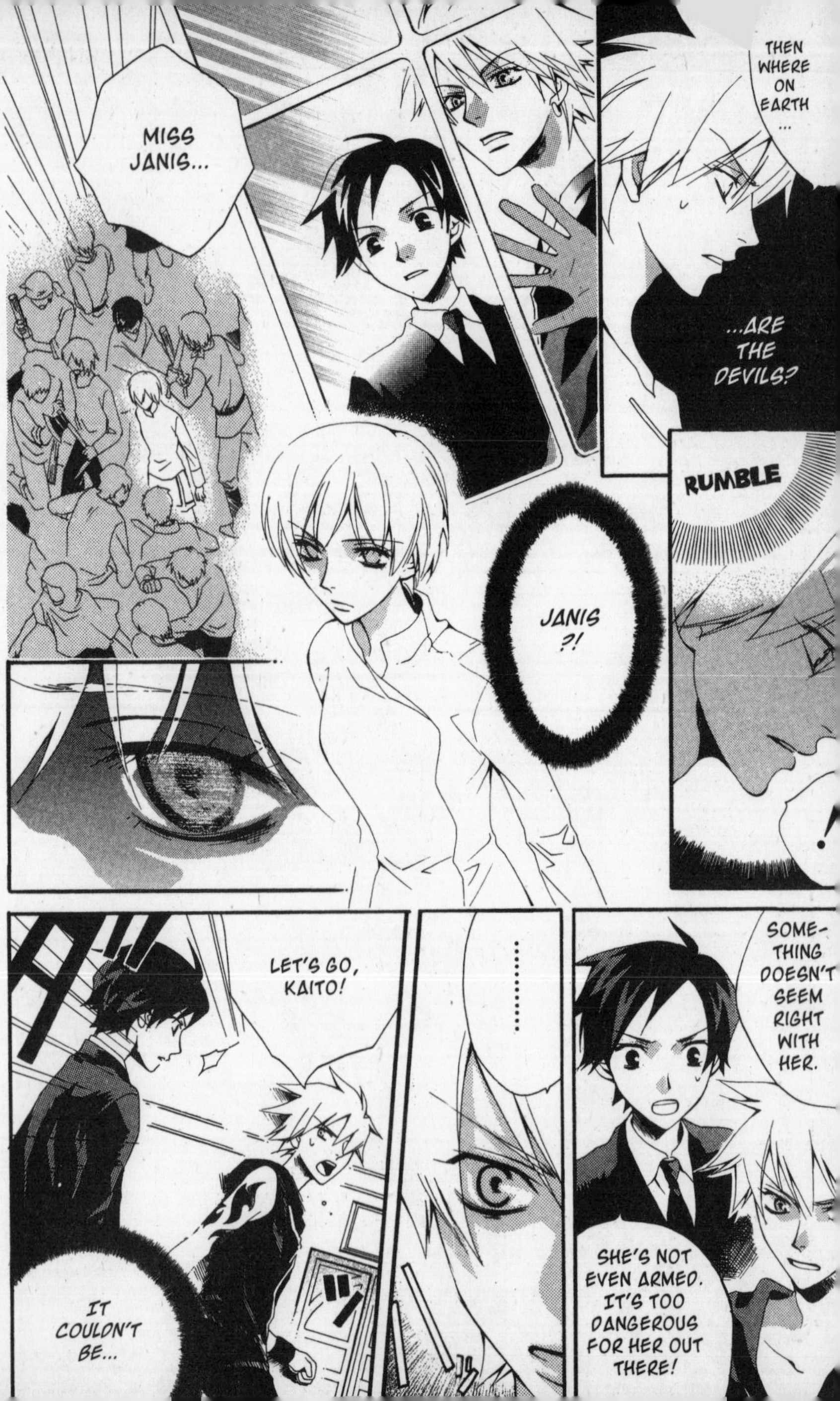
THEN WHERE ON EARTH ...
...ARE THE DEVILS?
MISS JANIS...
RUMBLE
!
JANIS ?!
SOME-THING DOESN'T SEEM RIGHT WITH HER.
SHE'S NOT EVEN ARMED. IT'S TOO DANGEROUS FOR HER OUT THERE!
....
LET'S GO, KAITO!
IT COULDN'T BE...

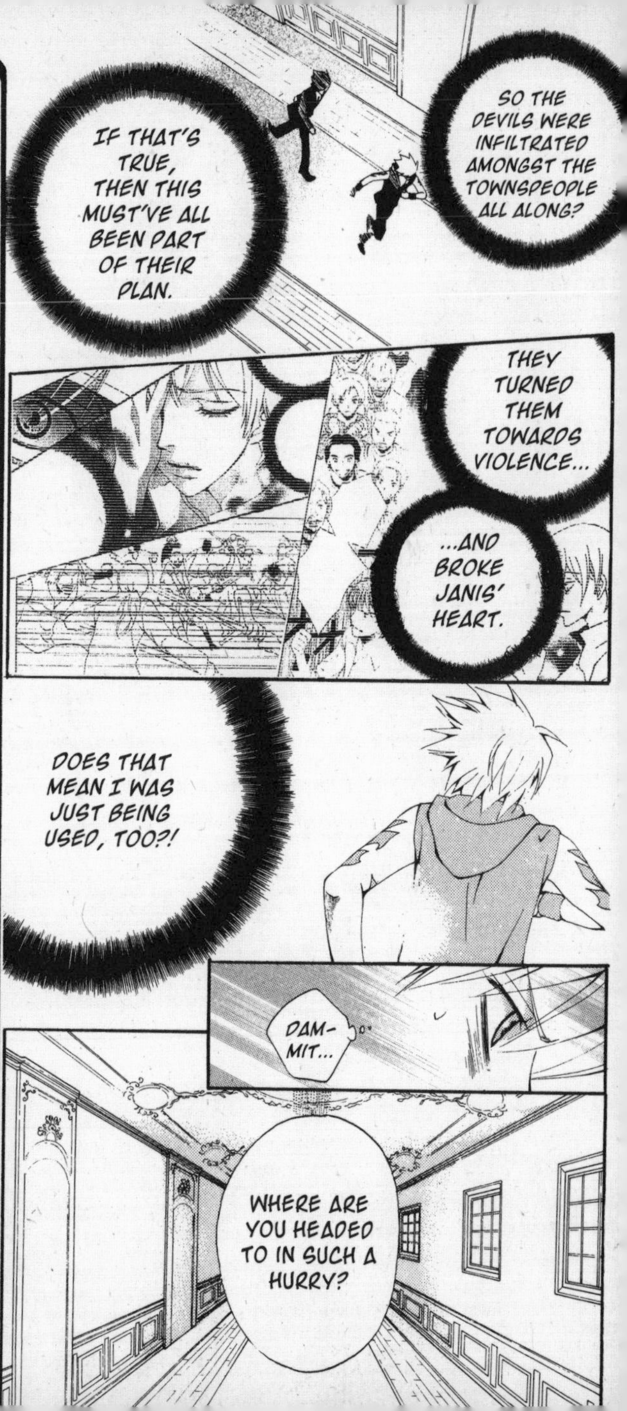
SO THE DEVILS WERE INFILTRATED AMONGST THE TOWNSPEOPLE ALL ALONG?
IF THAT'S TRUE, THEN THIS MUST'VE ALL BEEN PART OF THEIR PLAN.
THEY TURNED THEM TOWARDS VIOLENCE...
...AND BROKE JANIS' HEART.
DOES THAT MEAN I WAS JUST BEING USED, TOO?!
DAM-MIT...
WHERE ARE YOU HEADED TO IN SUCH A HURRY?

SR

Sorry that my words have to be so small! This manga has so many panels and they're all so packed together. I really appreciate you squinting your eyes to read this trivial talk! Keep up the good work! There's just one commentary left.

And uh...oh, if you could, I would love to receive letters of your impressions.

TOKYOPOP
5900 Wilshire Blvd.
#2000
Los Angeles CA.
90036

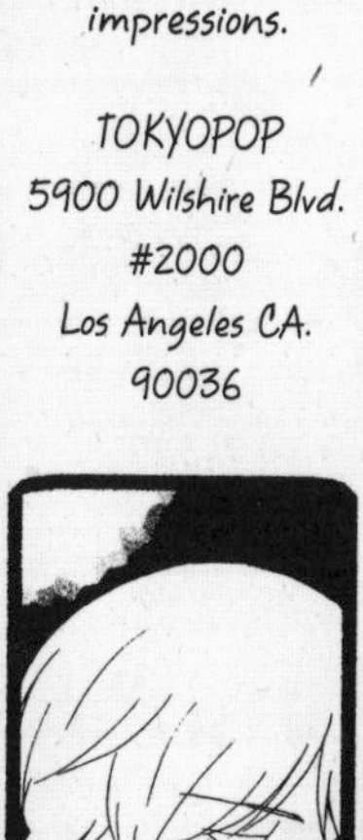

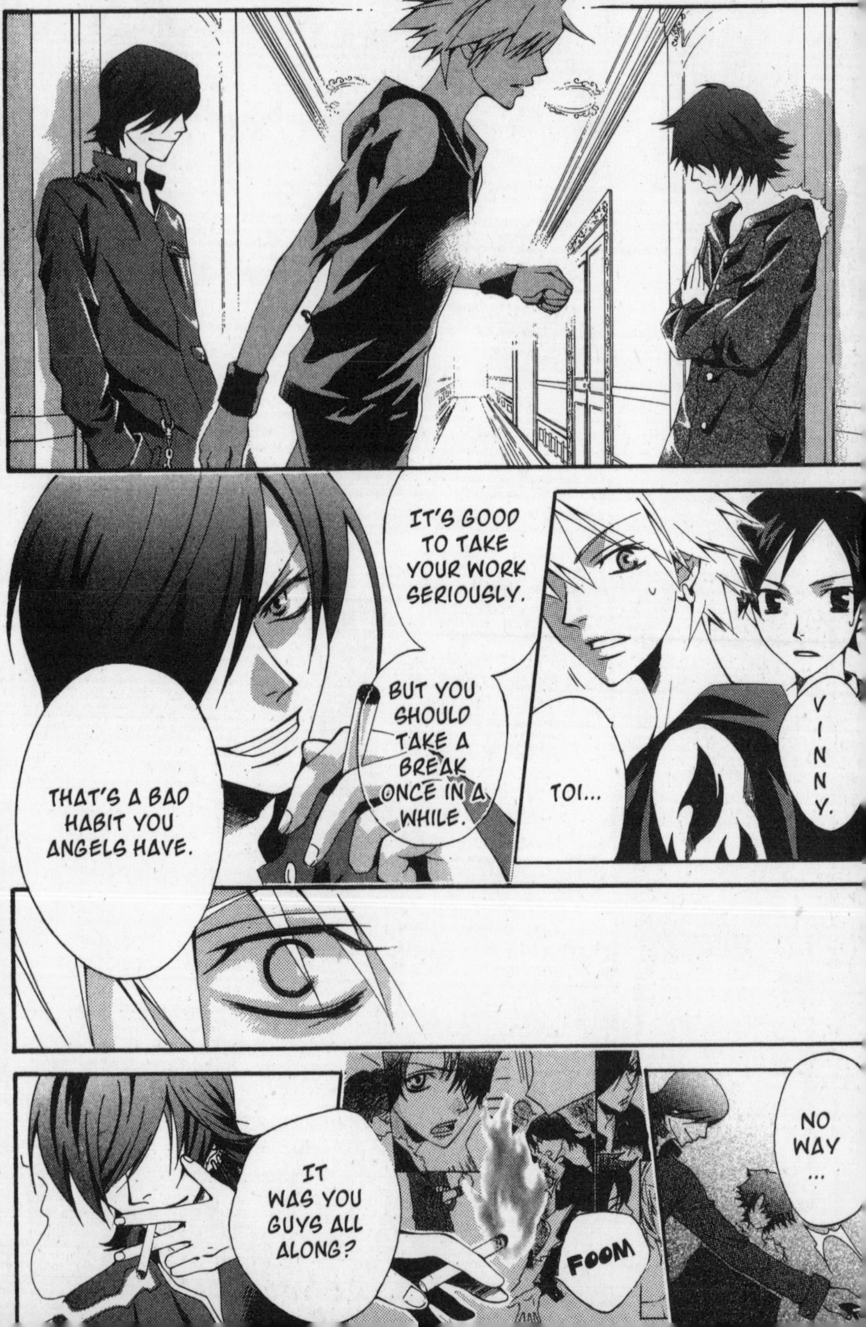
VINNY.
TOI...
IT'S GOOD TO TAKE YOUR WORK SERIOUSLY.
BUT YOU SHOULD TAKE A BREAK ONCE IN A WHILE.
THAT'S A BAD HABIT YOU ANGELS HAVE.
NO WAY ...
FOOM
IT WAS YOU GUYS ALL ALONG?

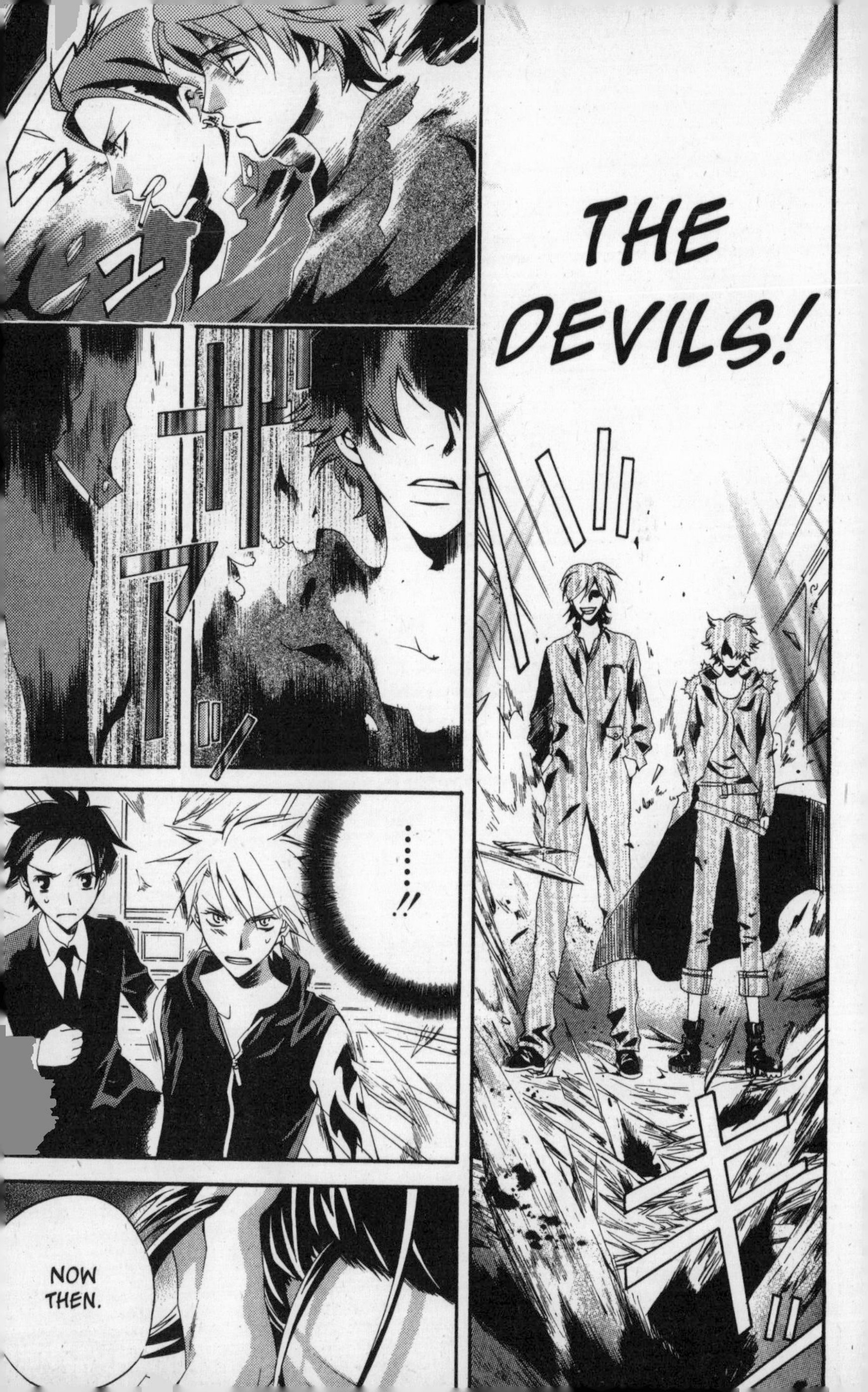
THE DEVILS!
......!!
NOW THEN.

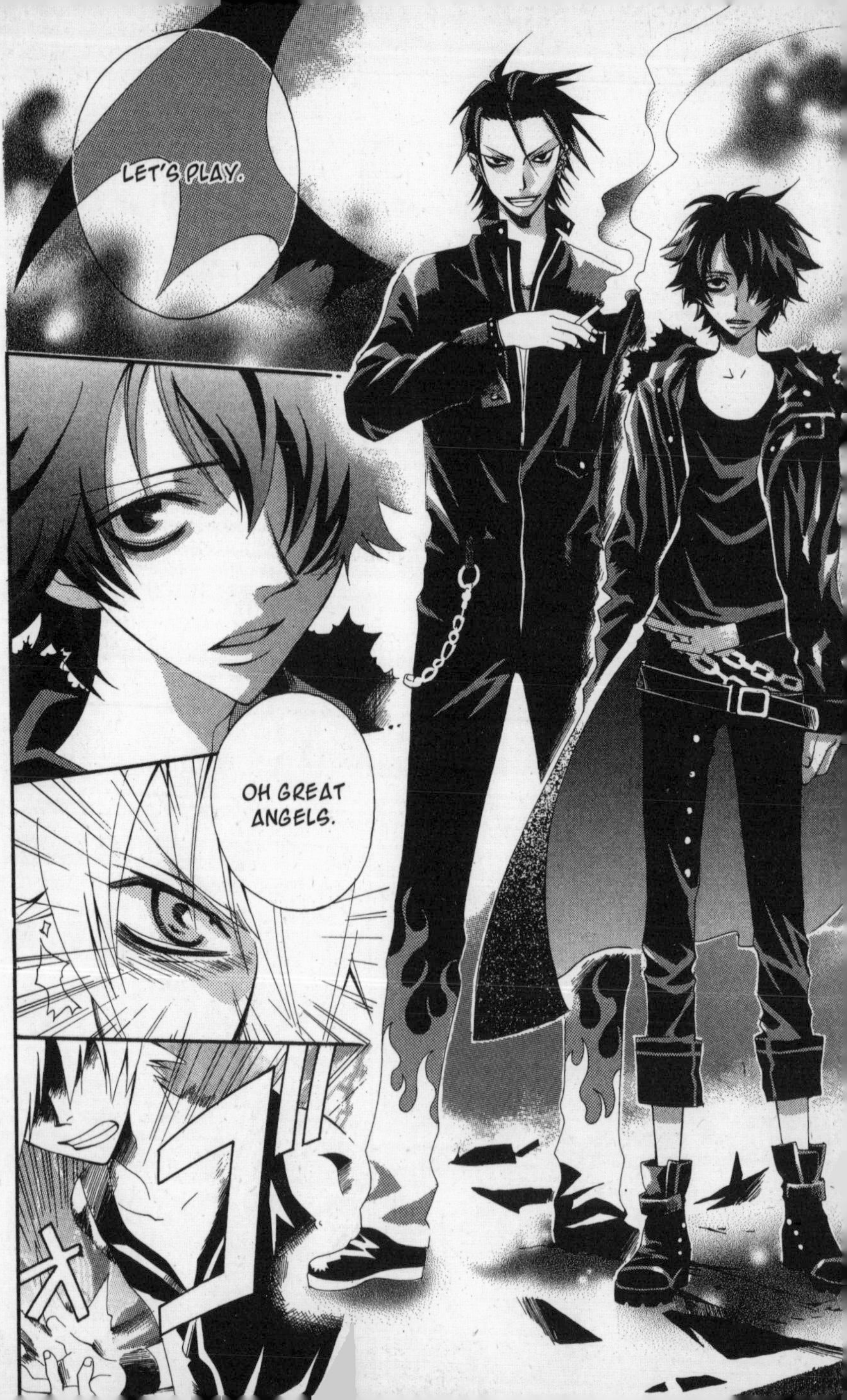
LET'S PLAY.
OH GREAT ANGELS.

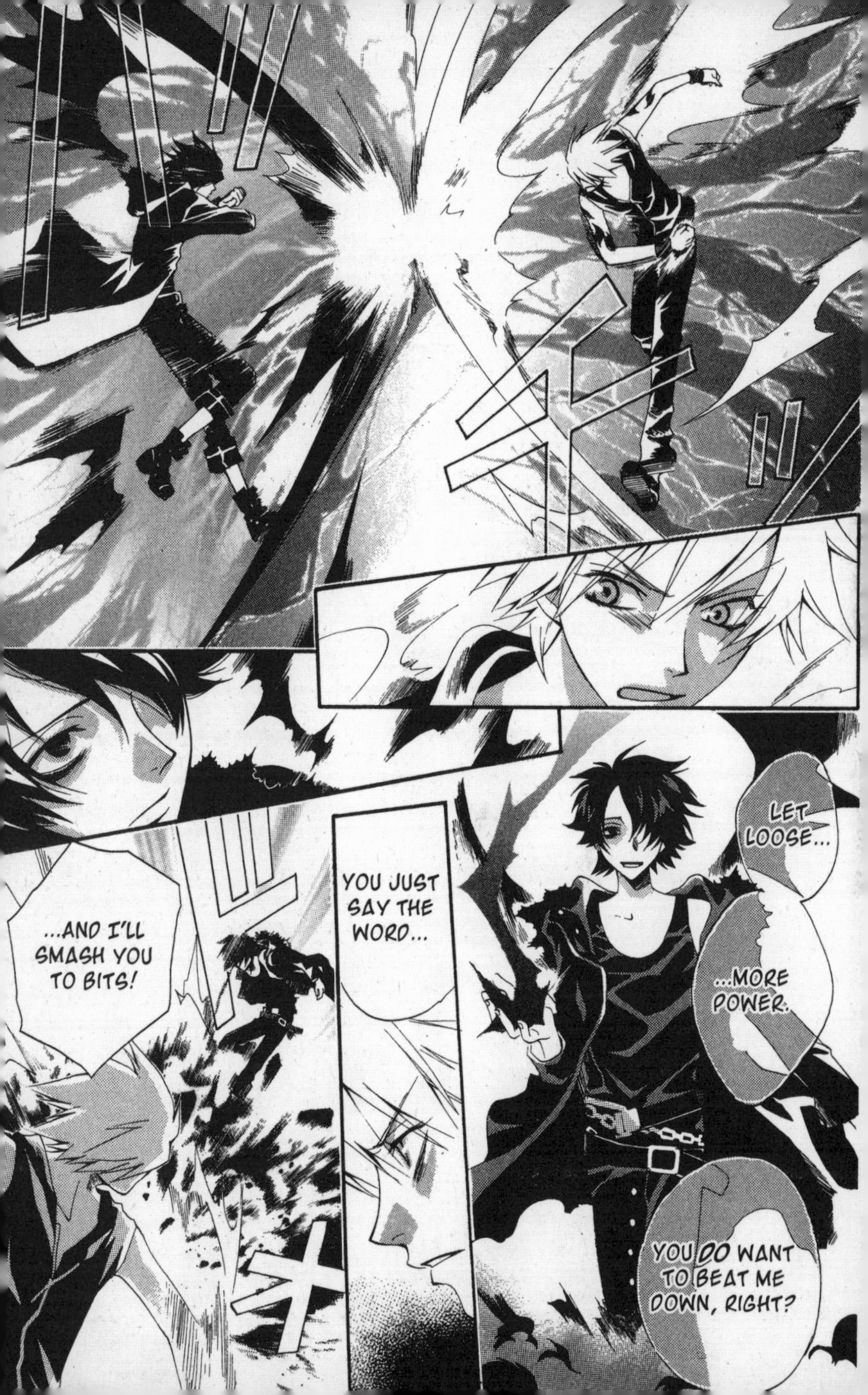
LET LOOSE...
...MORE POWER.
YOU DO WANT TO BEAT ME DOWN, RIGHT?
YOU JUST SAY THE WORD...
...AND I'LL SMASH YOU TO BITS!

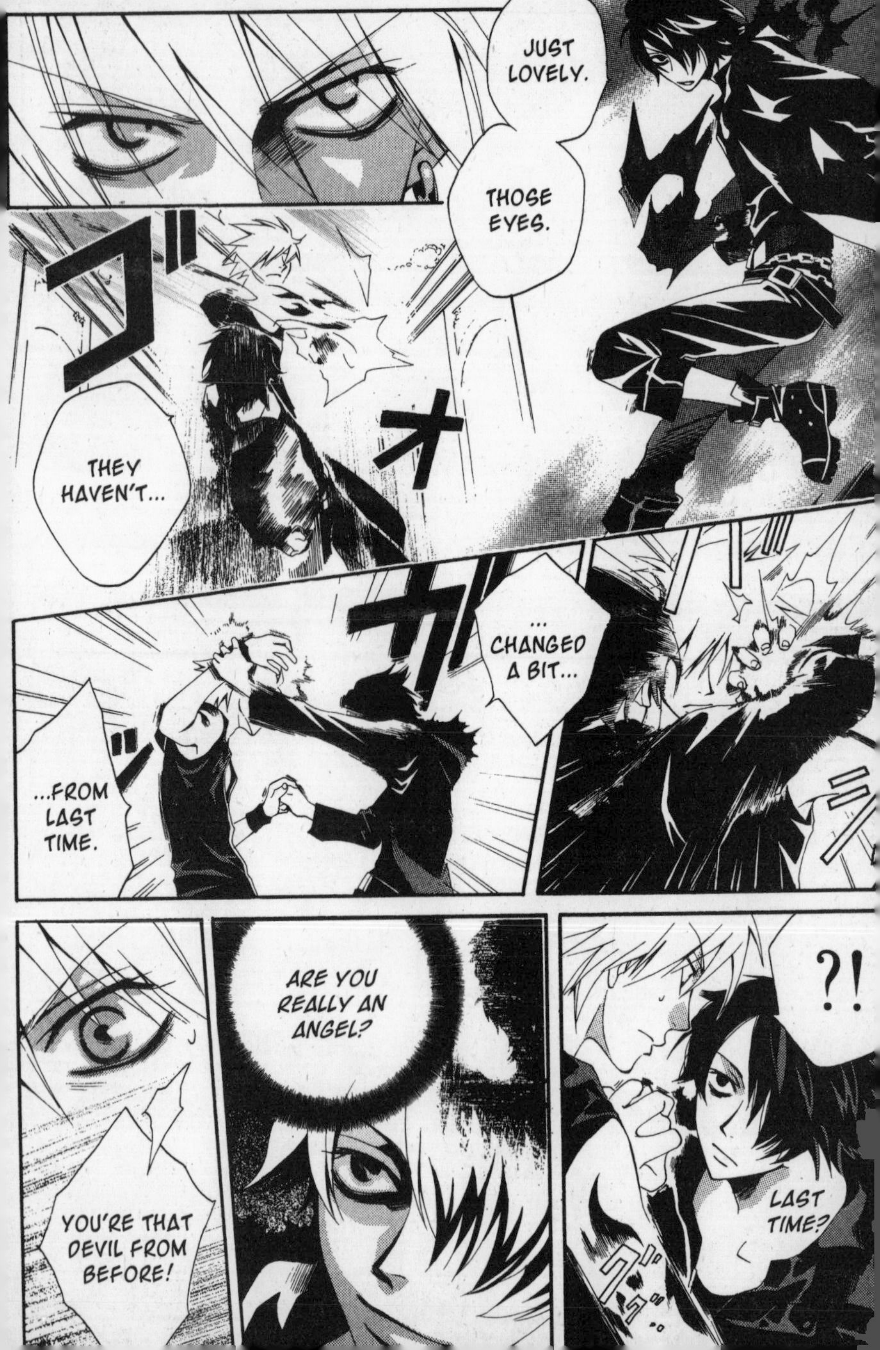
JUST LOVELY.
THOSE EYES.
THEY HAVEN'T...
...CHANGED A BIT...
...FROM LAST TIME.
?!
LAST TIME?
ARE YOU REALLY AN ANGEL?
YOU'RE THAT DEVIL FROM BEFORE!

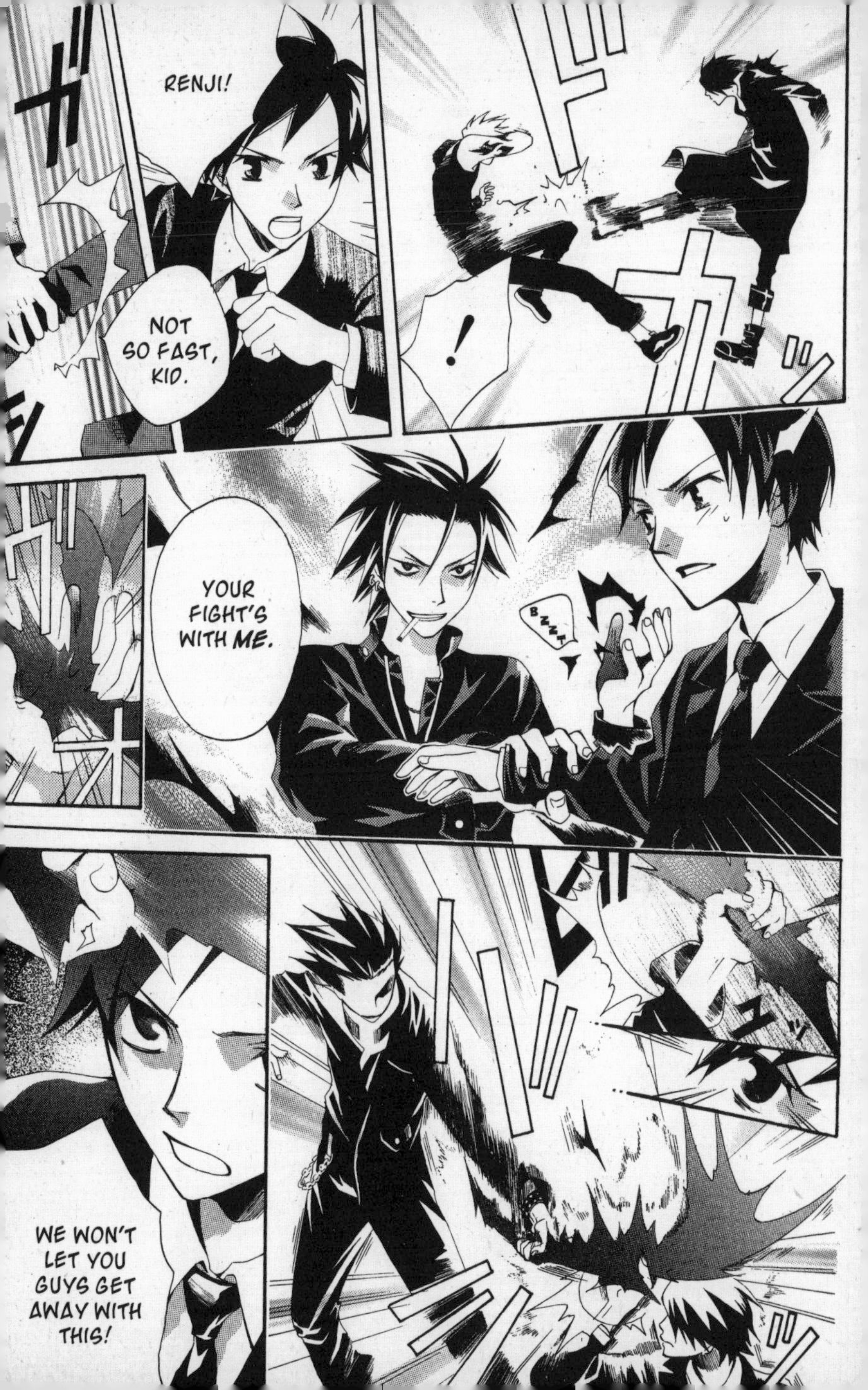
!
RENJI!
NOT SO FAST, KID.
YOUR FIGHT'S WITH ME.
BZZT
WE WON'T LET YOU GUYS GET AWAY WITH THIS!

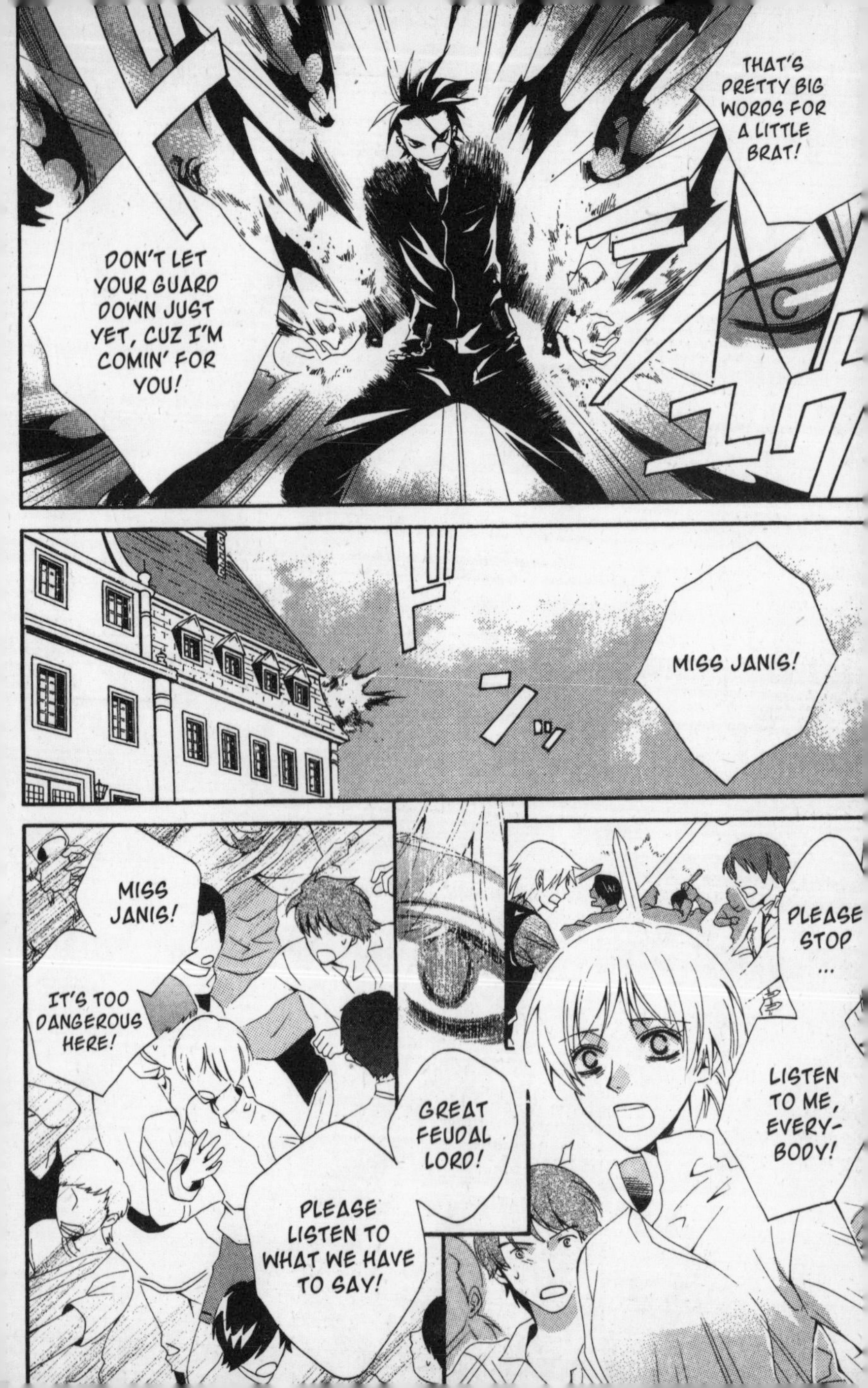
THAT'S PRETTY BIG WORDS FOR A LITTLE BRAT!
DON'T LET YOUR GUARD DOWN JUST YET, CUZ I'M COMIN' FOR YOU!
MISS JANIS!
PLEASE STOP ...
LISTEN TO ME, EVERY-BODY!
MISS JANIS!
IT'S TOO DANGEROUS HERE!
GREAT FEUDAL LORD!
PLEASE LISTEN TO WHAT WE HAVE TO SAY!

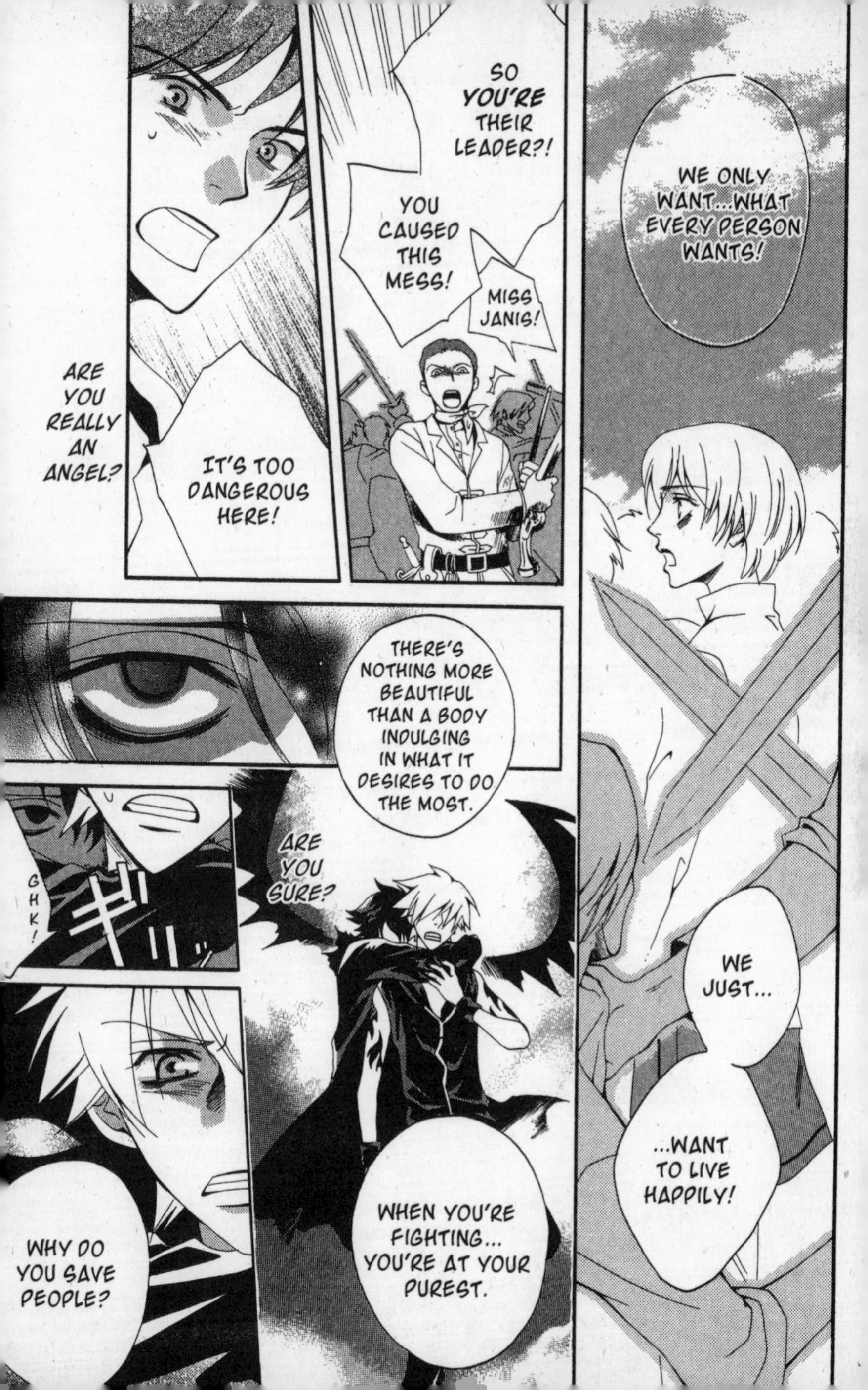
WE ONLY WANT...WHAT EVERY PERSON WANTS!
WE JUST...
...WANT TO LIVE HAPPILY!
SO *YOU'RE* THEIR LEADER?!
YOU CAUSED THIS MESS!
MISS JANIS!
IT'S TOO DANGEROUS HERE!
ARE YOU REALLY AN ANGEL?
THERE'S NOTHING MORE BEAUTIFUL THAN A BODY INDULGING IN WHAT IT DESIRES TO DO THE MOST.
ARE YOU SURE?
GHK!
WHEN YOU'RE FIGHTING... YOU'RE AT YOUR PUREST.
WHY DO YOU SAVE PEOPLE?

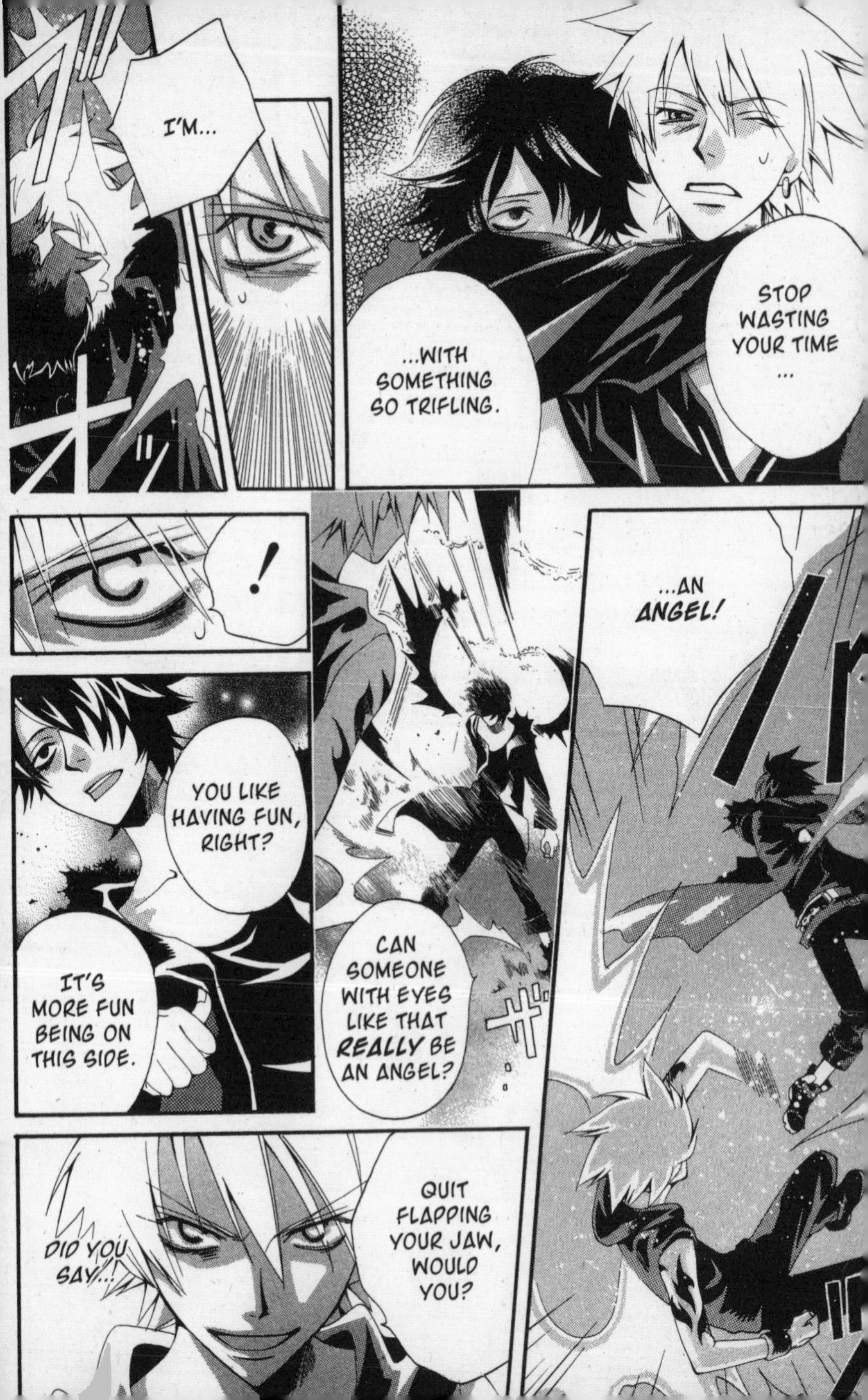
STOP WASTING YOUR TIME ...
...WITH SOMETHING SO TRIFLING.
I'M...
...AN ANGEL!
CAN SOMEONE WITH EYES LIKE THAT REALLY BE AN ANGEL?
!
YOU LIKE HAVING FUN, RIGHT?
IT'S MORE FUN BEING ON THIS SIDE.
QUIT FLAPPING YOUR JAW, WOULD YOU?
DID YOU SAY...!

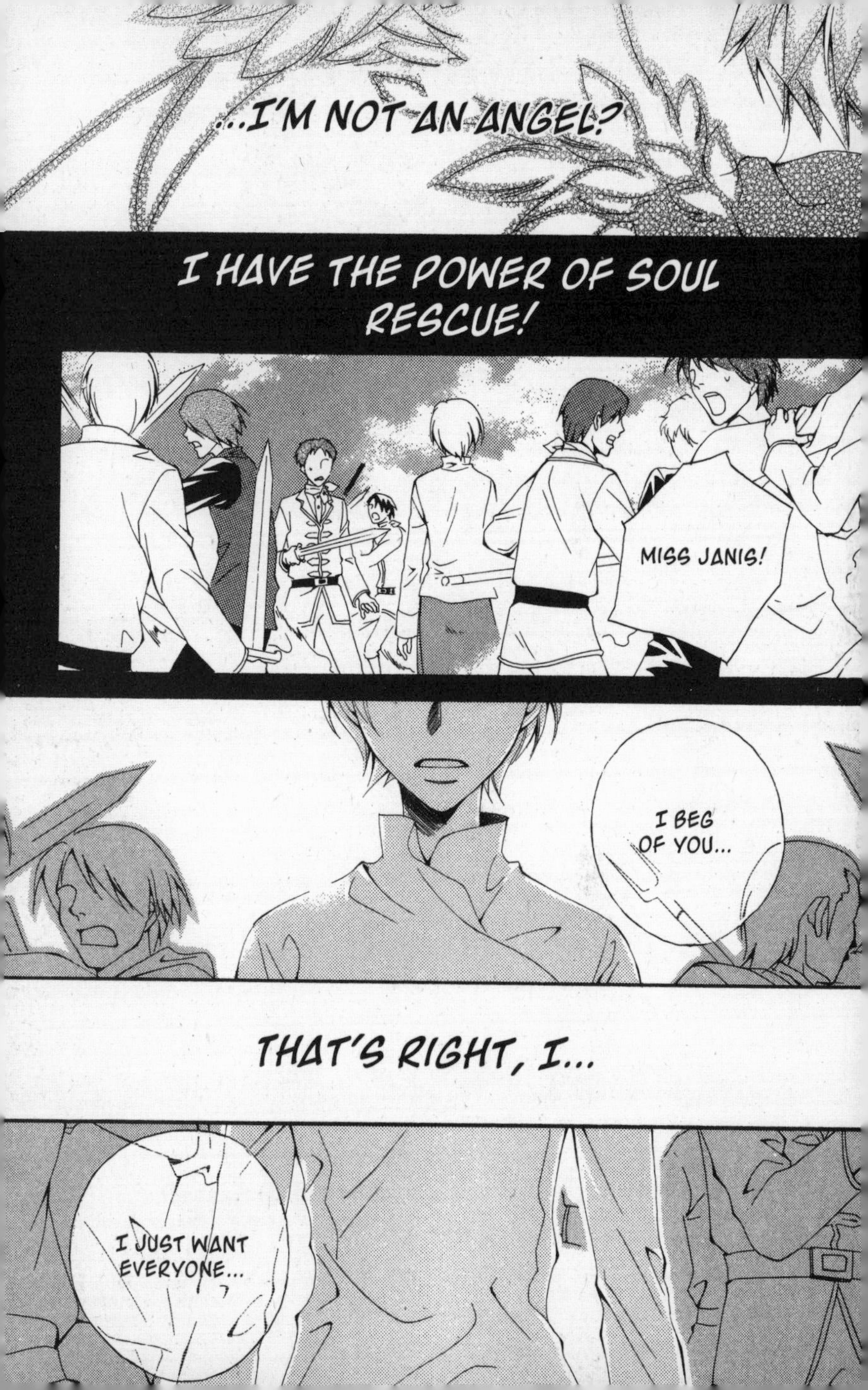
...I'M NOT AN ANGEL?
I HAVE THE POWER OF SOUL RESCUE!
MISS JANIS!
I BEG OF YOU...
THAT'S RIGHT, I...
I JUST WANT EVERYONE...

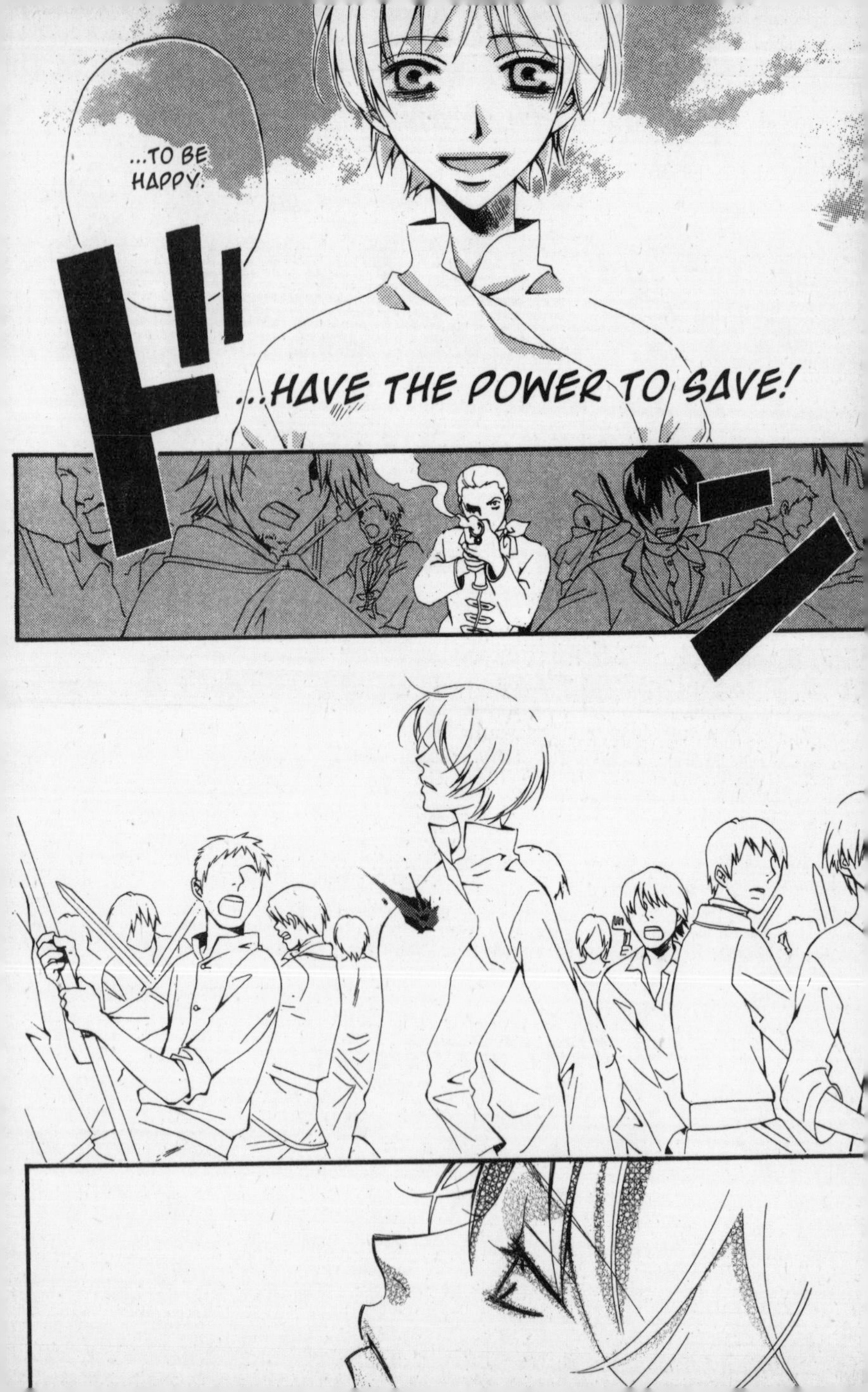
...TO BE HAPPY.
...HAVE THE POWER TO SAVE!

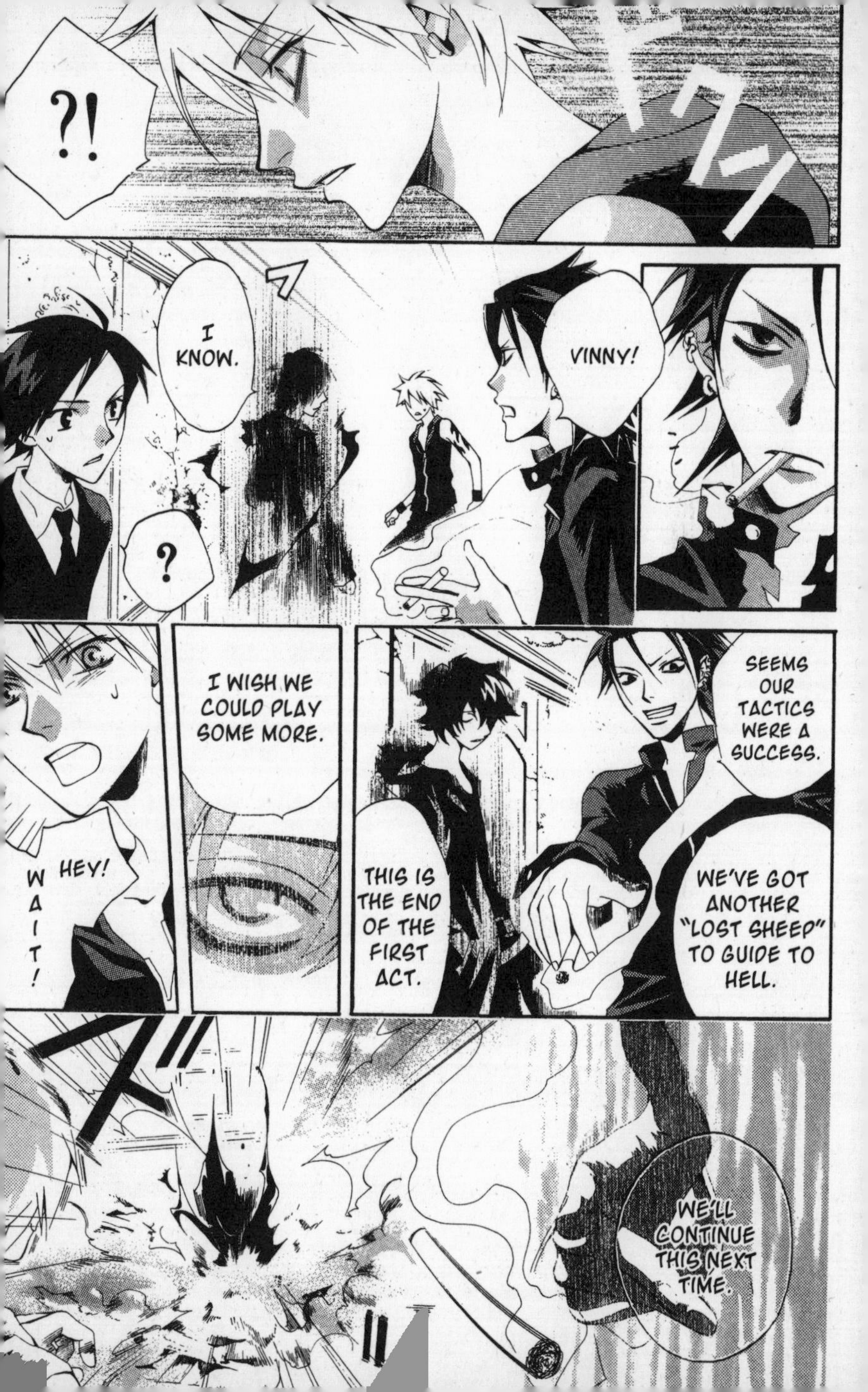
?!
VINNY!
I KNOW.
?
SEEMS OUR TACTICS WERE A SUCCESS.
WE'VE GOT ANOTHER "LOST SHEEP" TO GUIDE TO HELL.
THIS IS THE END OF THE FIRST ACT.
I WISH WE COULD PLAY SOME MORE.
WAIT!
HEY!
WE'LL CONTINUE THIS NEXT TIME.

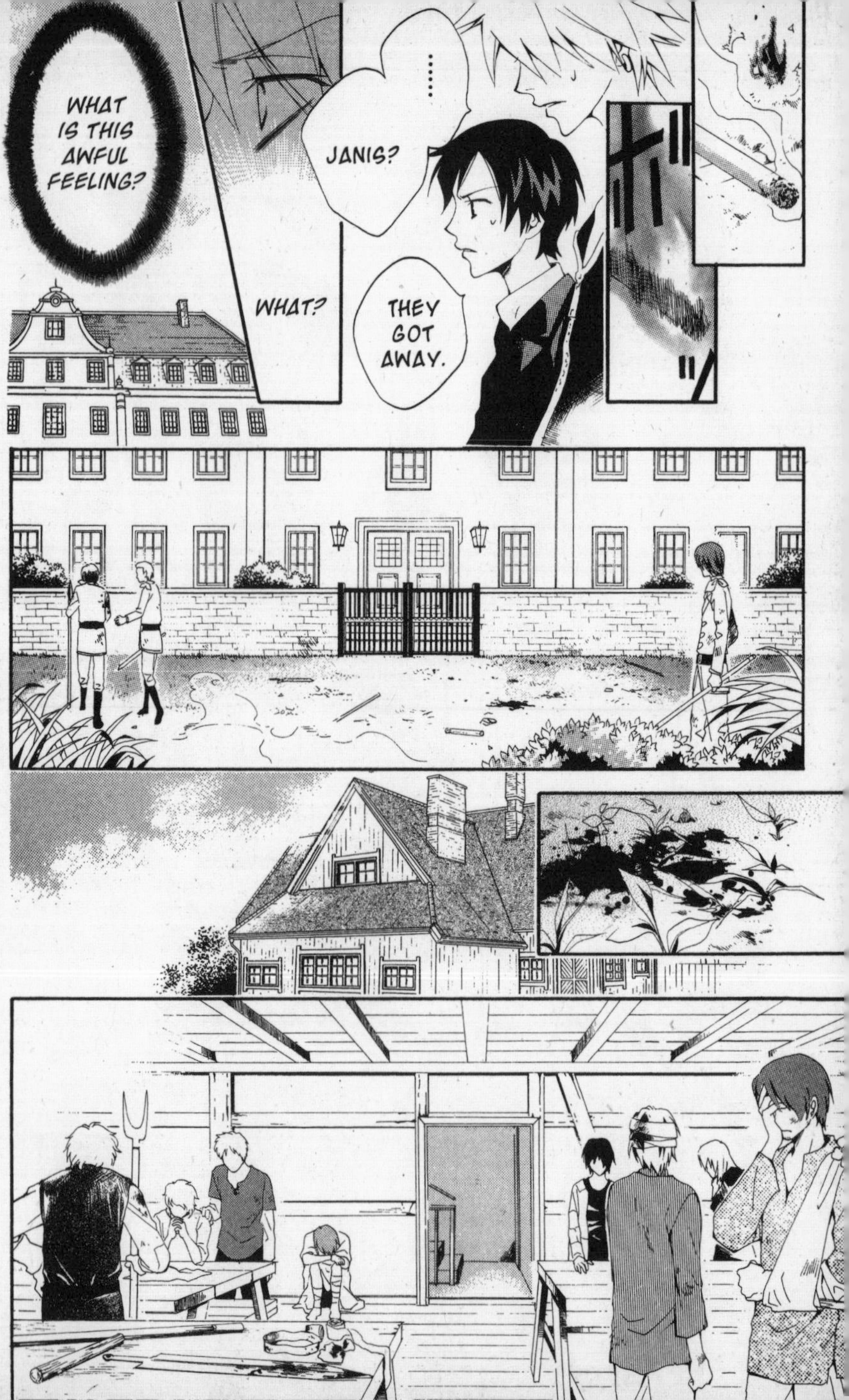

......
JANIS?
THEY GOT AWAY.
WHAT?
WHAT IS THIS AWFUL FEELING?

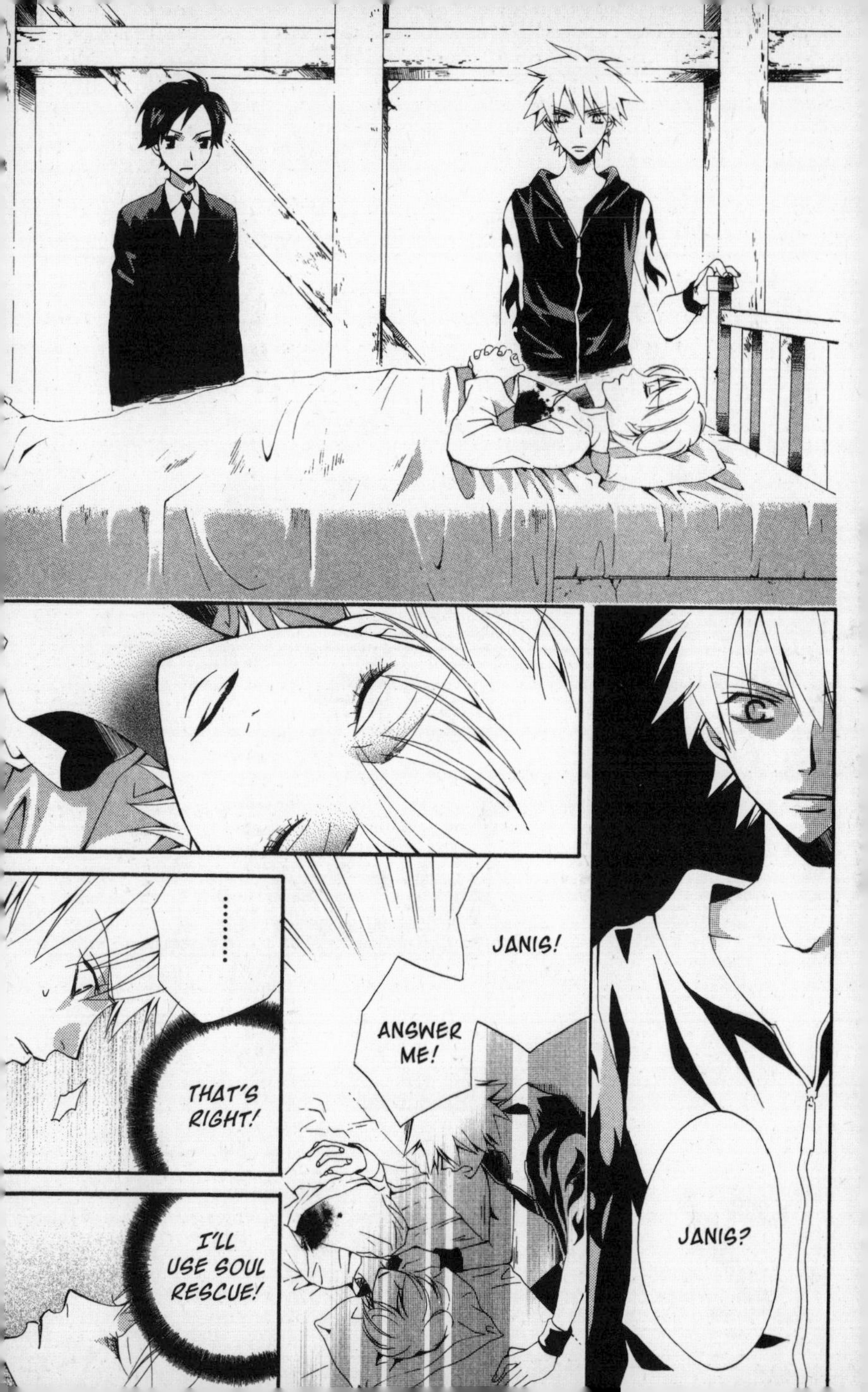
JANIS?
JANIS!
ANSWER ME!
....
THAT'S RIGHT!
I'LL USE SOUL RESCUE!

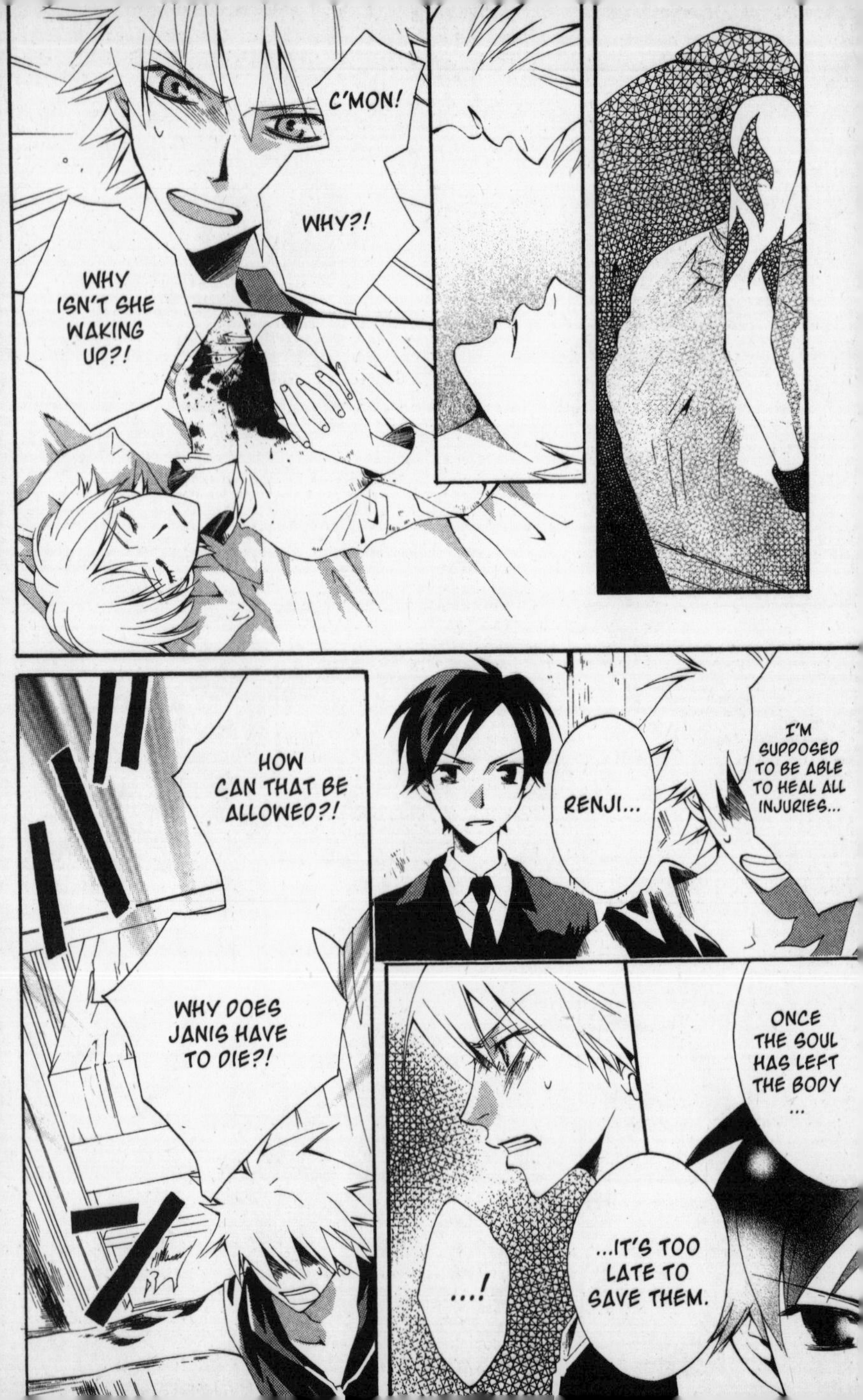
C'MON!
WHY?!
WHY ISN'T SHE WAKING UP?!
I'M SUPPOSED TO BE ABLE TO HEAL ALL INJURIES...
RENJI...
ONCE THE SOUL HAS LEFT THE BODY...
...IT'S TOO LATE TO SAVE THEM.
...!
HOW CAN THAT BE ALLOWED?!
WHY DOES JANIS HAVE TO DIE?!

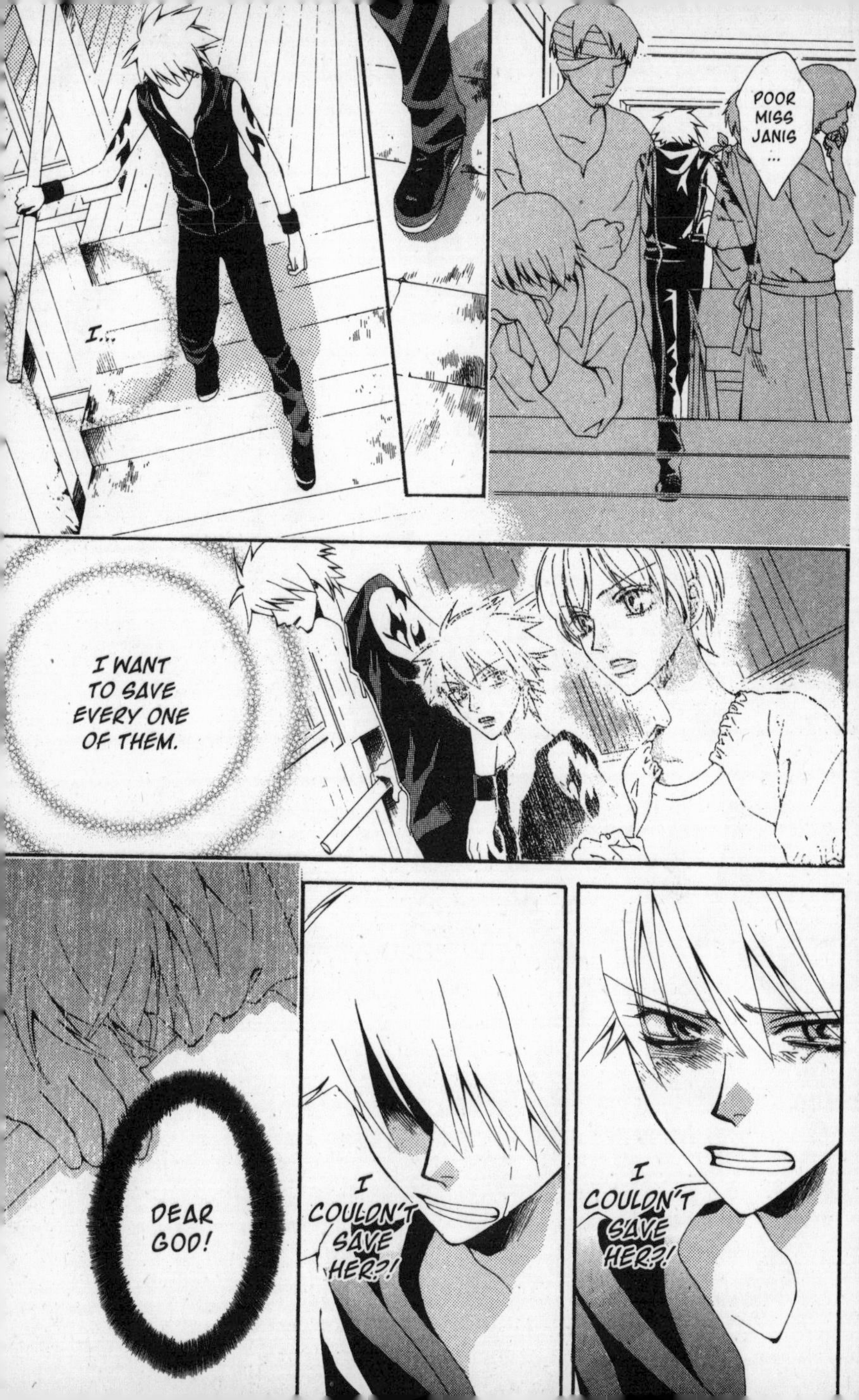
POOR MISS JANIS ...
I...
I WANT TO SAVE EVERY ONE OF THEM.
I COULDN'T SAVE HER?!
I COULDN'T SAVE HER?!
DEAR GOD!

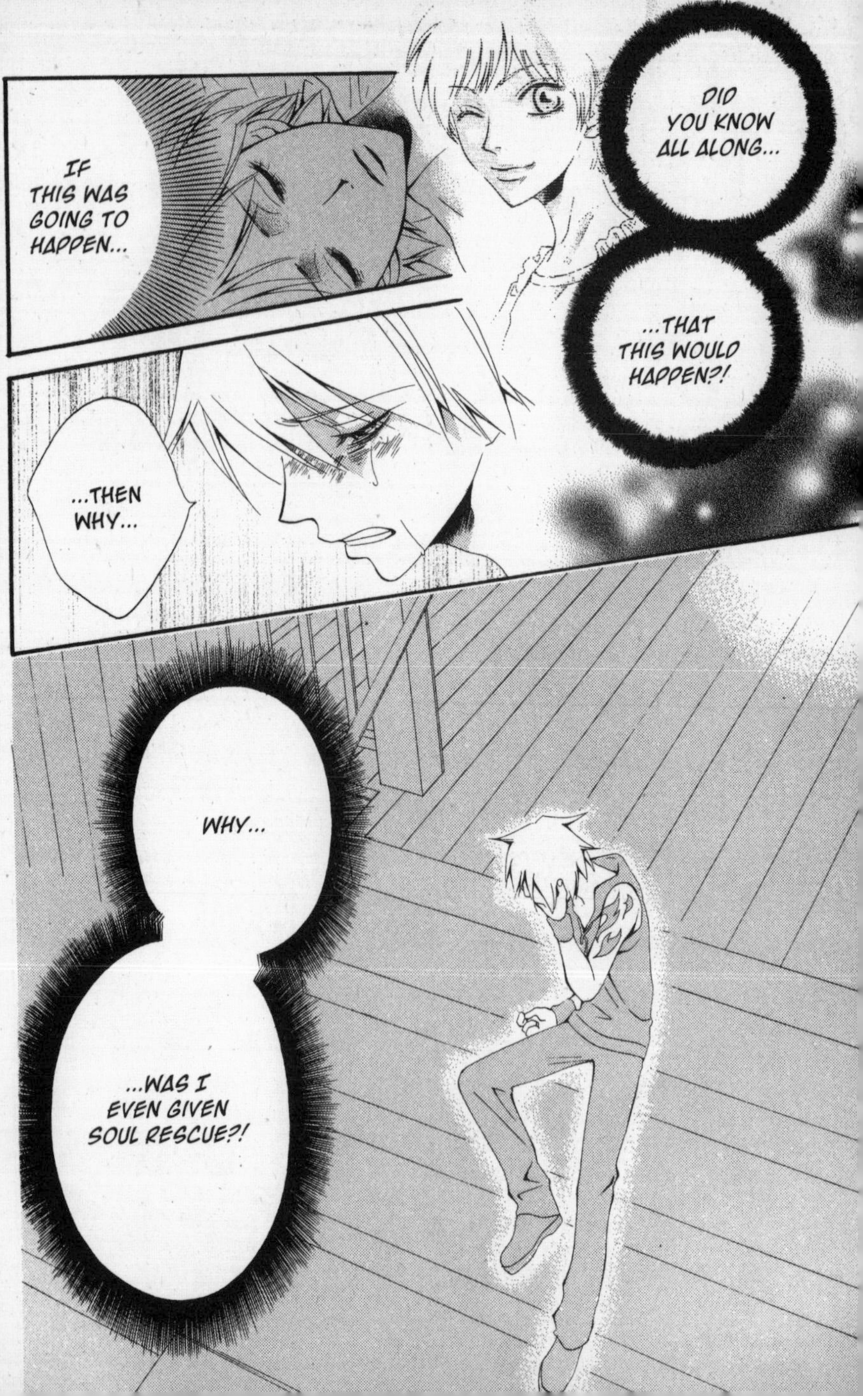
DID YOU KNOW ALL ALONG...
...THAT THIS WOULD HAPPEN?!
IF THIS WAS GOING TO HAPPEN...
...THEN WHY...
WHY...
...WAS I EVEN GIVEN SOUL RESCUE?!

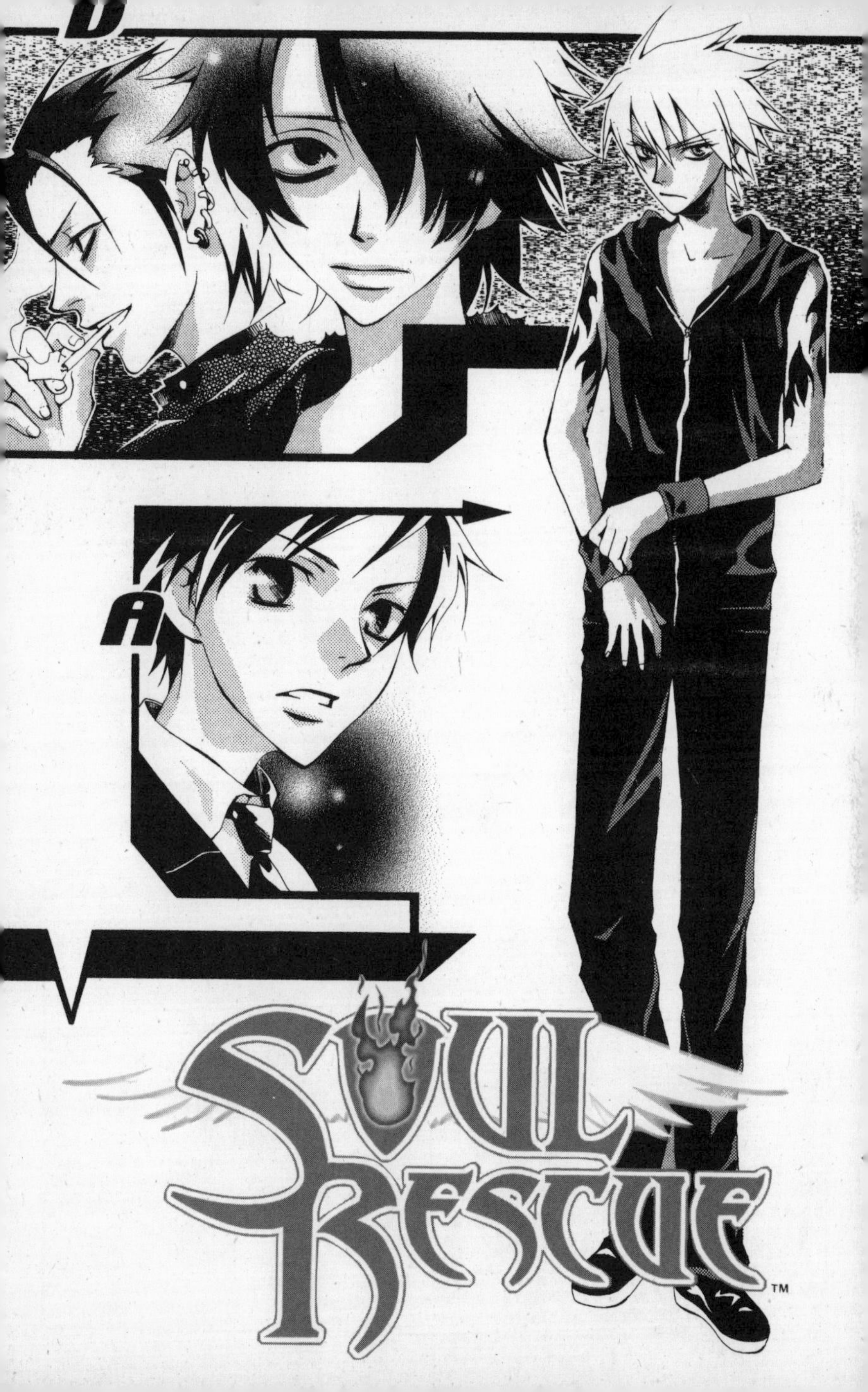
D
A
SOUL RESCUE™

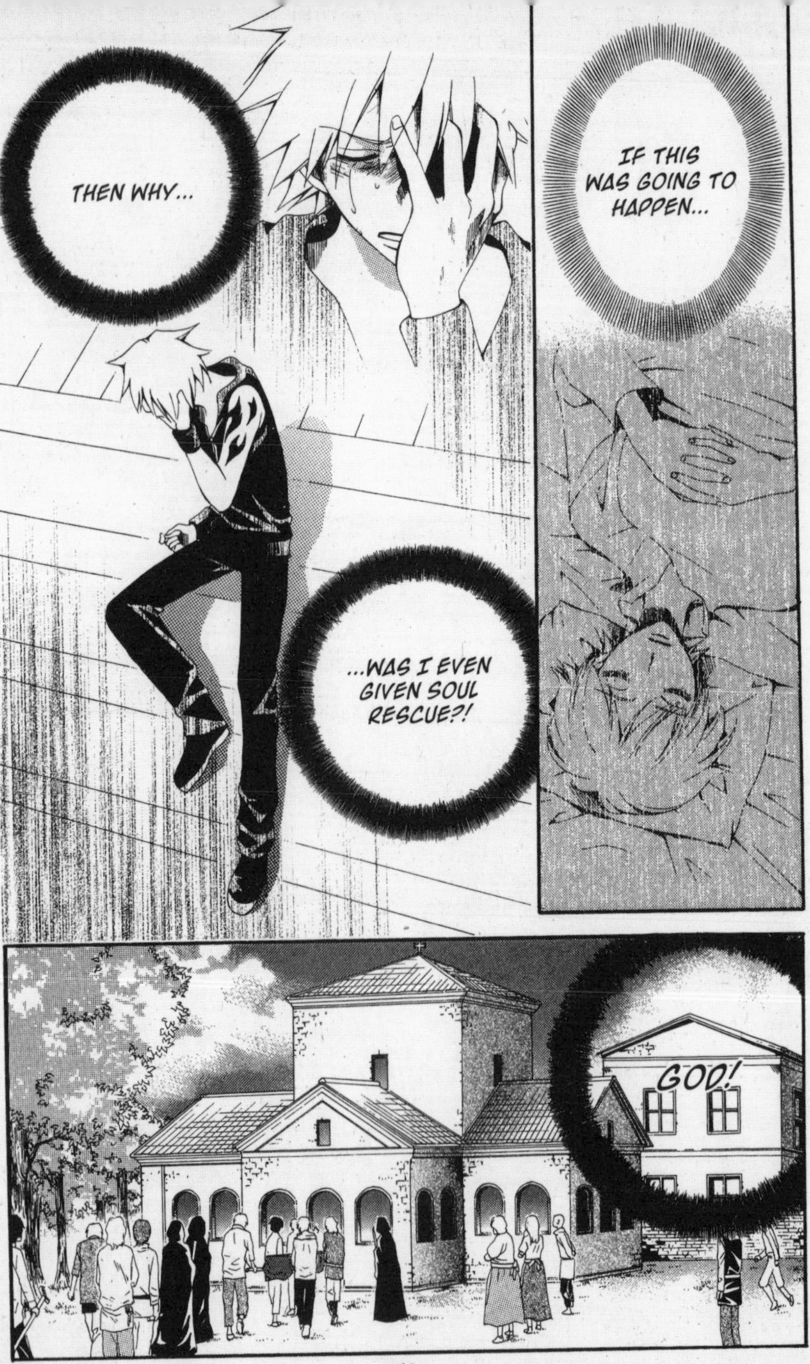
IF THIS WAS GOING TO HAPPEN...
THEN WHY...
...WAS I EVEN GIVEN SOUL RESCUE?!
GOD!

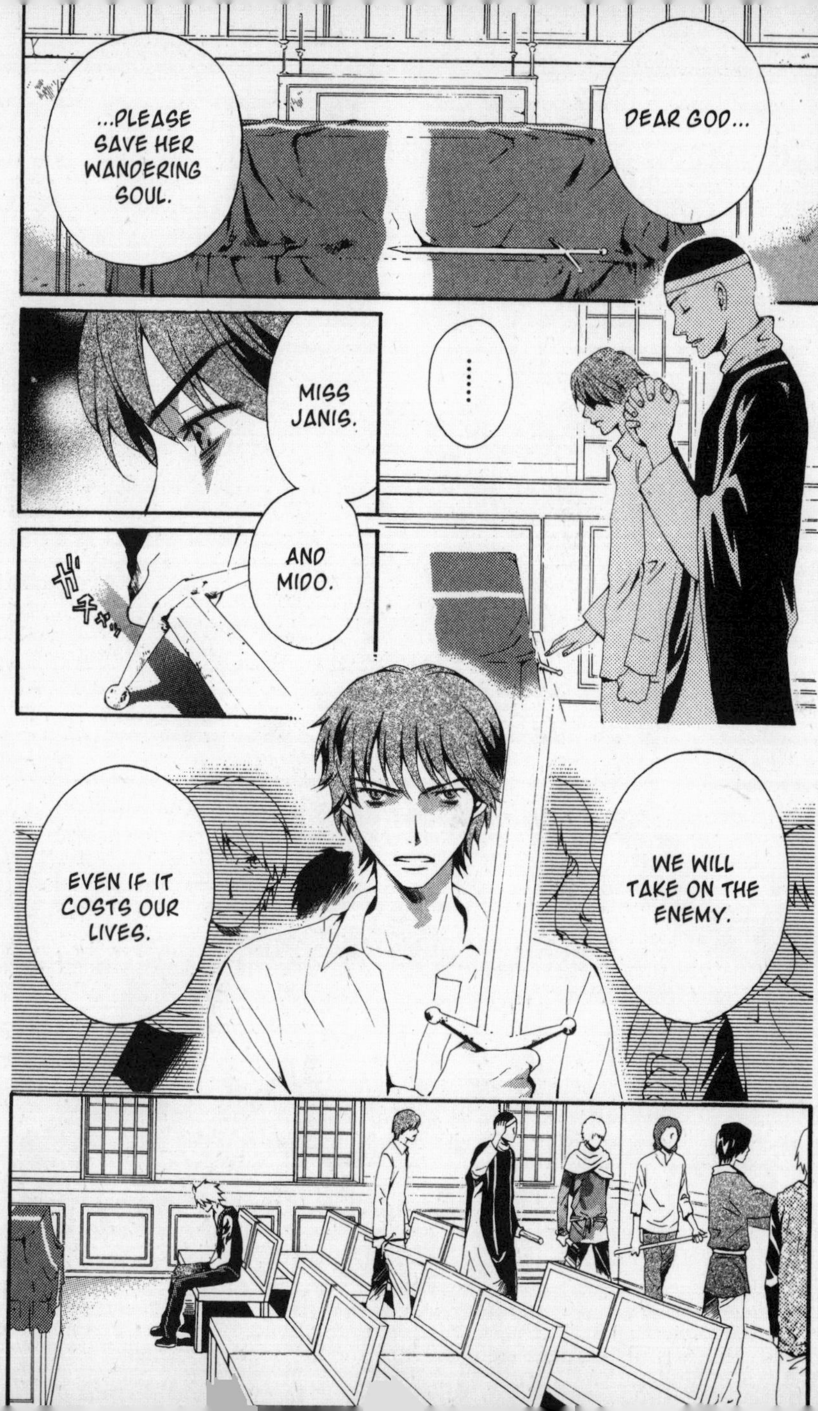
DEAR GOD...
...PLEASE SAVE HER WANDERING SOUL.
......
MISS JANIS.
AND MIDO.
ガチャッ
WE WILL TAKE ON THE ENEMY.
EVEN IF IT COSTS OUR LIVES.

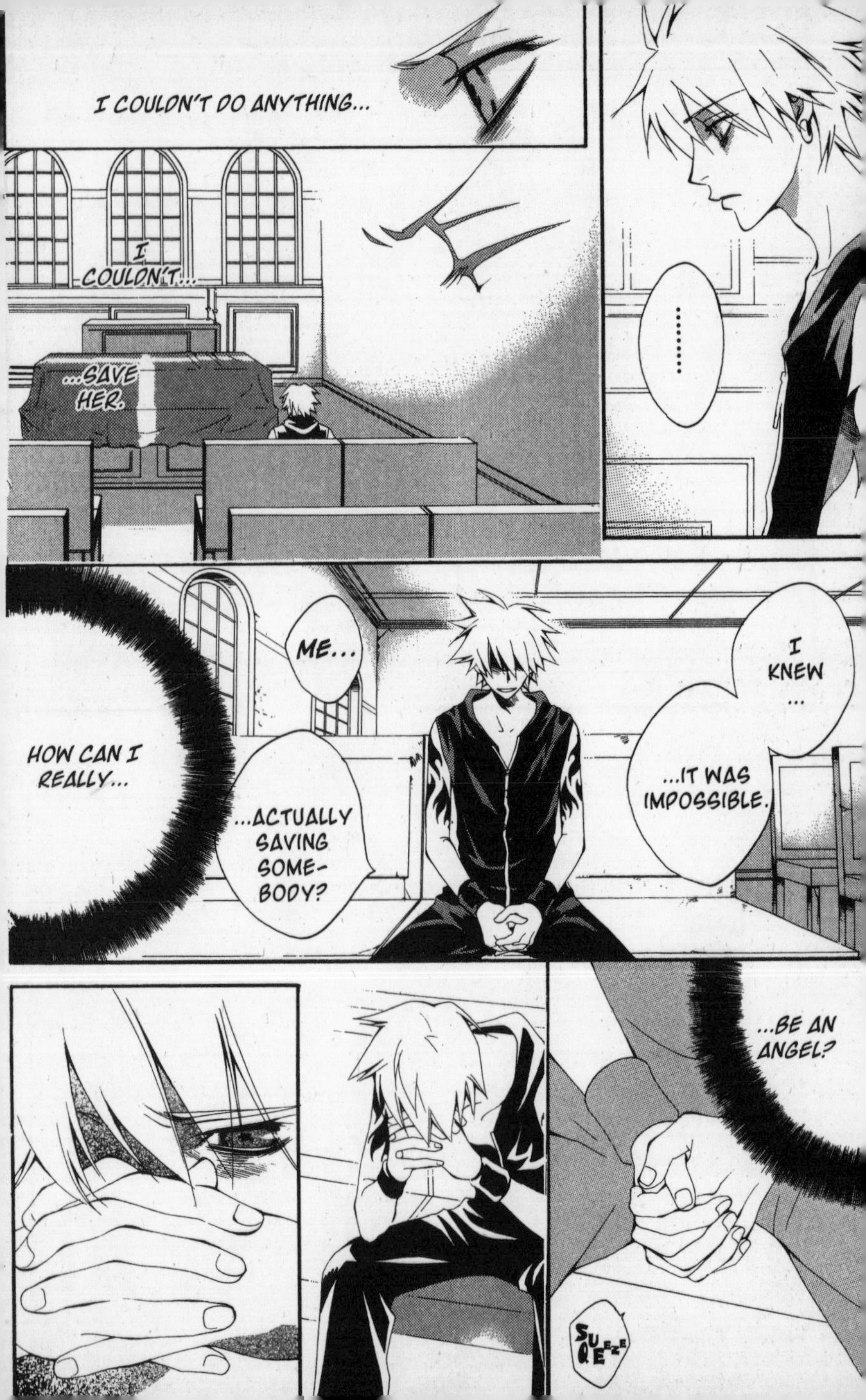
......
I COULDN'T DO ANYTHING...
I COULDN'T...
...SAVE HER.
I KNEW...
...IT WAS IMPOSSIBLE.
ME...
...ACTUALLY SAVING SOMEBODY?
HOW CAN I REALLY...
...BE AN ANGEL?
SQUEEZE

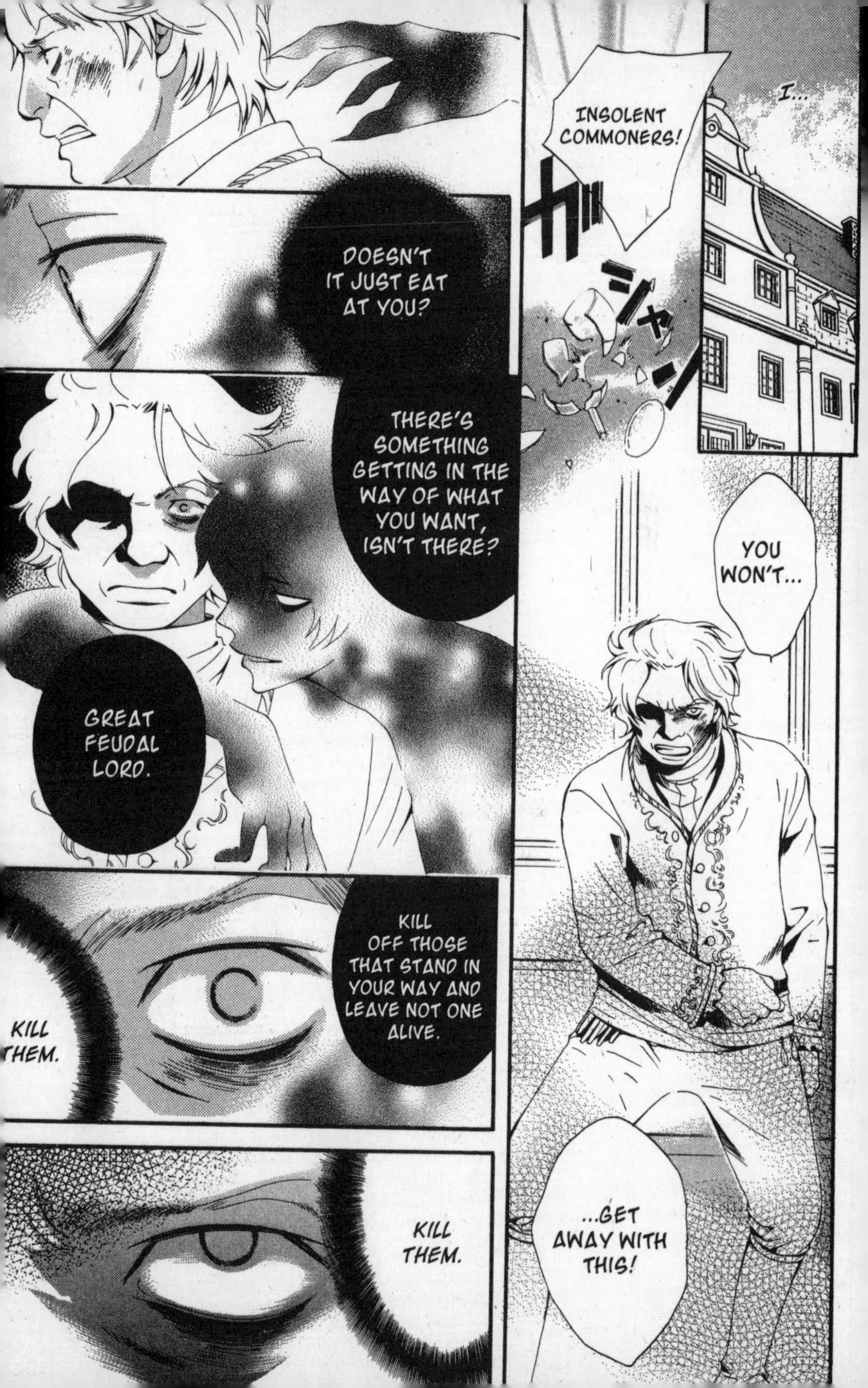

I...
INSOLENT COMMONERS!
YOU WON'T...
...GET AWAY WITH THIS!
DOESN'T IT JUST EAT AT YOU?
THERE'S SOMETHING GETTING IN THE WAY OF WHAT YOU WANT, ISN'T THERE?
GREAT FEUDAL LORD.
KILL OFF THOSE THAT STAND IN YOUR WAY AND LEAVE NOT ONE ALIVE.
KILL THEM.
KILL THEM.

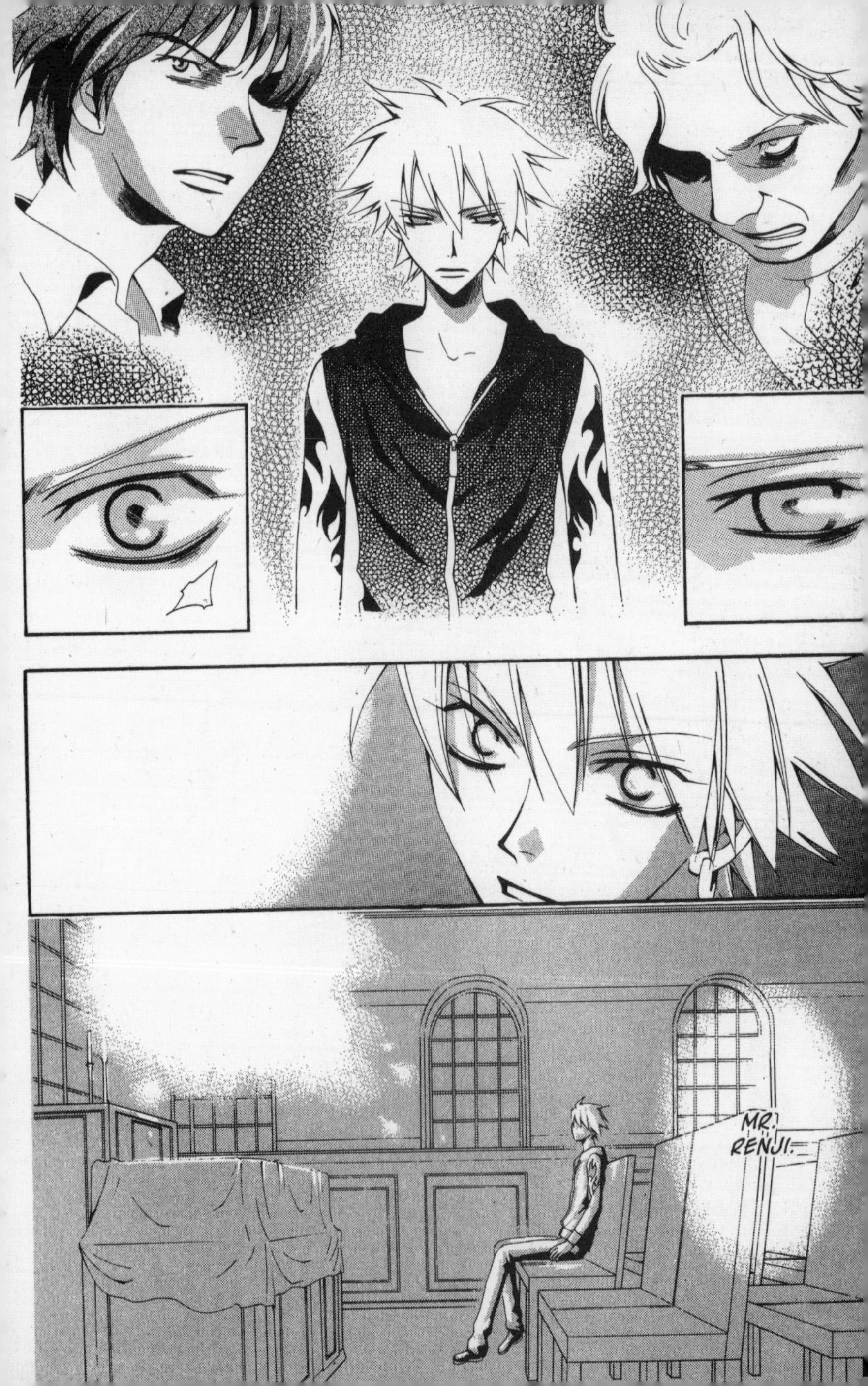
MR. RENJI...

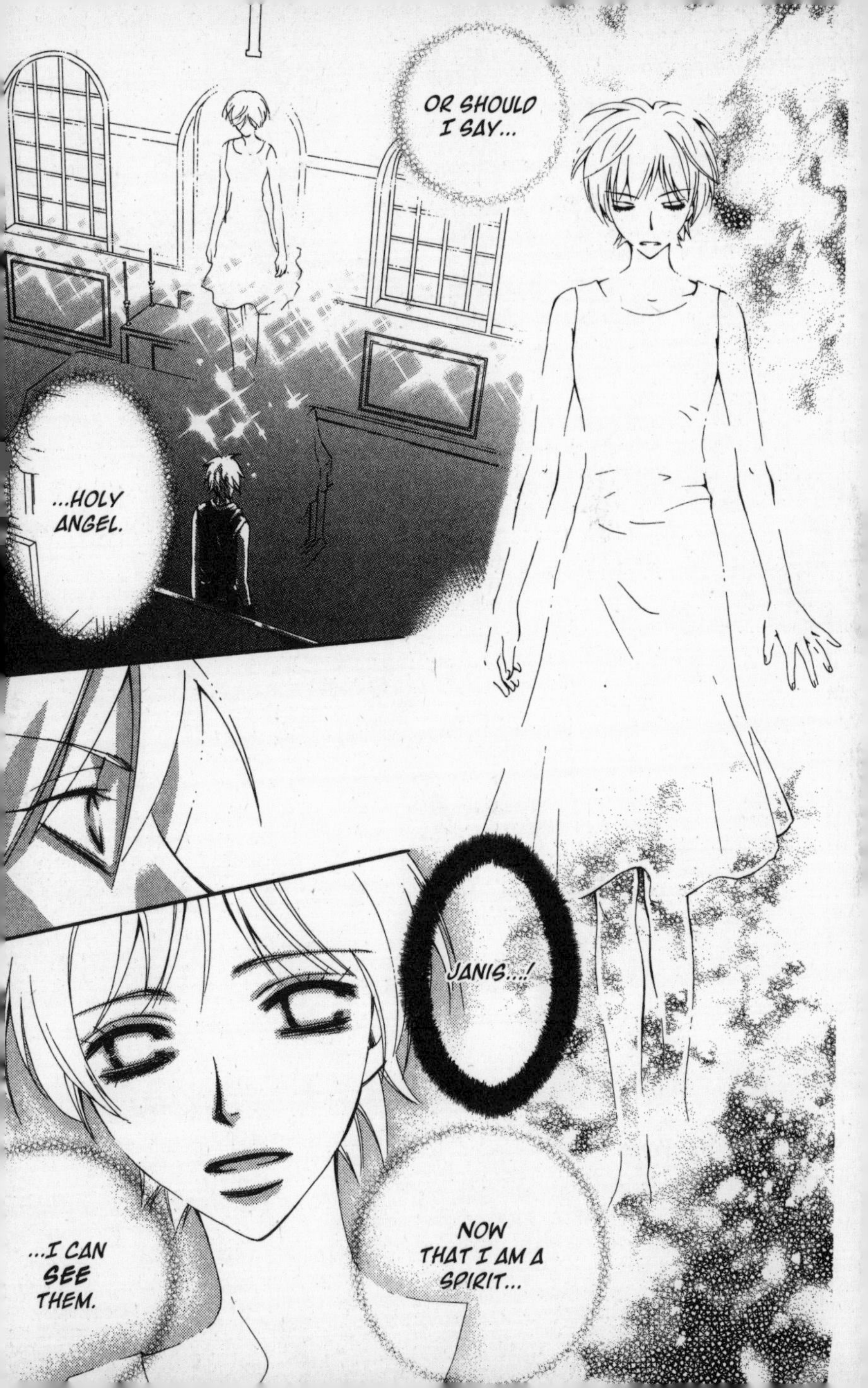
OR SHOULD I SAY...
...HOLY ANGEL.
JANIS...!
NOW THAT I AM A SPIRIT...
...I CAN SEE THEM.

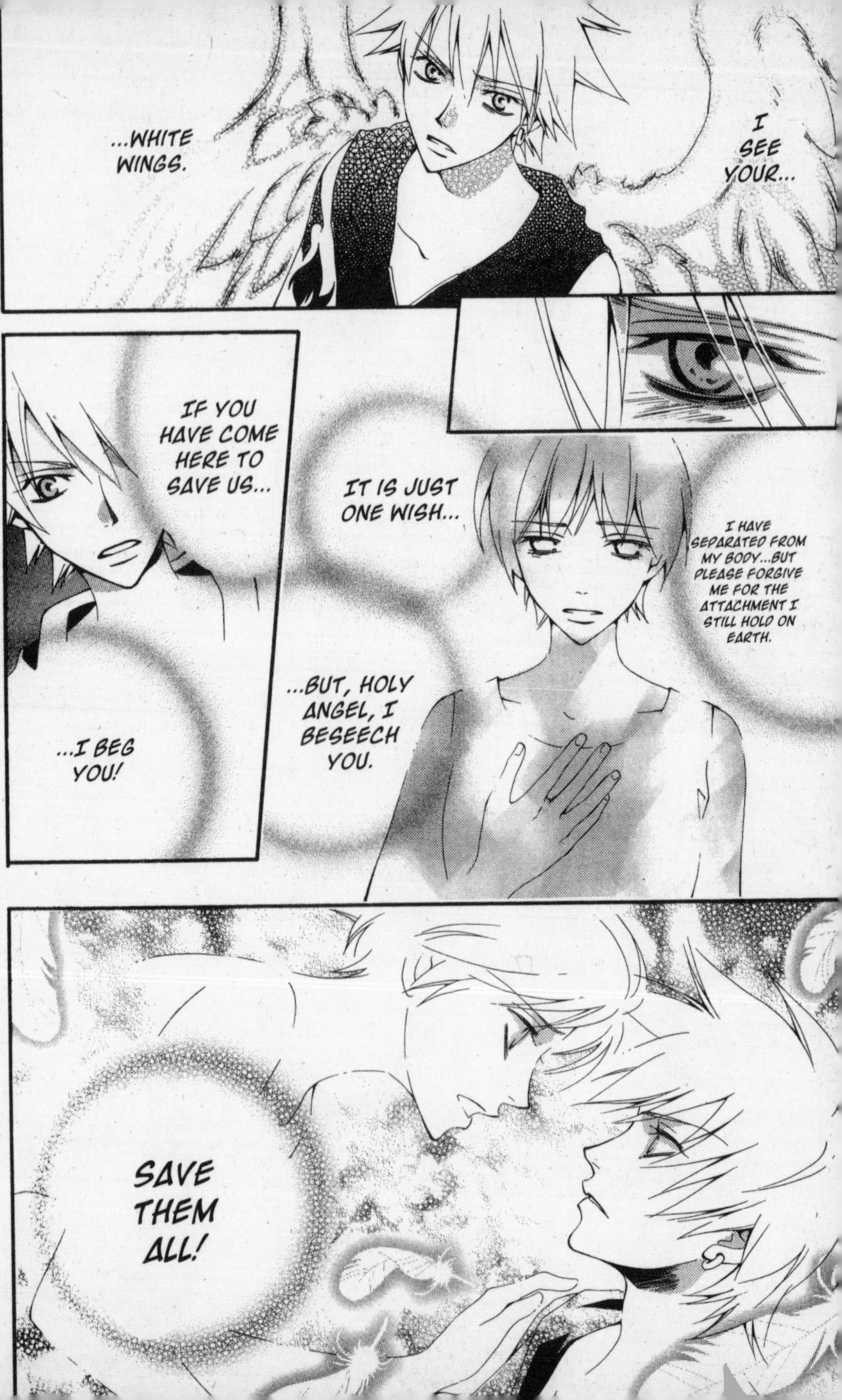
I SEE YOUR...
...WHITE WINGS.
I HAVE SEPARATED FROM MY BODY...BUT PLEASE FORGIVE ME FOR THE ATTACHMENT I STILL HOLD ON EARTH.
IT IS JUST ONE WISH...
...BUT, HOLY ANGEL, I BESEECH YOU.
IF YOU HAVE COME HERE TO SAVE US...
...I BEG YOU!
SAVE THEM ALL!

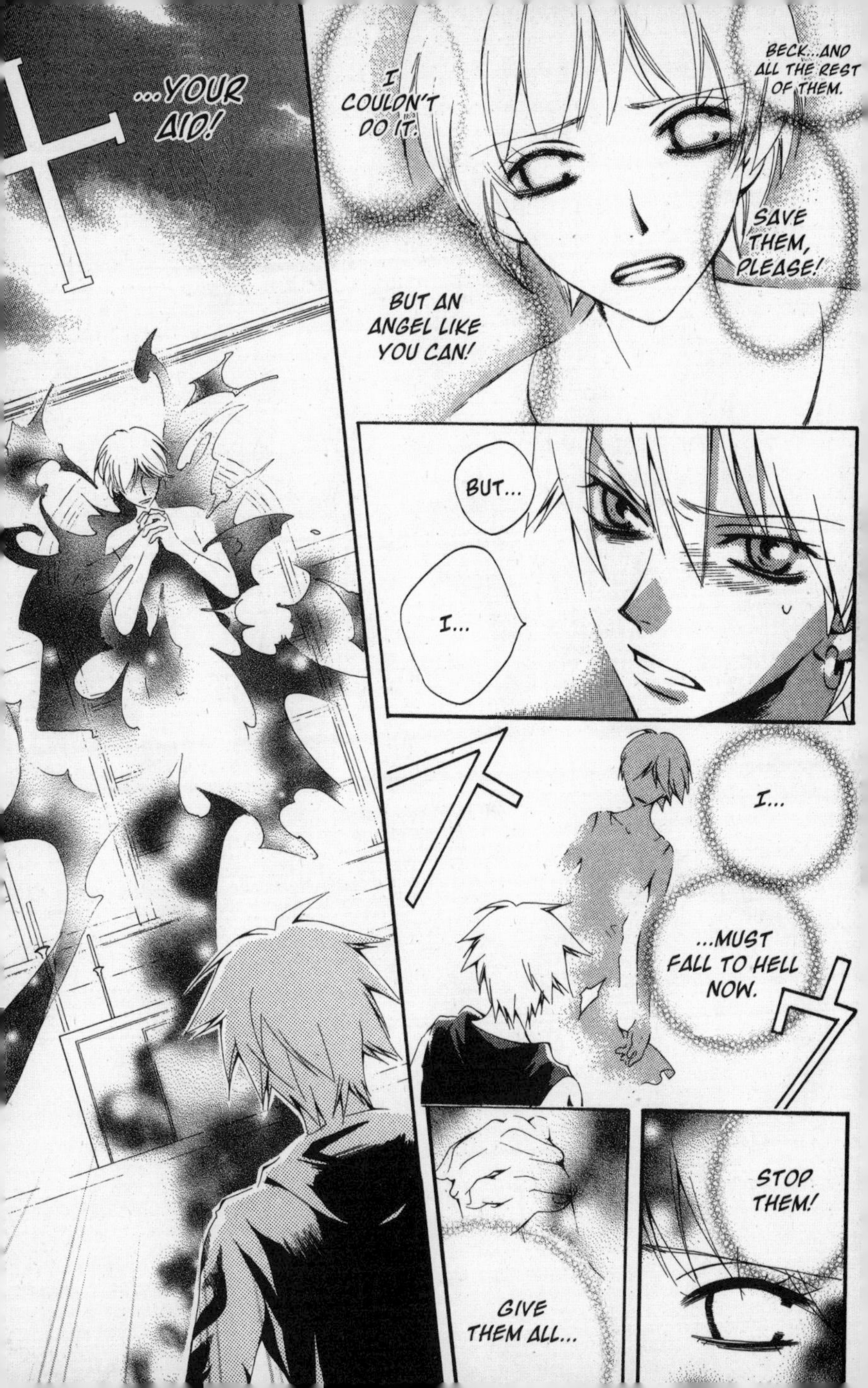
BECK...AND ALL THE REST OF THEM.
SAVE THEM, PLEASE!
I COULDN'T DO IT.
BUT AN ANGEL LIKE YOU CAN!
BUT...
I...
I...
...MUST FALL TO HELL NOW.
STOP THEM!
GIVE THEM ALL...
...YOUR AID!

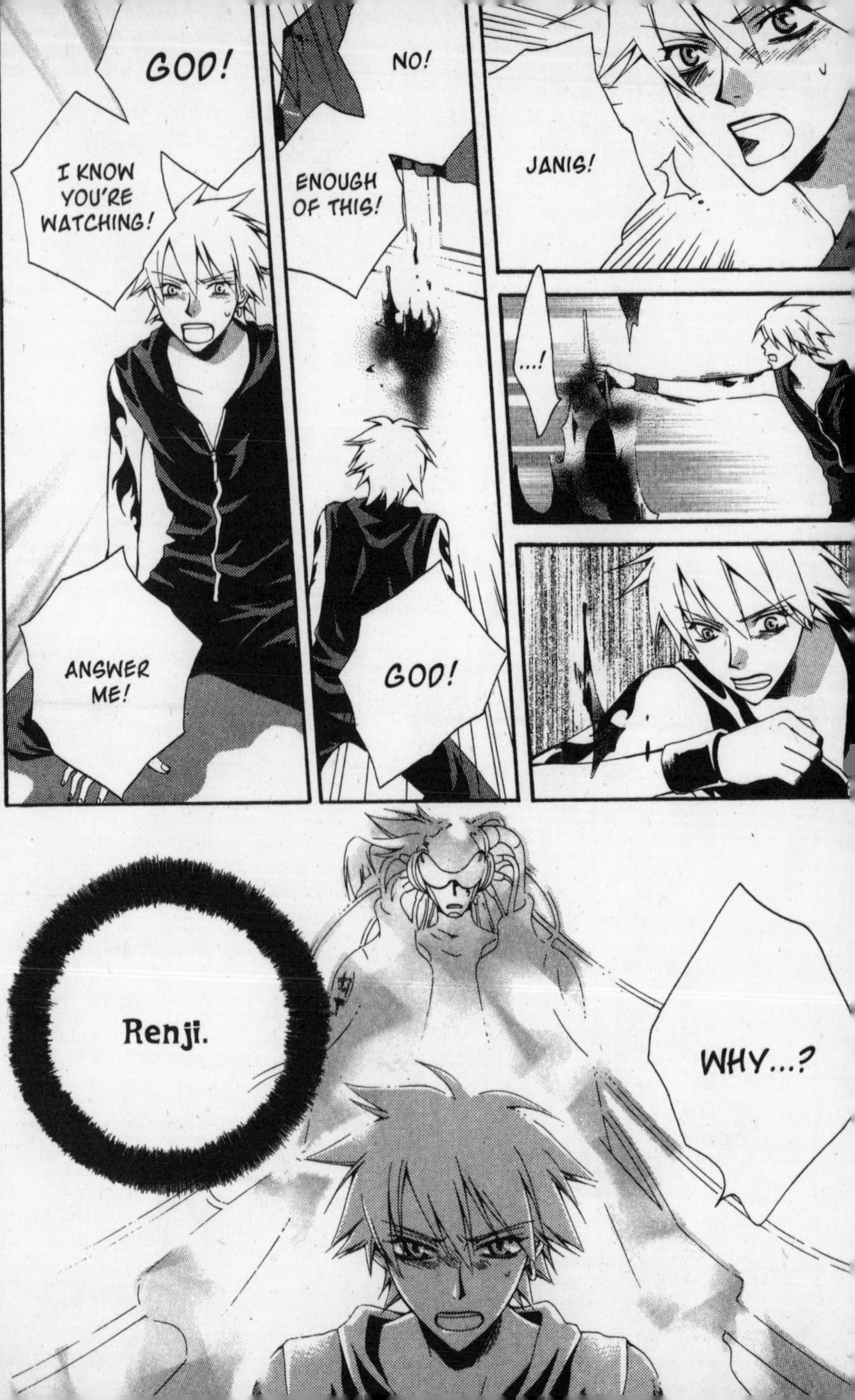
JANIS!
...!
NO!
ENOUGH OF THIS!
GOD!
GOD!
I KNOW YOU'RE WATCHING!
ANSWER ME!
WHY...?
Renji.

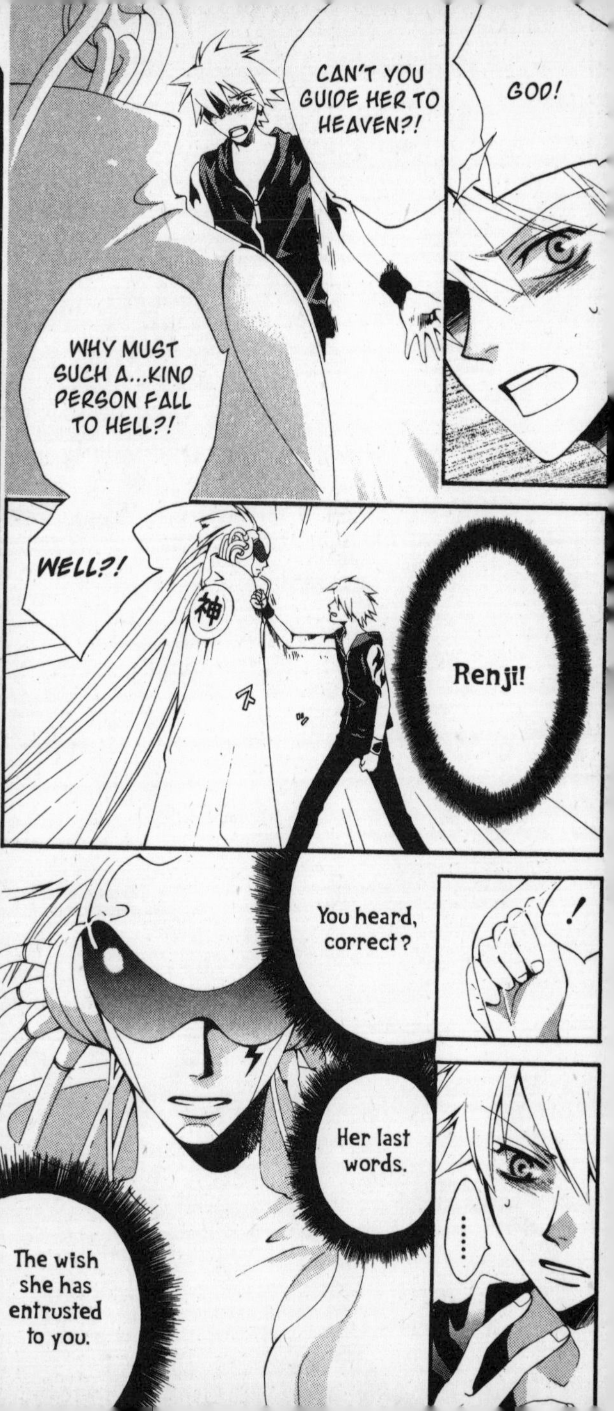
GOD!
CAN'T YOU GUIDE HER TO HEAVEN?!
WHY MUST SUCH A...KIND PERSON FALL TO HELL?!
WELL?!
Renji!
!
......
You heard, correct?
Her last words.
The wish she has entrusted to you.

SR

About this chapter:
I actually didn't want to draw people dying. But since it was necessary, I drew it.
What I wanted to draw in Soul Rescue was love and peace. That's what I truly believe to be important especially this day and age.

★★★★★★★★★★

Special Thanks!
⇩

As always, thanks to my wonderful family!
Necchii
Sayaka-san
Shimada-san
Yuuki-sempai
Ume
Eji
Shimi-san
Pin-chan
Everyone at Asaki Studios
Anyone else I owe thanks to?
Of course you out there reading this book!
Thank you!
I hope we meet again!

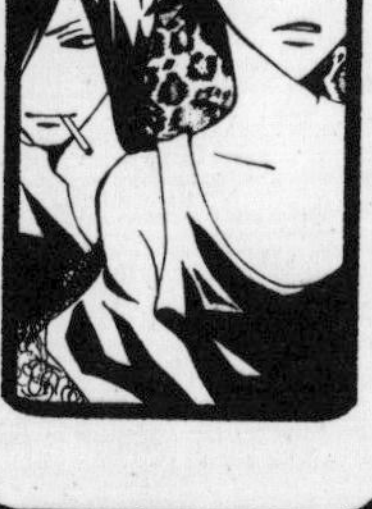

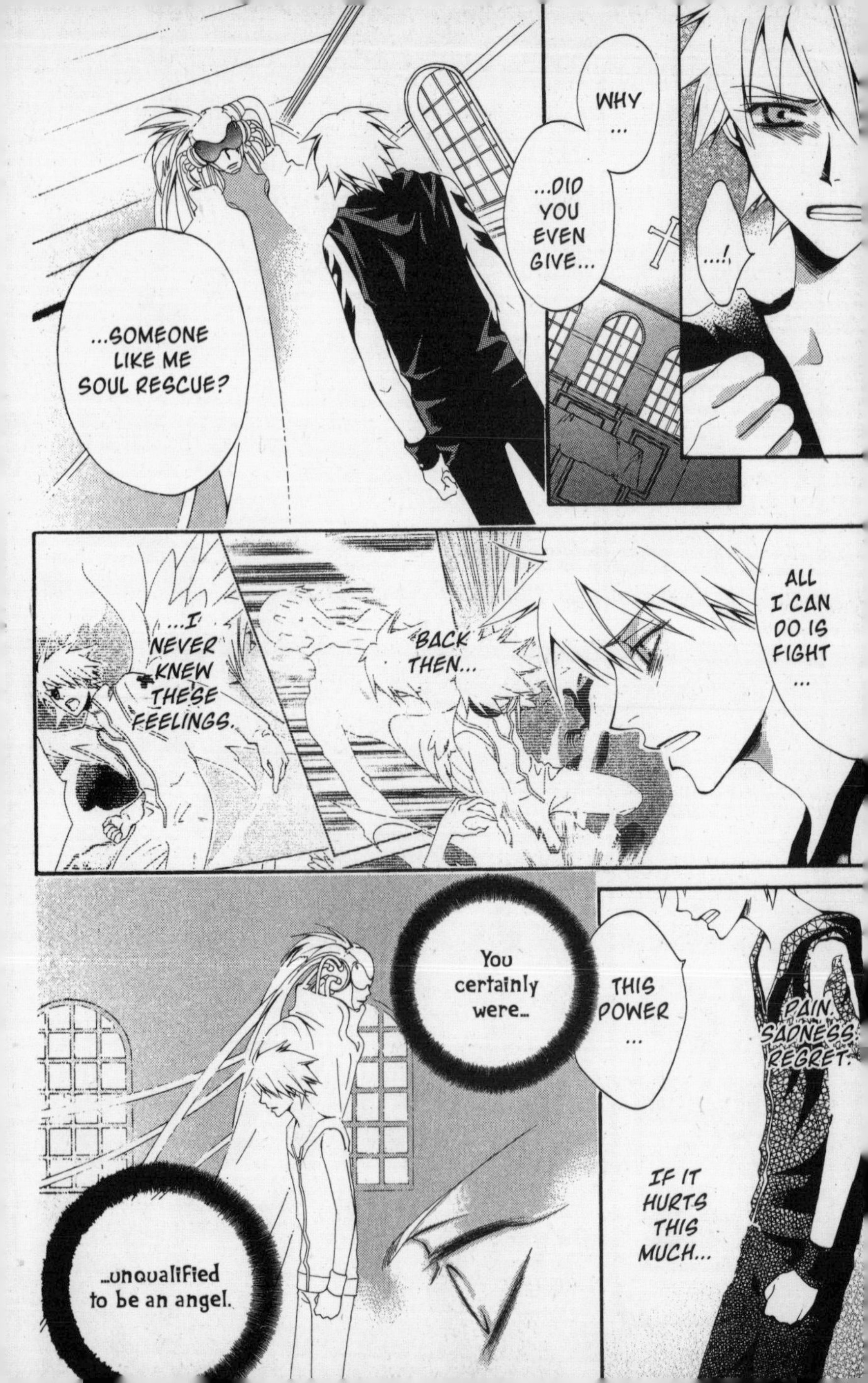
...!
WHY ...
...DID YOU EVEN GIVE...
...SOMEONE LIKE ME SOUL RESCUE?
ALL I CAN DO IS FIGHT ...
BACK THEN...
...I NEVER KNEW THESE FEELINGS.
PAIN. SADNESS. REGRET.
THIS POWER ...
IF IT HURTS THIS MUCH...
You certainly were..
...unqualified to be an angel.

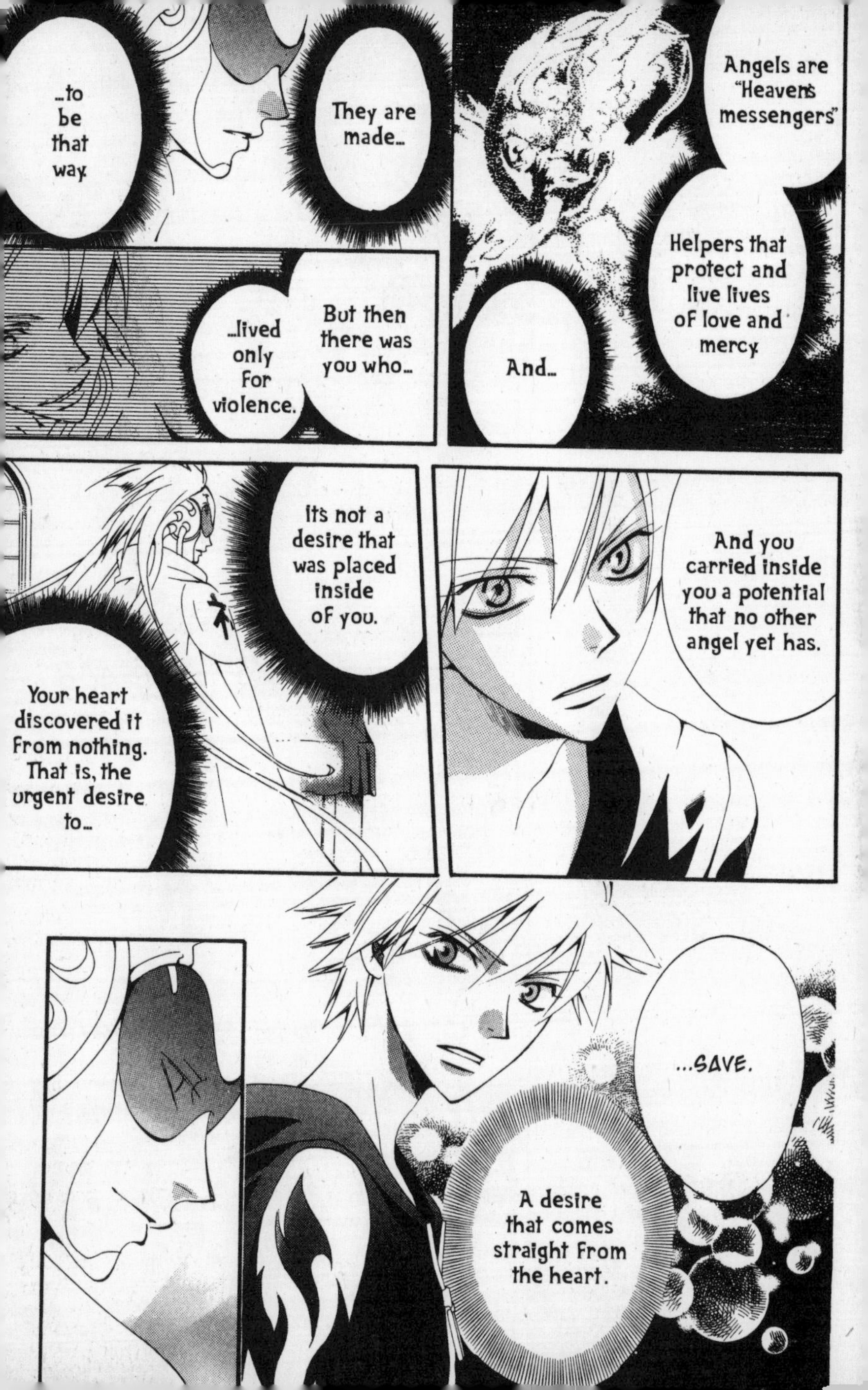

Angels are "Heaven's messengers"
Helpers that protect and live lives of love and mercy.
And...
They are made...
...to be that way.
But then there was you who...
...lived only for violence.
And you carried inside you a potential that no other angel yet has.
It's not a desire that was placed inside of you.
Your heart discovered it from nothing. That is, the urgent desire to...
...SAVE.
A desire that comes straight from the heart.

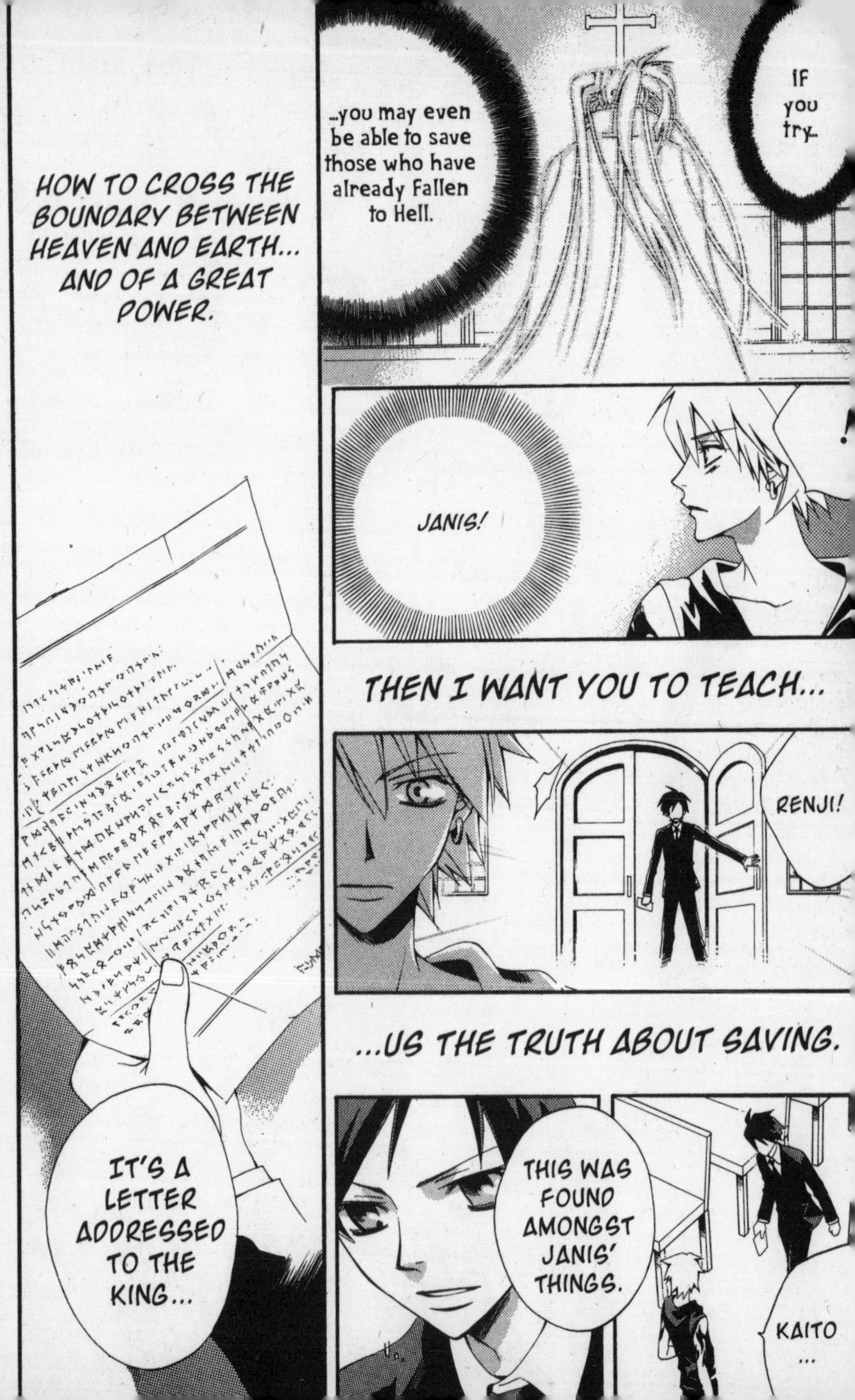
IF you try...
...you may even be able to save those who have already fallen to Hell.
JANIS!
THEN I WANT YOU TO TEACH...
RENJI!
...US THE TRUTH ABOUT SAVING.
KAITO ...
THIS WAS FOUND AMONGST JANIS' THINGS.
HOW TO CROSS THE BOUNDARY BETWEEN HEAVEN AND EARTH... AND OF A GREAT POWER.
IT'S A LETTER ADDRESSED TO THE KING...

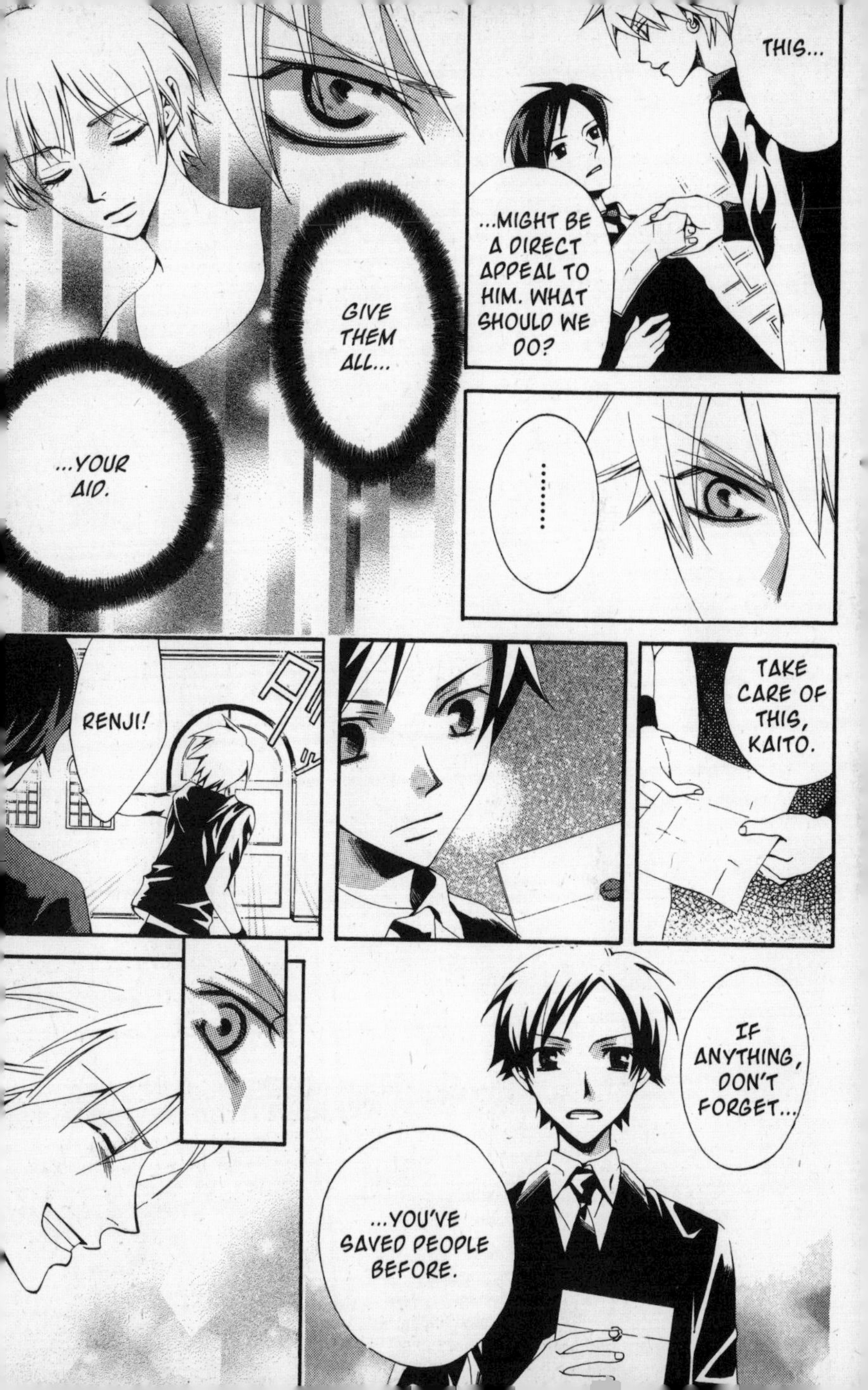
THIS...
...MIGHT BE A DIRECT APPEAL TO HIM. WHAT SHOULD WE DO?
......
GIVE THEM ALL...
...YOUR AID.
TAKE CARE OF THIS, KAITO.
RENJI!
IF ANYTHING, DON'T FORGET...
...YOU'VE SAVED PEOPLE BEFORE.

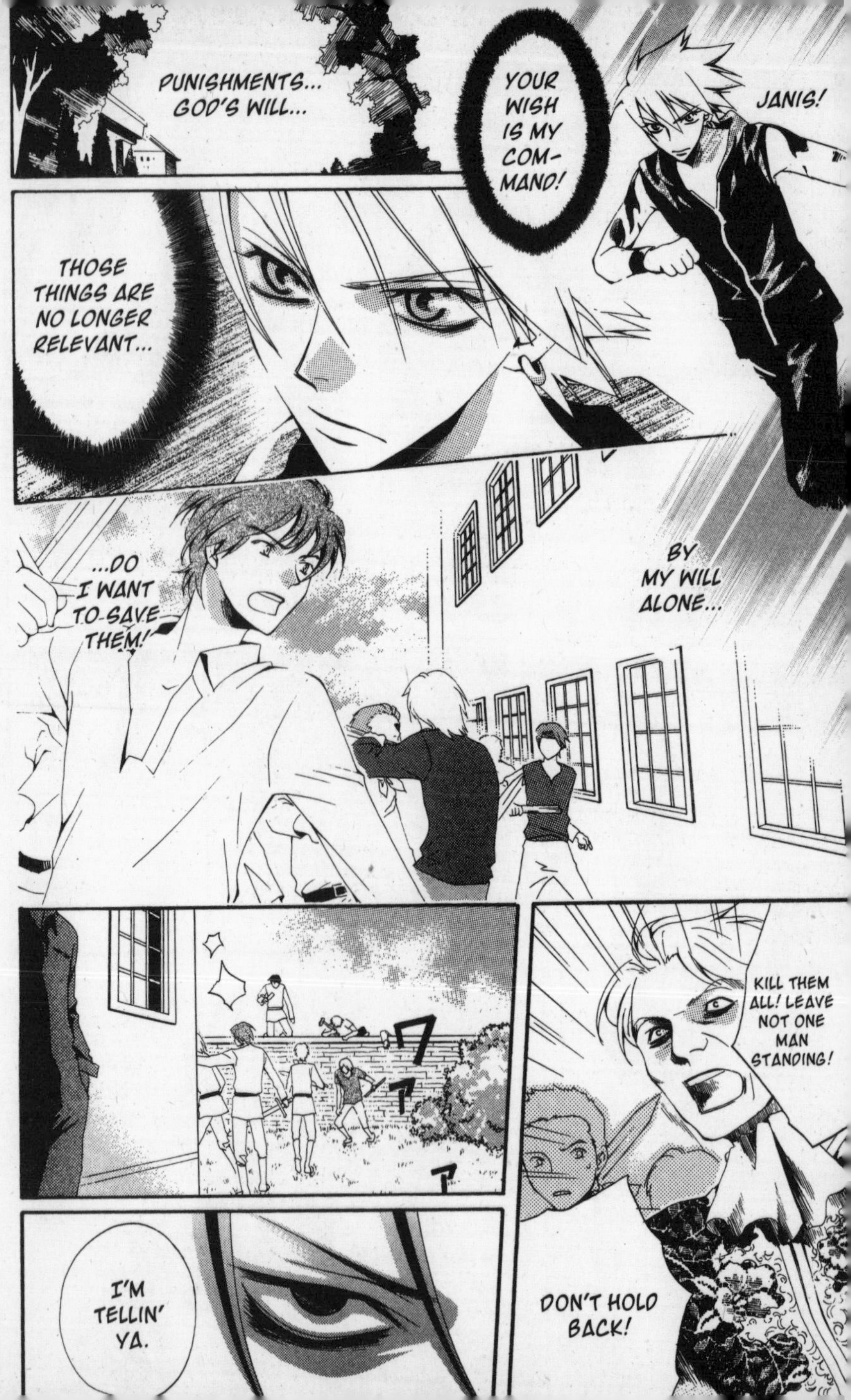
JANIS!
YOUR WISH IS MY COM-MAND!
PUNISHMENTS... GOD'S WILL...
THOSE THINGS ARE NO LONGER RELEVANT...
BY MY WILL ALONE...
...DO I WANT TO SAVE THEM!
KILL THEM ALL! LEAVE NOT ONE MAN STANDING!
DON'T HOLD BACK!
I'M TELLIN' YA.

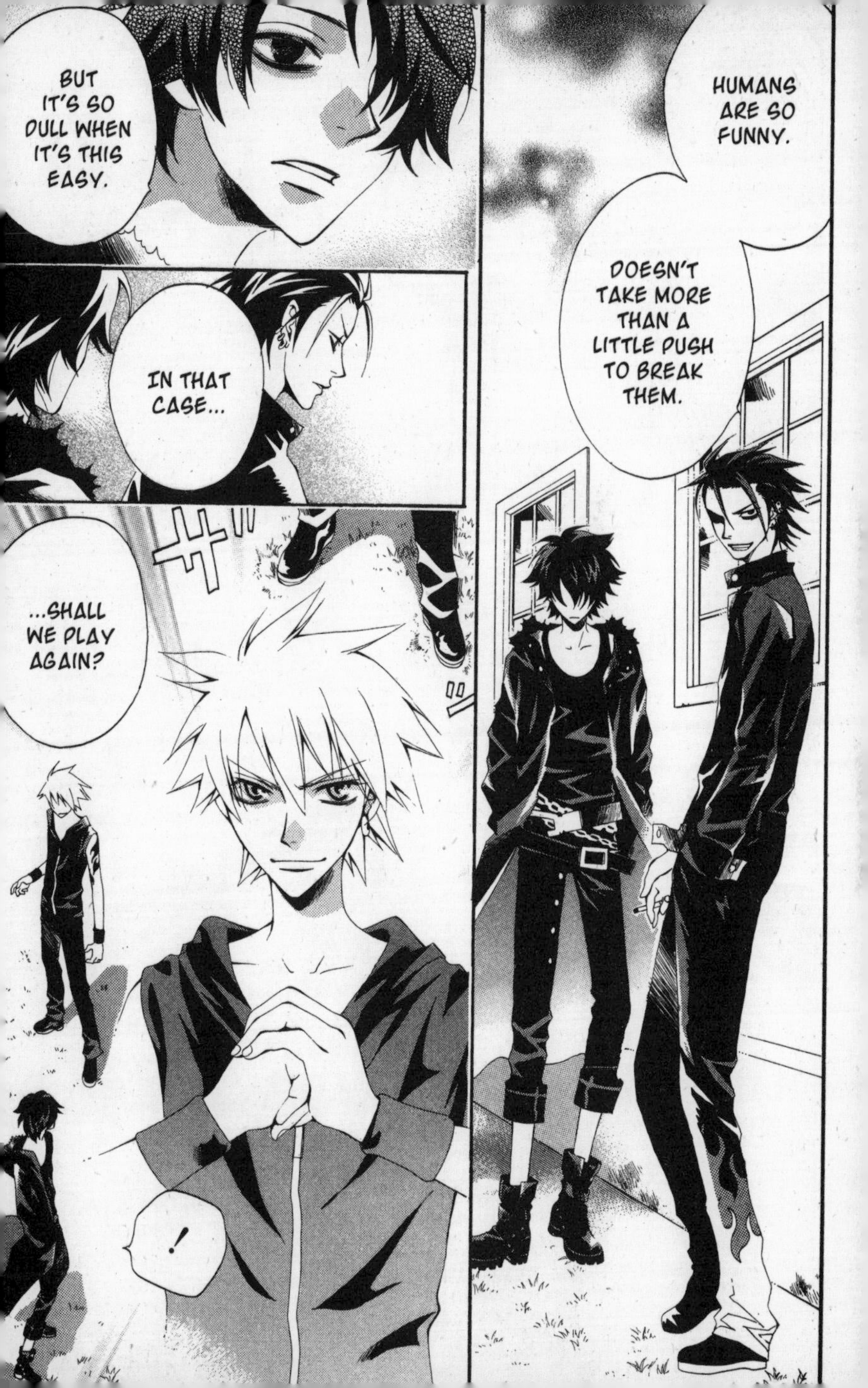
HUMANS ARE SO FUNNY.
DOESN'T TAKE MORE THAN A LITTLE PUSH TO BREAK THEM.
BUT IT'S SO DULL WHEN IT'S THIS EASY.
IN THAT CASE...
...SHALL WE PLAY AGAIN?
!

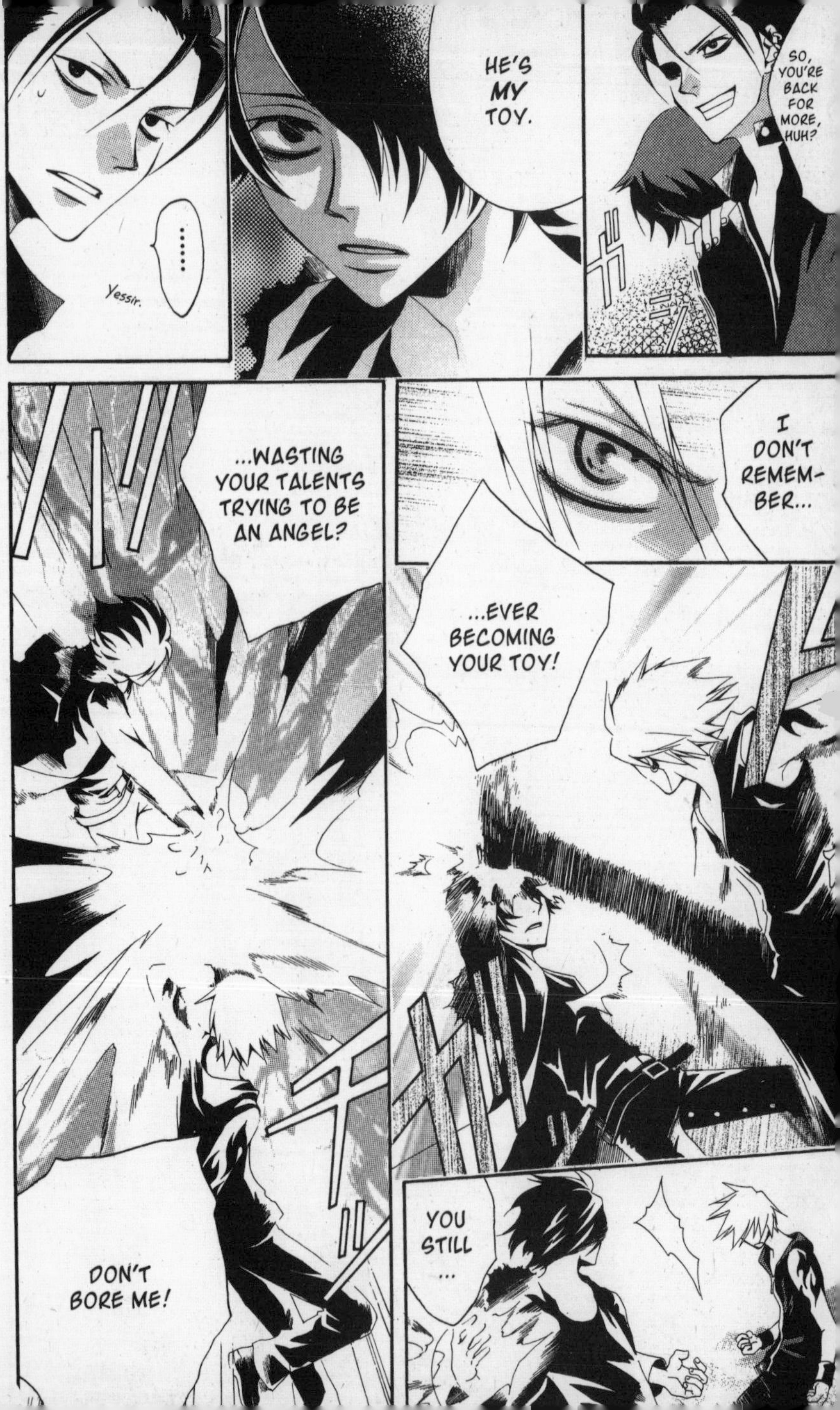
SO, YOU'RE BACK FOR MORE, HUH?
HE'S MY TOY.
......
Yessir.
I DON'T REMEMBER...
...EVER BECOMING YOUR TOY!
YOU STILL ...
...WASTING YOUR TALENTS TRYING TO BE AN ANGEL?
DON'T BORE ME!

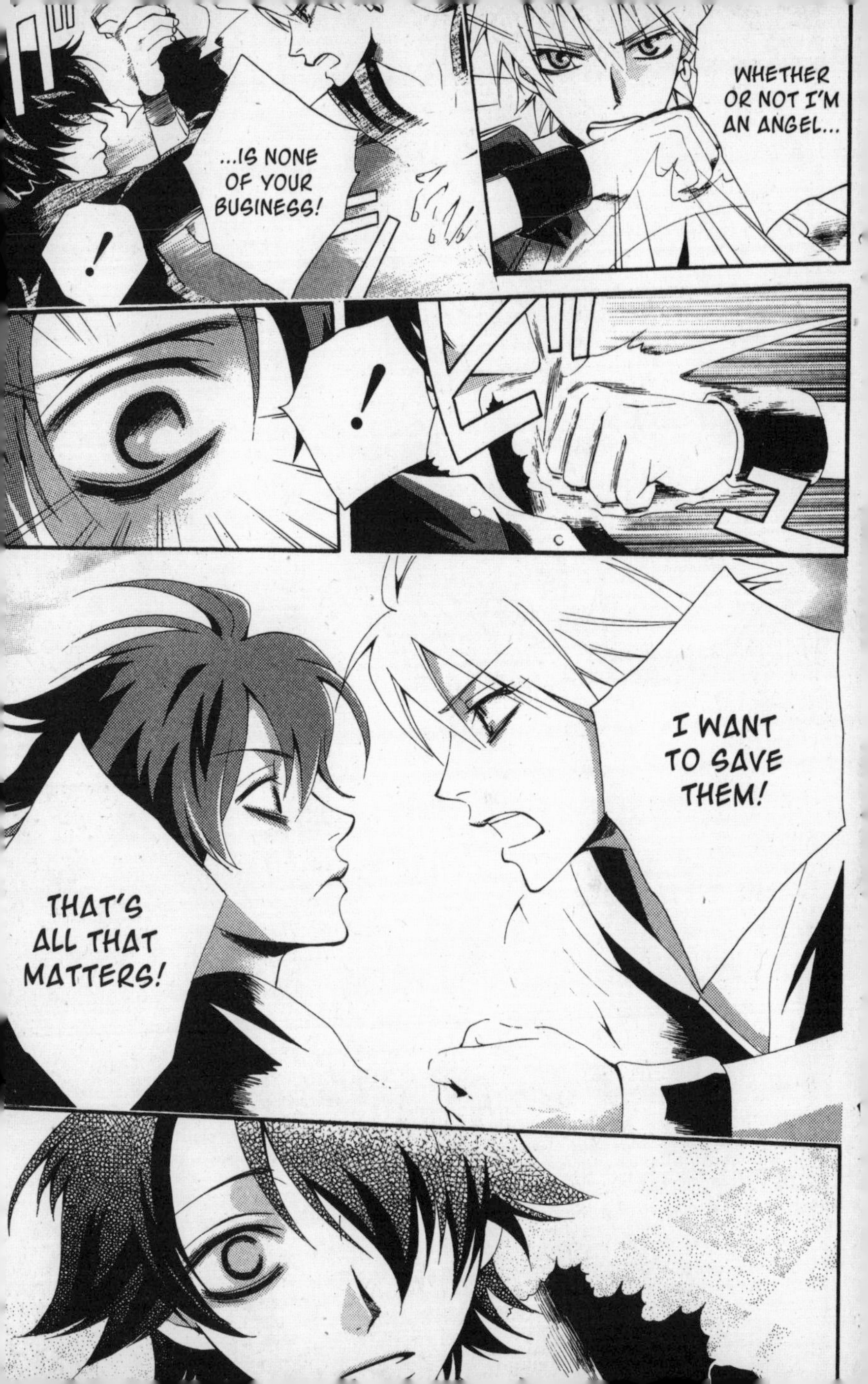

WHETHER OR NOT I'M AN ANGEL...
...IS NONE OF YOUR BUSINESS!
!
!
I WANT TO SAVE THEM!
THAT'S ALL THAT MATTERS!

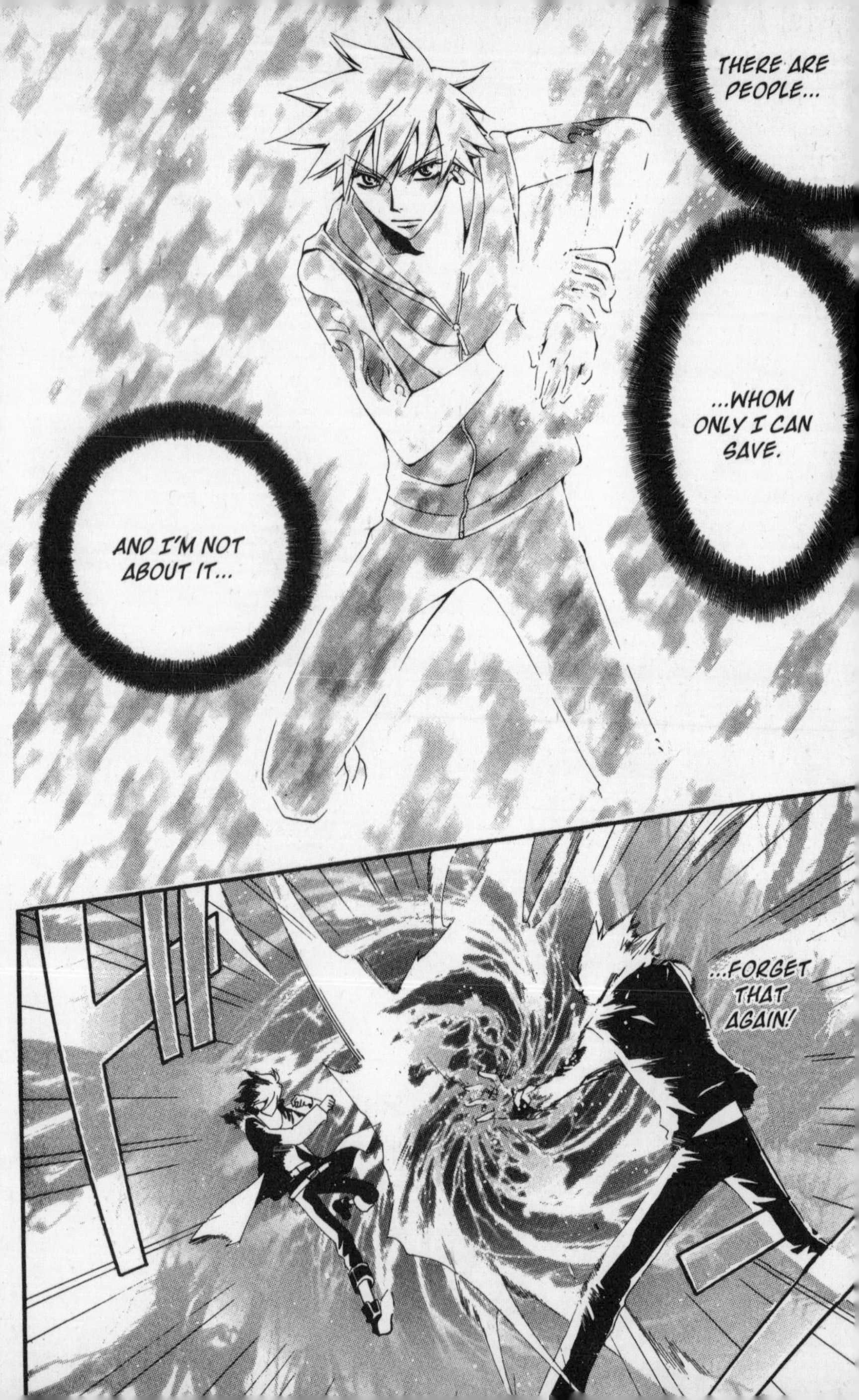
THERE ARE PEOPLE...
...WHOM ONLY I CAN SAVE.
AND I'M NOT ABOUT IT...
...FORGET THAT AGAIN!

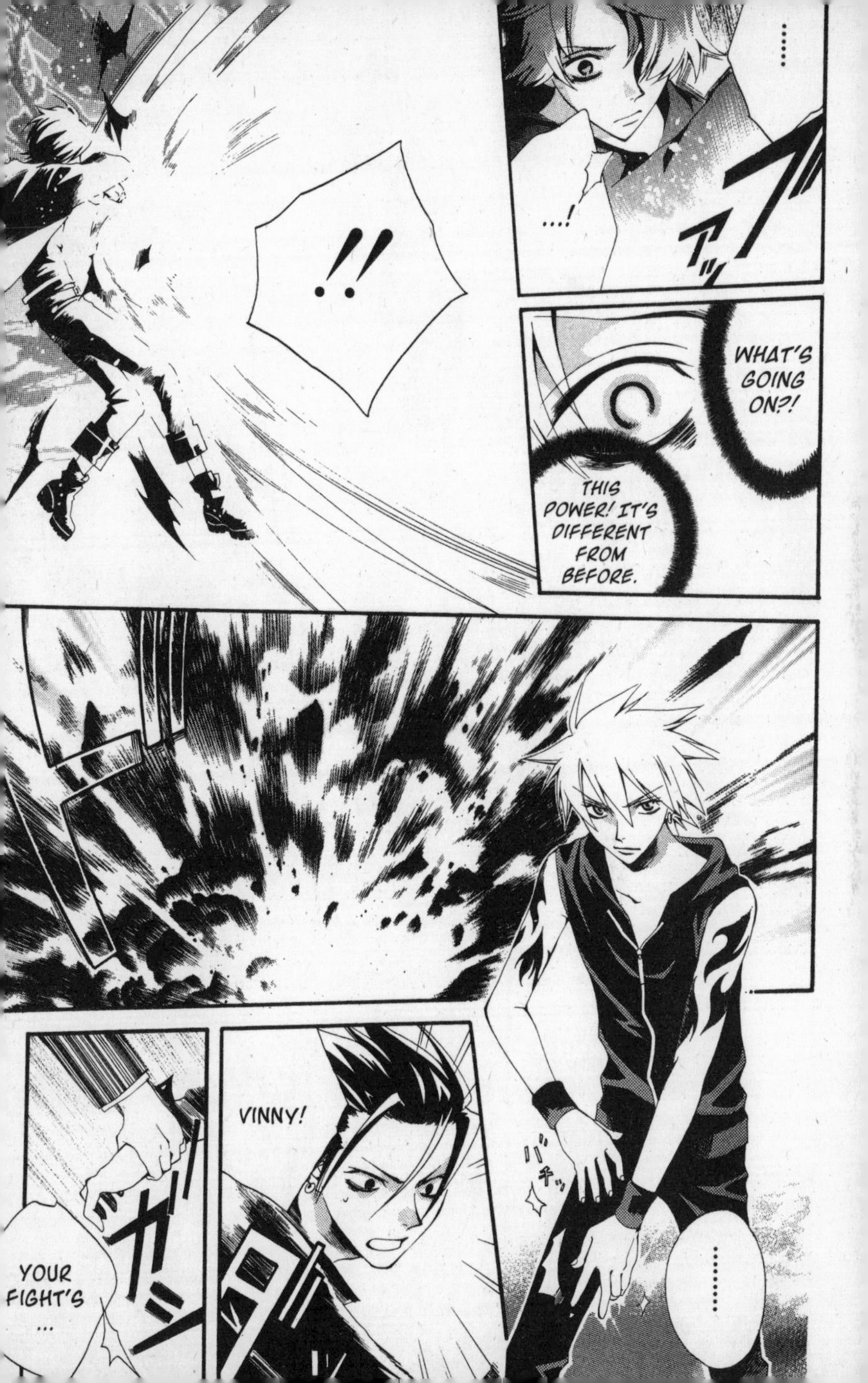
......
....!
ア ッ
!!
WHAT'S GOING ON?!
THIS POWER! IT'S DIFFERENT FROM BEFORE.
......
バ チ ッ
VINNY!
YOUR FIGHT'S ...

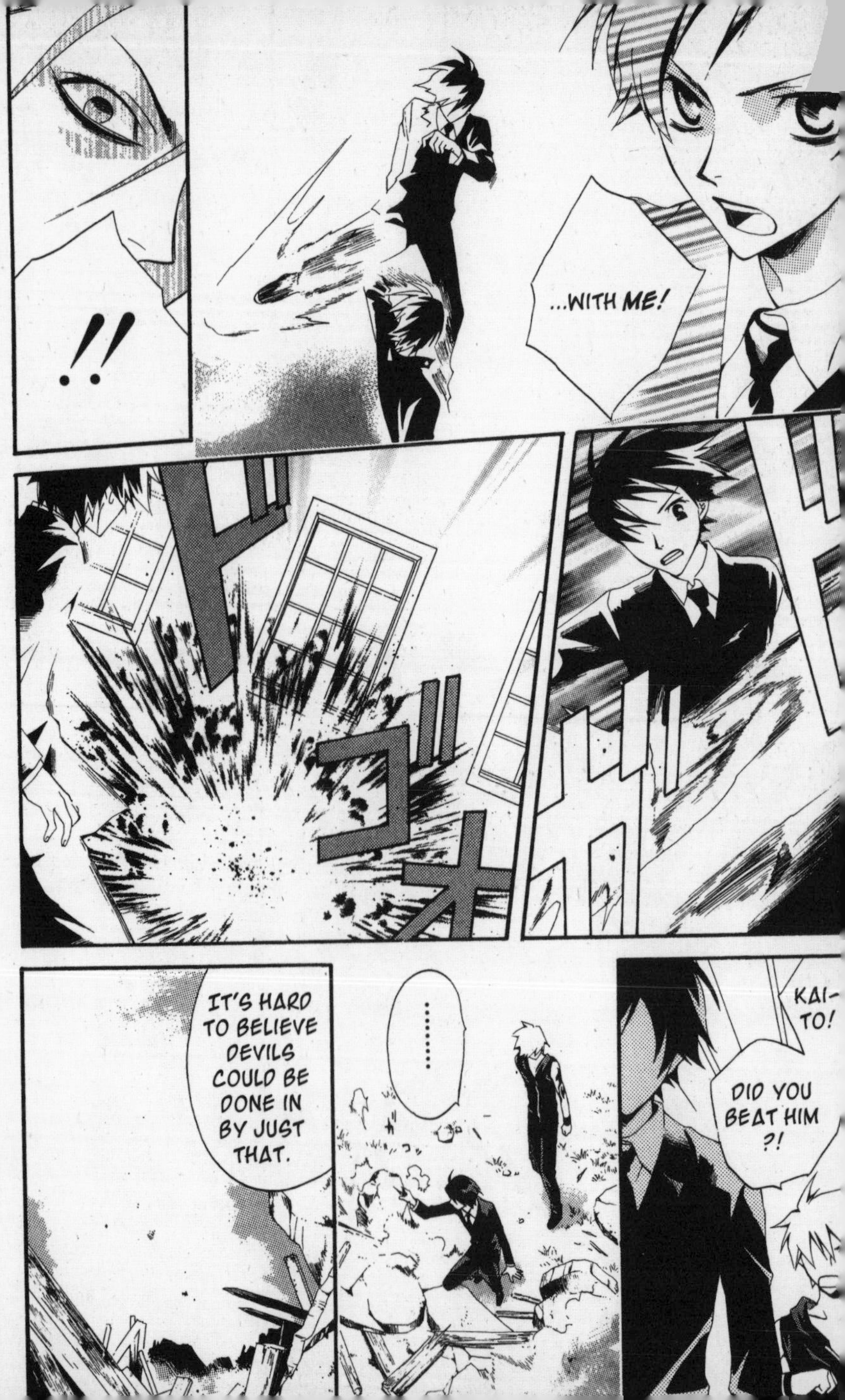
...WITH ME!
!!
KAI-TO!
DID YOU BEAT HIM ?!
....
IT'S HARD TO BELIEVE DEVILS COULD BE DONE IN BY JUST THAT.

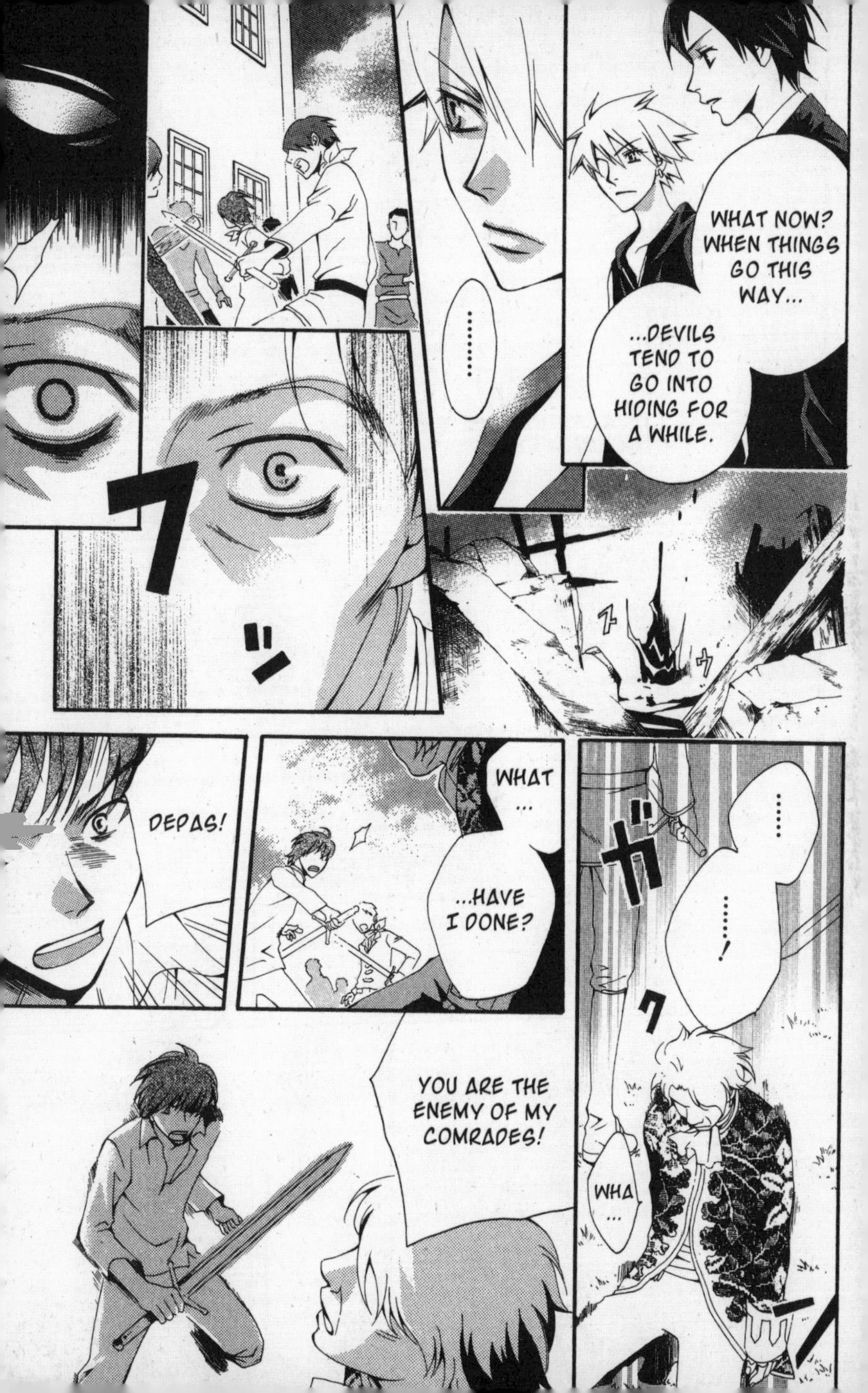
WHAT NOW? WHEN THINGS GO THIS WAY...
...DEVILS TEND TO GO INTO HIDING FOR A WHILE.
....
......
......!
WHA ...
WHAT ...
...HAVE I DONE?
DEPAS!
YOU ARE THE ENEMY OF MY COMRADES!

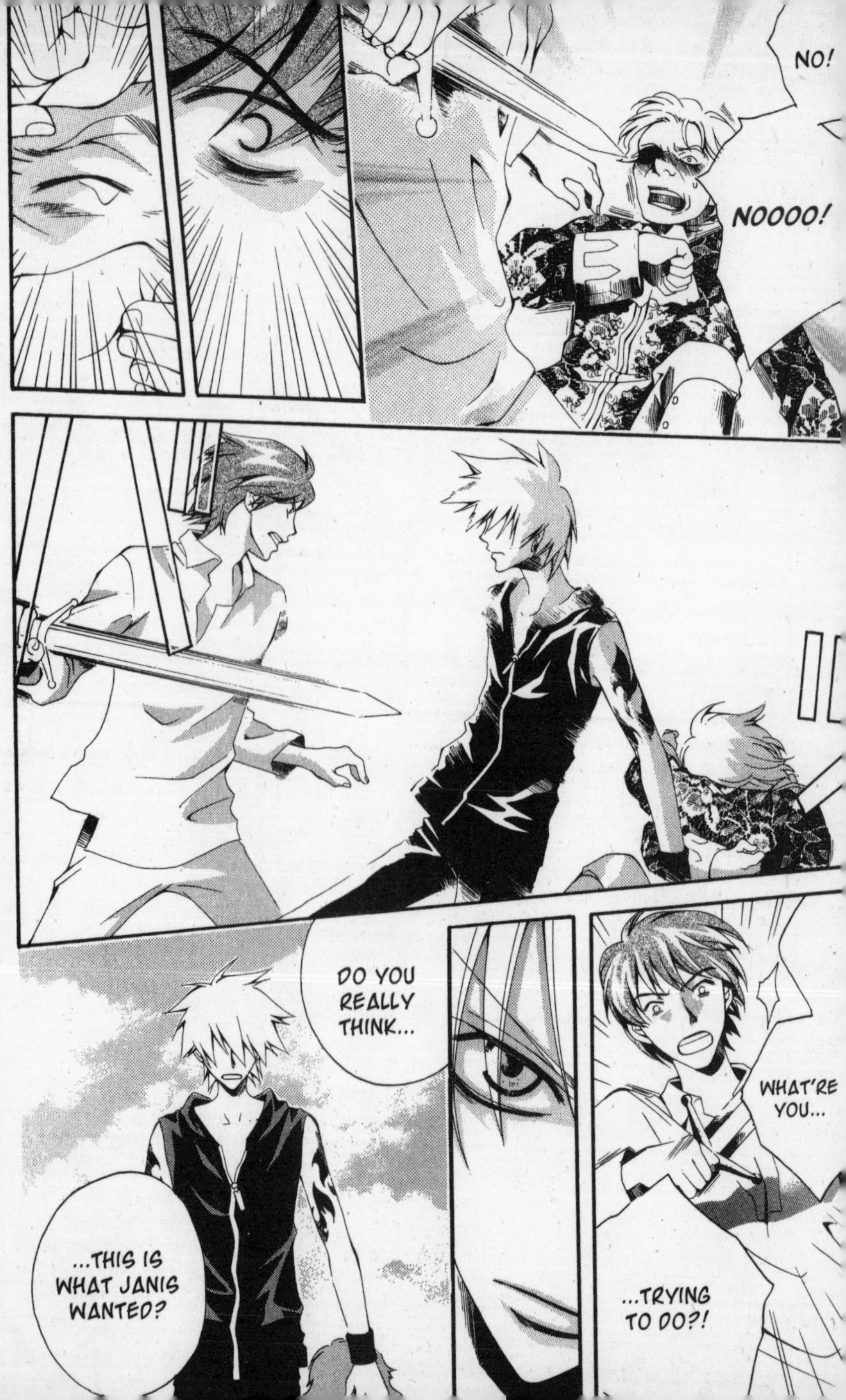
NO!
NOOOO!
WHAT'RE YOU...
...TRYING TO DO?!
DO YOU REALLY THINK...
...THIS IS WHAT JANIS WANTED?

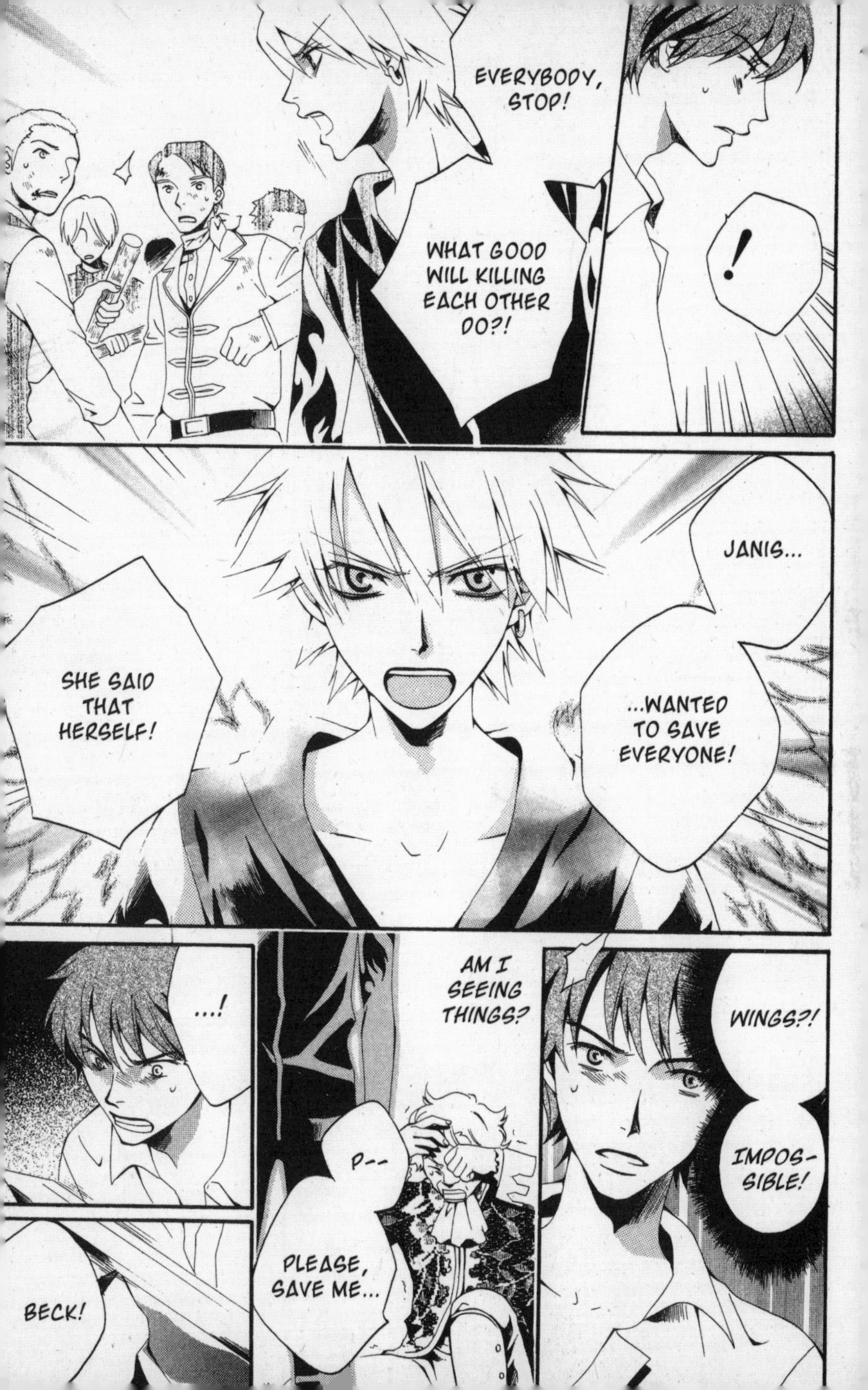
!
EVERYBODY, STOP!
WHAT GOOD WILL KILLING EACH OTHER DO?!
JANIS...
...WANTED TO SAVE EVERYONE!
SHE SAID THAT HERSELF!
WINGS?!
IMPOSSIBLE!
AM I SEEING THINGS?
P--
PLEASE, SAVE ME...
...!
BECK!

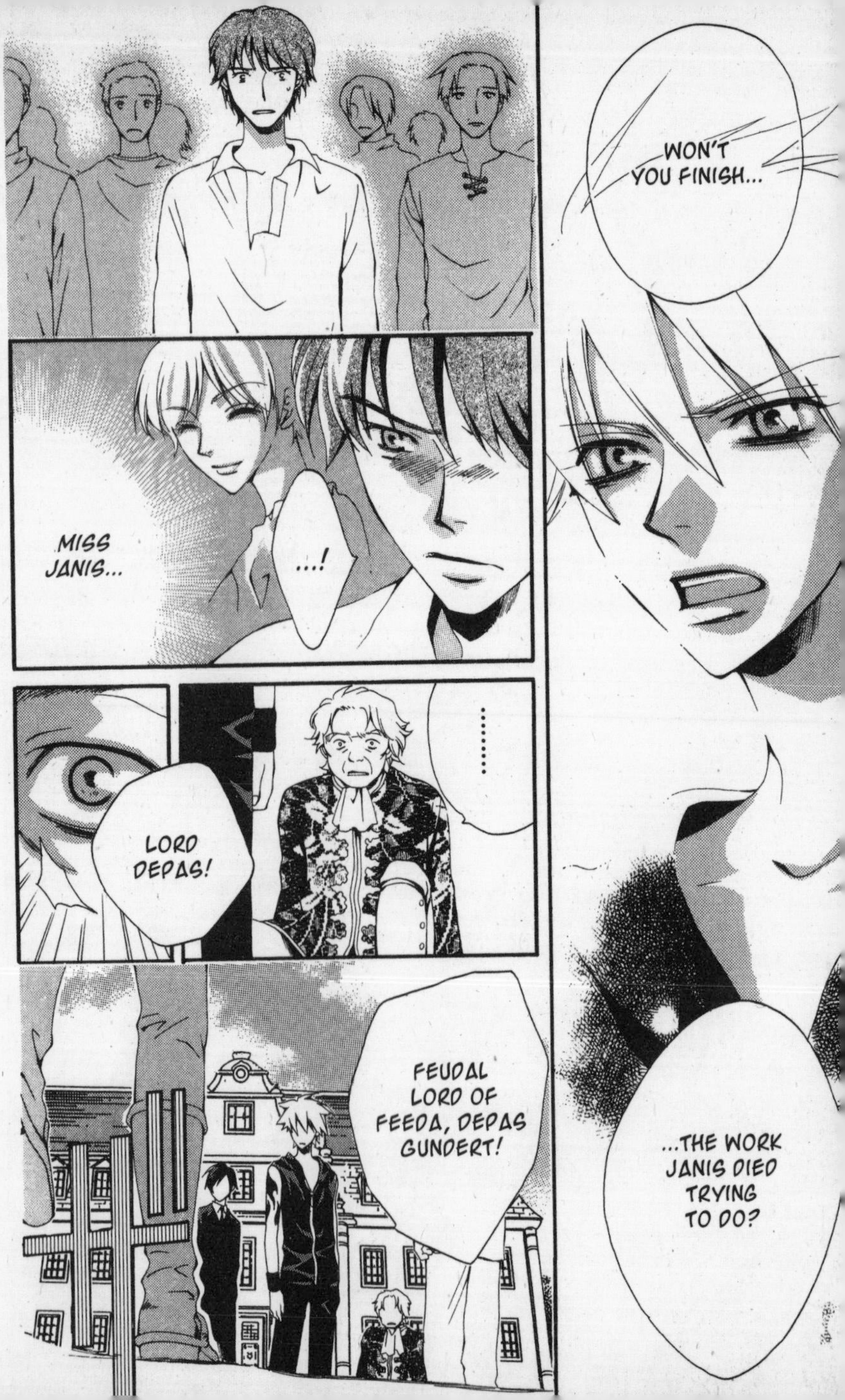
WON'T YOU FINISH...
...THE WORK JANIS DIED TRYING TO DO?
...!
MISS JANIS...
......
LORD DEPAS!
FEUDAL LORD OF FEEDA, DEPAS GUNDERT!

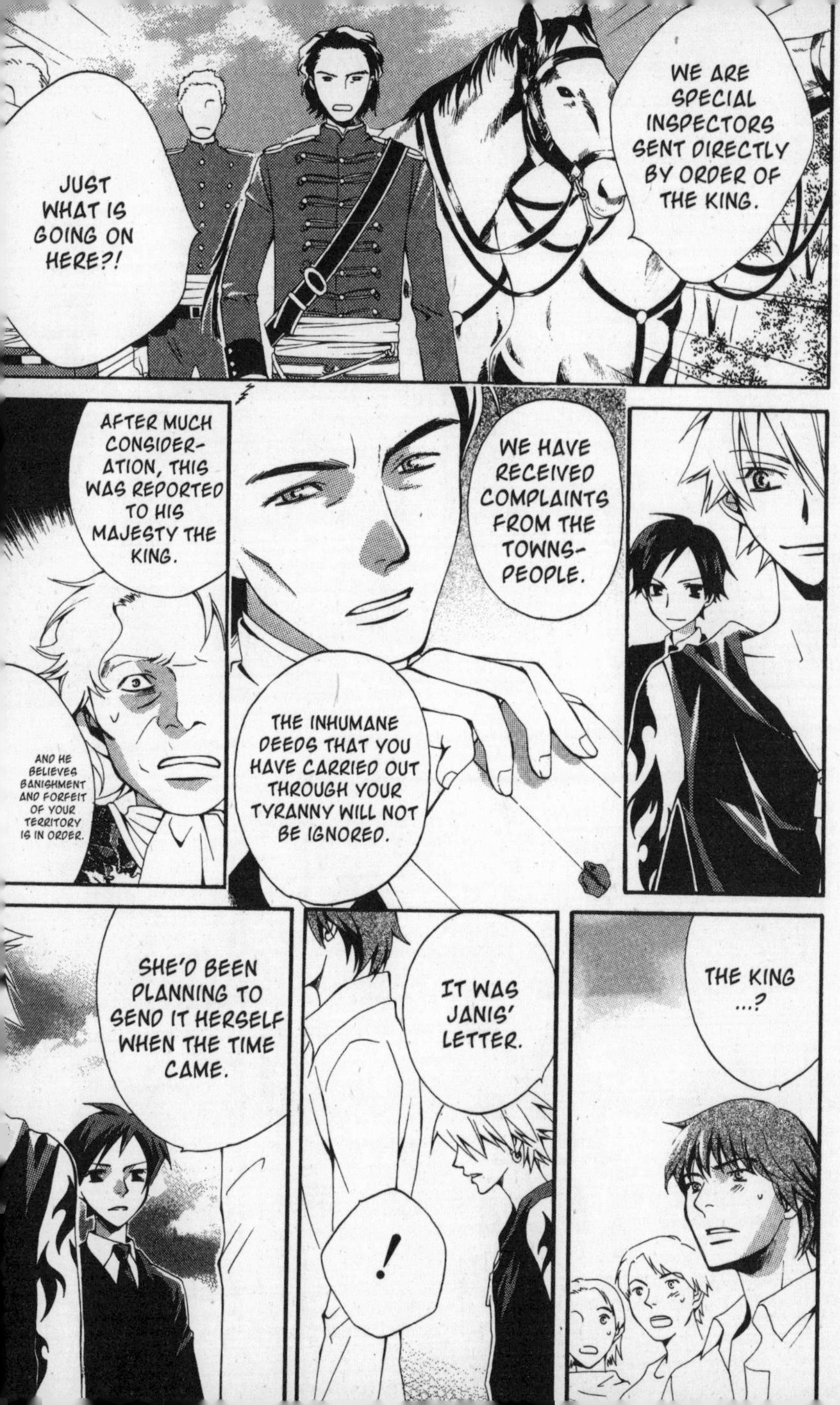
WE ARE SPECIAL INSPECTORS SENT DIRECTLY BY ORDER OF THE KING.
JUST WHAT IS GOING ON HERE?!
WE HAVE RECEIVED COMPLAINTS FROM THE TOWNSPEOPLE.
AFTER MUCH CONSIDERATION, THIS WAS REPORTED TO HIS MAJESTY THE KING.
THE INHUMANE DEEDS THAT YOU HAVE CARRIED OUT THROUGH YOUR TYRANNY WILL NOT BE IGNORED.
AND HE BELIEVES BANISHMENT AND FORFEIT OF YOUR TERRITORY IS IN ORDER.
THE KING ...?
IT WAS JANIS' LETTER.
!
SHE'D BEEN PLANNING TO SEND IT HERSELF WHEN THE TIME CAME.

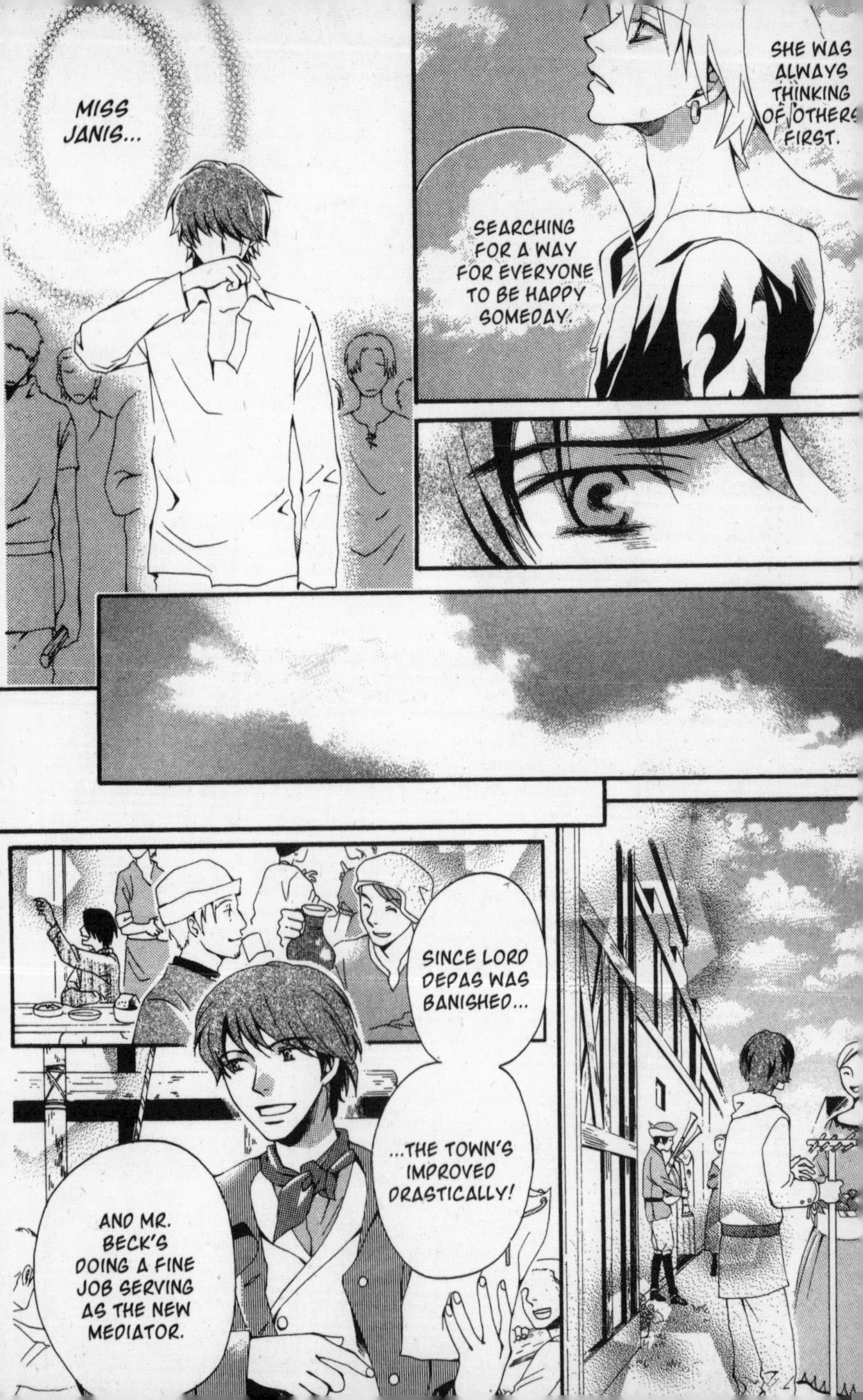

SHE WAS ALWAYS THINKING OF OTHERS FIRST.
SEARCHING FOR A WAY FOR EVERYONE TO BE HAPPY SOMEDAY.
MISS JANIS...
SINCE LORD DEPAS WAS BANISHED...
...THE TOWN'S IMPROVED DRASTICALLY!
AND MR. BECK'S DOING A FINE JOB SERVING AS THE NEW MEDIATOR.

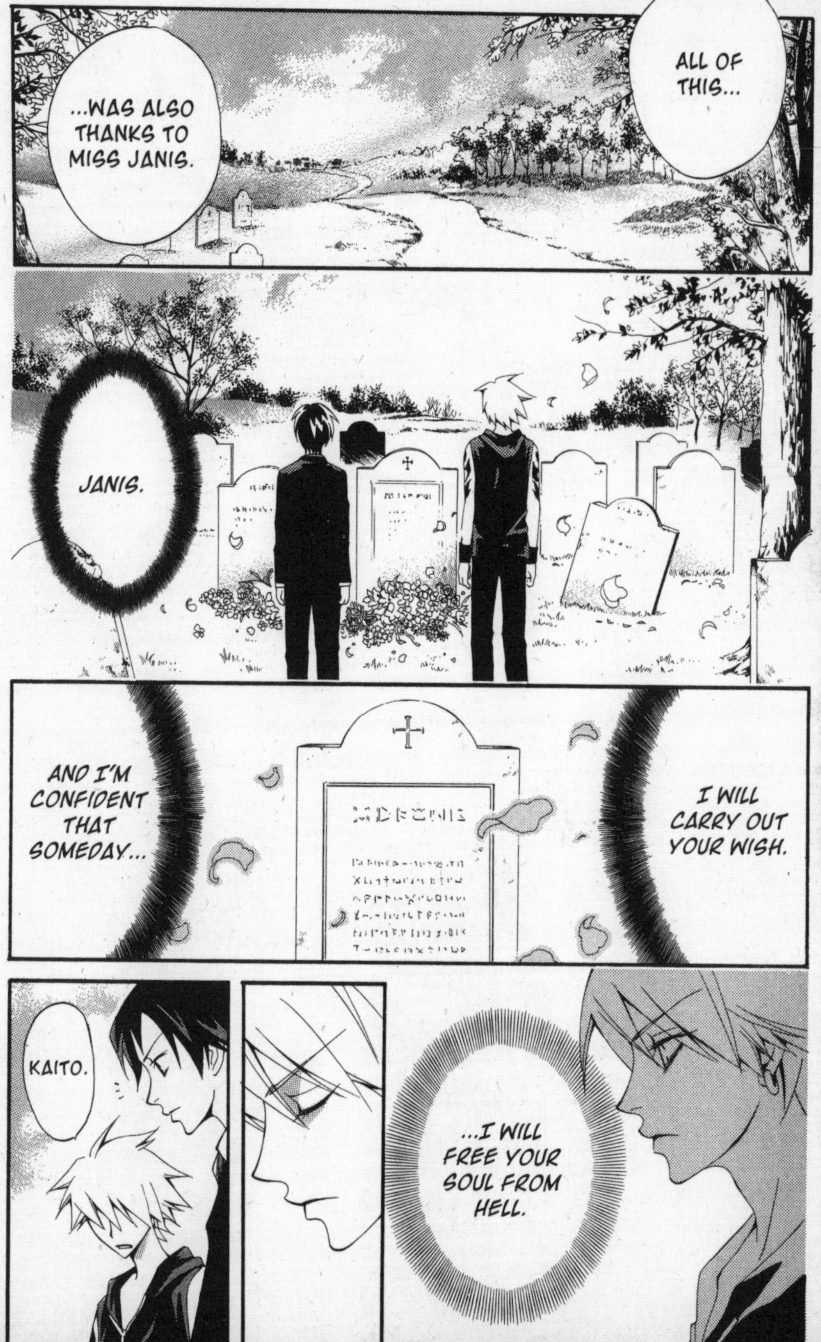
ALL OF THIS...
...WAS ALSO THANKS TO MISS JANIS.
JANIS.
I WILL CARRY OUT YOUR WISH.
AND I'M CONFIDENT THAT SOMEDAY...
...I WILL FREE YOUR SOUL FROM HELL.
KAITO.

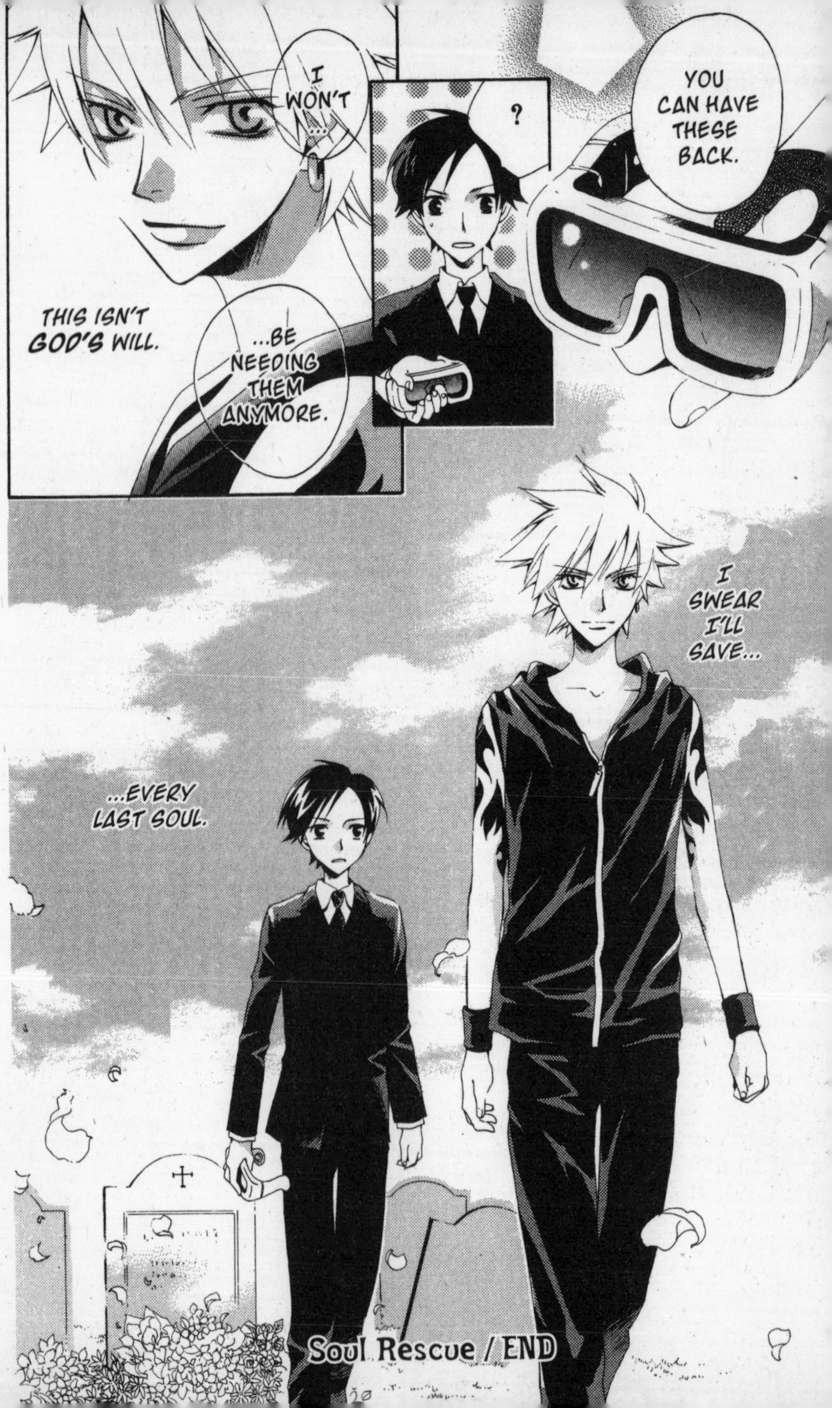
YOU CAN HAVE THESE BACK.
?
I WON'T ...
...BE NEEDING THEM ANYMORE.
THIS ISN'T GOD'S WILL.
I SWEAR I'LL SAVE...
...EVERY LAST SOUL.
Soul Rescue / END

Bonus: I tried doing a school thing. So here is...

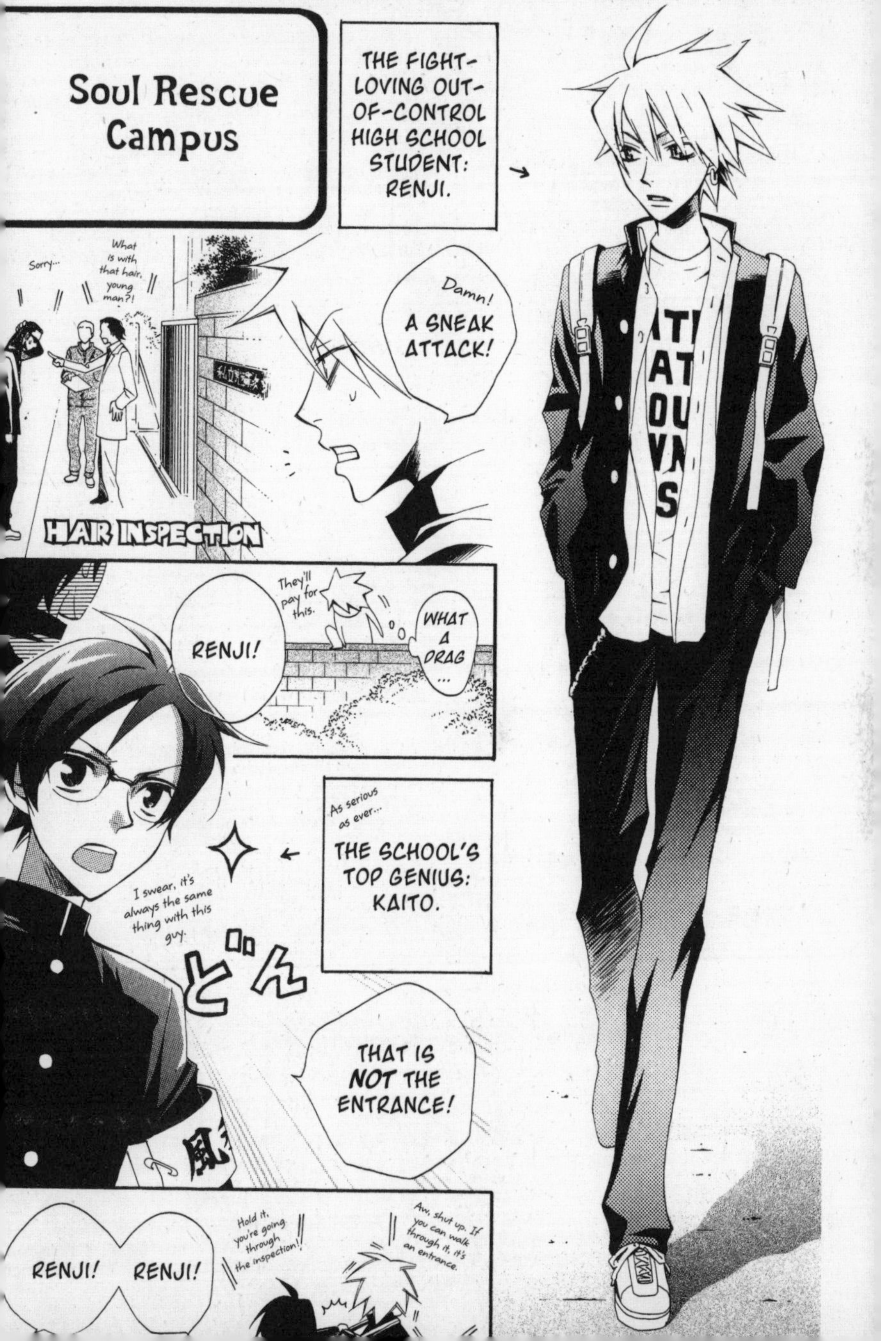
THE FIGHT-LOVING OUT-OF-CONTROL HIGH SCHOOL STUDENT: RENJI.
Soul Rescue Campus
Damn! A SNEAK ATTACK!
What is with that hair, young man?!
Sorry...
HAIR INSPECTION
WHAT A DRAG...
They'll pay for this.
RENJI!
As serious as ever...
THE SCHOOL'S TOP GENIUS: KAITO.
I swear, it's always the same thing with this guy.
どん
THAT IS NOT THE ENTRANCE!
Aw, shut up. If you can walk through it, it's an entrance.
Hold it, you're going through the inspection!
RENJI!
RENJI!

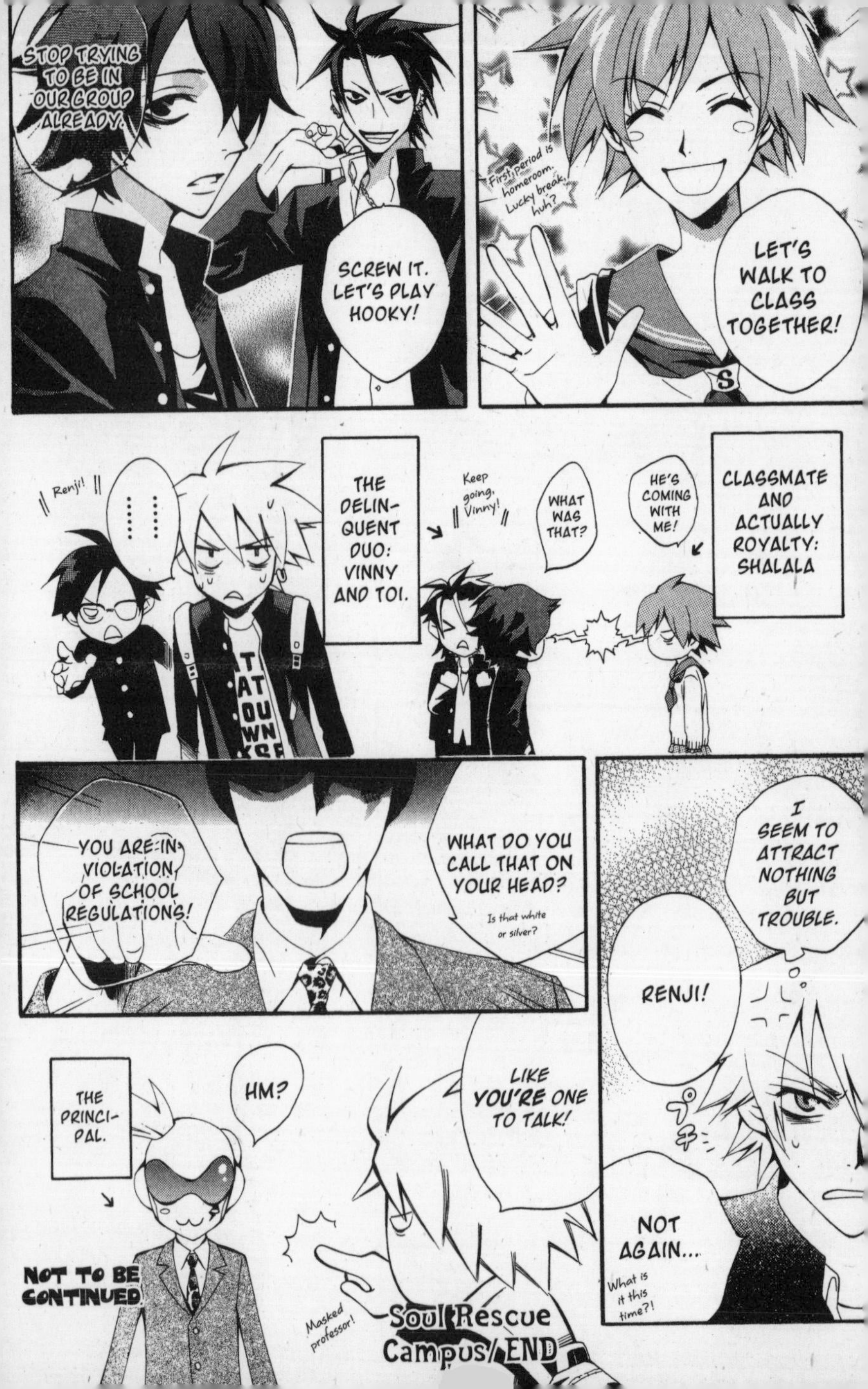
First period is homeroom. Lucky break, huh?
LET'S WALK TO CLASS TOGETHER!
STOP TRYING TO BE IN OUR GROUP ALREADY.
SCREW IT. LET'S PLAY HOOKY!
CLASSMATE AND ACTUALLY ROYALTY: SHALALA
HE'S COMING WITH ME!
WHAT WAS THAT?
Keep going, Vinny!
THE DELIN-QUENT DUO: VINNY AND TOI.
......
Renji!
I SEEM TO ATTRACT NOTHING BUT TROUBLE.
RENJI!
NOT AGAIN...
What is it this time?!
WHAT DO YOU CALL THAT ON YOUR HEAD?
Is that white or silver?
YOU ARE IN VIOLATION OF SCHOOL REGULATIONS!
LIKE YOU'RE ONE TO TALK!
HM?
THE PRINCI-PAL.
Masked professor!
NOT TO BE CONTINUED.
Soul Rescue Campus/END

In the next Volume of

Renji and Kaito continue their world tour of saving
souls, when they happen upon Princess Shalala
again — but this time, she's being Forced to wed to
an island king! Can Renji intervene long enough
to rescue the damsel in distress without breaking
the cardinal law of Angels — Falling in love?!
And more deadly encounters with the devilish
duo Toi and Vinny in Japan Force our heroes to
understand the true power of Friendship!

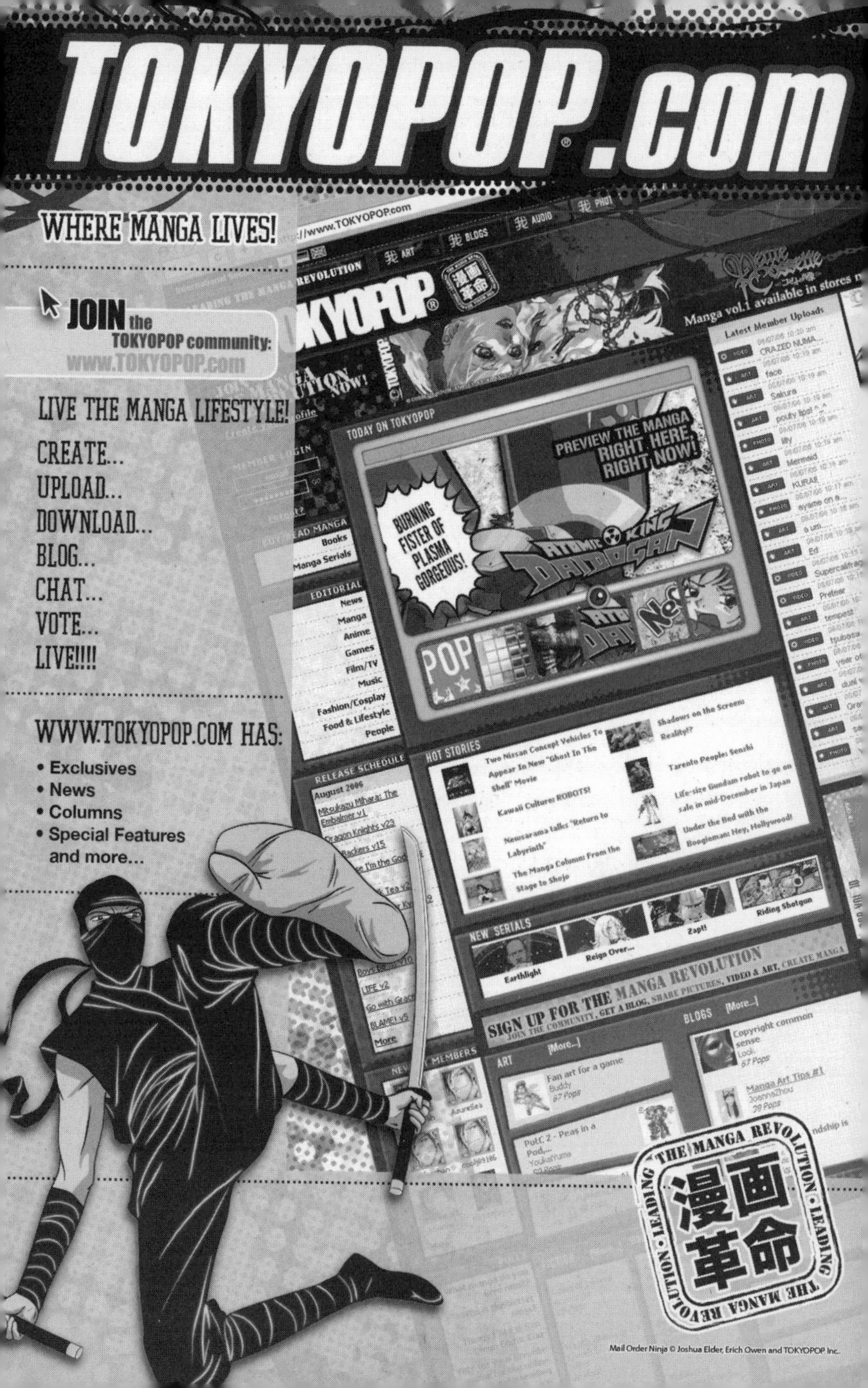
TOKYOPOP®.com
WHERE MANGA LIVES!
JOIN the TOKYOPOP community: www.TOKYOPOP.com
LIVE THE MANGA LIFESTYLE!
CREATE...
UPLOAD...
DOWNLOAD...
BLOG...
CHAT...
VOTE...
LIVE!!!!
WWW.TOKYOPOP.COM HAS:
• Exclusives
• News
• Columns
• Special Features and more...
PREVIEW THE MANGA RIGHT HERE, RIGHT NOW!
BURNING FISTER OF PLASMA GORGEOUS!
SIGN UP FOR THE MANGA REVOLUTION
THE MANGA REVOLUTION 漫画革命 LEADING THE MANGA REVOLUTION

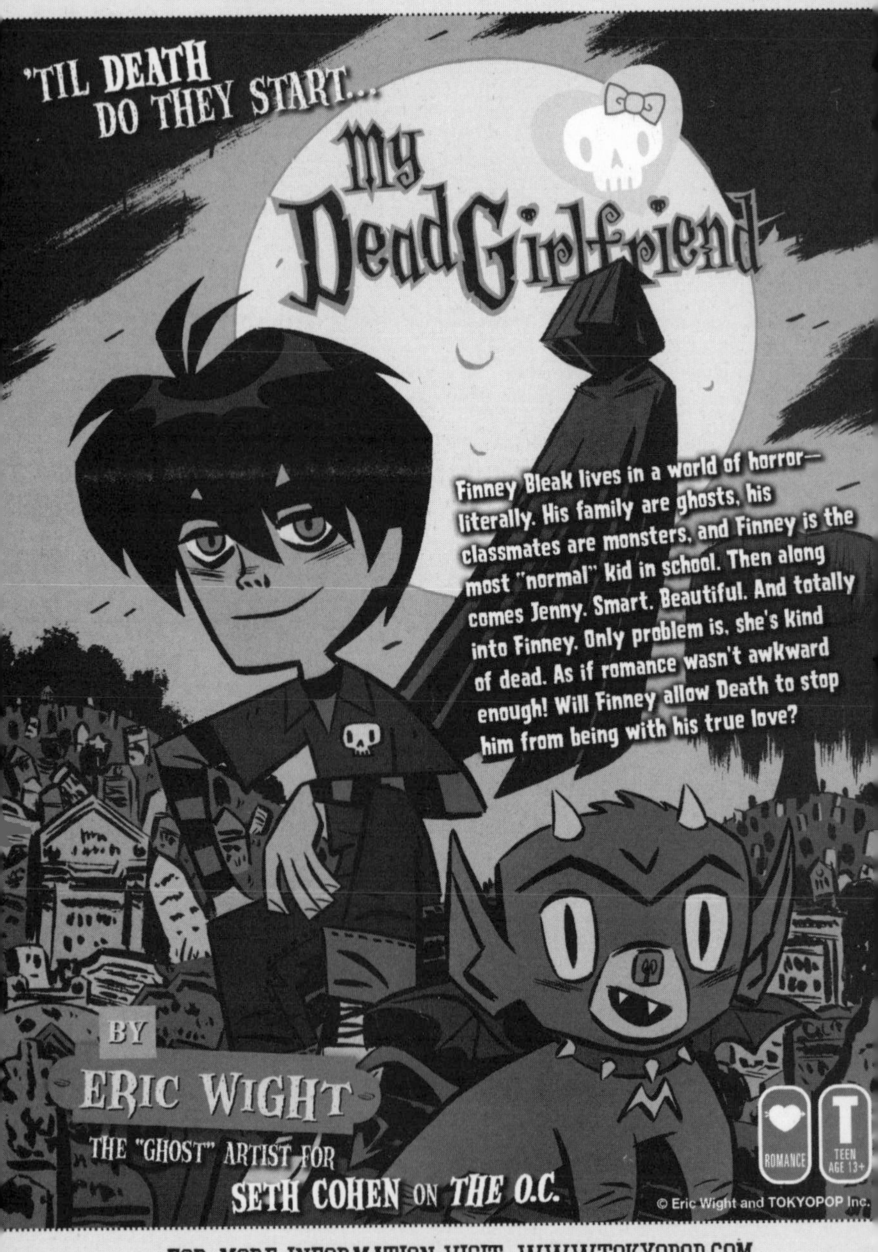
'TIL DEATH DO THEY START...
My Dead Girlfriend
Finney Bleak lives in a world of horror—literally. His family are ghosts, his classmates are monsters, and Finney is the most "normal" kid in school. Then along comes Jenny. Smart. Beautiful. And totally into Finney. Only problem is, she's kind of dead. As if romance wasn't awkward enough! Will Finney allow Death to stop him from being with his true love?
BY
ERIC WIGHT
THE "GHOST" ARTIST FOR SETH COHEN ON THE O.C.
ROMANCE
T
TEEN AGE 13+
© Eric Wight and TOKYOPOP Inc.

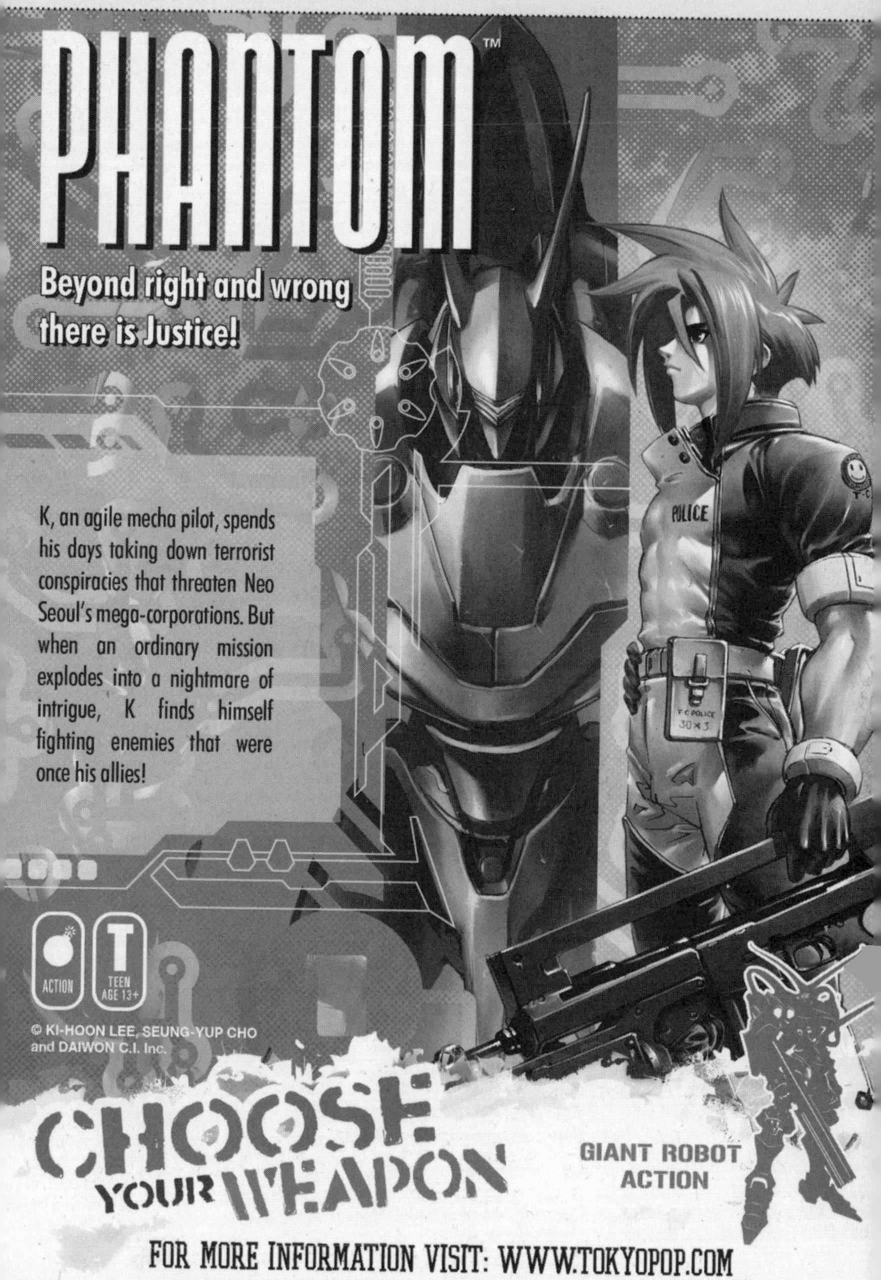
PHANTOM™
Beyond right and wrong there is Justice!
K, an agile mecha pilot, spends his days taking down terrorist conspiracies that threaten Neo Seoul's mega-corporations. But when an ordinary mission explodes into a nightmare of intrigue, K finds himself fighting enemies that were once his allies!
POLICE
ACTION
T
TEEN AGE 13+
© KI-HOON LEE, SEUNG-YUP CHO and DAIWON C.I. Inc.
CHOOSE YOUR WEAPON
GIANT ROBOT ACTION
FOR MORE INFORMATION VISIT: WWW.TOKYOPOP.COM

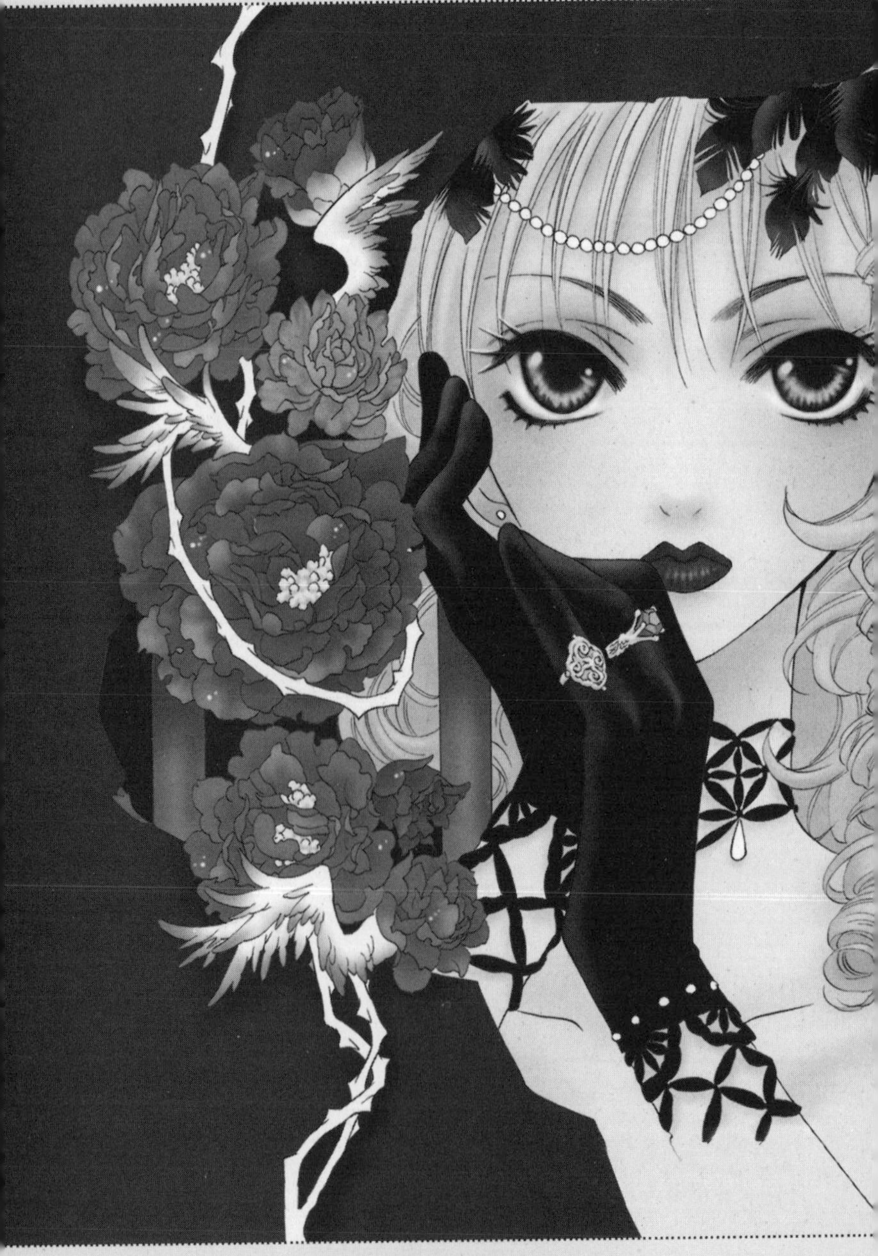

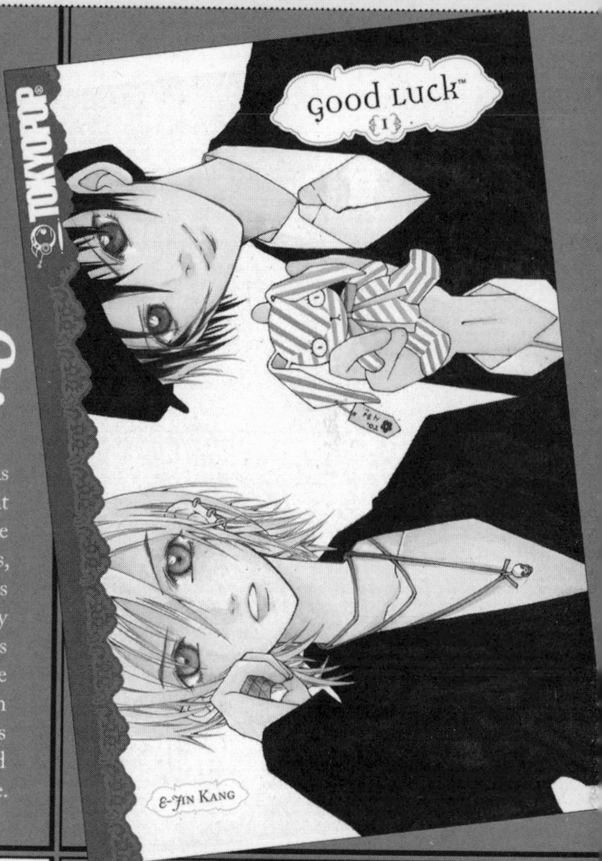
TOKYOPOP
good Luck™
1
E-JIN KANG

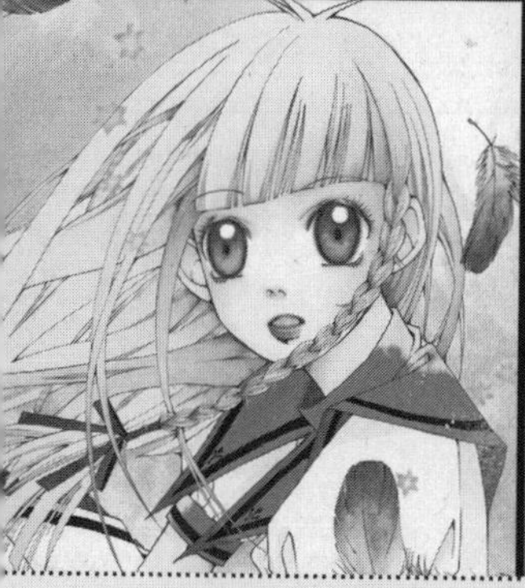

STOP!

This is the back of the book.
You wouldn't want to spoil a great ending!

This book is printed "manga-style," in the authentic Japanese right-to-left format. Since none of the artwork has been flipped or altered, readers get to experience the story just as the creator intended. You've been asking for it, so TOKYOPOP® delivered: authentic, hot-off-the-press, and far more fun!

DIRECTIONS

If this is your first time reading manga-style, here's a quick guide to help you understand how it works.

It's easy... just start in the top right panel and follow the numbers. Have fun, and look for more 100% authentic manga from TOKYOPOP®!